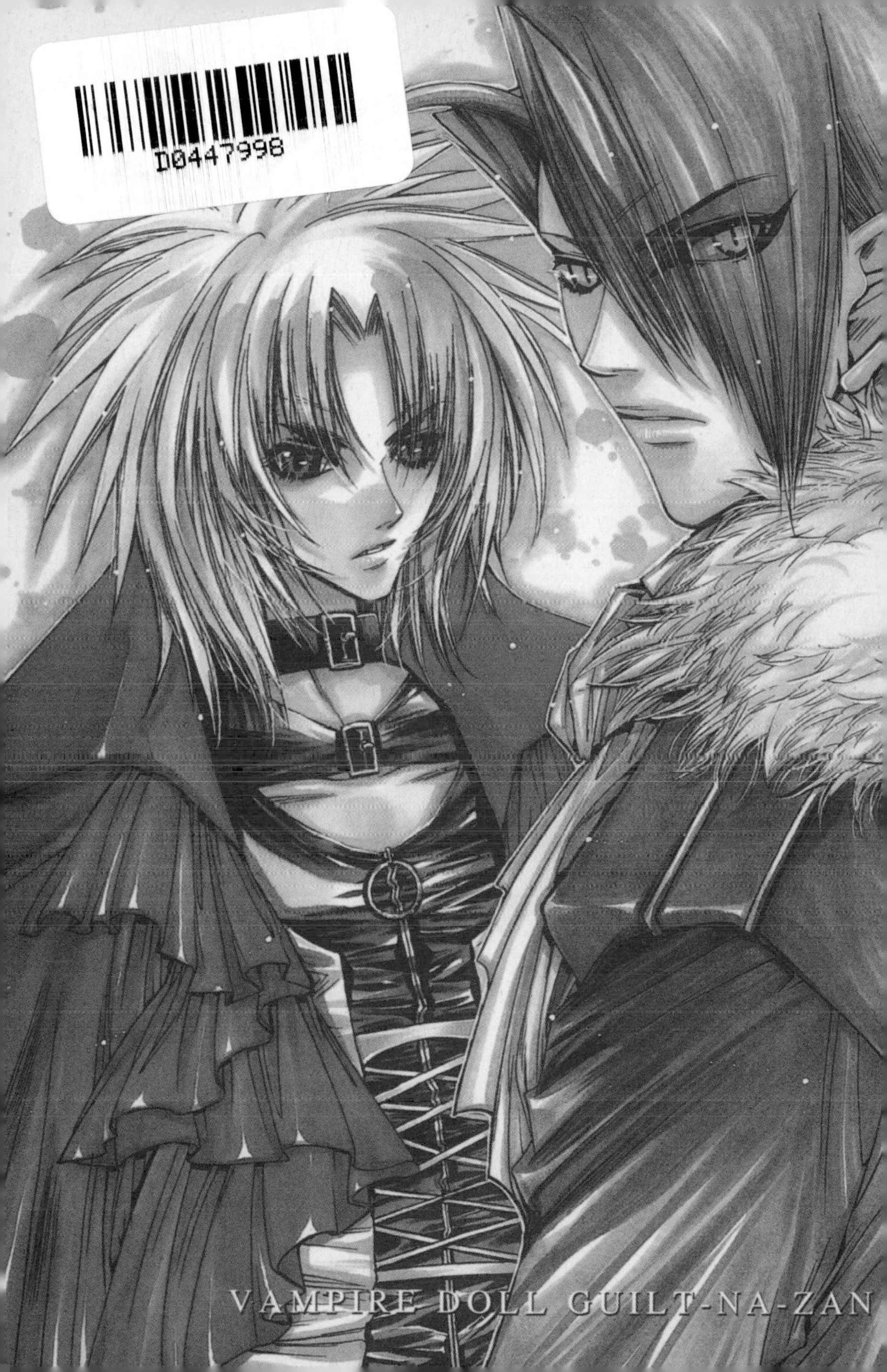
VAMPIRE DOLL GUILT-NA-ZAN

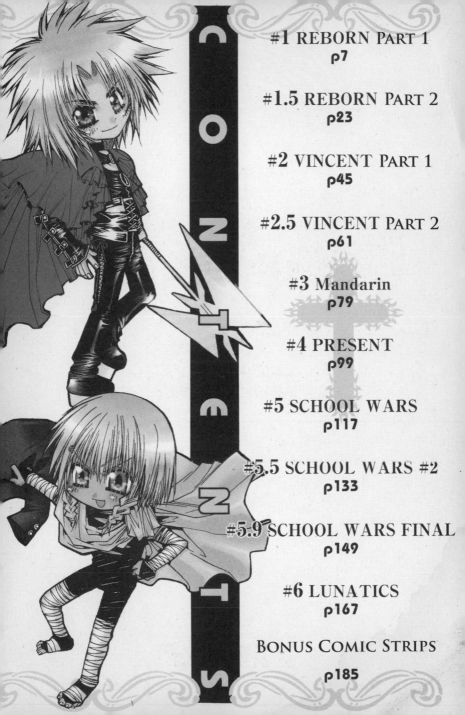

CONTENTS

Vampire Doll

Guilt-na-Zan

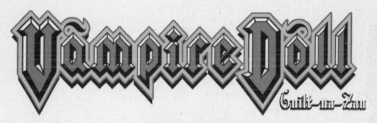

VOLUME 1

CREATED BY
ERIKA KARI

TOKYOPOP®

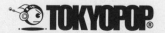

HAMBURG // LONDON // LOS ANGELES // TOKYO

Vampire Doll Vol. 1
Created by Erika Kari

Translation - Yoohae Yang
English Adaptation - Patricia Duffield
Copy Editor - Peter Ahlstrom
Retouch and Lettering - Camellia Cox
Production Artist - Bowen Park
Cover Design - Kyle Plummer

Editor - Alexis Kirsch
Digital Imaging Manager - Chris Buford
Production Manager - Elisabeth Brizzi
VP of Production - Ron Klamert
Editor-in-Chief - Rob Tokar
Publisher - Mike Kiley
President and C.O.O. - John Parker
C.E.O. and Chief Creative Officer - Stuart Levy

A  Manga

TOKYOPOP Inc.
5900 Wilshire Blvd. Suite 2000
Los Angeles, CA 90036

E-mail: info@TOKYOPOP.com
Come visit us online at www.TOKYOPOP.com

ISBN: 1-59816-519-4

First TOKYOPOP printing: September 2006
10 9 8 7 6 5 4 3
Printed in the USA

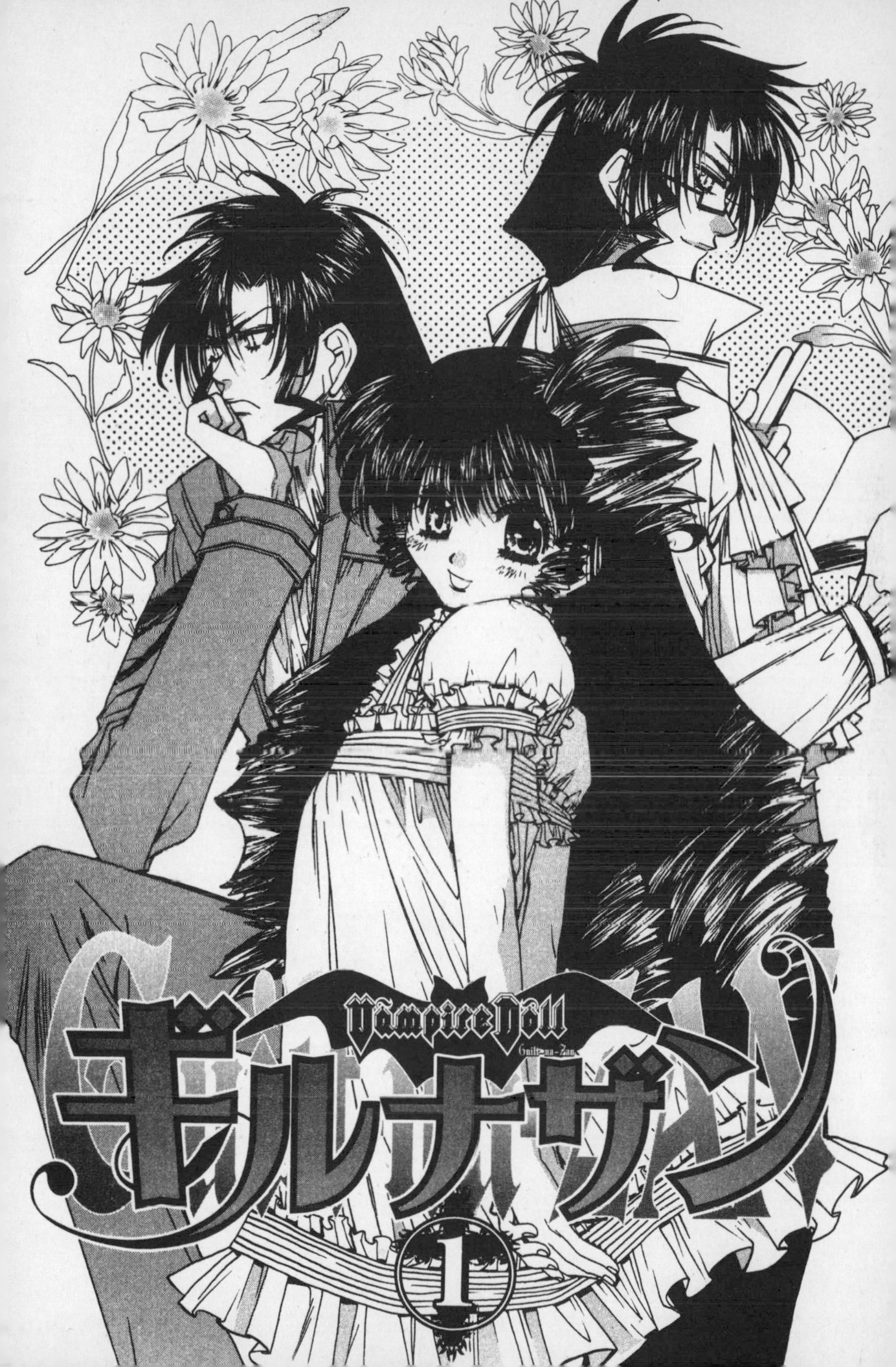
Vampire Doll
ギルナザン
Guilt-na-Zan
1

Main Characters

GUILT-NA

LONG AGO, HE WAS KNOWN AS THE LORD OF VAMPIRES, THE MOST FEARED OF ALL HIS KIND. PLEASE READ THIS BOOK TO FIND OUT WHY HE'S NOW A GIRL.

GUILT-NA-ZAN

THIS IS WHAT GUILT-NA-ZAN USED TO LOOK LIKE. PLEASE READ THIS BOOK TO FIND OUT IF HE'LL EVER BE ABLE TO RECLAIM HIS ORIGINAL FORM.

KYOJI

HE IS A VERY SKILLED EXORCIST. PLEASE READ THIS BOOK TO FIND OUT HOW EVIL HE IS.

TONAE

ON THE SURFACE, SHE APPEARS ALMOST EXACTLY LIKE GUILT-NA. PLEASE READ THIS BOOK TO FIND OUT WHY SUCH A PURE AND GUILELESS GIRL LOOKS LIKE HIM.

VINCENT

HE LOOKS HANDSOME AND COOL. PLEASE READ THE BOOK TO FIND OUT IF HE'S REALLY AS COOL AS HE SEEMS.

KYOICHI

HE IS THE BIGGEST IDIOT IN THE ENTIRE WORLD. PLEASE READ THE BOOK TO FIND OUT JUST HOW STUPID HE IS.

????

PLEASE READ THE BOOK TO FIND OUT WHETHER OR NOT HIS NAME WILL BE REVEALED.

SHIZUKA

ONE OF TONAE'S CLASSMATES, SHE IS ALSO THE STUDENT PRESIDENT. PLEASE READ THE BOOK TO FIND OUT WHAT KIND OF GIRL SHE IS.

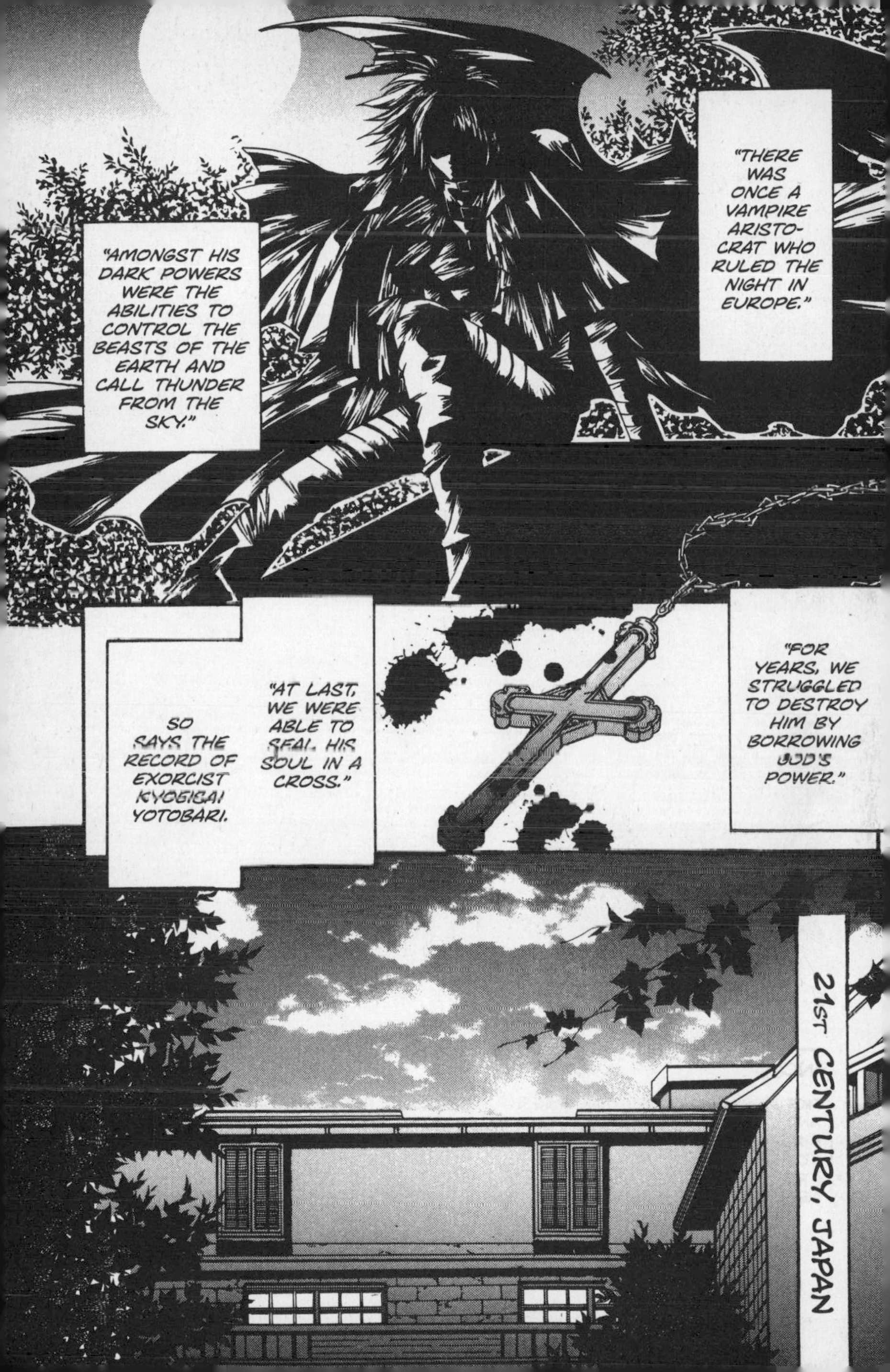
"THERE WAS ONCE A VAMPIRE ARISTOCRAT WHO RULED THE NIGHT IN EUROPE."
"AMONGST HIS DARK POWERS WERE THE ABILITIES TO CONTROL THE BEASTS OF THE EARTH AND CALL THUNDER FROM THE SKY."
"FOR YEARS, WE STRUGGLED TO DESTROY HIM BY BORROWING GOD'S POWER."
"AT LAST, WE WERE ABLE TO SEAL HIS SOUL IN A CROSS."
SO SAYS THE RECORD OF EXORCIST KYOGISAI YOTOBARI.
21ST CENTURY, JAPAN

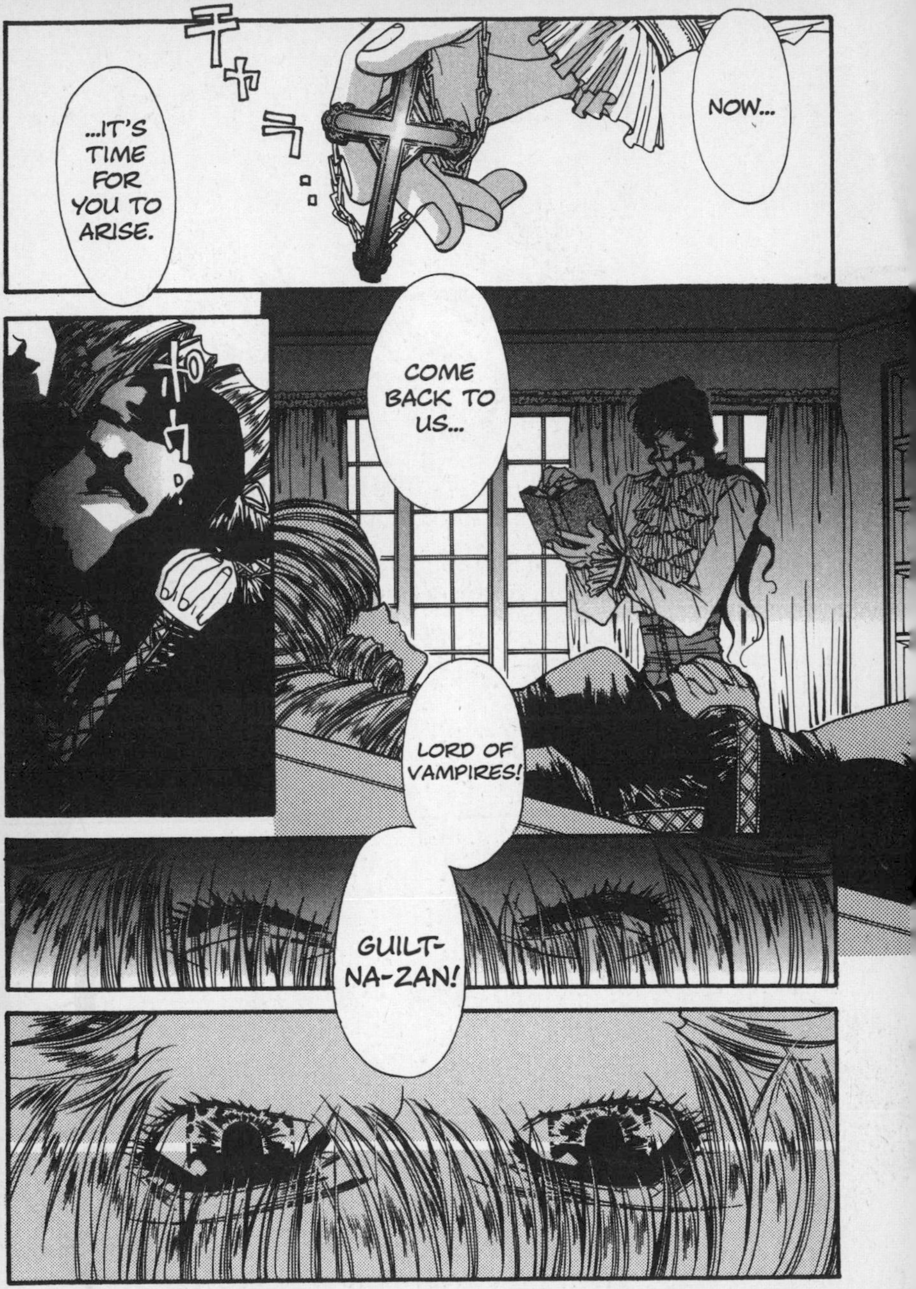
NOW...
チャラ
...IT'S TIME FOR YOU TO ARISE.
COME BACK TO US...
LORD OF VAMPIRES!
GUILT-NA-ZAN!

♯1 REBORN Part 1

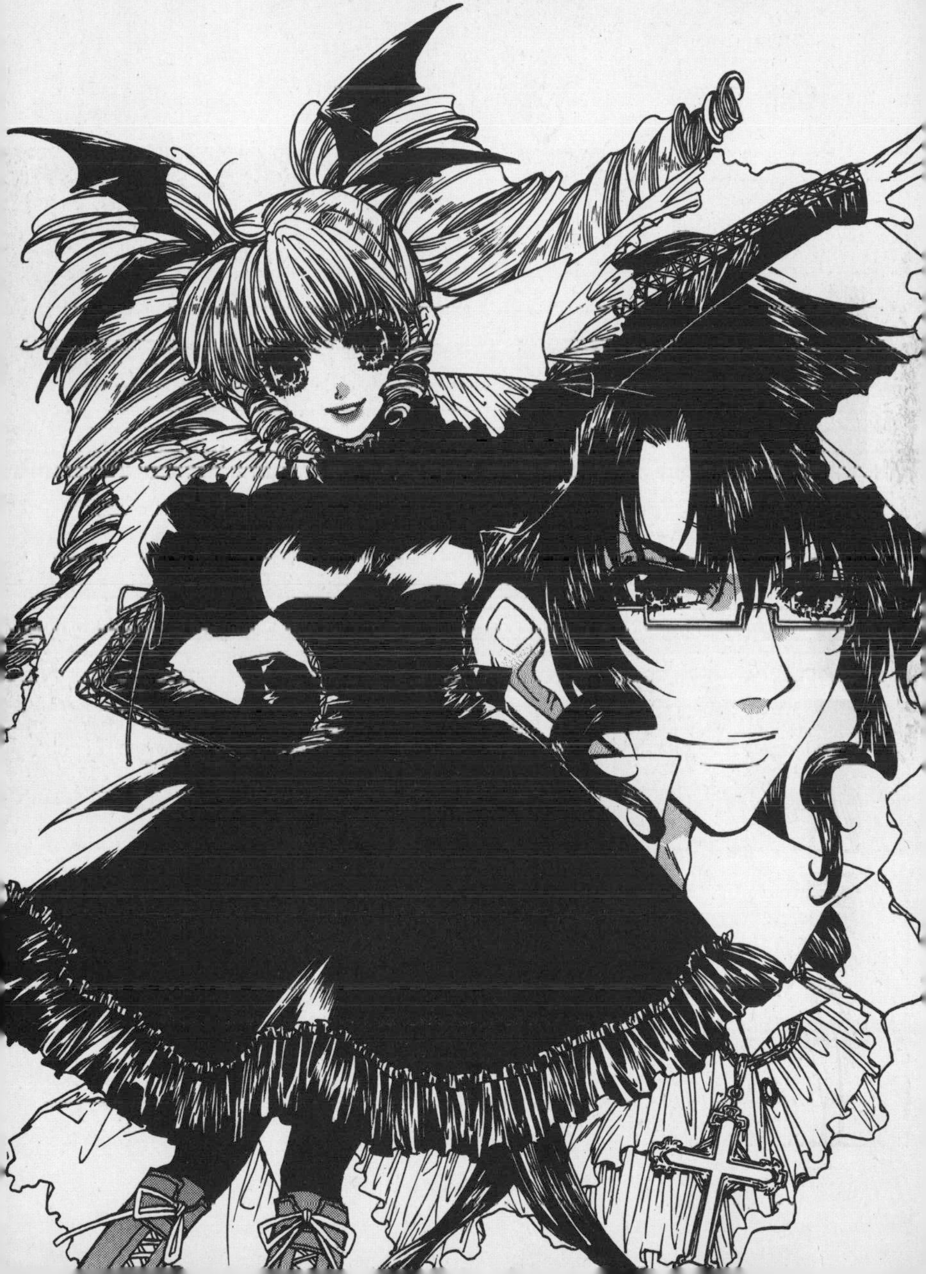

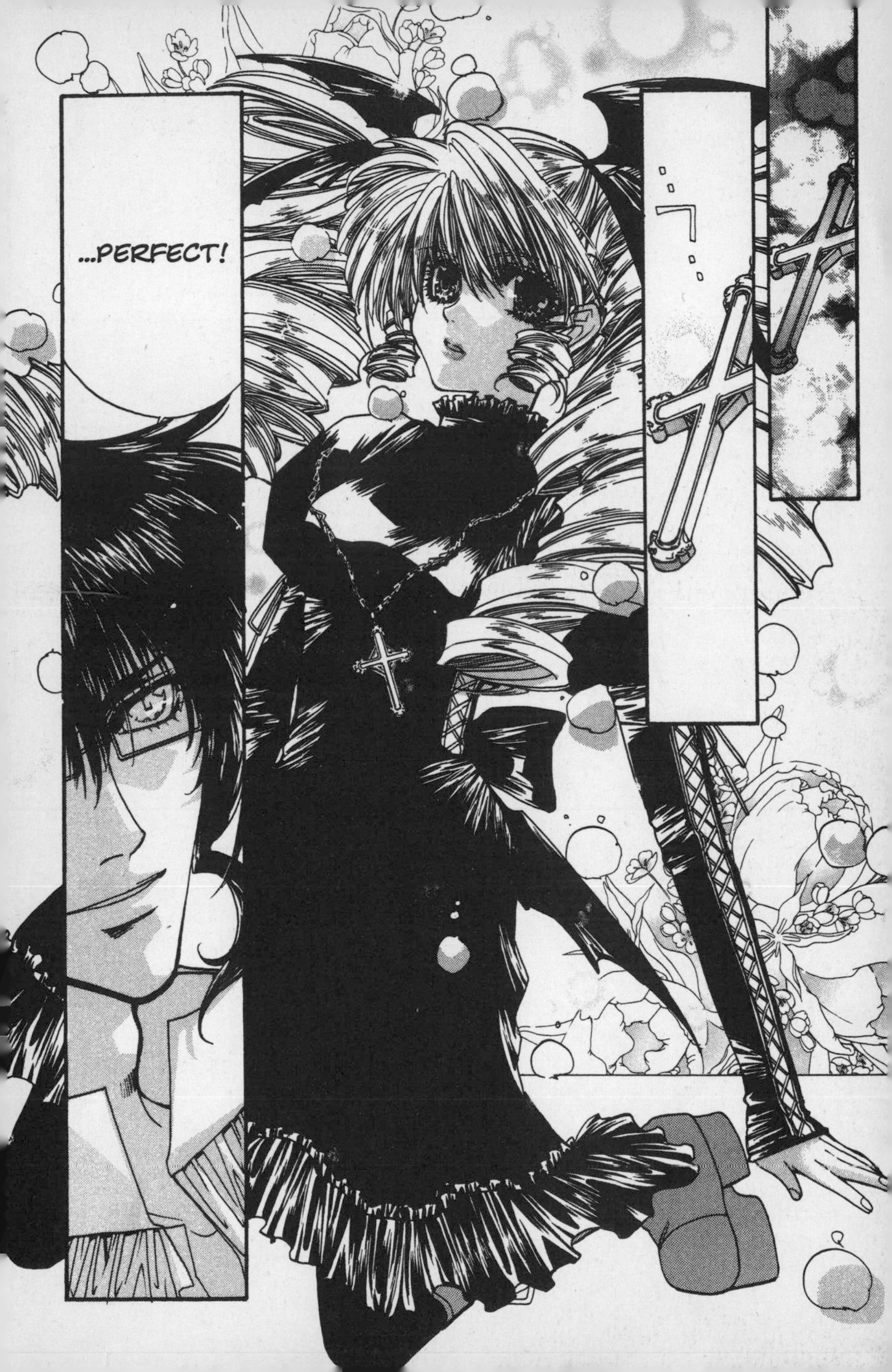
...PERFECT!

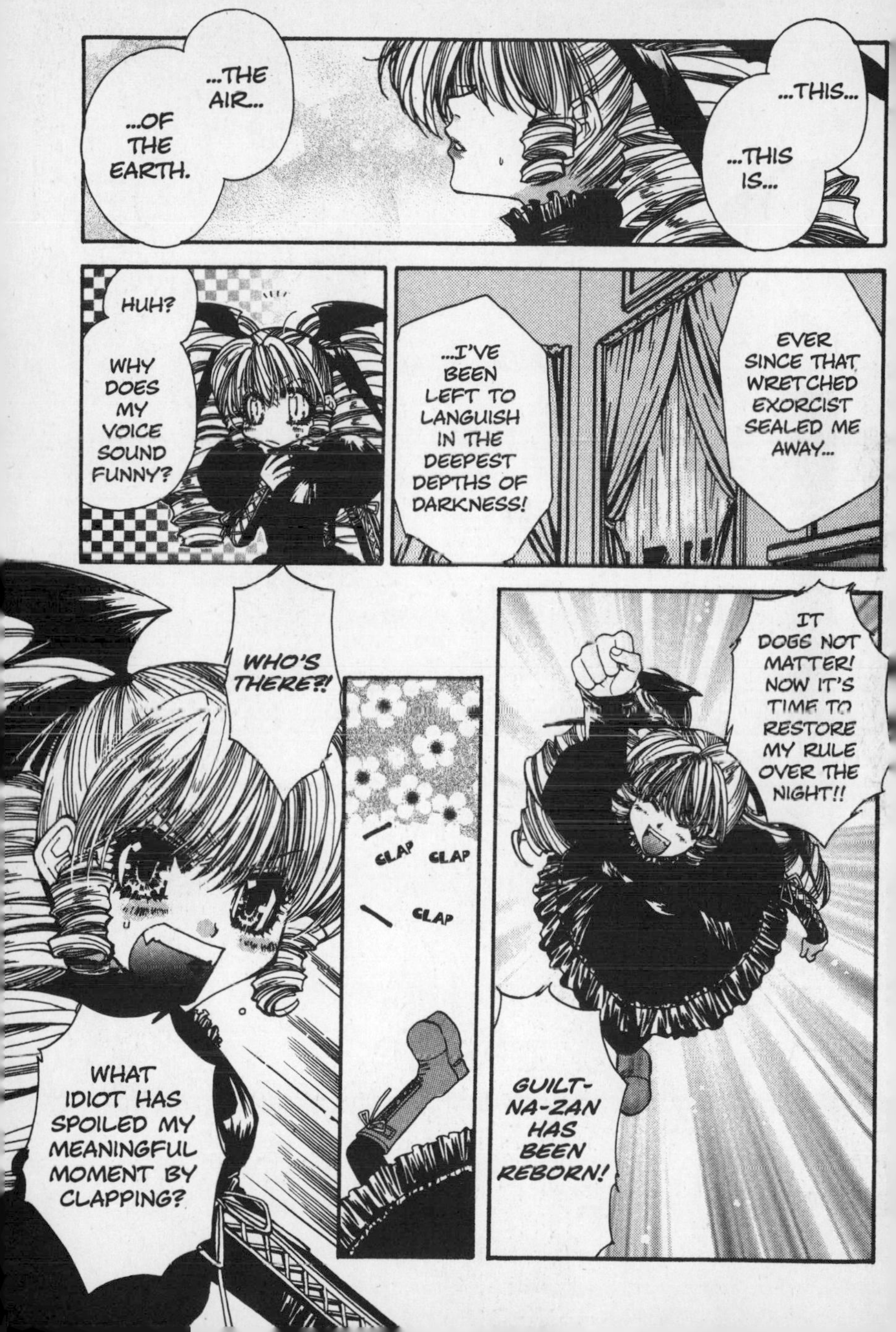
...THIS...
...THIS IS...
...THE AIR...
...OF THE EARTH.
EVER SINCE THAT WRETCHED EXORCIST SEALED ME AWAY...
...I'VE BEEN LEFT TO LANGUISH IN THE DEEPEST DEPTHS OF DARKNESS!
HUH?
WHY DOES MY VOICE SOUND FUNNY?
IT DOES NOT MATTER! NOW IT'S TIME TO RESTORE MY RULE OVER THE NIGHT!!
GUILT-NA-ZAN HAS BEEN REBORN!
CLAP
CLAP
CLAP
WHO'S THERE?!
WHAT IDIOT HAS SPOILED MY MEANINGFUL MOMENT BY CLAPPING?

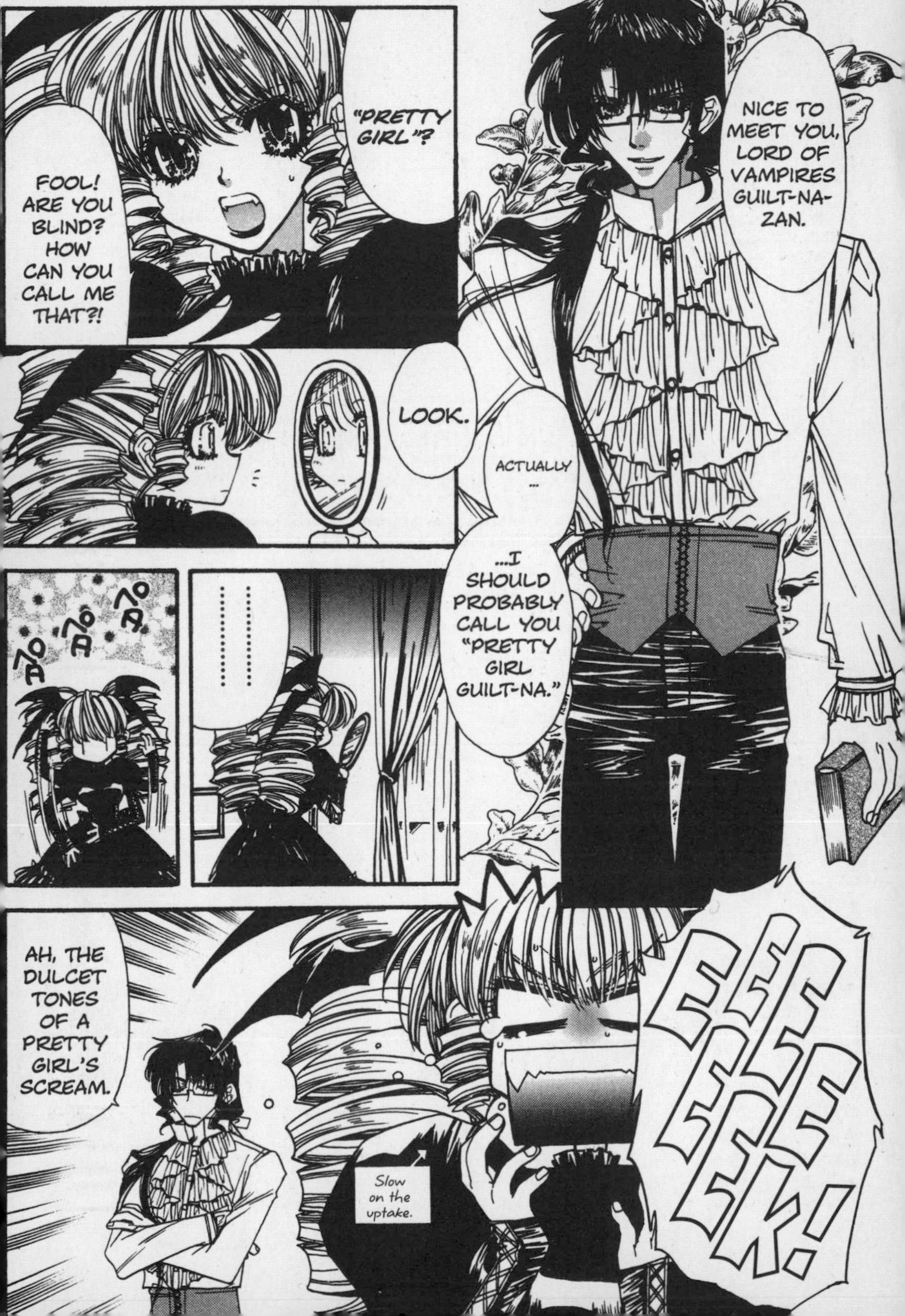
NICE TO MEET YOU, LORD OF VAMPIRES GUILT-NA-ZAN.
ACTUALLY ...
...I SHOULD PROBABLY CALL YOU "PRETTY GIRL GUILT-NA."
"PRETTY GIRL"?
FOOL! ARE YOU BLIND? HOW CAN YOU CALL ME THAT?!
LOOK.
......
^o^A
^o^A
^o^A
EEEEEEEEK!
Slow on the uptake.
AH, THE DULCET TONES OF A PRETTY GIRL'S SCREAM.

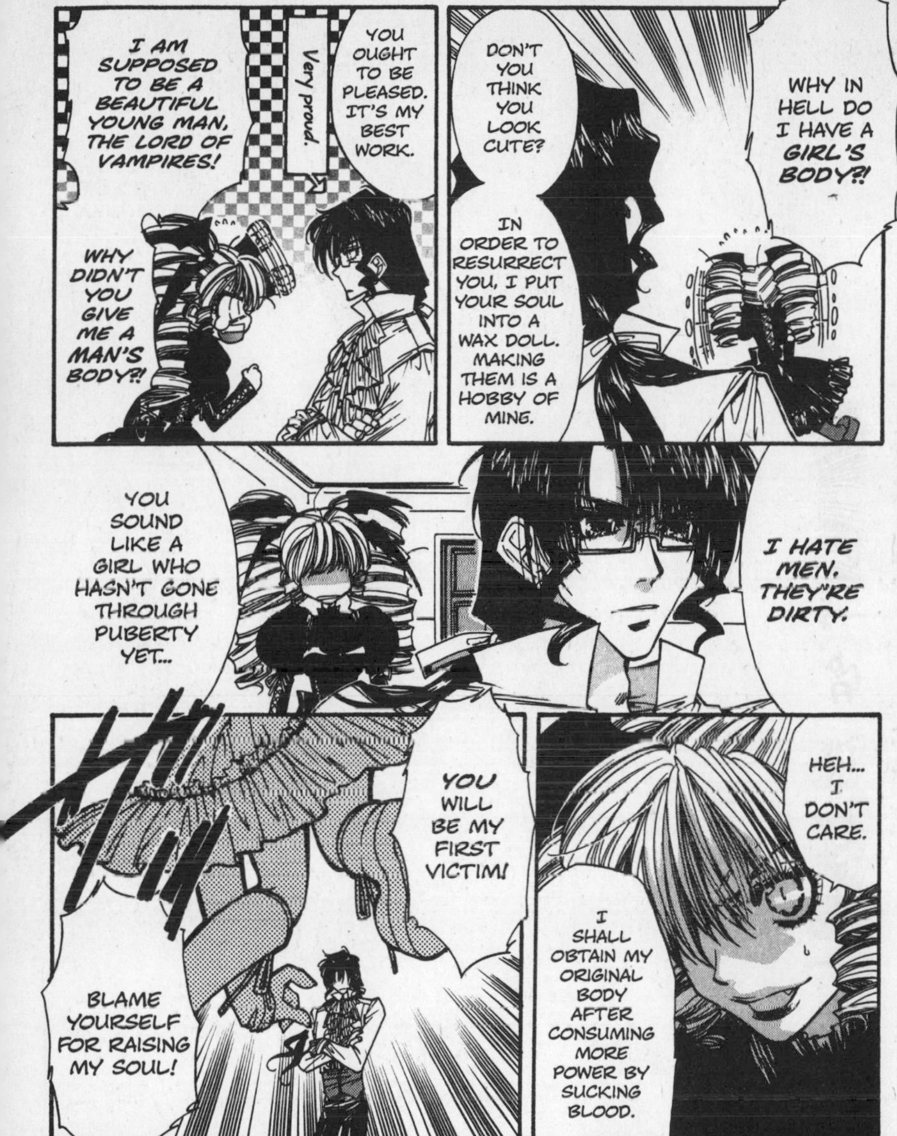
WHY IN HELL DO I HAVE A GIRL'S BODY?!
DON'T YOU THINK YOU LOOK CUTE?
IN ORDER TO RESURRECT YOU, I PUT YOUR SOUL INTO A WAX DOLL. MAKING THEM IS A HOBBY OF MINE.
YOU OUGHT TO BE PLEASED. IT'S MY BEST WORK.
Very proud.
I AM SUPPOSED TO BE A BEAUTIFUL YOUNG MAN, THE LORD OF VAMPIRES!
WHY DIDN'T YOU GIVE ME A MAN'S BODY?!
I HATE MEN. THEY'RE DIRTY.
YOU SOUND LIKE A GIRL WHO HASN'T GONE THROUGH PUBERTY YET...
HEH... I DON'T CARE.
I SHALL OBTAIN MY ORIGINAL BODY AFTER CONSUMING MORE POWER BY SUCKING BLOOD.
YOU WILL BE MY FIRST VICTIM!
BLAME YOURSELF FOR RAISING MY SOUL!
HEH

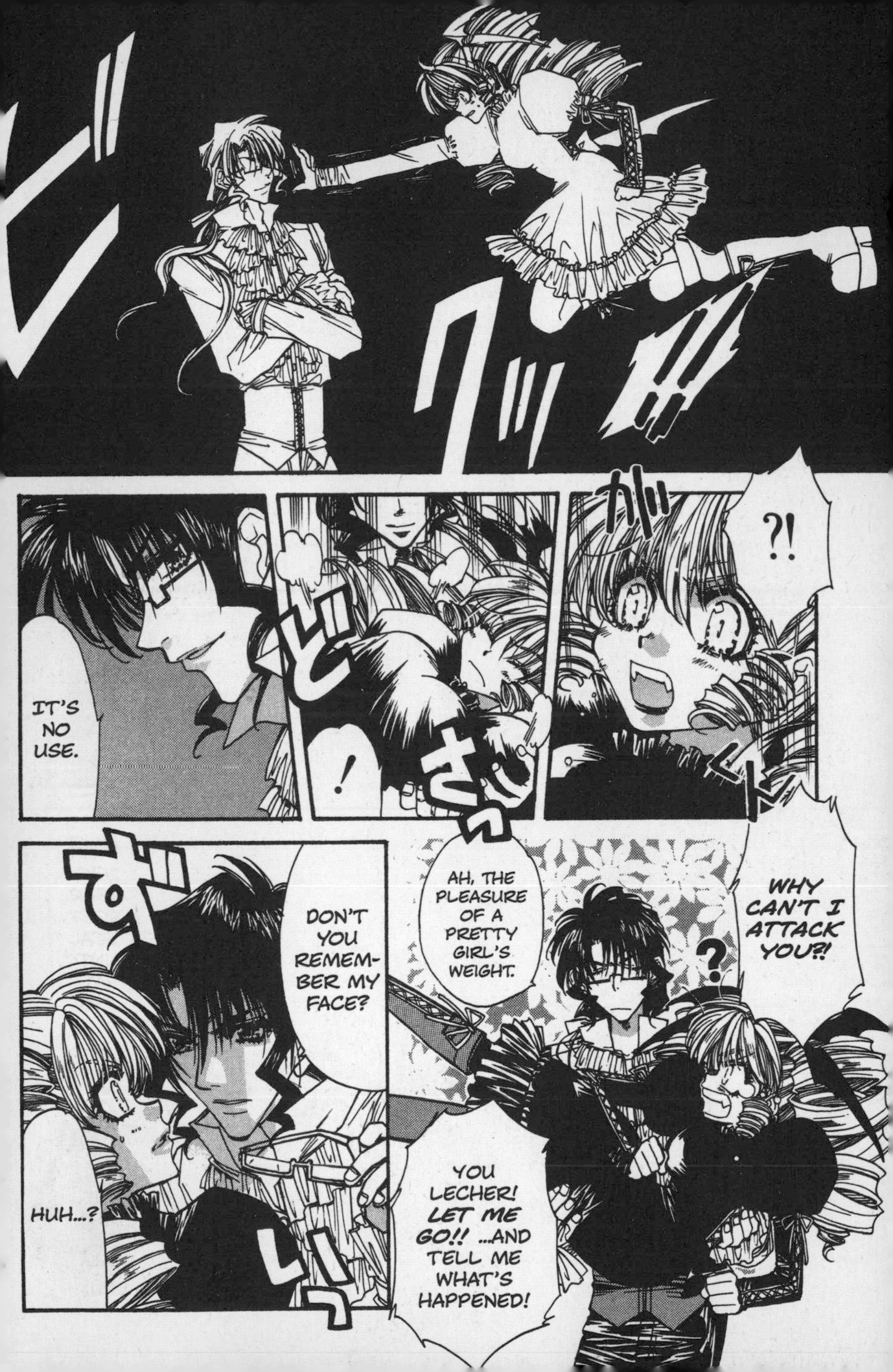

?!
!
IT'S NO USE.
WHY CAN'T I ATTACK YOU?!
?
AH, THE PLEASURE OF A PRETTY GIRL'S WEIGHT.
YOU LECHER! LET ME GO!! ...AND TELL ME WHAT'S HAPPENED!
DON'T YOU REMEMBER MY FACE?
HUH...?

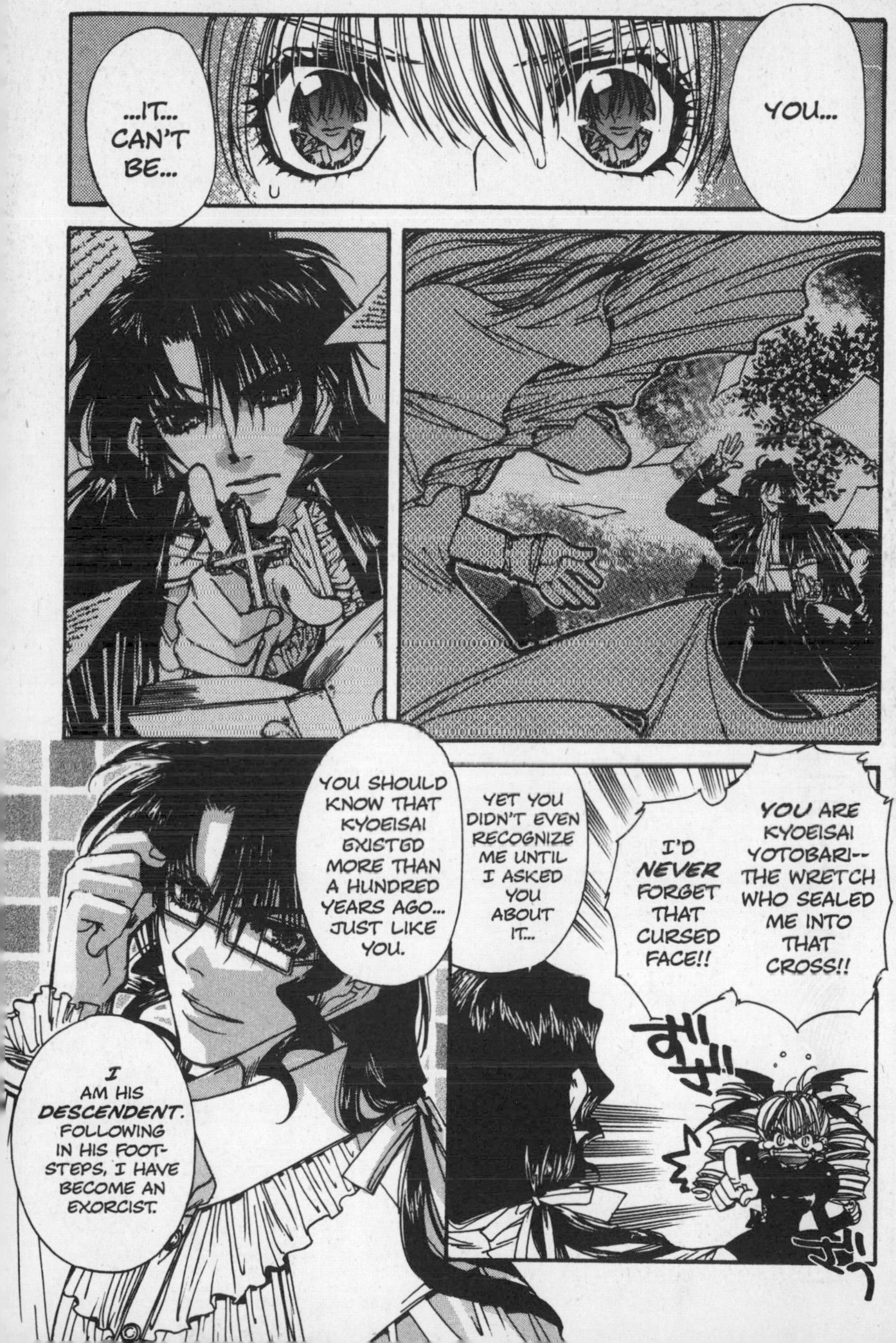
YOU...
...IT... CAN'T BE...
YOU ARE KYOEISAI YOTOBARI-- THE WRETCH WHO SEALED ME INTO THAT CROSS!!
I'D NEVER FORGET THAT CURSED FACE!!
YET YOU DIDN'T EVEN RECOGNIZE ME UNTIL I ASKED YOU ABOUT IT...
YOU SHOULD KNOW THAT KYOEISAI EXISTED MORE THAN A HUNDRED YEARS AGO... JUST LIKE YOU.
I AM HIS DESCENDENT. FOLLOWING IN HIS FOOT-STEPS, I HAVE BECOME AN EXORCIST.

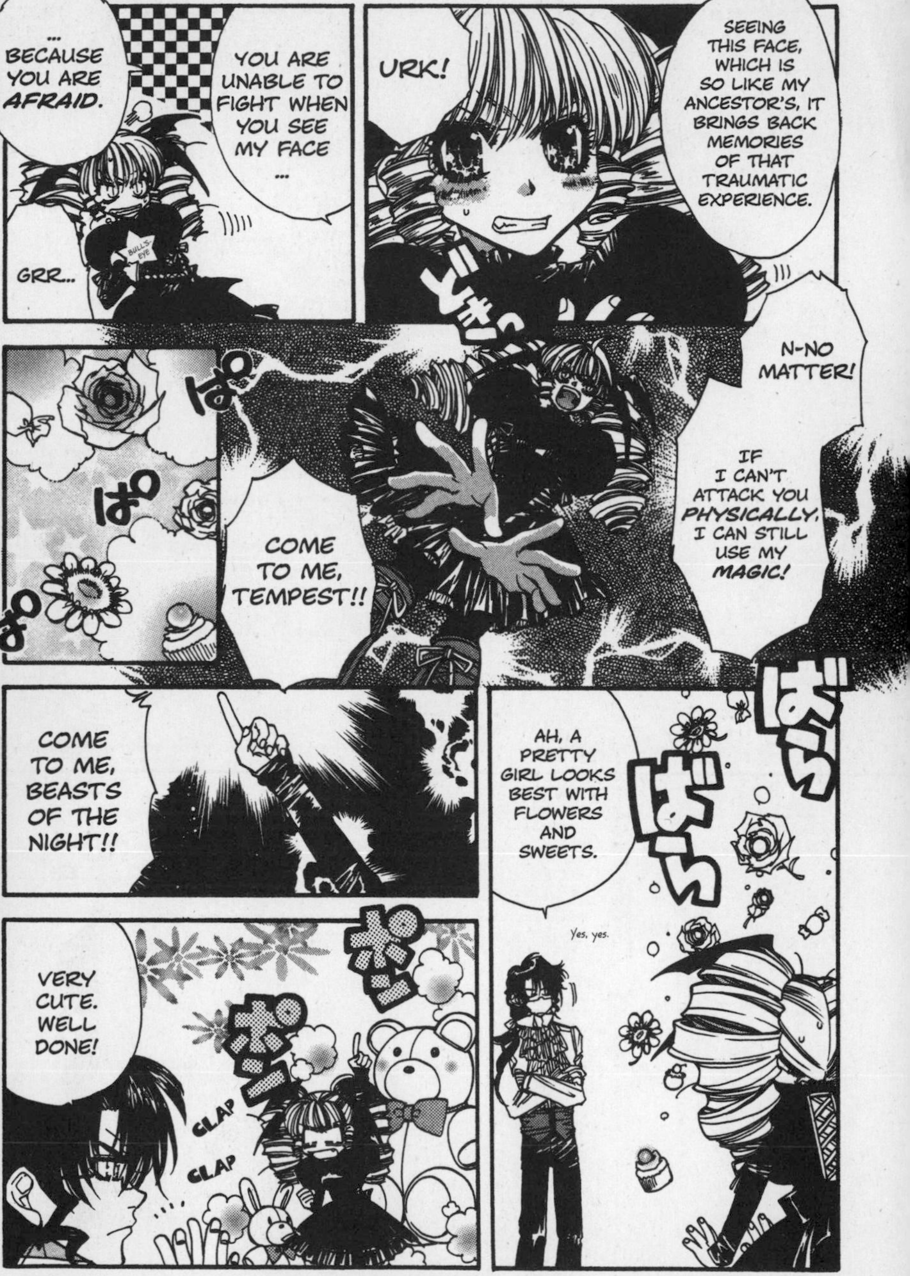
SEEING THIS FACE, WHICH IS SO LIKE MY ANCESTOR'S, IT BRINGS BACK MEMORIES OF THAT TRAUMATIC EXPERIENCE.
URK!
YOU ARE UNABLE TO FIGHT WHEN YOU SEE MY FACE ...
... BECAUSE YOU ARE AFRAID.
BULL'S-EYE
GRR...
N-NO MATTER!
IF I CAN'T ATTACK YOU PHYSICALLY, I CAN STILL USE MY MAGIC!
COME TO ME, TEMPEST!!
ぱ
ぱ
ぱ
ばら
ばら
AH, A PRETTY GIRL LOOKS BEST WITH FLOWERS AND SWEETS.
Yes, yes.
COME TO ME, BEASTS OF THE NIGHT!!
ポン
ポン
VERY CUTE. WELL DONE!
CLAP
CLAP
...

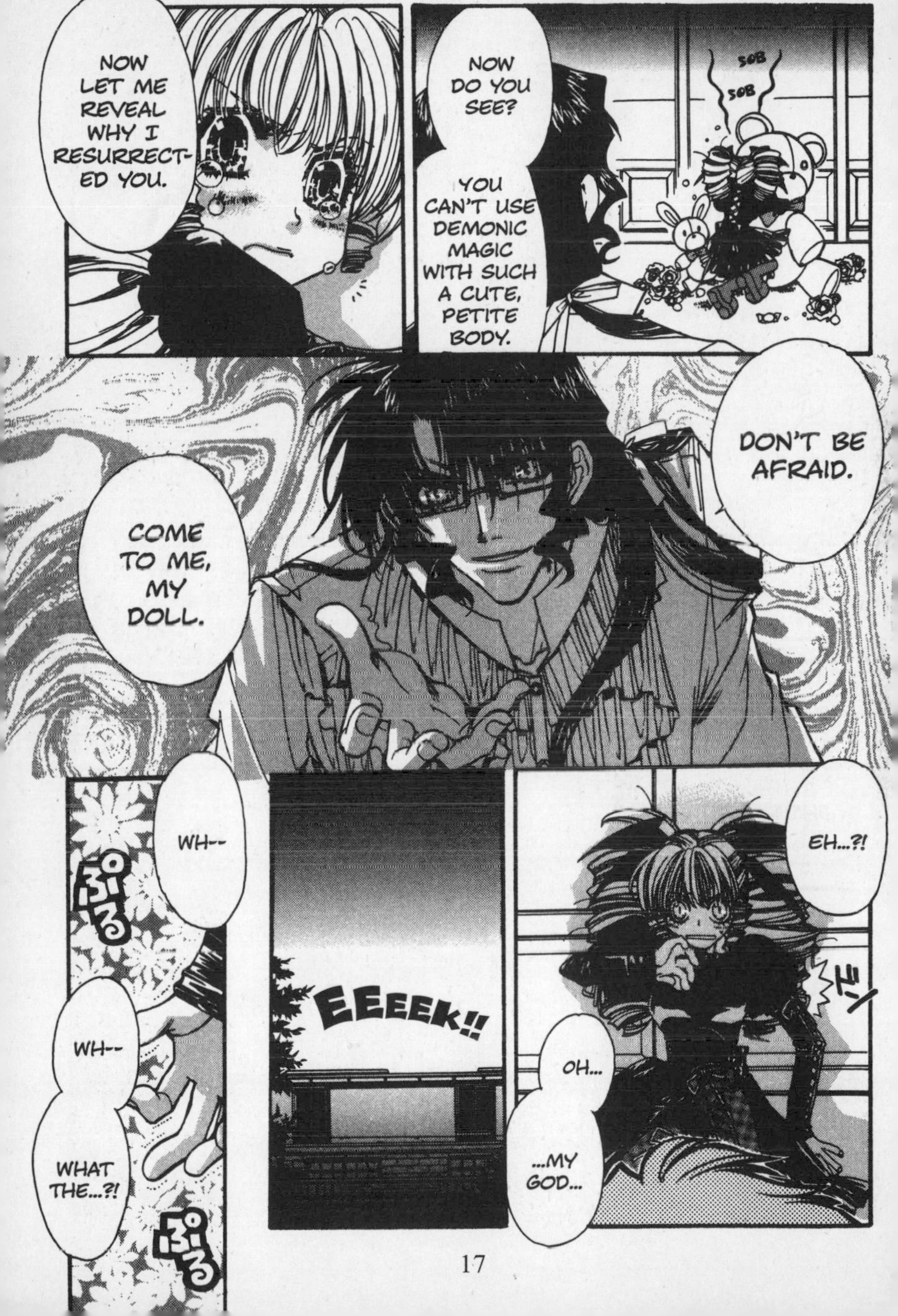
NOW DO YOU SEE?
YOU CAN'T USE DEMONIC MAGIC WITH SUCH A CUTE, PETITE BODY.
SOB
SOB
NOW LET ME REVEAL WHY I RESURRECT-ED YOU.
DON'T BE AFRAID.
COME TO ME, MY DOLL.
EH...?!
OH...
...MY GOD...
EEEEK!!
WH--
WH--
WHAT THE...?!

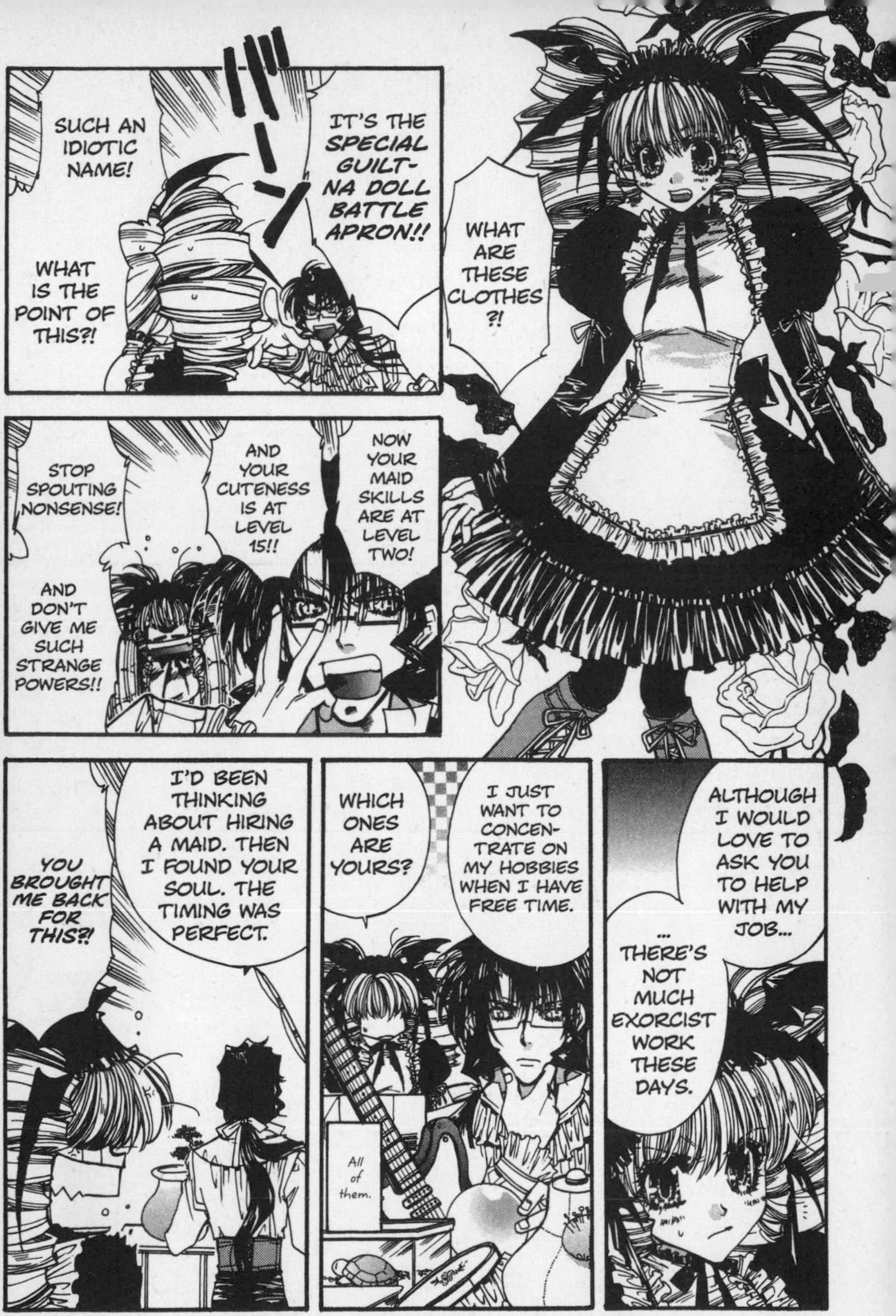
WHAT ARE THESE CLOTHES?!
IT'S THE SPECIAL GUILT-NA DOLL BATTLE APRON!!
SUCH AN IDIOTIC NAME!
WHAT IS THE POINT OF THIS?!
NOW YOUR MAID SKILLS ARE AT LEVEL TWO!
AND YOUR CUTENESS IS AT LEVEL 15!!
STOP SPOUTING NONSENSE!
AND DON'T GIVE ME SUCH STRANGE POWERS!!
ALTHOUGH I WOULD LOVE TO ASK YOU TO HELP WITH MY JOB...
...THERE'S NOT MUCH EXORCIST WORK THESE DAYS.
I JUST WANT TO CONCENTRATE ON MY HOBBIES WHEN I HAVE FREE TIME.
WHICH ONES ARE YOURS?
All of them.
I'D BEEN THINKING ABOUT HIRING A MAID. THEN I FOUND YOUR SOUL. THE TIMING WAS PERFECT.
YOU BROUGHT ME BACK FOR THIS?!

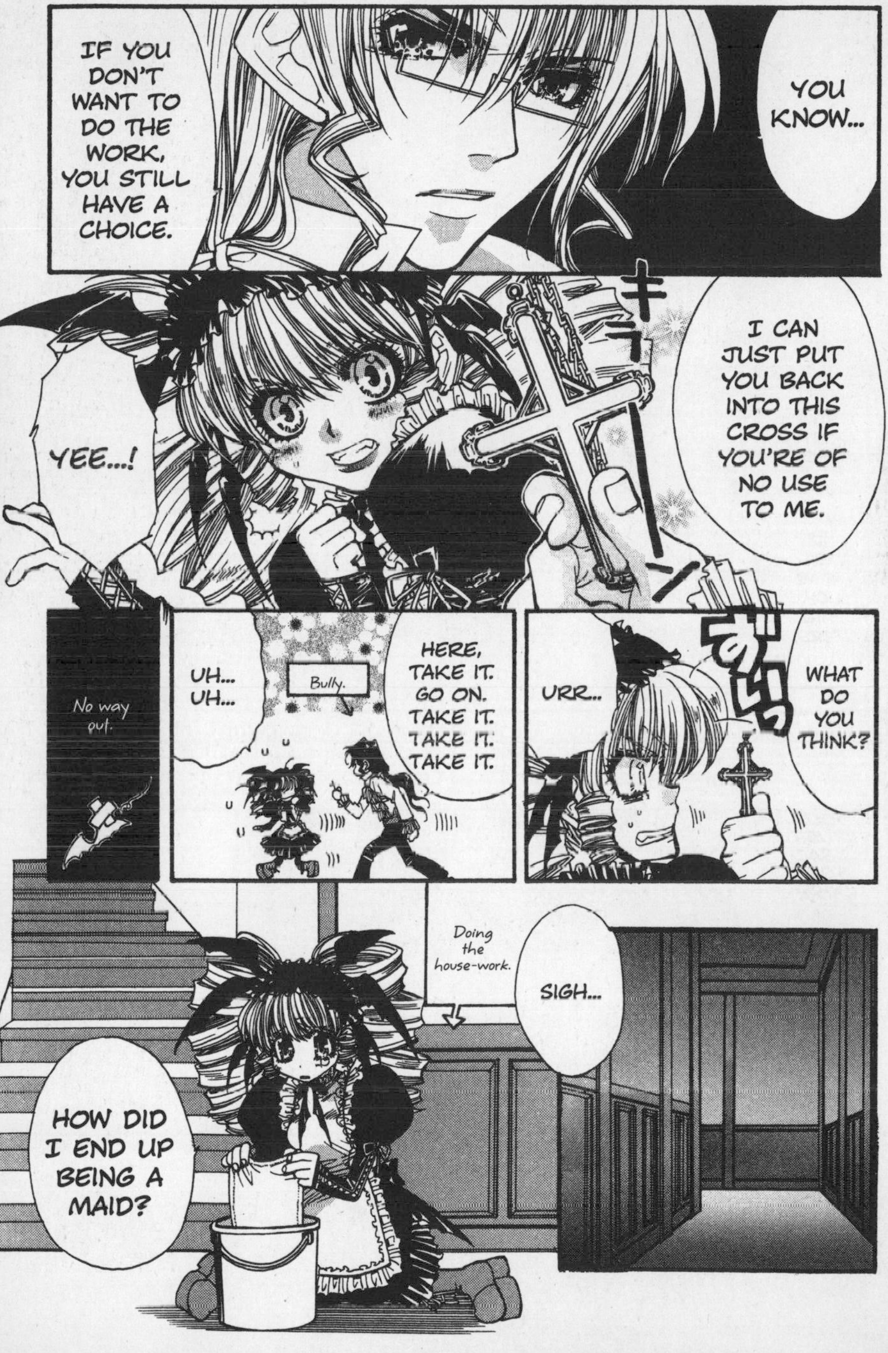
YOU KNOW...
IF YOU DON'T WANT TO DO THE WORK, YOU STILL HAVE A CHOICE.
I CAN JUST PUT YOU BACK INTO THIS CROSS IF YOU'RE OF NO USE TO ME.
YEE...!
WHAT DO YOU THINK?
URR..
HERE, TAKE IT. GO ON. TAKE IT. TAKE IT. TAKE IT.
Bully.
UH... UH...
No way out.
SIGH...
Doing the house-work.
HOW DID I END UP BEING A MAID?

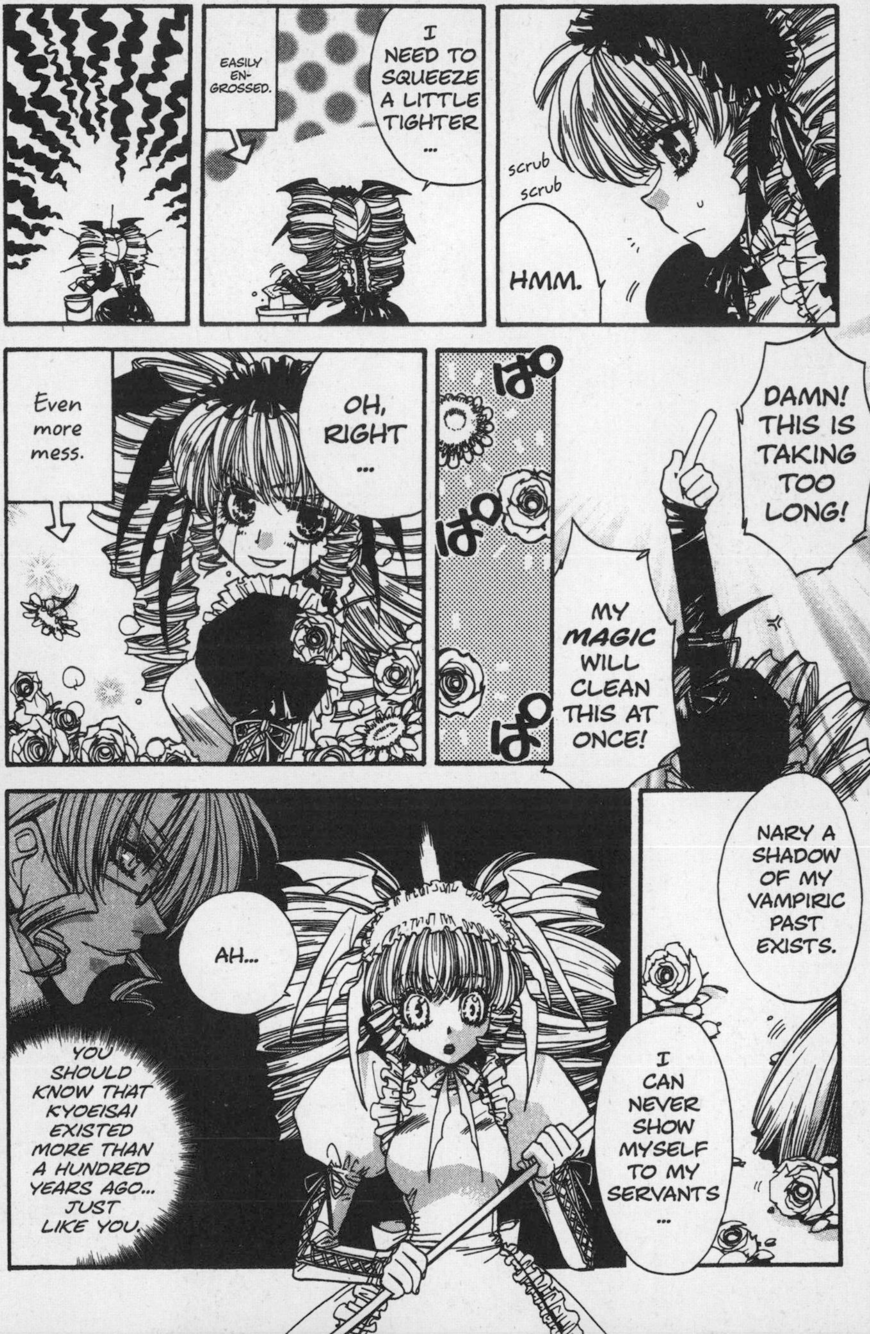
scrub scrub
HMM.
I NEED TO SQUEEZE A LITTLE TIGHTER ...
EASILY EN-GROSSED.
DAMN! THIS IS TAKING TOO LONG!
MY MAGIC WILL CLEAN THIS AT ONCE!
ぱ ぱ ぱ
OH, RIGHT ...
Even more mess.
NARY A SHADOW OF MY VAMPIRIC PAST EXISTS.
I CAN NEVER SHOW MYSELF TO MY SERVANTS ...
AH...
YOU SHOULD KNOW THAT KYOEISAI EXISTED MORE THAN A HUNDRED YEARS AGO... JUST LIKE YOU.

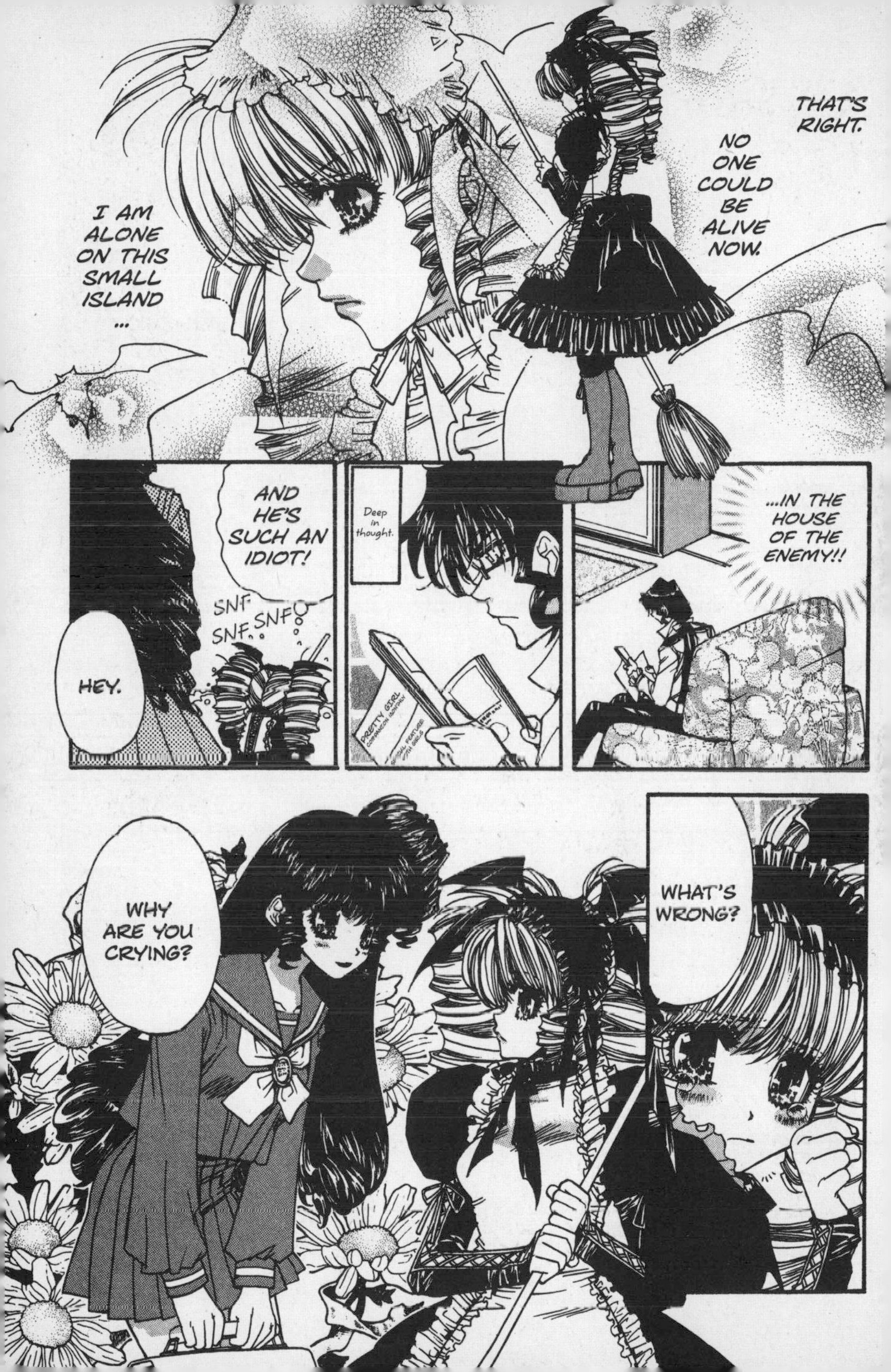
THAT'S RIGHT.
NO ONE COULD BE ALIVE NOW.
I AM ALONE ON THIS SMALL ISLAND ...
...IN THE HOUSE OF THE ENEMY!!
Deep in thought.
PRETTY GIRL
AND HE'S SUCH AN IDIOT!
SNF SNF SNF
HEY.
WHAT'S WRONG?
WHY ARE YOU CRYING?

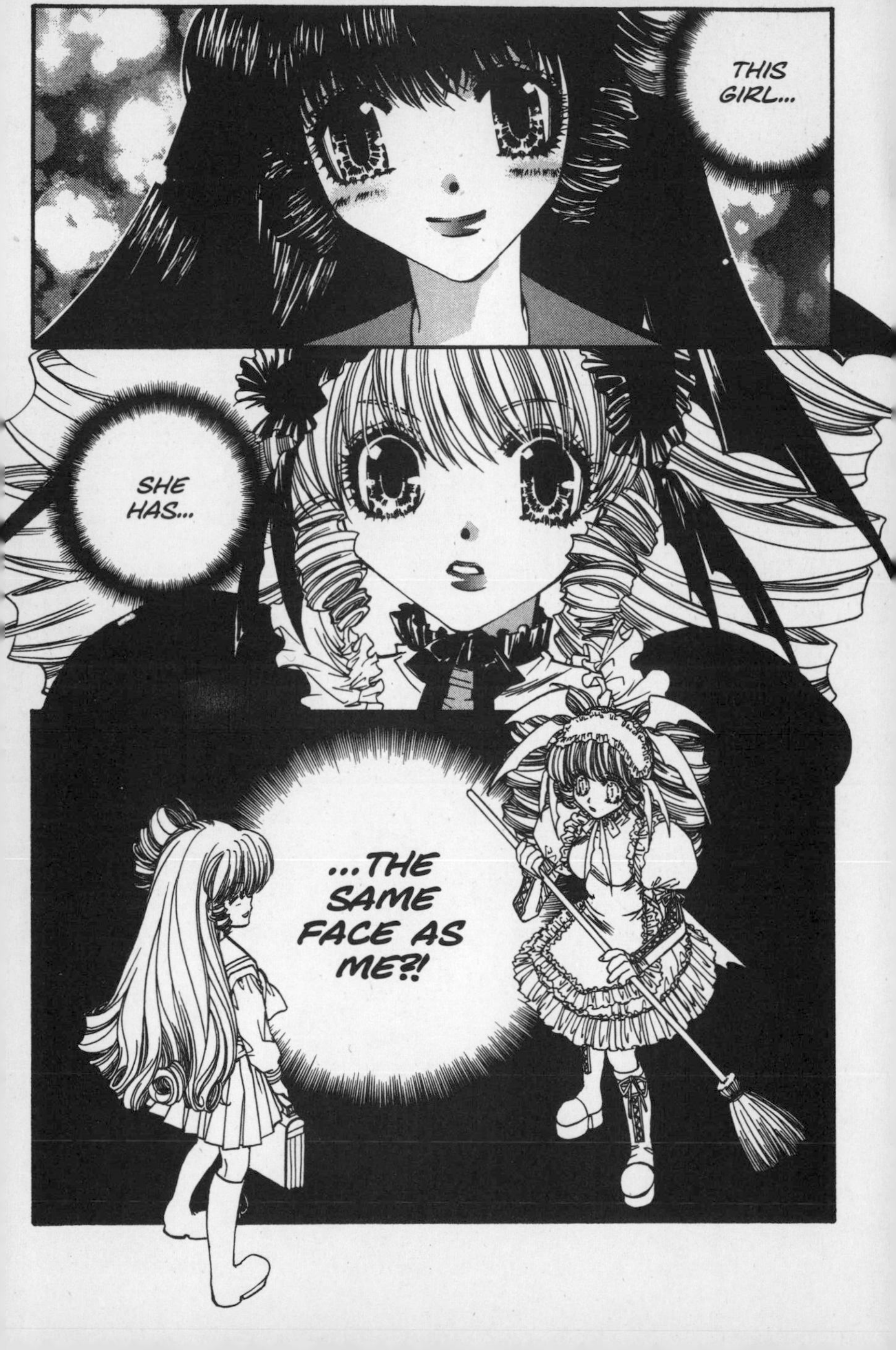
THIS GIRL...
SHE HAS...
...THE SAME FACE AS ME?!

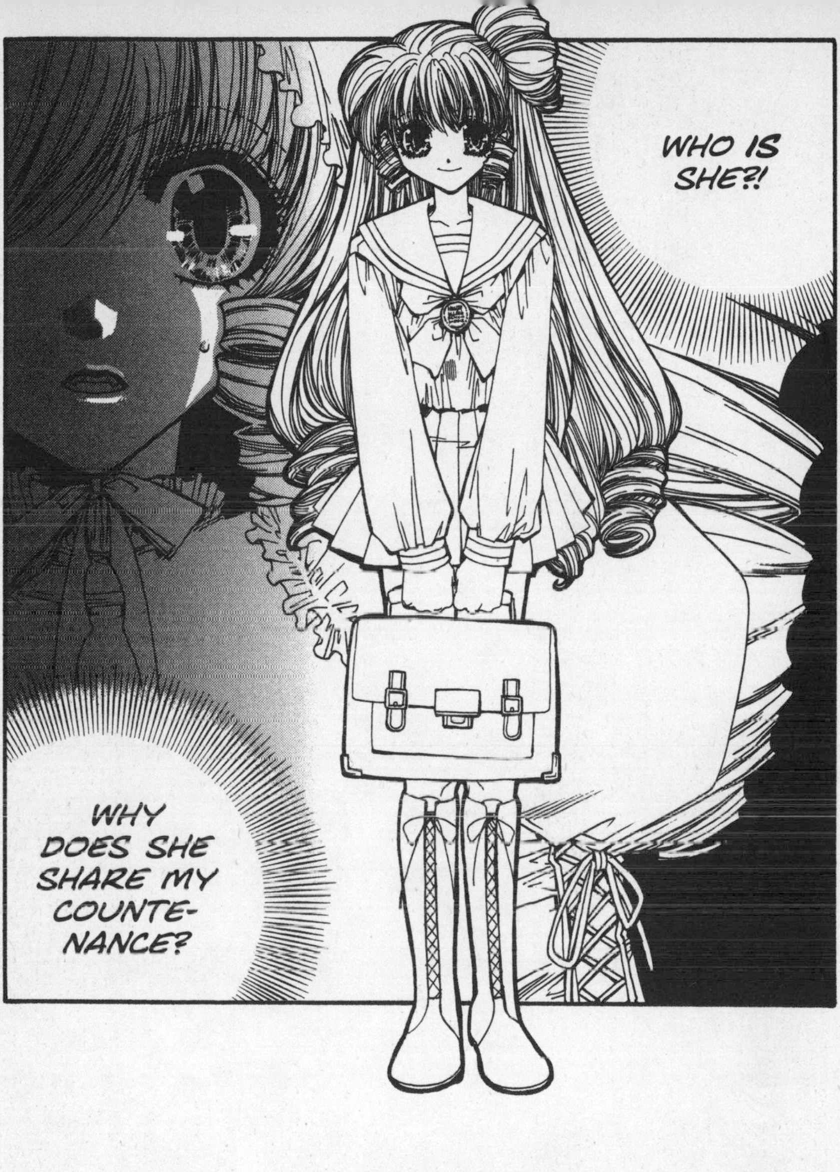
WHO IS SHE?!
WHY DOES SHE SHARE MY COUNTE-NANCE?

♯1.5 REBORN Part 2

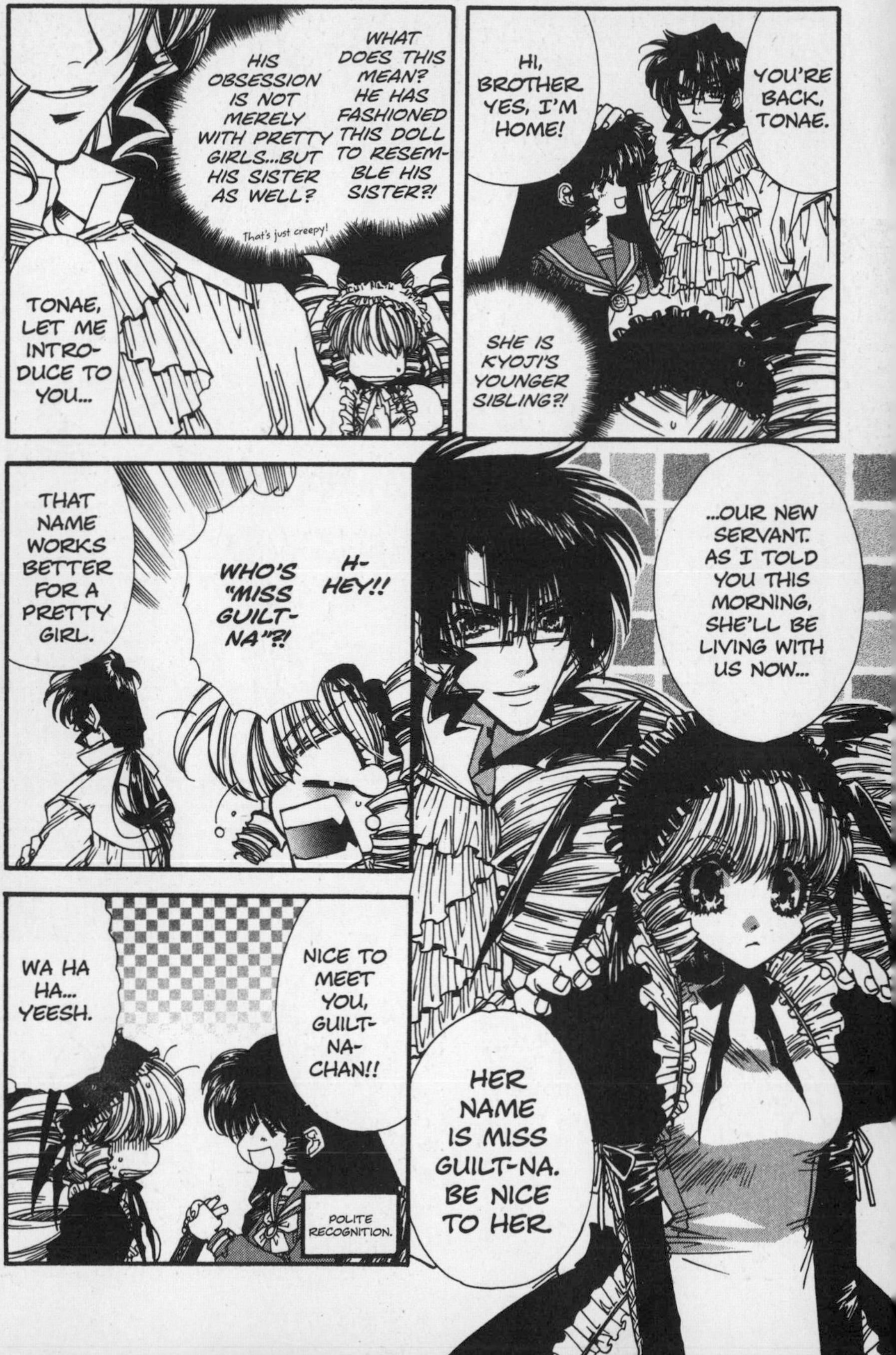
YOU'RE BACK, TONAE.
HI, BROTHER YES, I'M HOME!
SHE IS KYOJI'S YOUNGER SIBLING?!
WHAT DOES THIS MEAN? HE HAS FASHIONED THIS DOLL TO RESEMBLE HIS SISTER?!
HIS OBSESSION IS NOT MERELY WITH PRETTY GIRLS...BUT HIS SISTER AS WELL?
That's just creepy!
TONAE, LET ME INTRODUCE TO YOU...
...OUR NEW SERVANT. AS I TOLD YOU THIS MORNING, SHE'LL BE LIVING WITH US NOW...
HER NAME IS MISS GUILT-NA. BE NICE TO HER
H-HEY!!
WHO'S "MISS GUILT-NA"?!
THAT NAME WORKS BETTER FOR A PRETTY GIRL.
NICE TO MEET YOU, GUILT-NA-CHAN!!
WA HA HA... YEESH.
POLITE RECOGNITION.

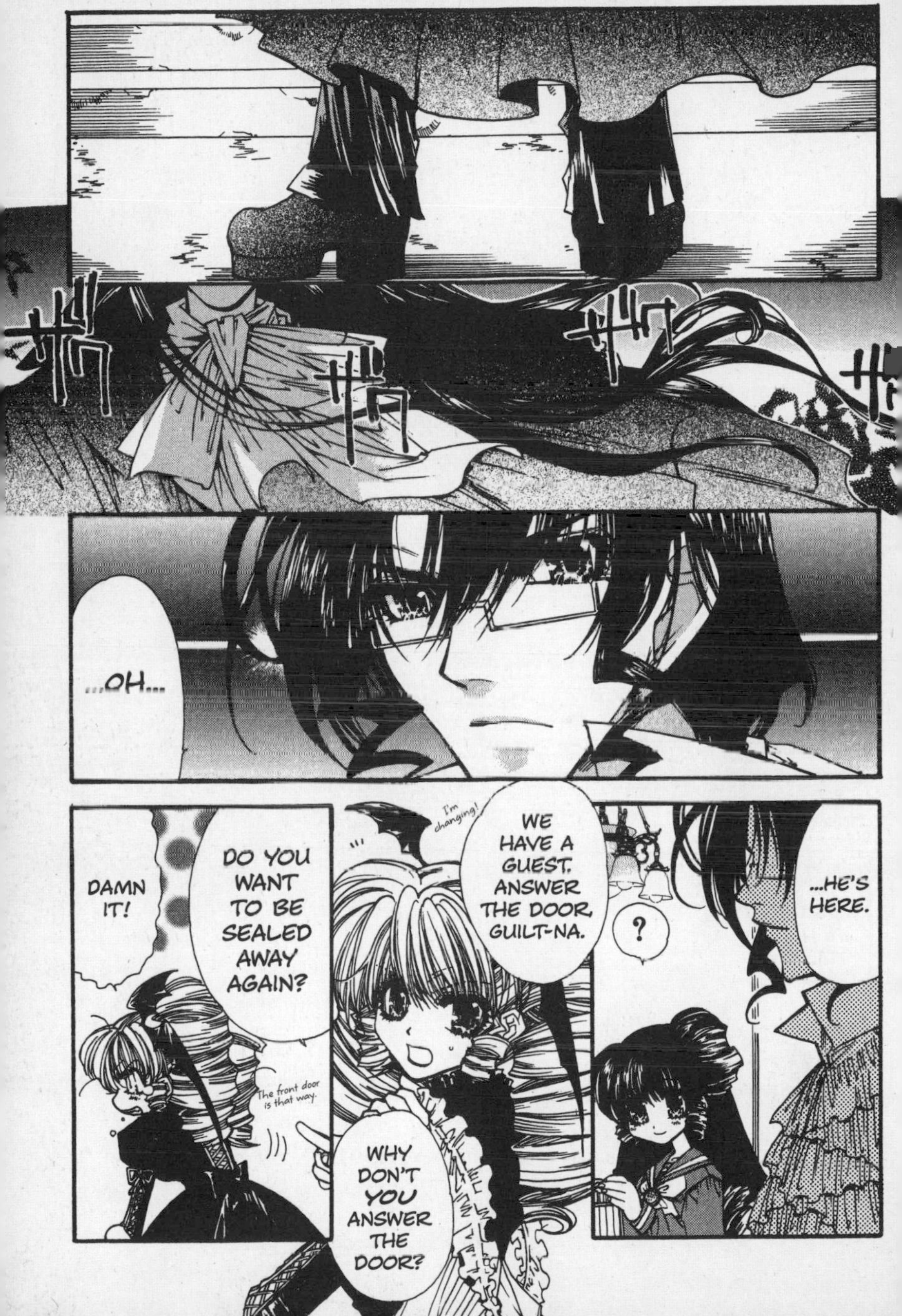
...OH...
...HE'S HERE.
?
WE HAVE A GUEST. ANSWER THE DOOR, GUILT-NA.
I'm changing!
WHY DON'T YOU ANSWER THE DOOR?
DO YOU WANT TO BE SEALED AWAY AGAIN?
The front door is that way.
DAMN IT!

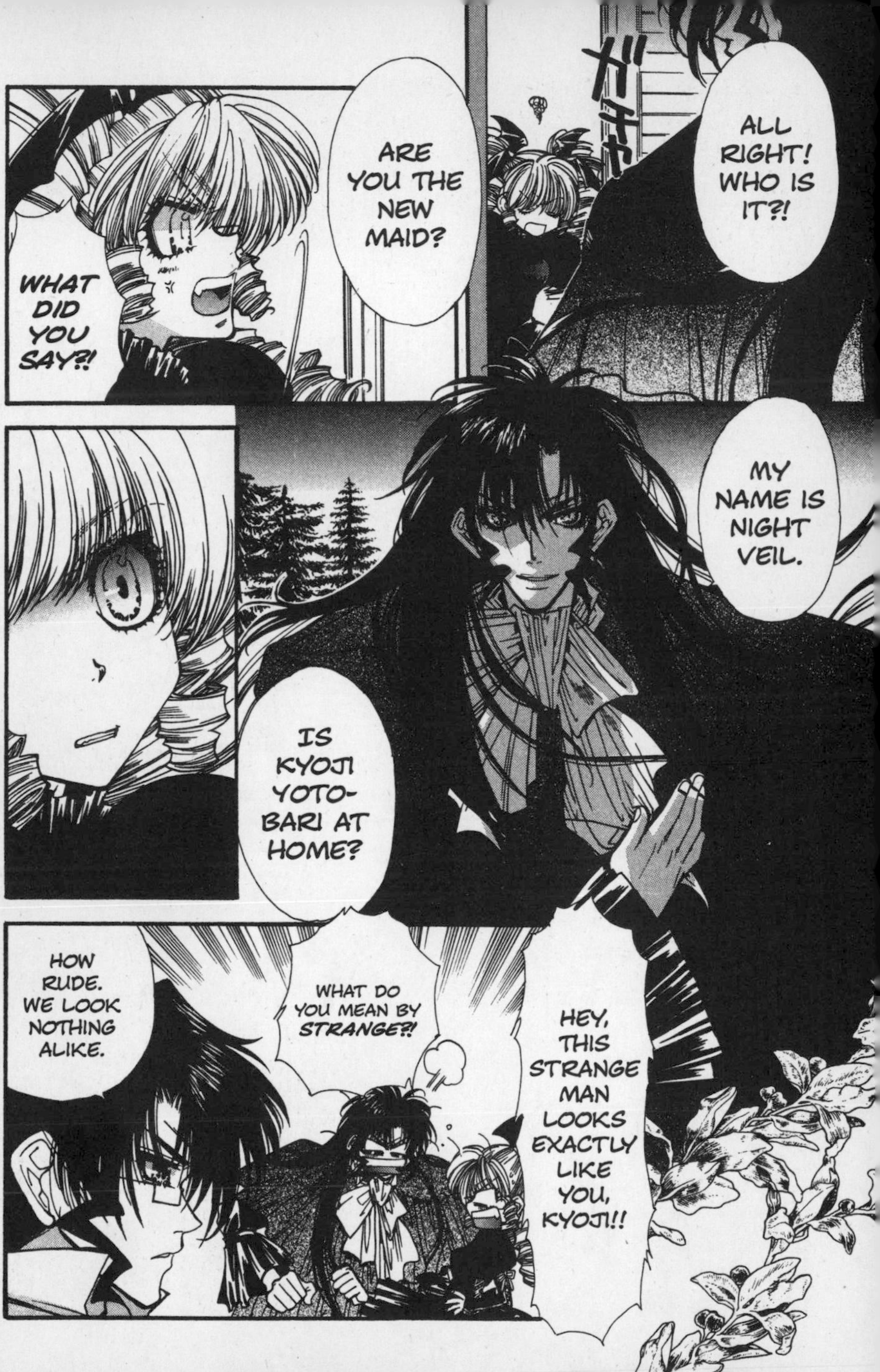
ALL RIGHT! WHO IS IT?!
ARE YOU THE NEW MAID?
WHAT DID YOU SAY?!
MY NAME IS NIGHT VEIL.
IS KYOJI YOTOBARI AT HOME?
HEY, THIS STRANGE MAN LOOKS EXACTLY LIKE YOU, KYOJI!!
WHAT DO YOU MEAN BY *STRANGE*?!
HOW RUDE. WE LOOK NOTHING ALIKE.

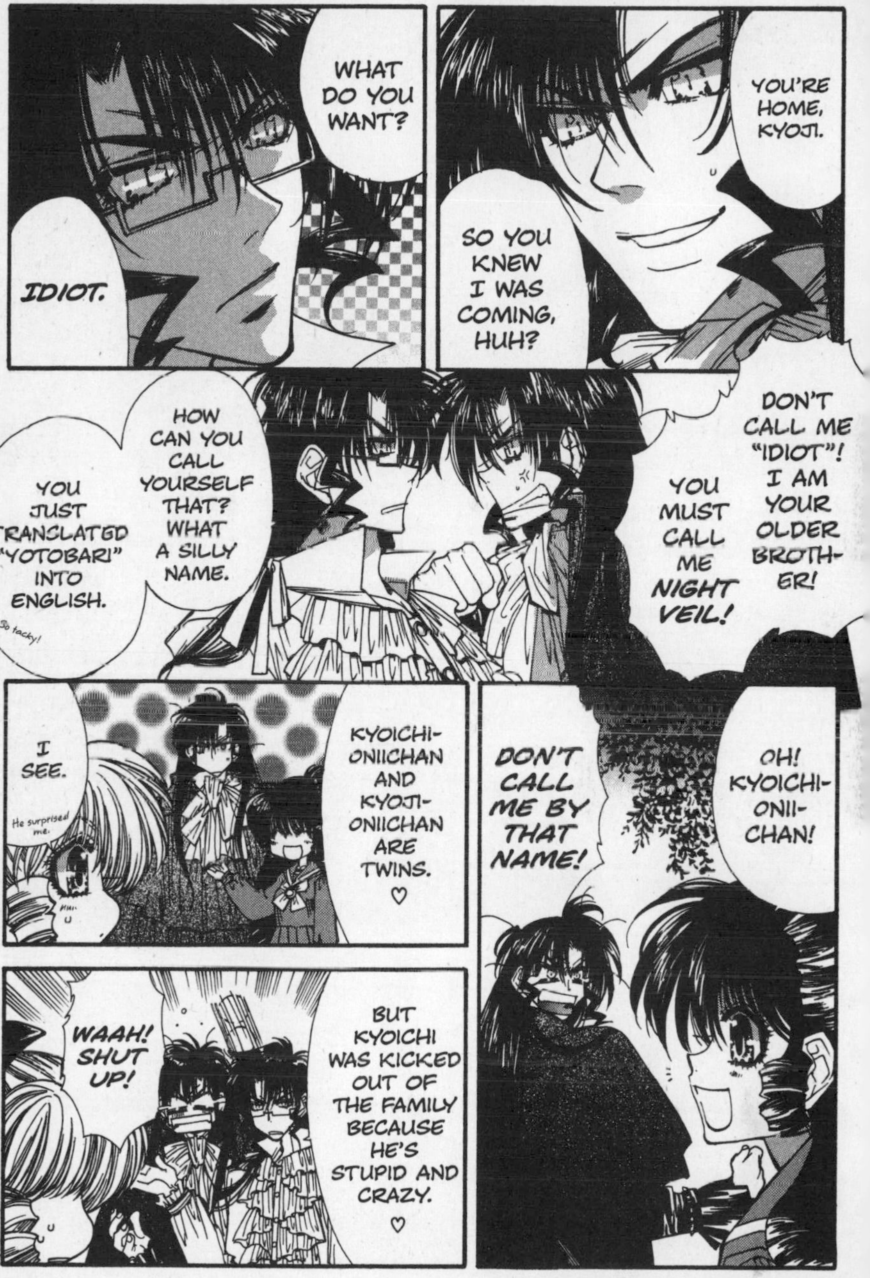
YOU'RE HOME, KYOJI.
SO YOU KNEW I WAS COMING, HUH?
WHAT DO YOU WANT?
IDIOT.
DON'T CALL ME "IDIOT"! I AM YOUR OLDER BROTH-ER!
YOU MUST CALL ME NIGHT VEIL!
HOW CAN YOU CALL YOURSELF THAT? WHAT A SILLY NAME.
YOU JUST TRANSLATED "YOTOBARI" INTO ENGLISH.
So tacky!
OH! KYOICHI-ONII-CHAN!
DON'T CALL ME BY THAT NAME!
KYOICHI-ONIICHAN AND KYOJI-ONIICHAN ARE TWINS. ♡
I SEE.
He surprised me.
BUT KYOICHI WAS KICKED OUT OF THE FAMILY BECAUSE HE'S STUPID AND CRAZY. ♡
WAAH! SHUT UP!

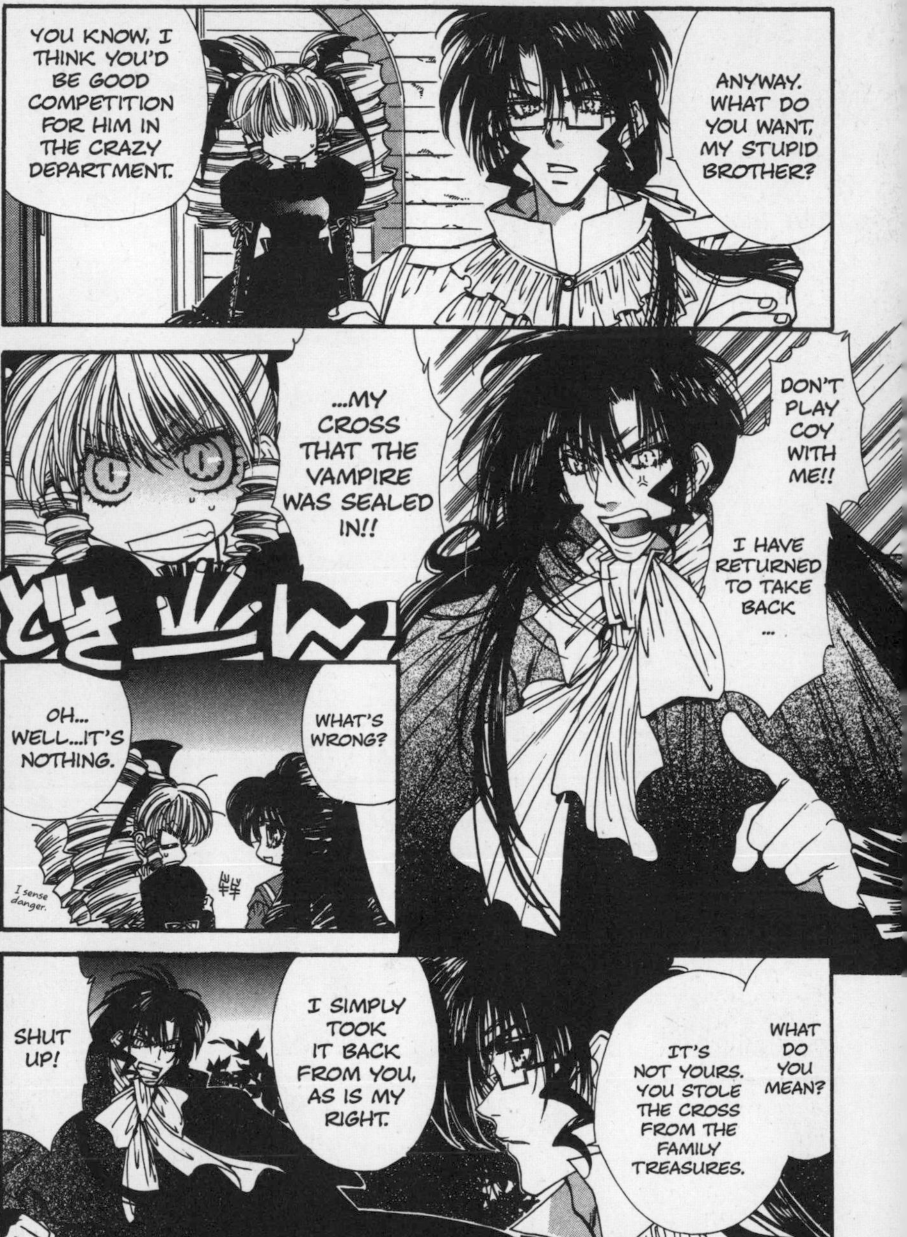
ANYWAY. WHAT DO YOU WANT, MY STUPID BROTHER?
YOU KNOW, I THINK YOU'D BE GOOD COMPETITION FOR HIM IN THE CRAZY DEPARTMENT.
DON'T PLAY COY WITH ME!!
I HAVE RETURNED TO TAKE BACK ...
...MY CROSS THAT THE VAMPIRE WAS SEALED IN!!
ときーん
WHAT'S WRONG?
OH... WELL...IT'S NOTHING.
I sense danger.
WHAT DO YOU MEAN?
IT'S NOT YOURS. YOU STOLE THE CROSS FROM THE FAMILY TREASURES.
I SIMPLY TOOK IT BACK FROM YOU, AS IS MY RIGHT.
SHUT UP!

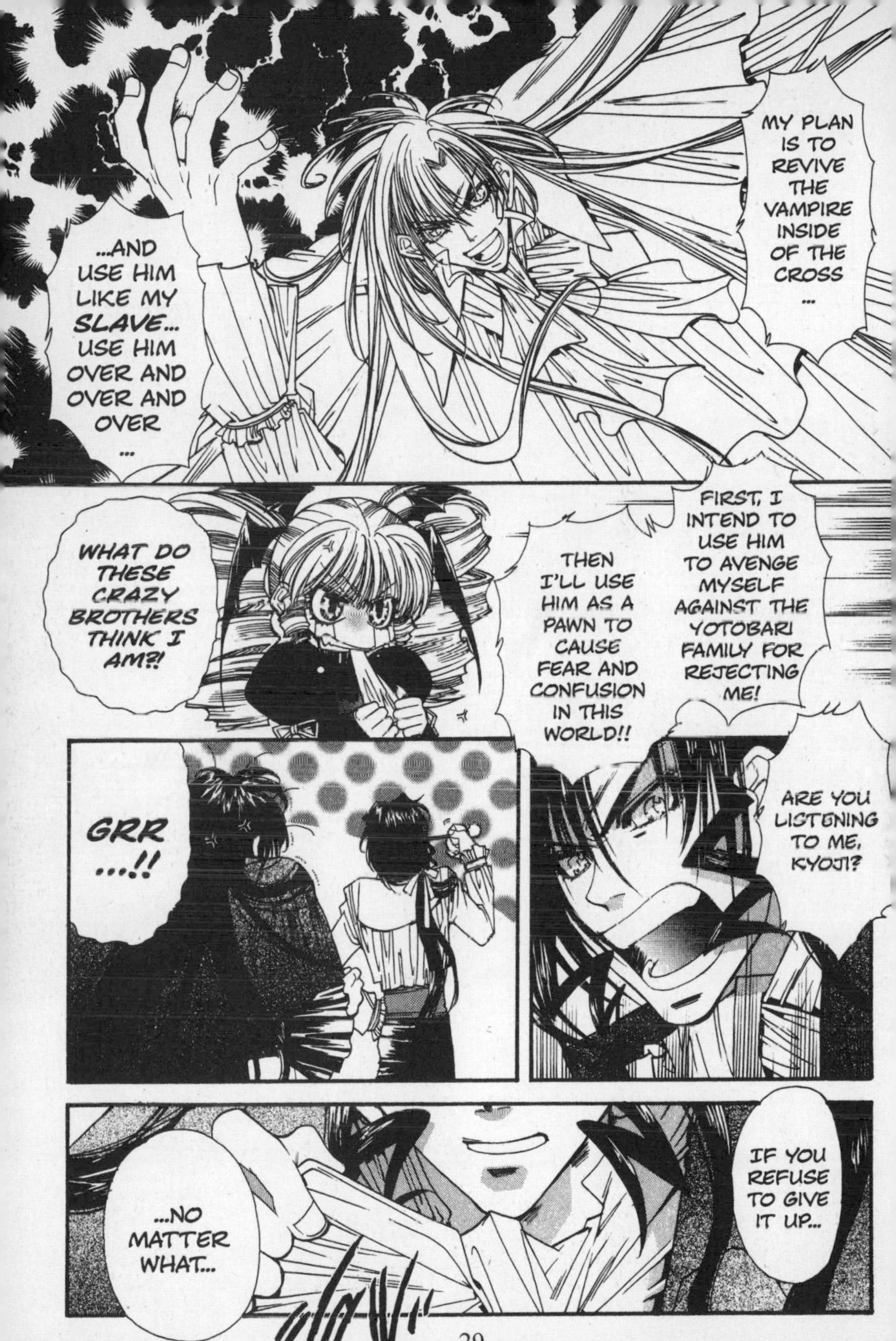
MY PLAN IS TO REVIVE THE VAMPIRE INSIDE OF THE CROSS ...
...AND USE HIM LIKE MY SLAVE... USE HIM OVER AND OVER AND OVER ...
FIRST, I INTEND TO USE HIM TO AVENGE MYSELF AGAINST THE YOTOBARI FAMILY FOR REJECTING ME!
THEN I'LL USE HIM AS A PAWN TO CAUSE FEAR AND CONFUSION IN THIS WORLD!!
WHAT DO THESE CRAZY BROTHERS THINK I AM?!
ARE YOU LISTENING TO ME, KYOJI?
GRR ...!!
IF YOU REFUSE TO GIVE IT UP...
...NO MATTER WHAT...

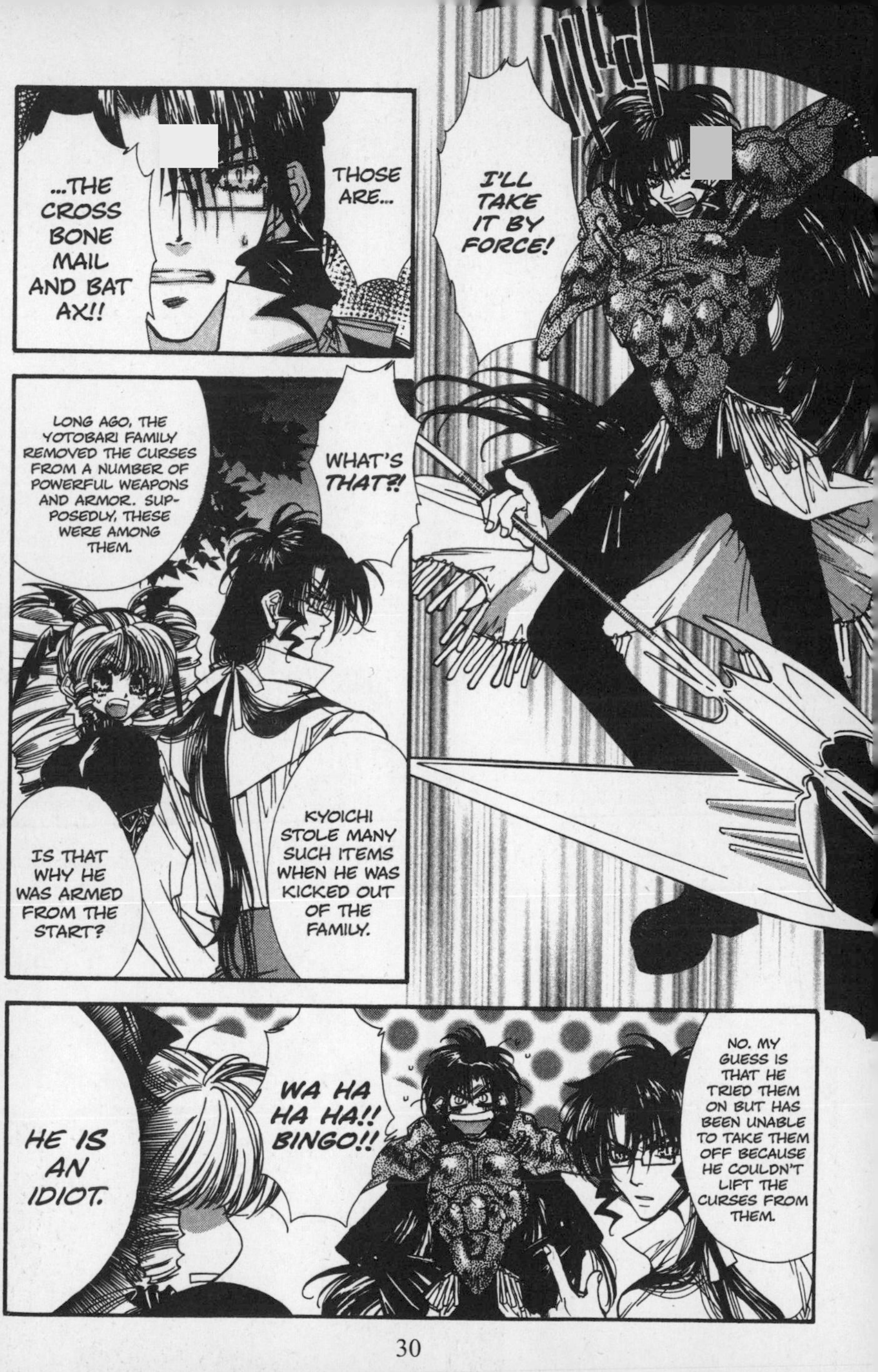
I'LL TAKE IT BY FORCE!
THOSE ARE...
...THE CROSS BONE MAIL AND BAT AX!!
WHAT'S THAT?!
LONG AGO, THE YOTOBARI FAMILY REMOVED THE CURSES FROM A NUMBER OF POWERFUL WEAPONS AND ARMOR. SUP-POSEDLY, THESE WERE AMONG THEM.
KYOICHI STOLE MANY SUCH ITEMS WHEN HE WAS KICKED OUT OF THE FAMILY.
IS THAT WHY HE WAS ARMED FROM THE START?
NO. MY GUESS IS THAT HE TRIED THEM ON BUT HAS BEEN UNABLE TO TAKE THEM OFF BECAUSE HE COULDN'T LIFT THE CURSES FROM THEM.
WA HA HA HA!! BINGO!!
HE IS AN IDIOT.

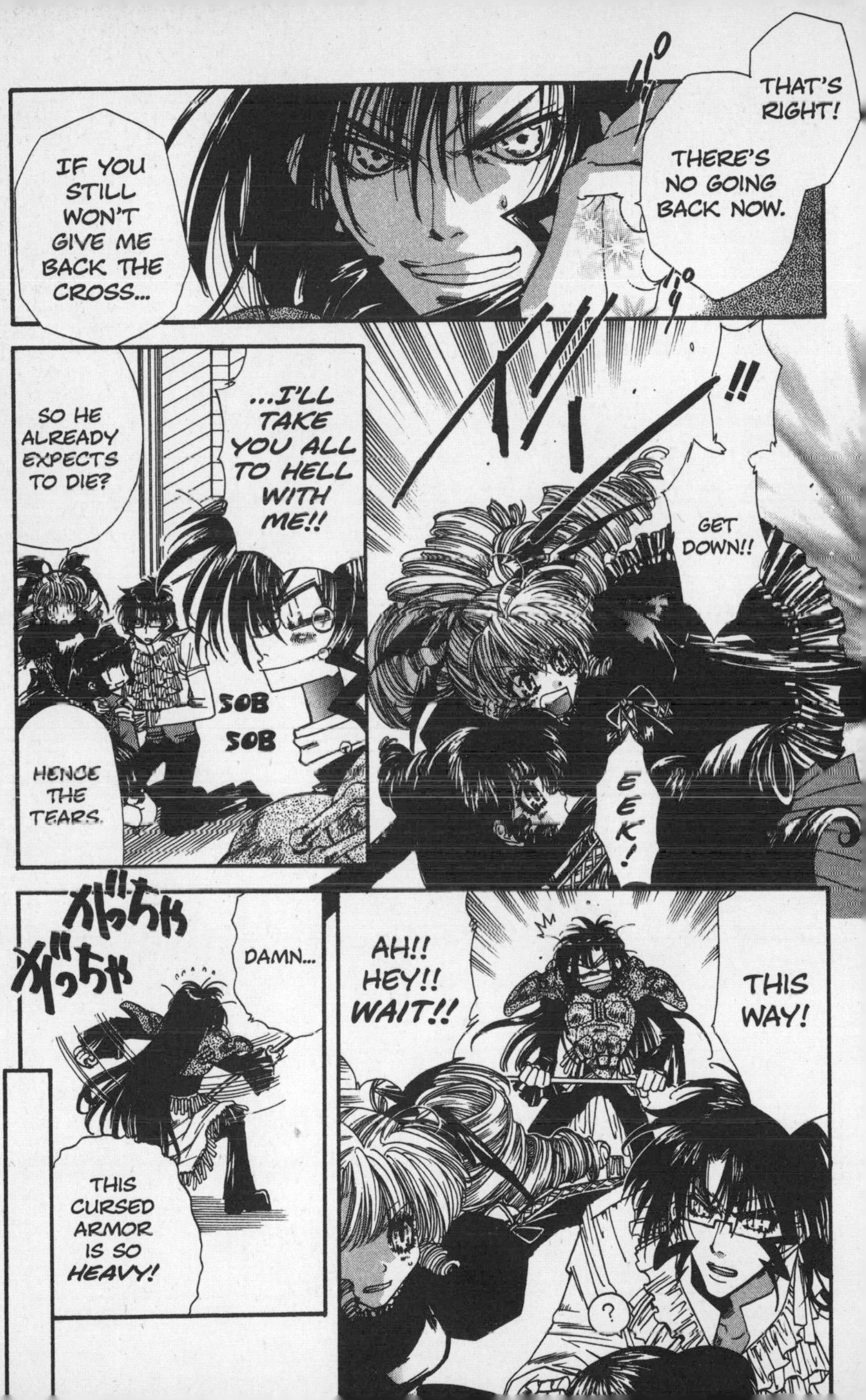
THAT'S RIGHT!
THERE'S NO GOING BACK NOW.
IF YOU STILL WON'T GIVE ME BACK THE CROSS...
!!
GET DOWN!!
EEK!
...I'LL TAKE YOU ALL TO HELL WITH ME!!
SO HE ALREADY EXPECTS TO DIE?
SOB SOB
HENCE THE TEARS.
THIS WAY!
AH!! HEY!! WAIT!!
DAMN...
THIS CURSED ARMOR IS SO HEAVY!

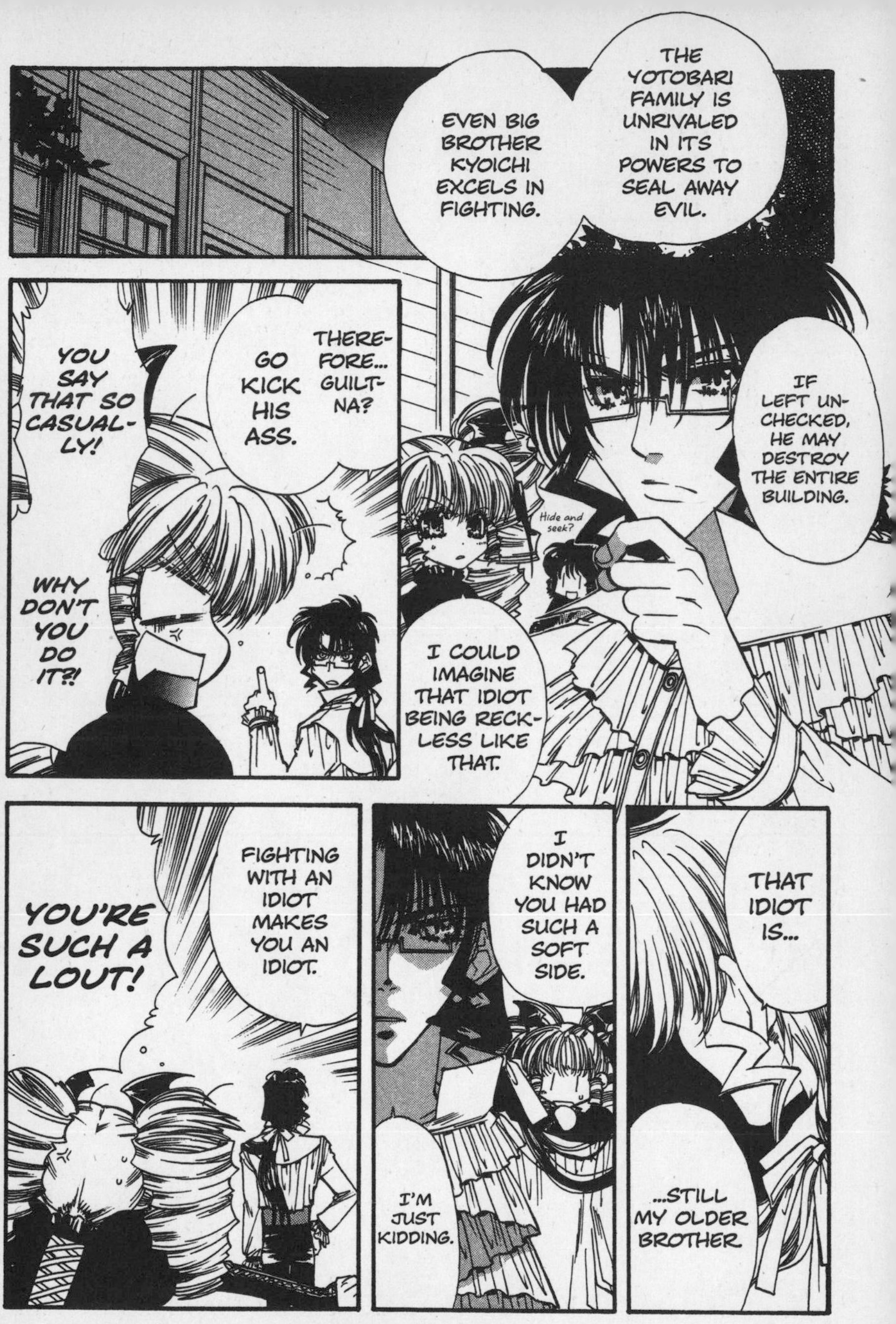
THE YOTOBARI FAMILY IS UNRIVALED IN ITS POWERS TO SEAL AWAY EVIL.
EVEN BIG BROTHER KYOICHI EXCELS IN FIGHTING.
IF LEFT UN-CHECKED, HE MAY DESTROY THE ENTIRE BUILDING.
Hide and seek?
I COULD IMAGINE THAT IDIOT BEING RECK-LESS LIKE THAT.
THERE-FORE... GUILT-NA?
GO KICK HIS ASS.
YOU SAY THAT SO CASUAL-LY!
WHY DON'T YOU DO IT?!
THAT IDIOT IS...
...STILL MY OLDER BROTHER.
I DIDN'T KNOW YOU HAD SUCH A SOFT SIDE.
I'M JUST KIDDING.
FIGHTING WITH AN IDIOT MAKES YOU AN IDIOT.
YOU'RE SUCH A LOUT!

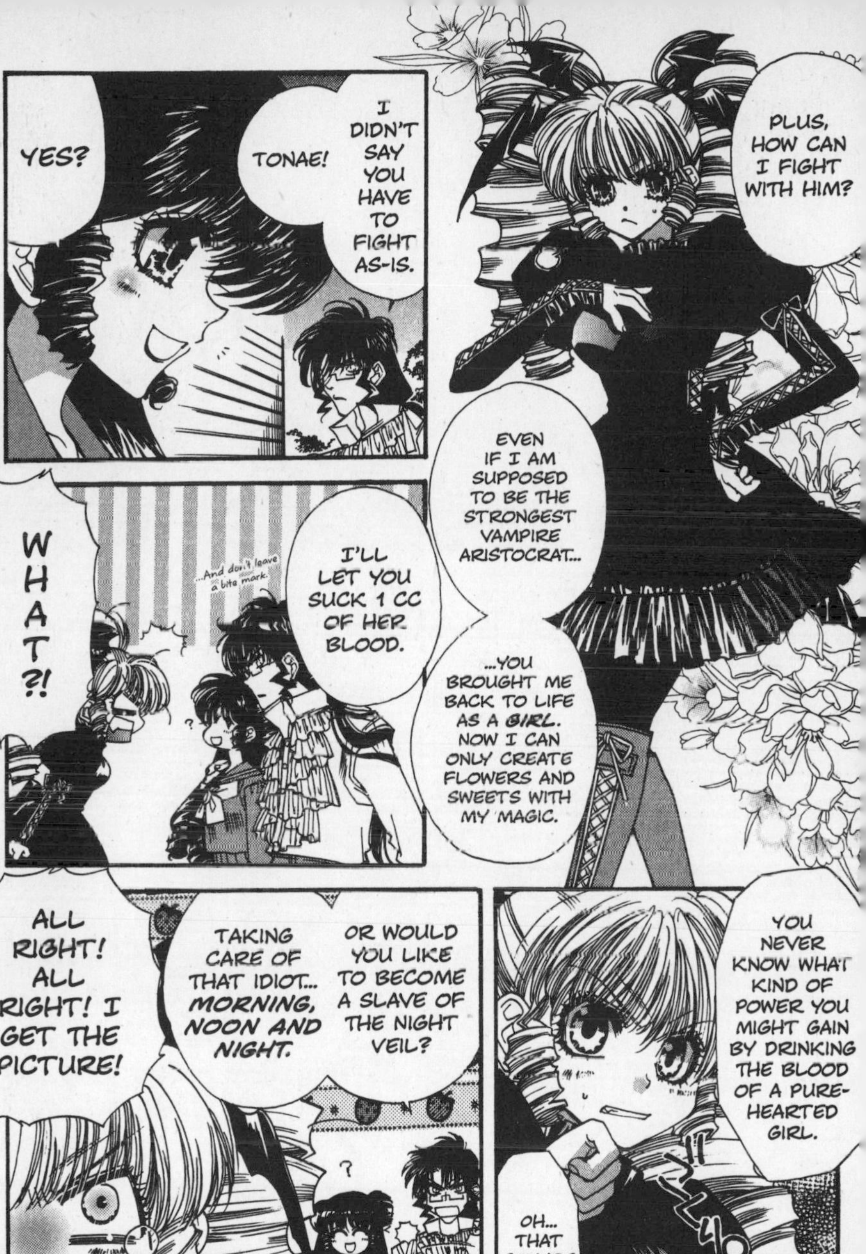
PLUS, HOW CAN I FIGHT WITH HIM?
EVEN IF I AM SUPPOSED TO BE THE STRONGEST VAMPIRE ARISTOCRAT...
...YOU BROUGHT ME BACK TO LIFE AS A *GIRL*. NOW I CAN ONLY CREATE FLOWERS AND SWEETS WITH MY MAGIC.
I DIDN'T SAY YOU HAVE TO FIGHT AS-IS.
TONAE!
YES?
I'LL LET YOU SUCK 1 CC OF HER BLOOD.
...And don't leave a bite mark.
WHAT?!
YOU NEVER KNOW WHAT KIND OF POWER YOU MIGHT GAIN BY DRINKING THE BLOOD OF A PURE-HEARTED GIRL.
OH... THAT SOUNDS ...
OR WOULD YOU LIKE TO BECOME A SLAVE OF THE NIGHT VEIL?
TAKING CARE OF THAT IDIOT... *MORNING, NOON AND NIGHT.*
ALL RIGHT! ALL RIGHT! I GET THE PICTURE!

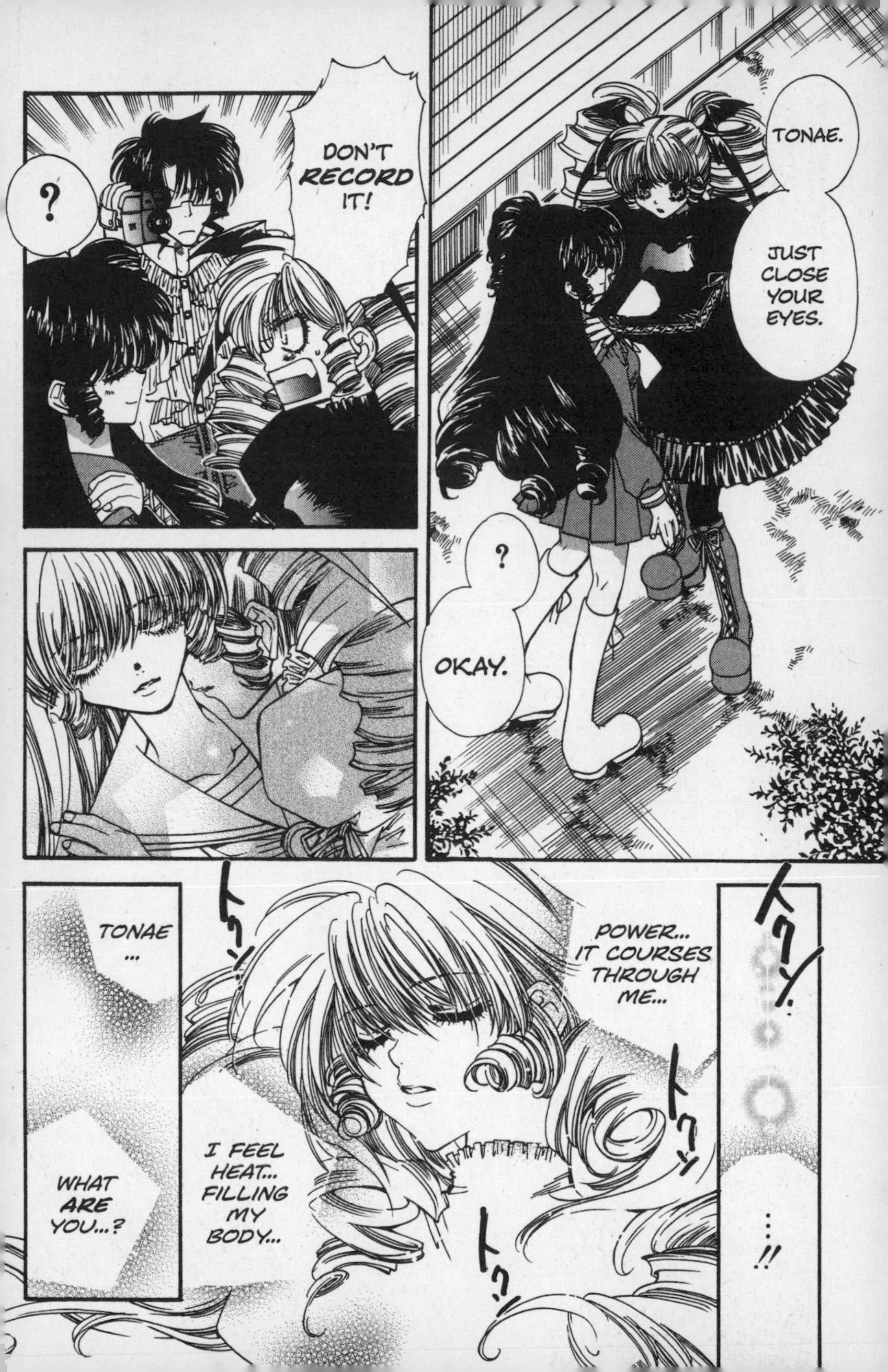
TONAE.
JUST CLOSE YOUR EYES.
?
OKAY.
DON'T RECORD IT!
?
トクン
...!!
POWER... IT COURSES THROUGH ME...
トクン
トクン
TONAE ...
I FEEL HEAT... FILLING MY BODY...
WHAT ARE YOU...?
トクン

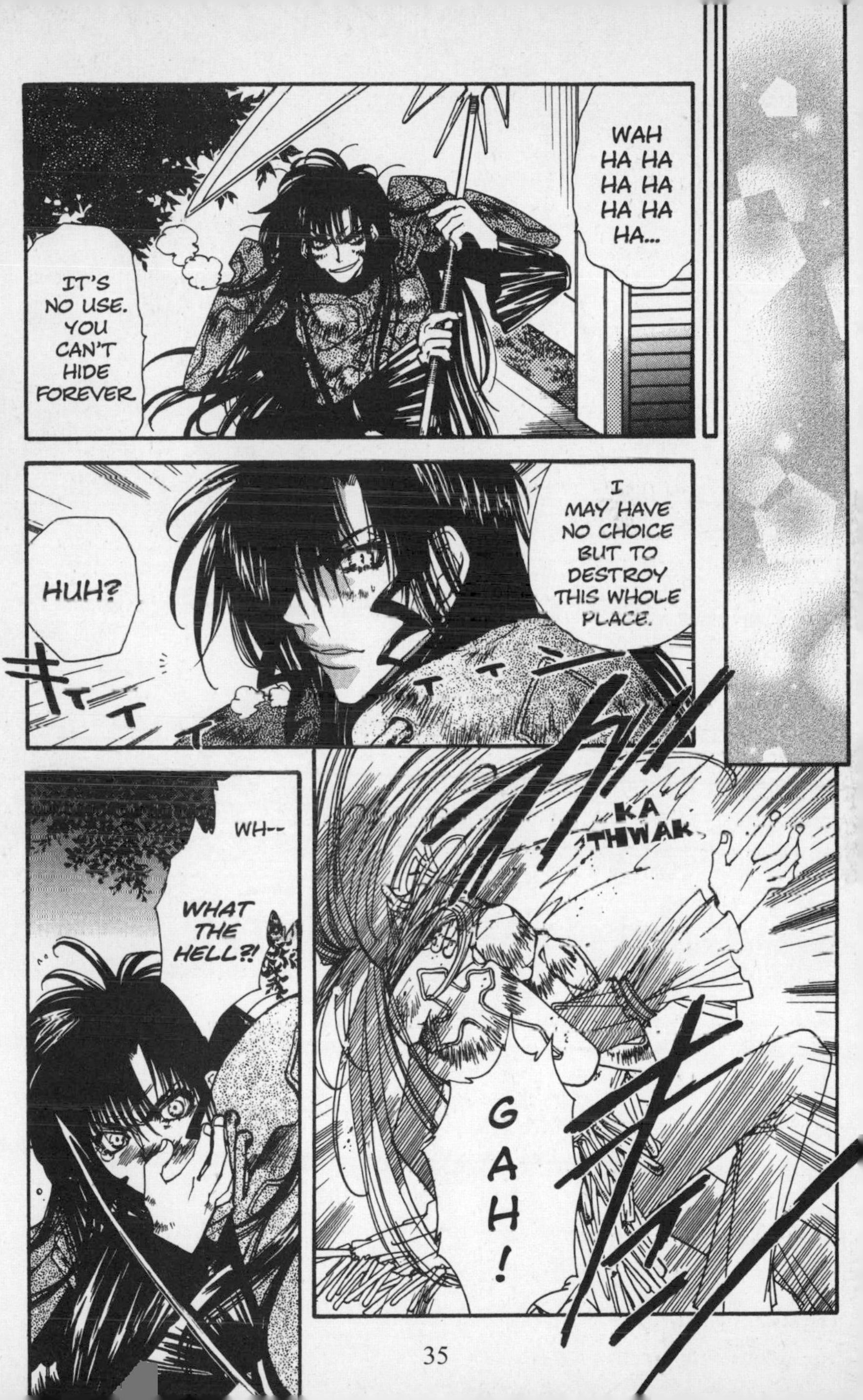
WAH HA HA HA HA HA HA HA...
IT'S NO USE. YOU CAN'T HIDE FOREVER.
I MAY HAVE NO CHOICE BUT TO DESTROY THIS WHOLE PLACE.
HUH?
KA THWAK
GAH!
WH--
WHAT THE HELL?!

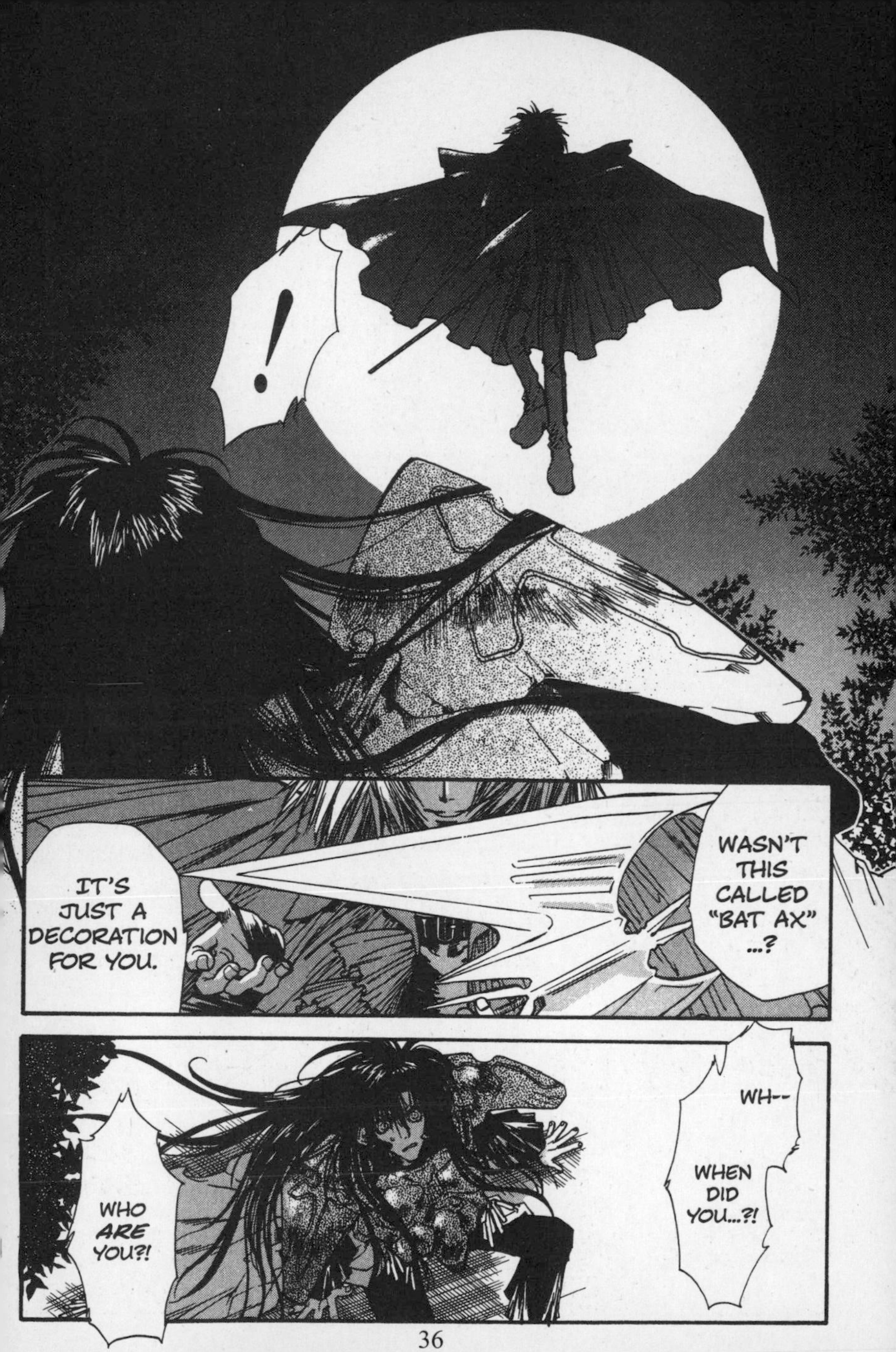
!
WASN'T THIS CALLED "BAT AX" ...?
IT'S JUST A DECORATION FOR YOU.
WH--
WHEN DID YOU...?!
WHO *ARE* YOU?!

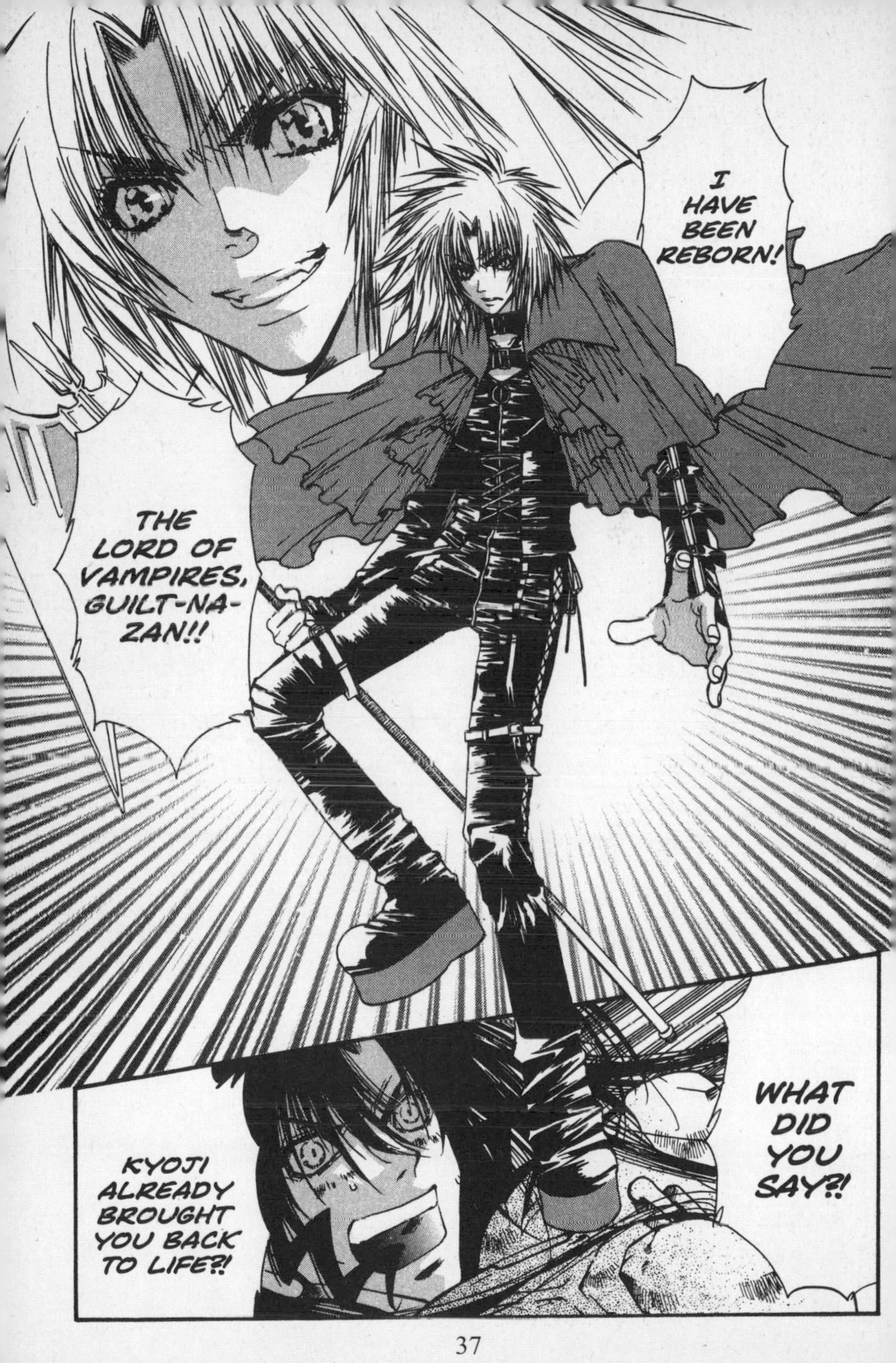
I HAVE BEEN REBORN!
THE LORD OF VAMPIRES, GUILT-NA-ZAN!!
WHAT DID YOU SAY?!
KYOJI ALREADY BROUGHT YOU BACK TO LIFE?!

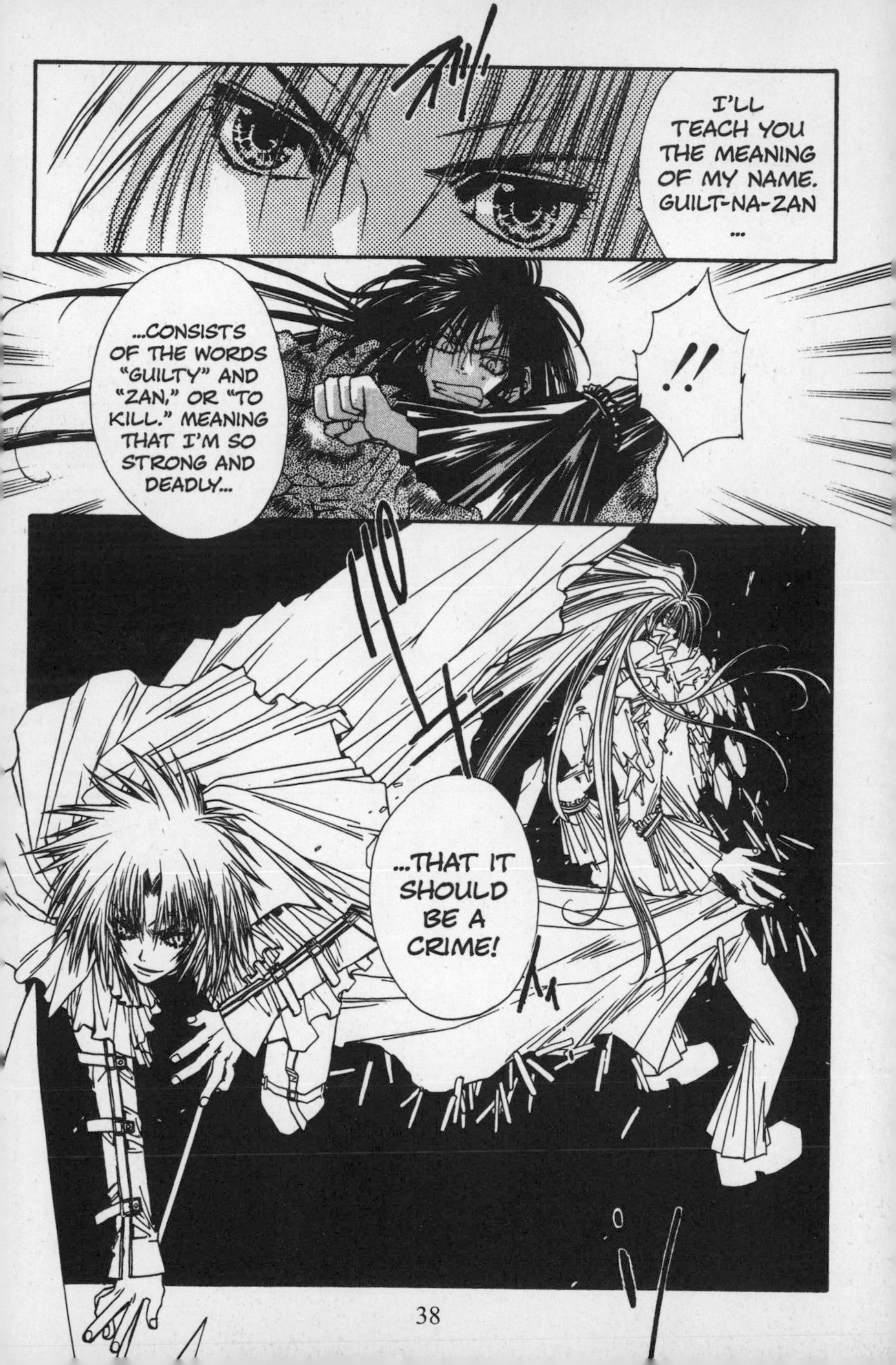
I'LL TEACH YOU THE MEANING OF MY NAME. GUILT-NA-ZAN ...
!!
...CONSISTS OF THE WORDS "GUILTY" AND "ZAN," OR "TO KILL." MEANING THAT I'M SO STRONG AND DEADLY...
...THAT IT SHOULD BE A CRIME!

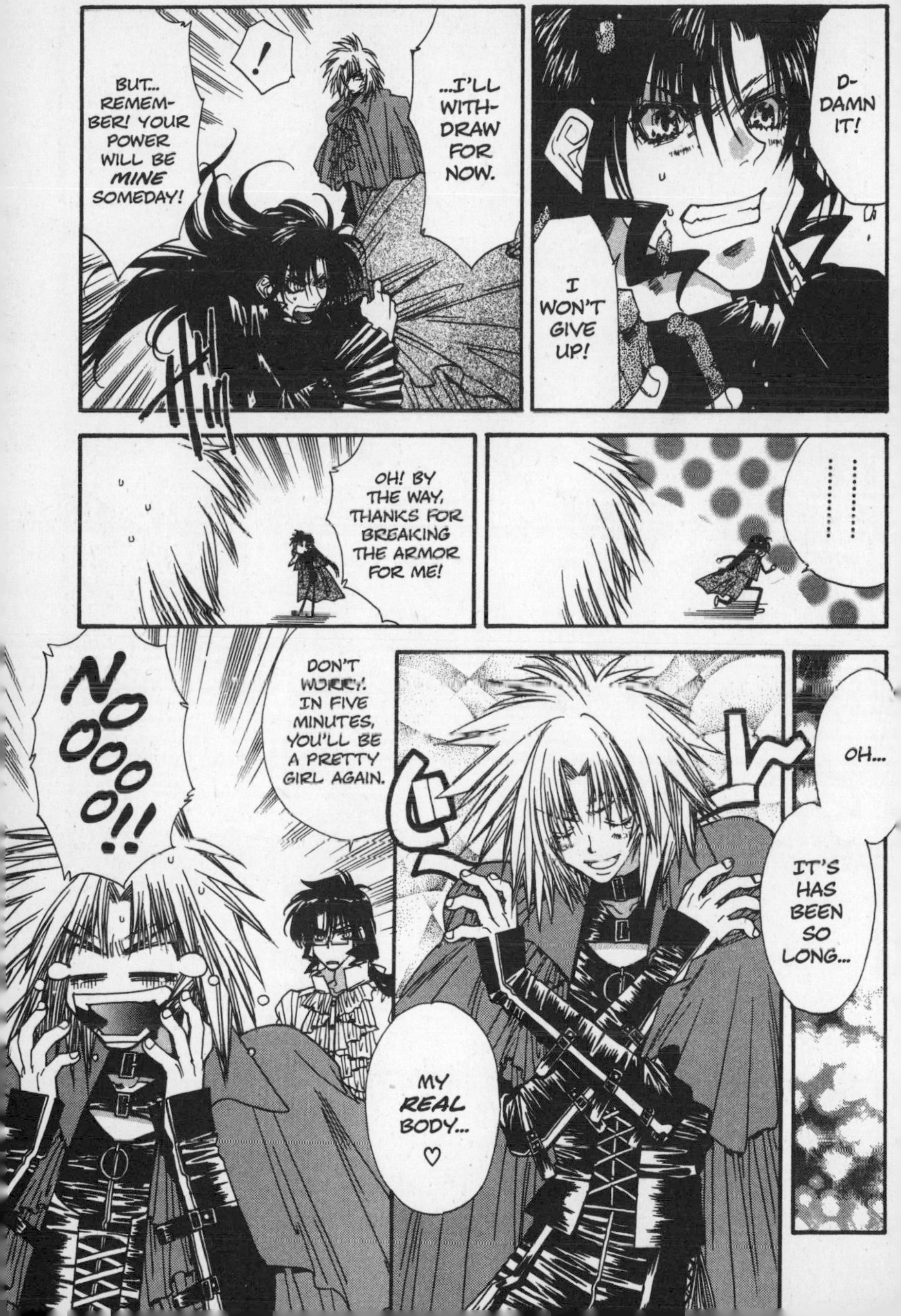
D-DAMN IT!
I WON'T GIVE UP!
...I'LL WITH-DRAW FOR NOW.
!
BUT... REMEM-BER! YOUR POWER WILL BE *MINE* SOMEDAY!
......
OH! BY THE WAY, THANKS FOR BREAKING THE ARMOR FOR ME!
OH...
IT'S HAS BEEN SO LONG...
MY *REAL* BODY... ♡
DON'T WORRY. IN FIVE MINUTES, YOU'LL BE A PRETTY GIRL AGAIN.
NOOOOOO!!

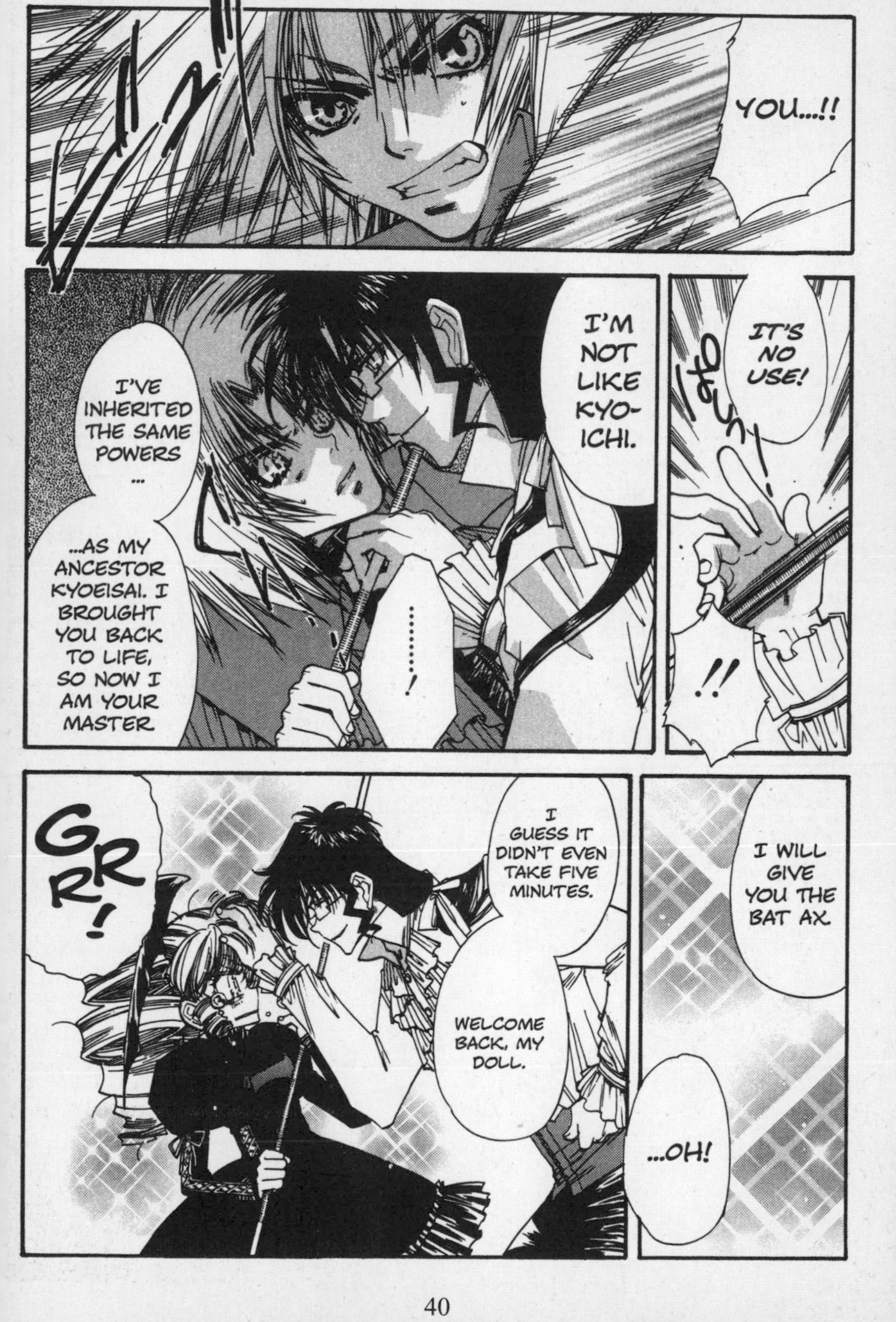
YOU...!!
IT'S NO USE!
!!
I'M NOT LIKE KYO-ICHI.
I'VE INHERITED THE SAME POWERS ...
...AS MY ANCESTOR KYOEISAI. I BROUGHT YOU BACK TO LIFE, SO NOW I AM YOUR MASTER
......!
I WILL GIVE YOU THE BAT AX.
...OH!
I GUESS IT DIDN'T EVEN TAKE FIVE MINUTES.
WELCOME BACK, MY DOLL.
GRR!

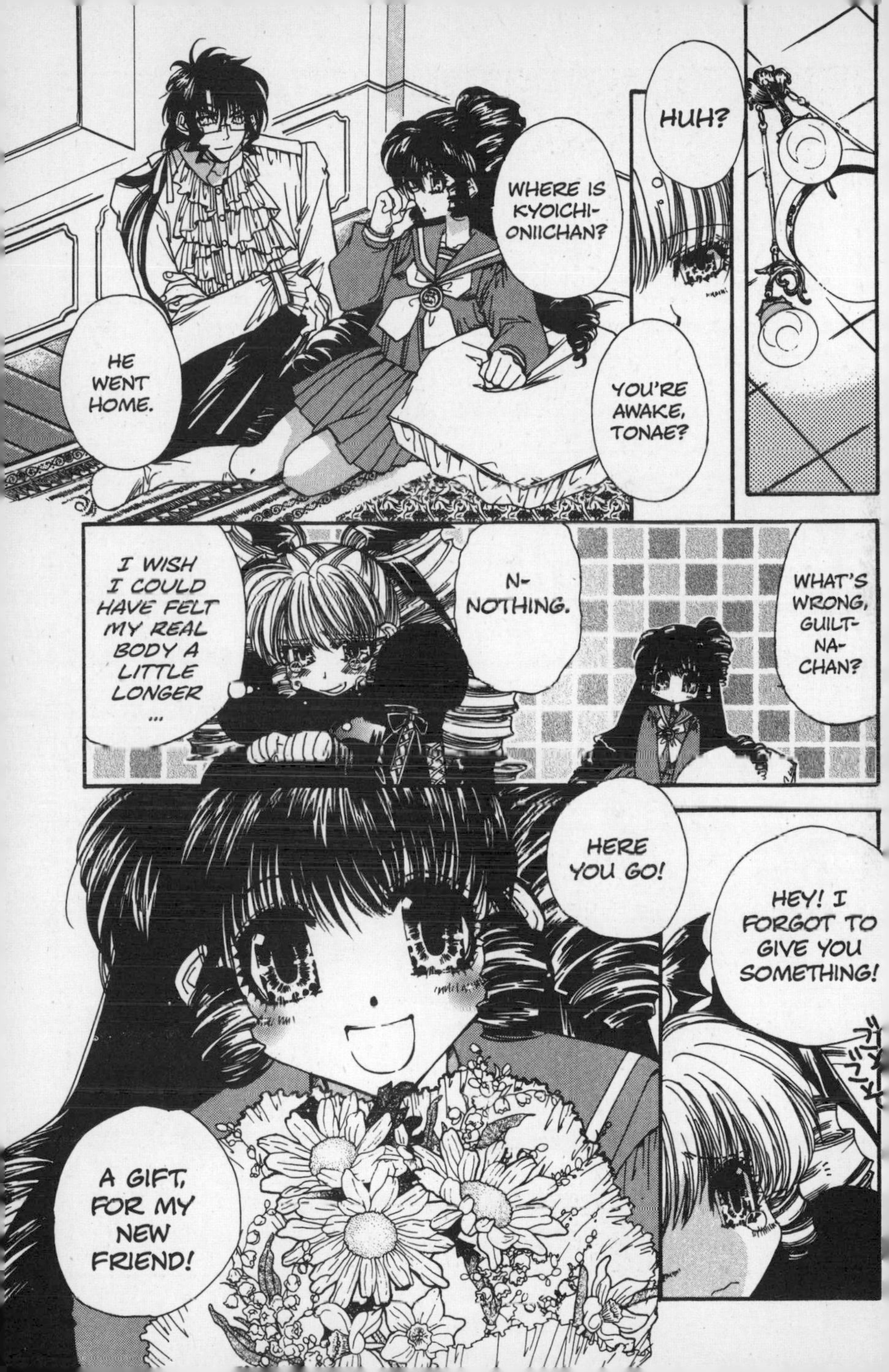
HUH?
YOU'RE AWAKE, TONAE?
WHERE IS KYOICHI-ONIICHAN?
HE WENT HOME.
WHAT'S WRONG, GUILT-NA-CHAN?
N-NOTHING.
I WISH I COULD HAVE FELT MY REAL BODY A LITTLE LONGER ...
HEY! I FORGOT TO GIVE YOU SOMETHING!
HERE YOU GO!
A GIFT, FOR MY NEW FRIEND!

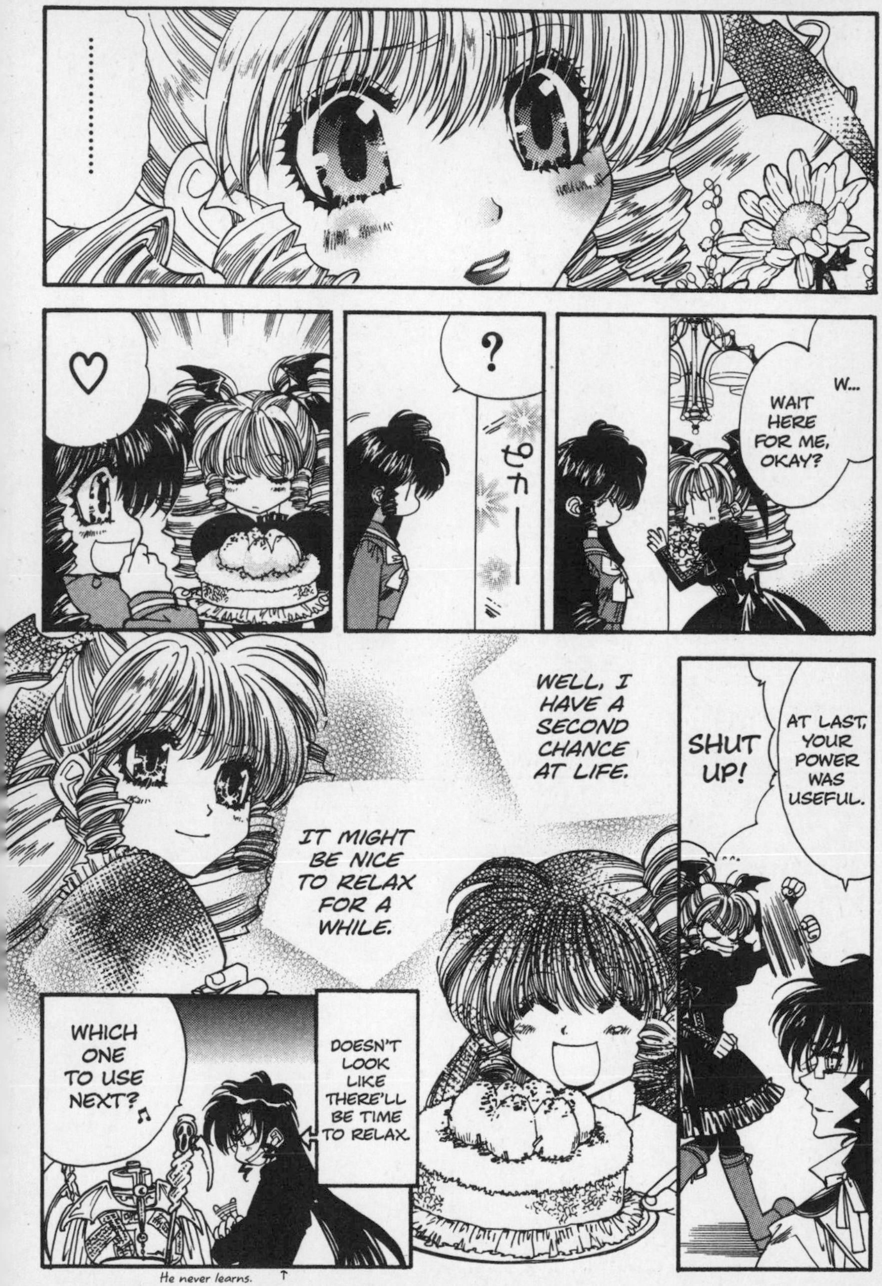
......
W...
WAIT HERE FOR ME, OKAY?
?
ピカー
♡
AT LAST, YOUR POWER WAS USEFUL.
SHUT UP!
...
WELL, I HAVE A SECOND CHANCE AT LIFE.
IT MIGHT BE NICE TO RELAX FOR A WHILE.
DOESN'T LOOK LIKE THERE'LL BE TIME TO RELAX.
WHICH ONE TO USE NEXT? ♪

He never learns. ↑

Reborn

BONUS COMIC STRIP

HIS OBSESSION IS NOT MERELY WITH PRETTY GIRLS... BUT HIS SISTER AS WELL?
SUCH A SILLY THOUGHT.
IT'S NOT TRUE?
I LIKE LITTLE GIRLS, TOO.
Spoken without hesitation!
AND PRETTY WOMEN?
HONESTLY, I DON'T CARE FOR THEM.
BUT...
IF A LITTLE GIRL MAGICALLY TRANSFORMS INTO A PRETTY WOMAN, THAT I LIKE.
His collection.
YOU ARE SICK.

VAMPIRE DOLL

REFLECTIONS

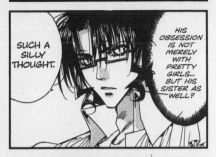

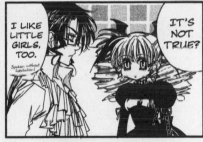

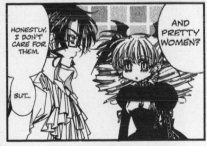

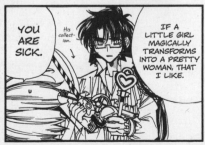

GUILT-NA-ZAN

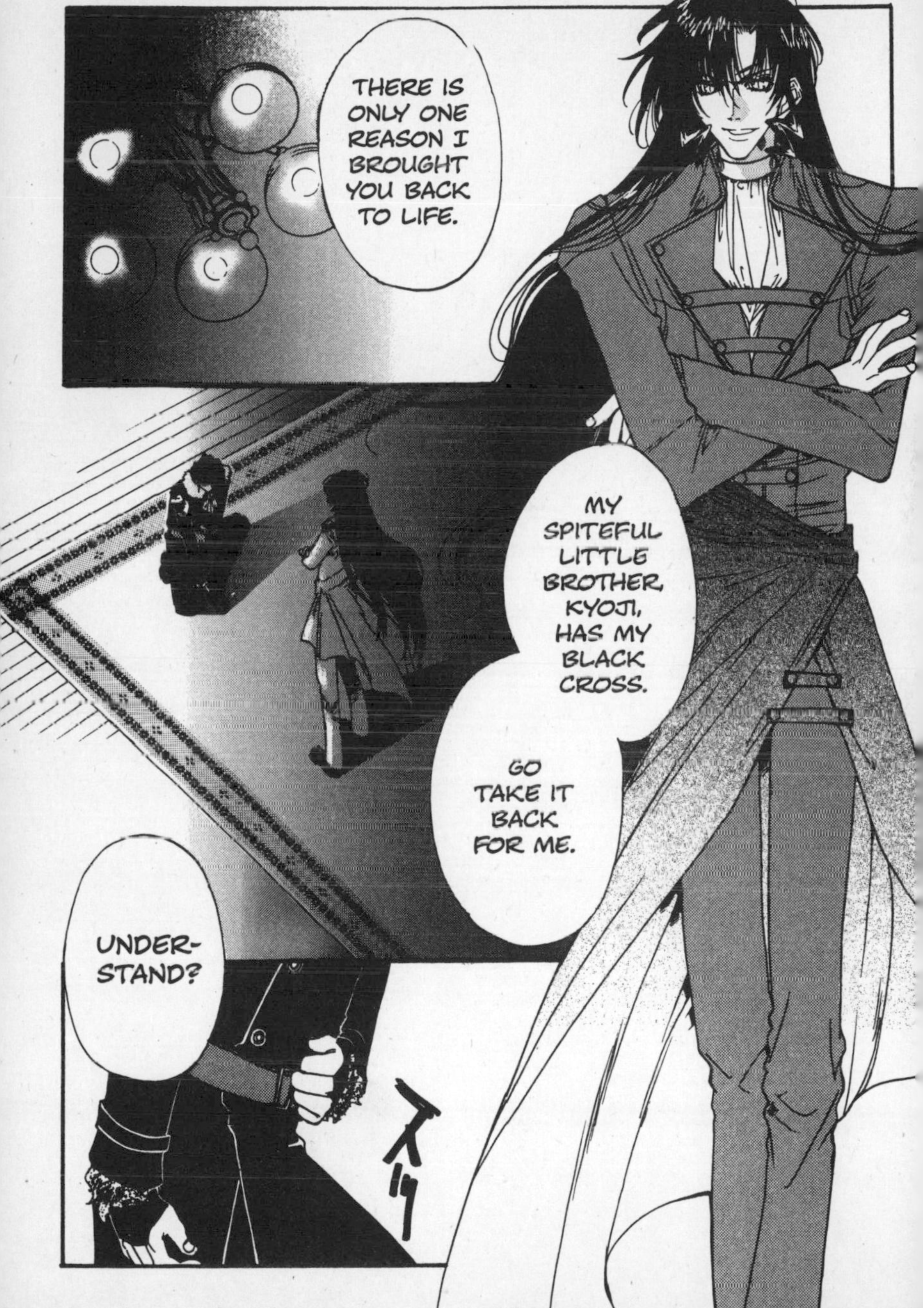
THERE IS ONLY ONE REASON I BROUGHT YOU BACK TO LIFE.
MY SPITEFUL LITTLE BROTHER, KYOJI, HAS MY BLACK CROSS.
GO TAKE IT BACK FOR ME.
UNDER-STAND?

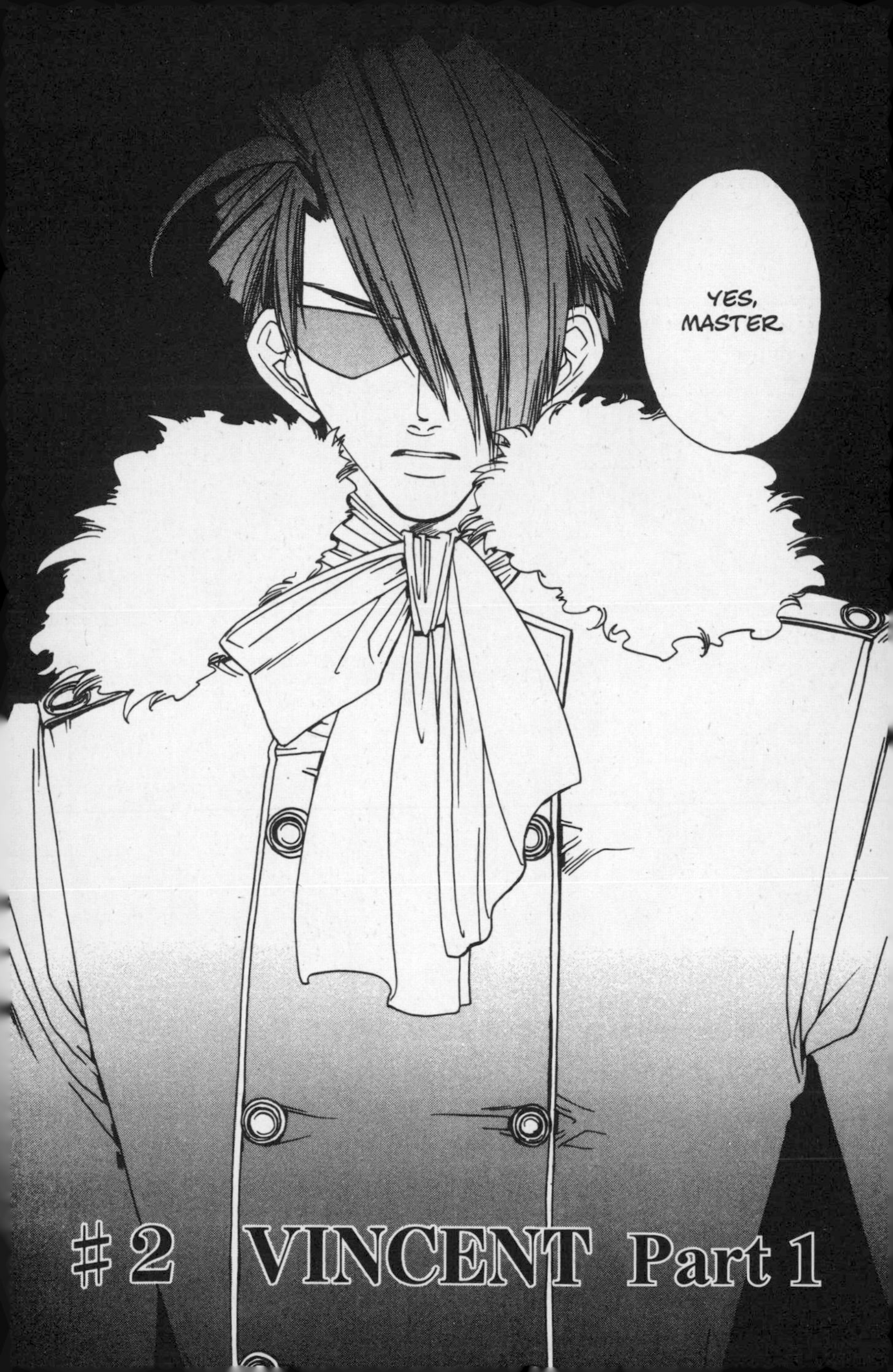
YES, MASTER
#2 VINCENT Part 1

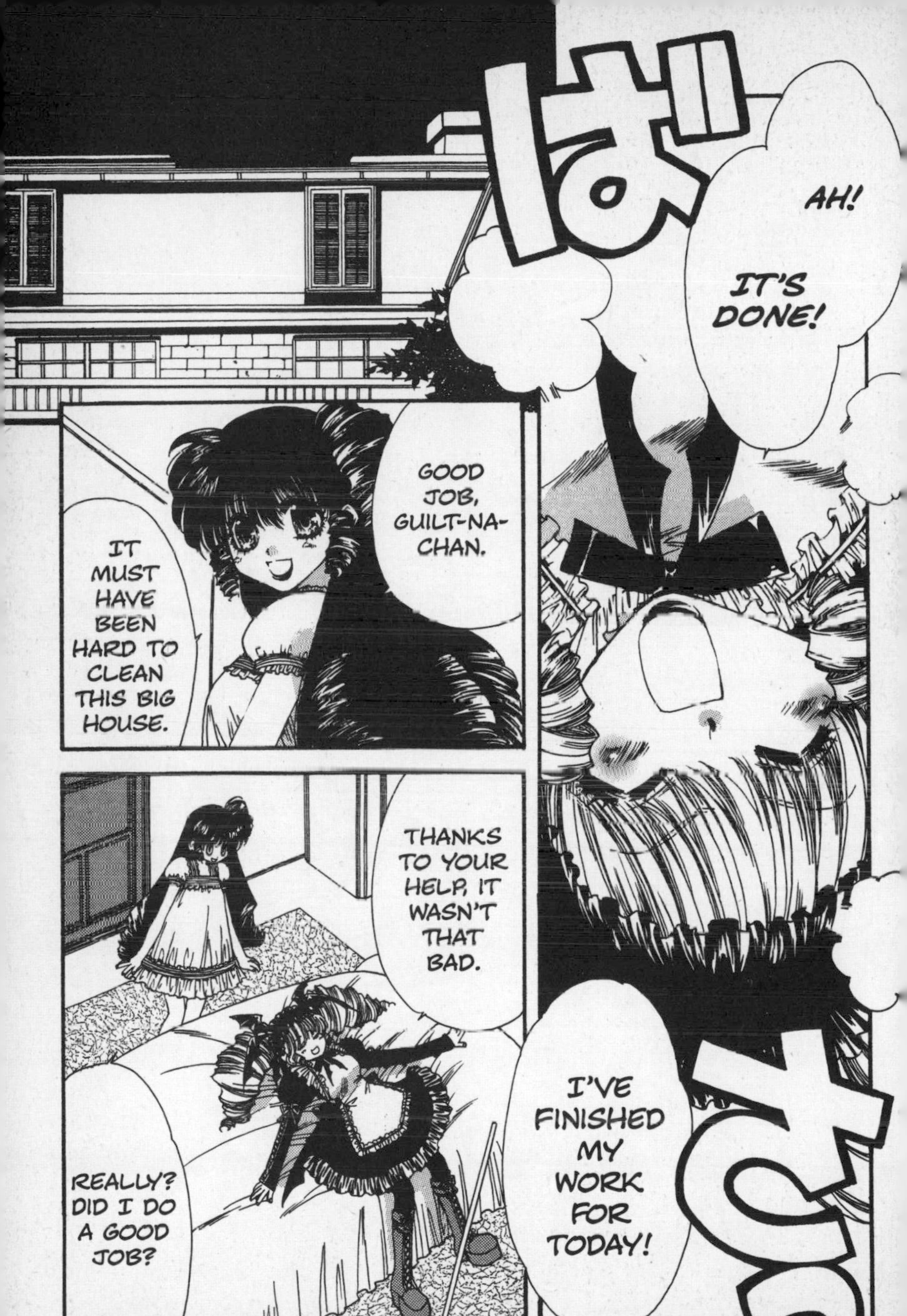
ば
AH!
IT'S DONE!
I'VE FINISHED MY WORK FOR TODAY!
GOOD JOB, GUILT-NA-CHAN.
IT MUST HAVE BEEN HARD TO CLEAN THIS BIG HOUSE.
THANKS TO YOUR HELP, IT WASN'T THAT BAD.
REALLY? DID I DO A GOOD JOB?

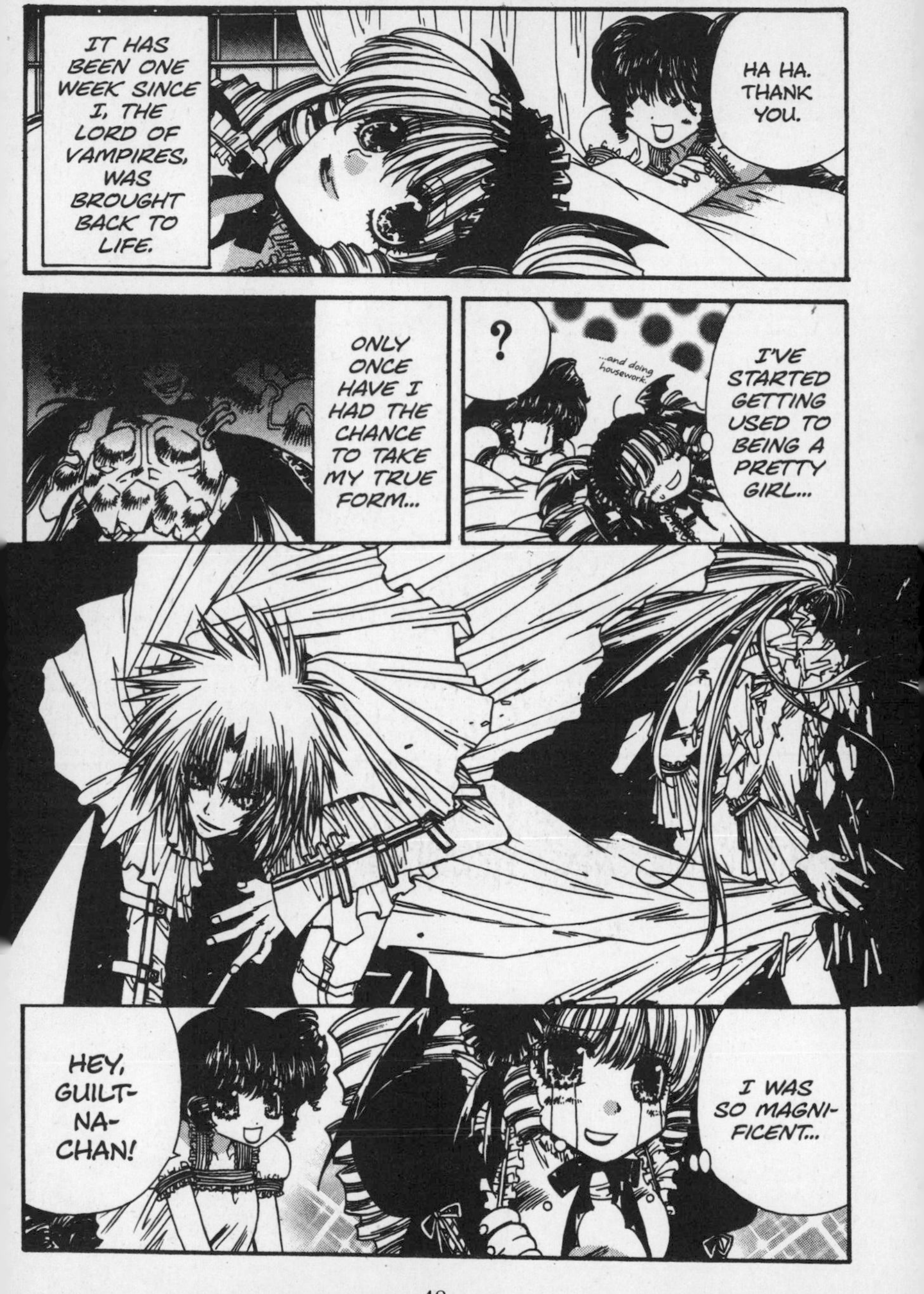
HA HA. THANK YOU.
IT HAS BEEN ONE WEEK SINCE I, THE LORD OF VAMPIRES, WAS BROUGHT BACK TO LIFE.
I'VE STARTED GETTING USED TO BEING A PRETTY GIRL...
...and doing housework.
?
ONLY ONCE HAVE I HAD THE CHANCE TO TAKE MY TRUE FORM...
I WAS SO MAGNIFICENT...
HEY, GUILT-NA-CHAN!

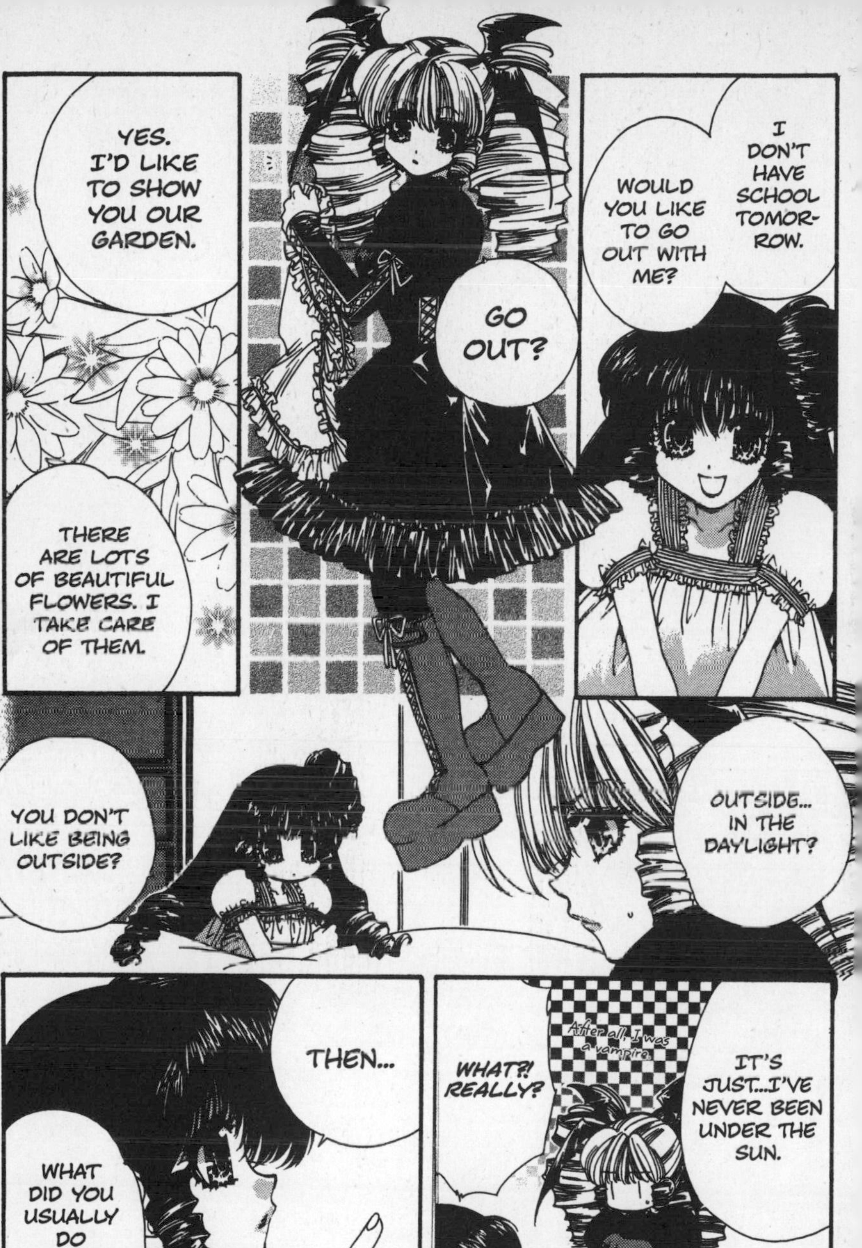
I DON'T HAVE SCHOOL TOMOR-ROW.
WOULD YOU LIKE TO GO OUT WITH ME?
GO OUT?
YES. I'D LIKE TO SHOW YOU OUR GARDEN.
THERE ARE LOTS OF BEAUTIFUL FLOWERS. I TAKE CARE OF THEM.
OUTSIDE... IN THE DAYLIGHT?
YOU DON'T LIKE BEING OUTSIDE?
IT'S JUST...I'VE NEVER BEEN UNDER THE SUN.
After all, I was a vampire.
WHAT?! REALLY?
THEN...
WHAT DID YOU USUALLY DO DURING THE DAY?

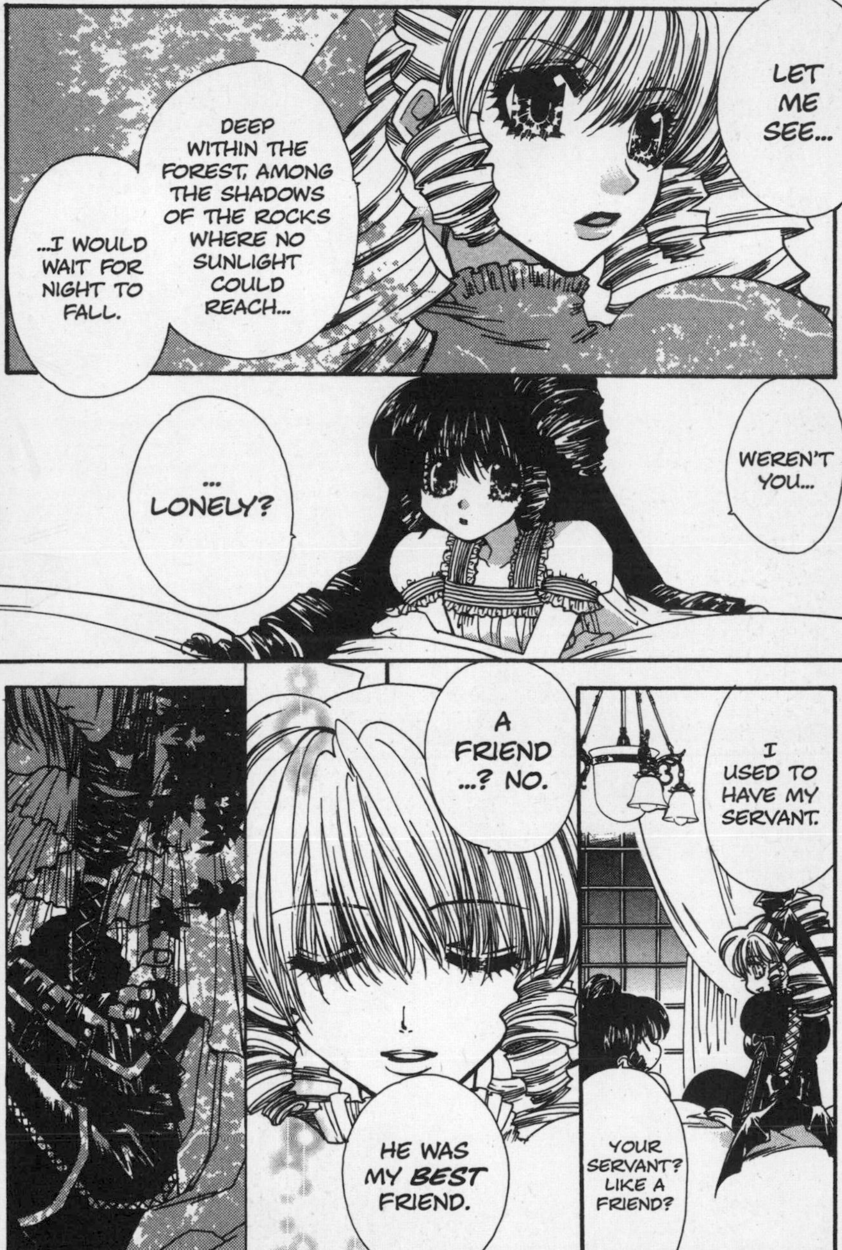
LET ME SEE...
DEEP WITHIN THE FOREST, AMONG THE SHADOWS OF THE ROCKS WHERE NO SUNLIGHT COULD REACH...
...I WOULD WAIT FOR NIGHT TO FALL.
WEREN'T YOU...
... LONELY?
I USED TO HAVE MY SERVANT.
YOUR SERVANT? LIKE A FRIEND?
A FRIEND ...? NO.
HE WAS MY *BEST* FRIEND.

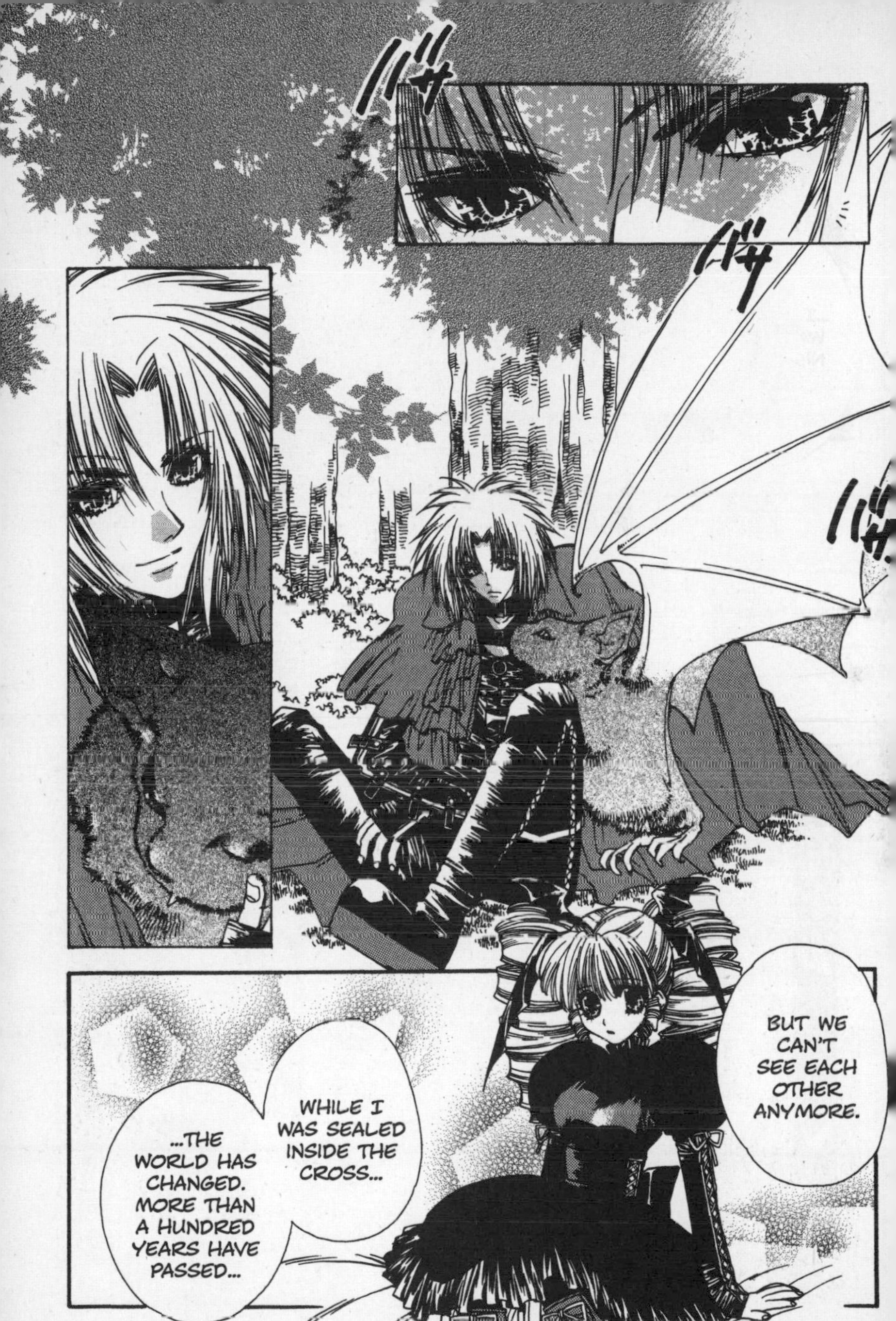
バサ
バサ
バサ
BUT WE CAN'T SEE EACH OTHER ANYMORE.
WHILE I WAS SEALED INSIDE THE CROSS...
...THE WORLD HAS CHANGED. MORE THAN A HUNDRED YEARS HAVE PASSED...

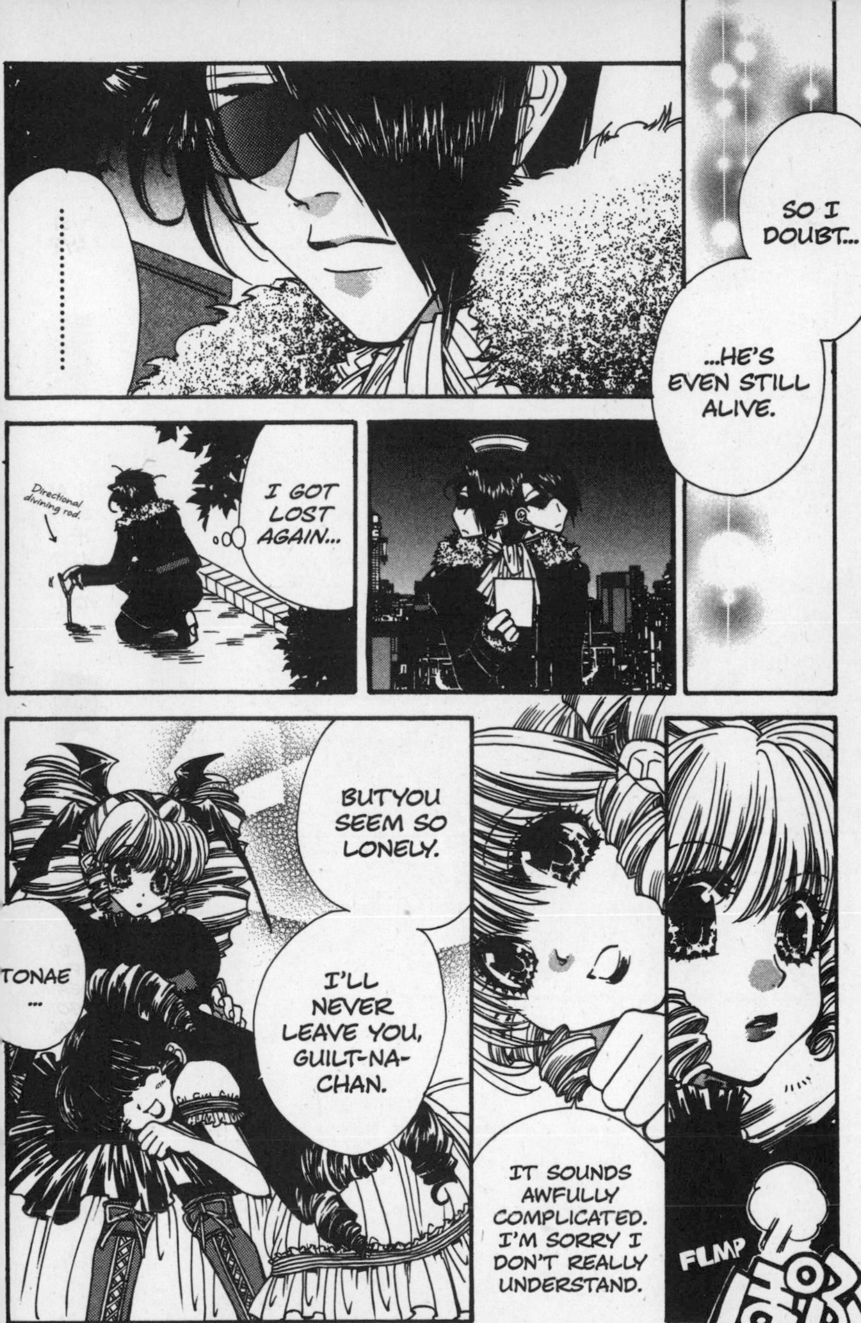
SO I DOUBT...
...HE'S EVEN STILL ALIVE.
......
Directional divining rod.
I GOT LOST AGAIN...
FLMP
IT SOUNDS AWFULLY COMPLICATED. I'M SORRY I DON'T REALLY UNDERSTAND.
BUT YOU SEEM SO LONELY.
I'LL NEVER LEAVE YOU, GUILT-NA-CHAN.
TONAE ...

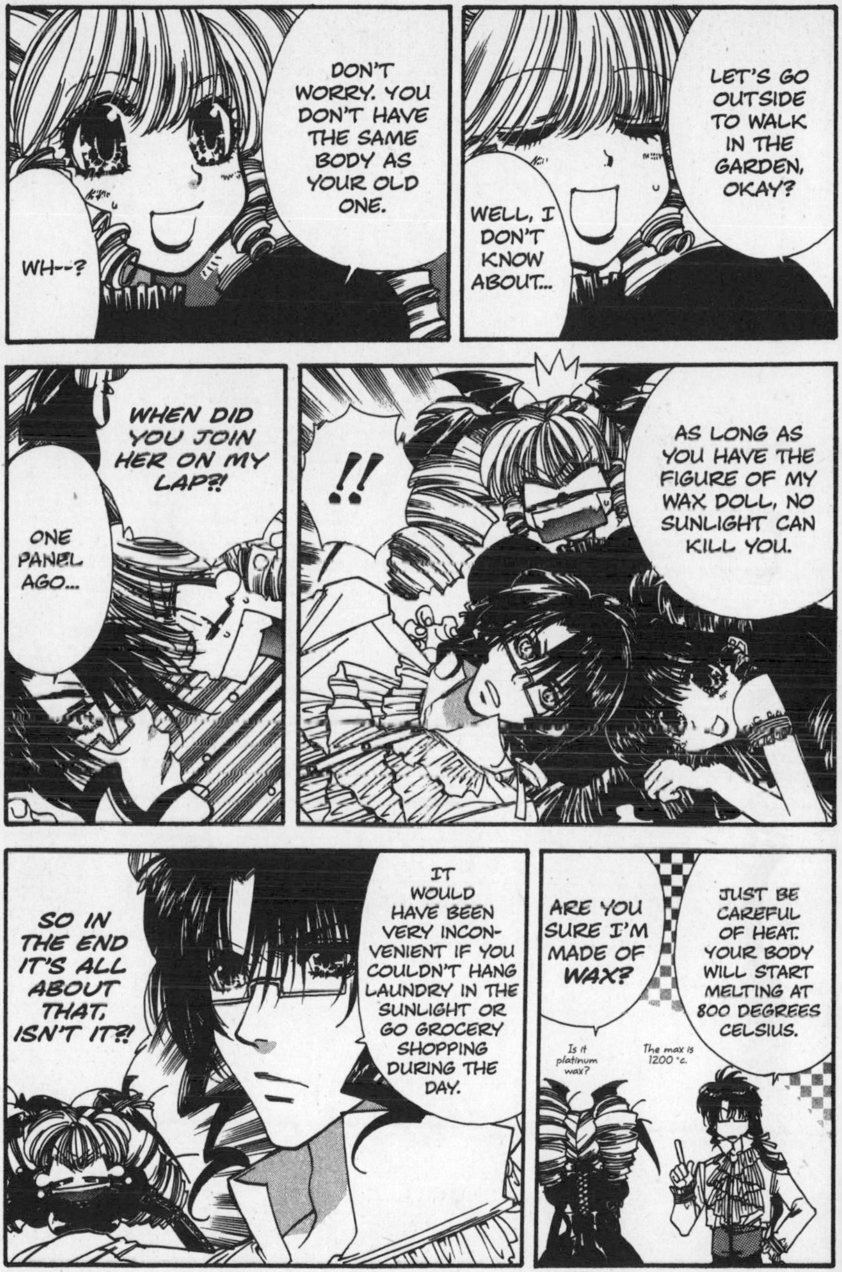
LET'S GO OUTSIDE TO WALK IN THE GARDEN, OKAY?
WELL, I DON'T KNOW ABOUT...
DON'T WORRY. YOU DON'T HAVE THE SAME BODY AS YOUR OLD ONE.
WH--?
AS LONG AS YOU HAVE THE FIGURE OF MY WAX DOLL, NO SUNLIGHT CAN KILL YOU.
!!
WHEN DID YOU JOIN HER ON MY LAP?!
ONE PANEL AGO...
JUST BE CAREFUL OF HEAT. YOUR BODY WILL START MELTING AT 800 DEGREES CELSIUS.
ARE YOU SURE I'M MADE OF WAX?
The max is 1200 °c.
Is it platinum wax?
IT WOULD HAVE BEEN VERY INCON-VENIENT IF YOU COULDN'T HANG LAUNDRY IN THE SUNLIGHT OR GO GROCERY SHOPPING DURING THE DAY.
SO IN THE END IT'S ALL ABOUT THAT, ISN'T IT?!

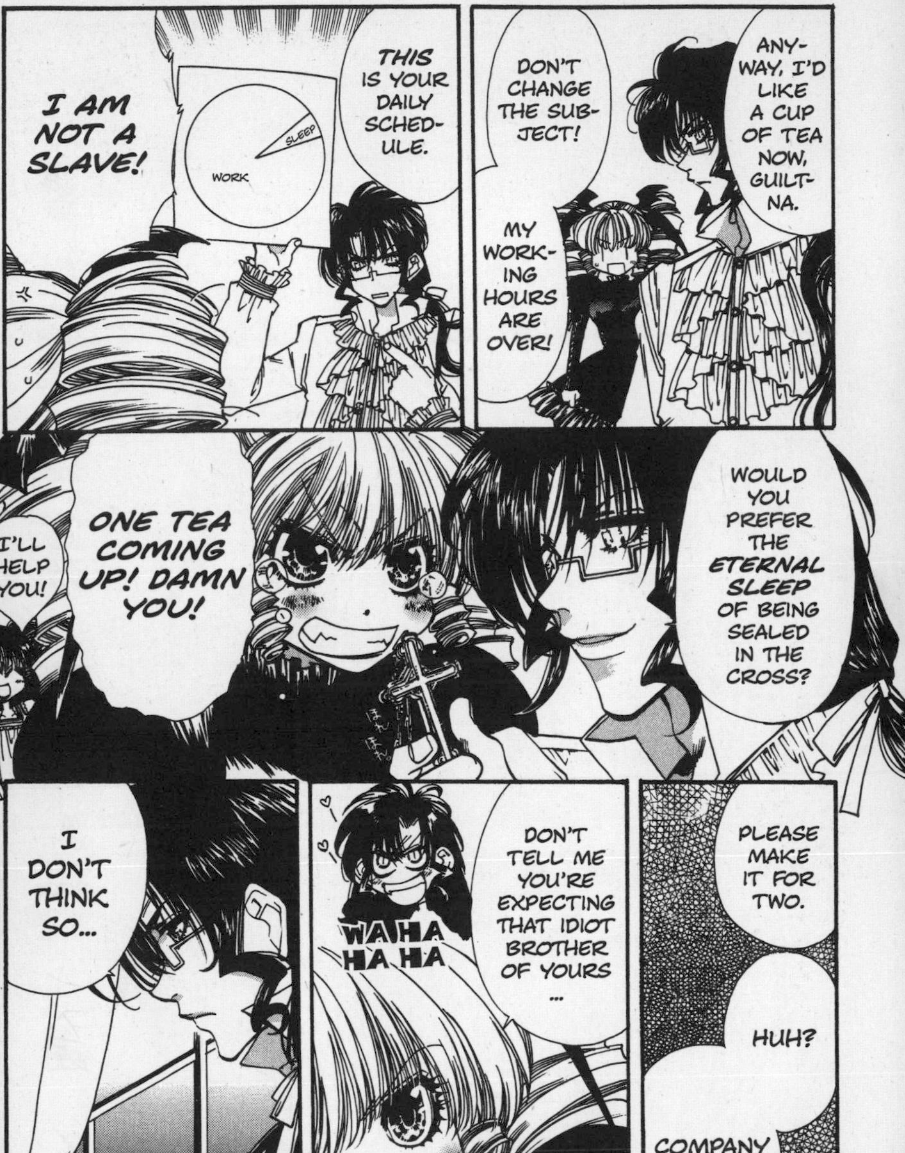
ANY-WAY, I'D LIKE A CUP OF TEA NOW, GUILT-NA.
DON'T CHANGE THE SUB-JECT!
MY WORK-ING HOURS ARE OVER!
THIS IS YOUR DAILY SCHED-ULE.
SLEEP
WORK
I AM NOT A SLAVE!
WOULD YOU PREFER THE ETERNAL SLEEP OF BEING SEALED IN THE CROSS?
ONE TEA COMING UP! DAMN YOU!
I'LL HELP YOU!
PLEASE MAKE IT FOR TWO.
HUH?
COMPANY AT THIS HOUR?
DON'T TELL ME YOU'RE EXPECTING THAT IDIOT BROTHER OF YOURS ...
WA HA HA HA
I DON'T THINK SO...

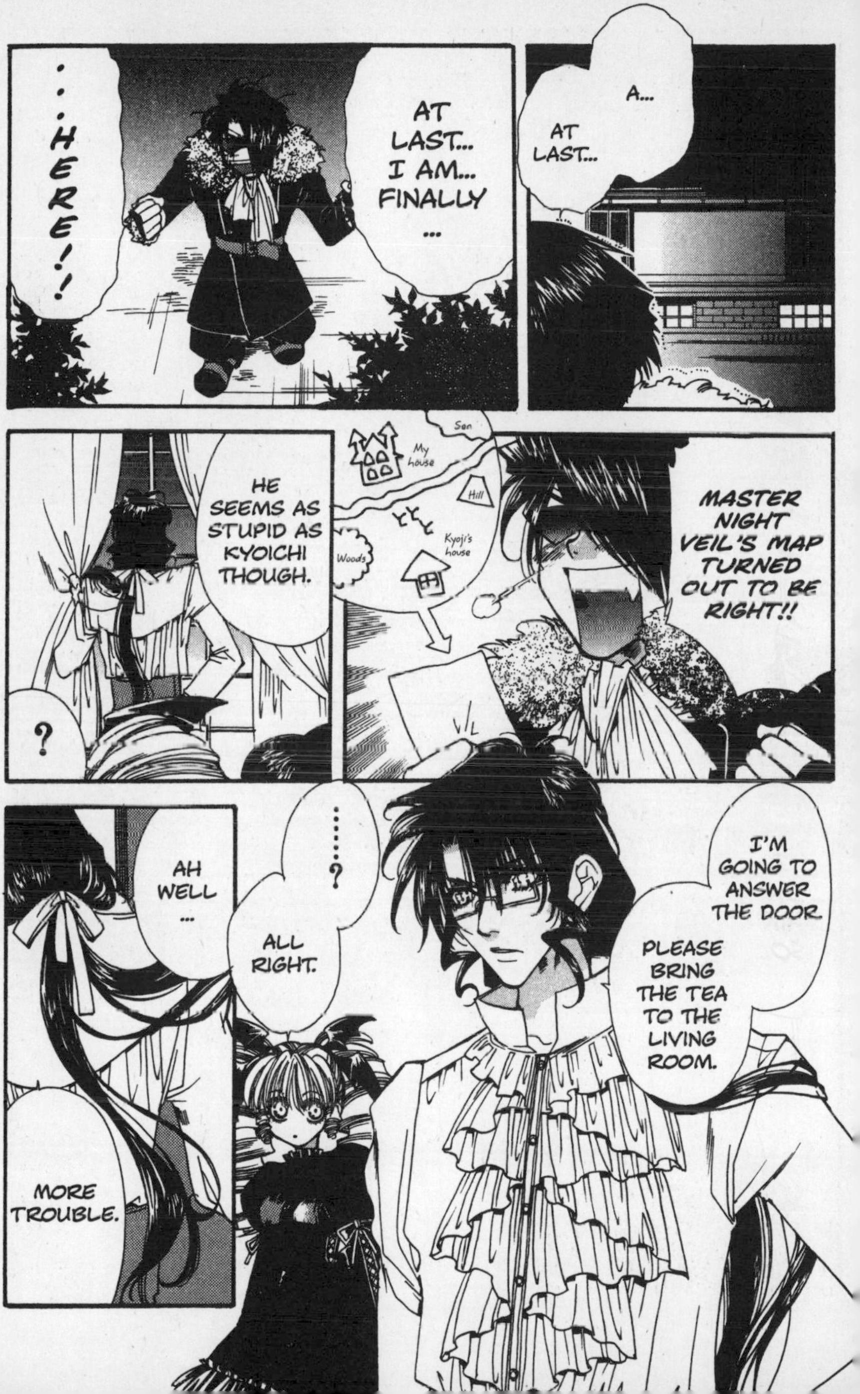
A...
AT LAST...
AT LAST... I AM... FINALLY ...
...HERE!!
Son
My house
Hill
Kyoji's house
Woods
MASTER NIGHT VEIL'S MAP TURNED OUT TO BE RIGHT!!
HE SEEMS AS STUPID AS KYOICHI THOUGH.
?
I'M GOING TO ANSWER THE DOOR.
PLEASE BRING THE TEA TO THE LIVING ROOM.
......?
ALL RIGHT.
AH WELL ...
MORE TROUBLE.

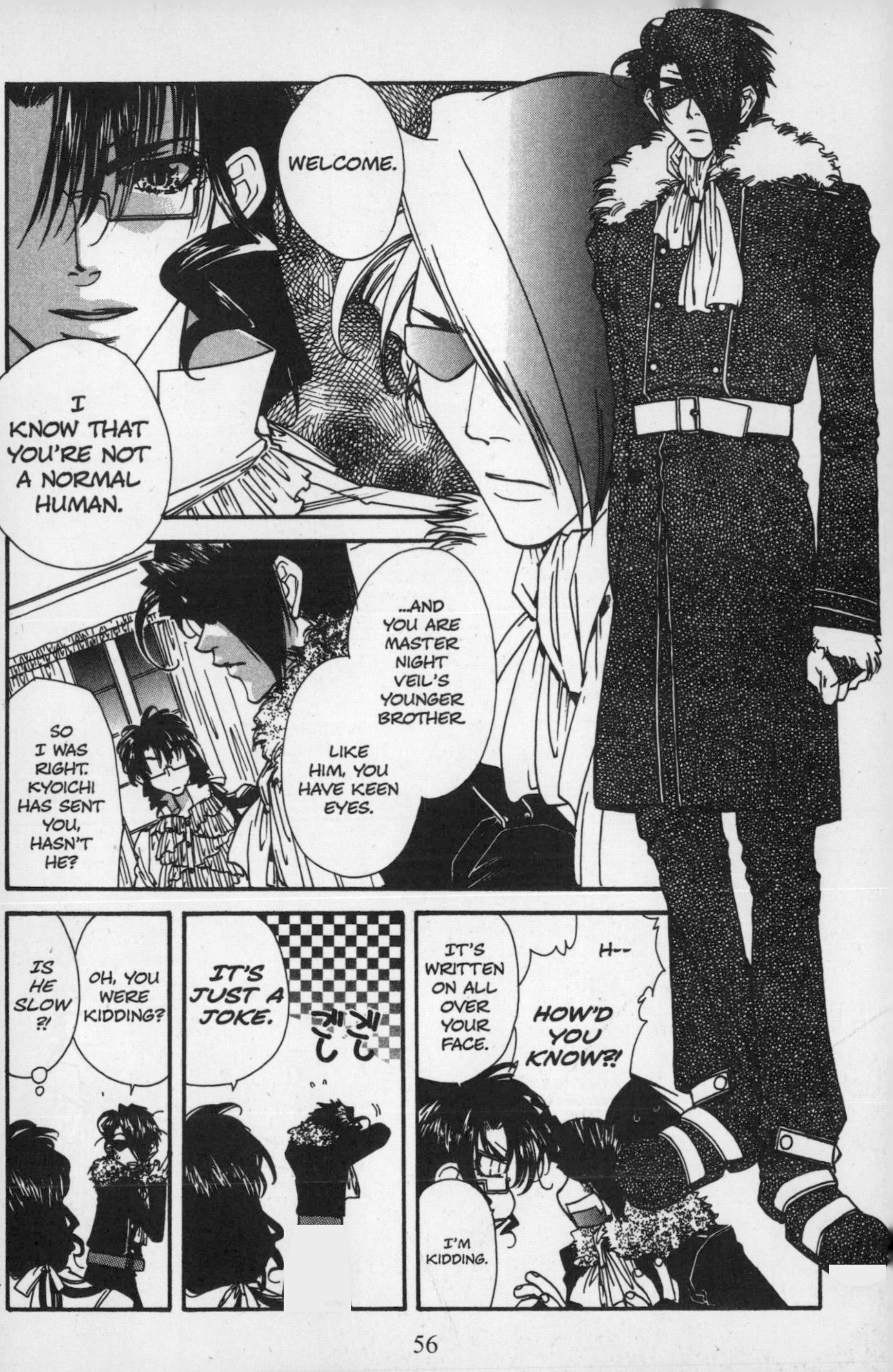

WELCOME.
I KNOW THAT YOU'RE NOT A NORMAL HUMAN.
...AND YOU ARE MASTER NIGHT VEIL'S YOUNGER BROTHER
LIKE HIM, YOU HAVE KEEN EYES.
SO I WAS RIGHT. KYOICHI HAS SENT YOU, HASN'T HE?
H--
HOW'D YOU KNOW?!
IT'S WRITTEN ON ALL OVER YOUR FACE.
I'M KIDDING.
IT'S JUST A JOKE.
OH, YOU WERE KIDDING?
IS HE SLOW?!

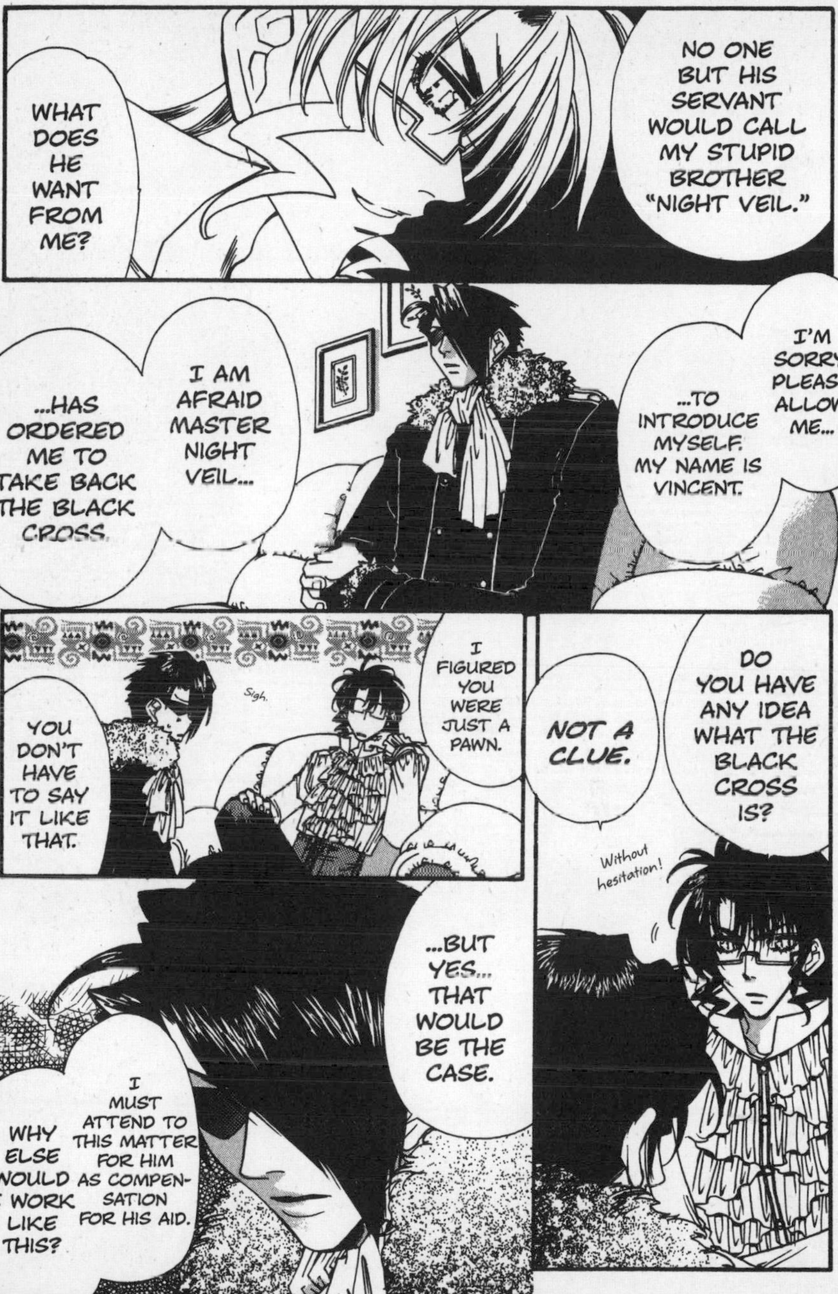
NO ONE BUT HIS SERVANT WOULD CALL MY STUPID BROTHER "NIGHT VEIL."
WHAT DOES HE WANT FROM ME?
I'M SORRY. PLEASE ALLOW ME...
...TO INTRODUCE MYSELF. MY NAME IS VINCENT.
I AM AFRAID MASTER NIGHT VEIL...
...HAS ORDERED ME TO TAKE BACK THE BLACK CROSS.
DO YOU HAVE ANY IDEA WHAT THE BLACK CROSS IS?
NOT A CLUE.
Without hesitation!
I FIGURED YOU WERE JUST A PAWN.
Sigh.
YOU DON'T HAVE TO SAY IT LIKE THAT.
...BUT YES... THAT WOULD BE THE CASE.
I MUST ATTEND TO THIS MATTER FOR HIM AS COMPEN-SATION FOR HIS AID.
WHY ELSE WOULD I WORK LIKE THIS?

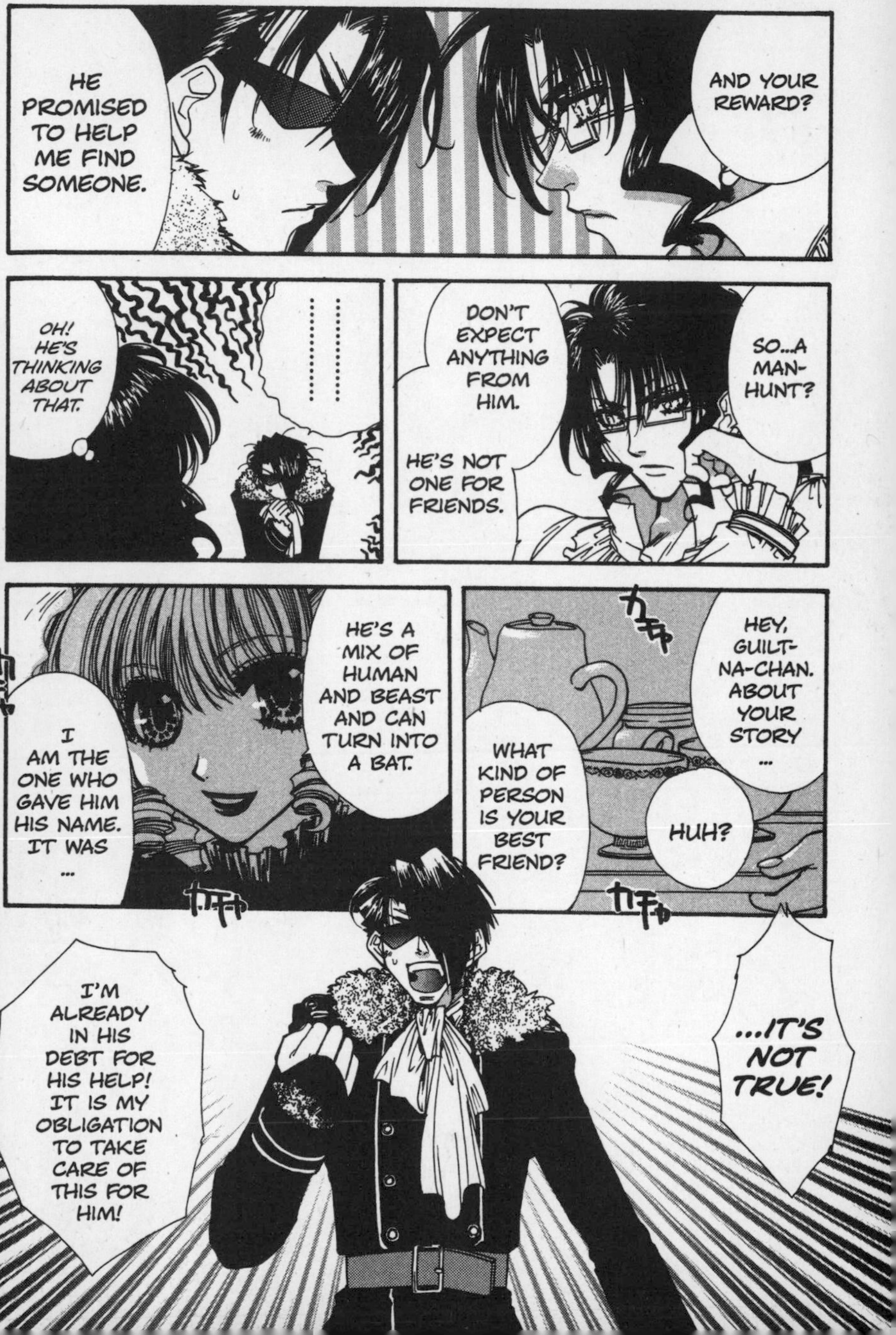
AND YOUR REWARD?
HE PROMISED TO HELP ME FIND SOMEONE.
SO...A MAN-HUNT?
DON'T EXPECT ANYTHING FROM HIM.
HE'S NOT ONE FOR FRIENDS.
......
OH! HE'S THINKING ABOUT THAT.
HEY, GUILT-NA-CHAN. ABOUT YOUR STORY ...
HUH?
WHAT KIND OF PERSON IS YOUR BEST FRIEND?
HE'S A MIX OF HUMAN AND BEAST AND CAN TURN INTO A BAT.
I AM THE ONE WHO GAVE HIM HIS NAME. IT WAS ...
...IT'S NOT TRUE!
I'M ALREADY IN HIS DEBT FOR HIS HELP! IT IS MY OBLIGATION TO TAKE CARE OF THIS FOR HIM!

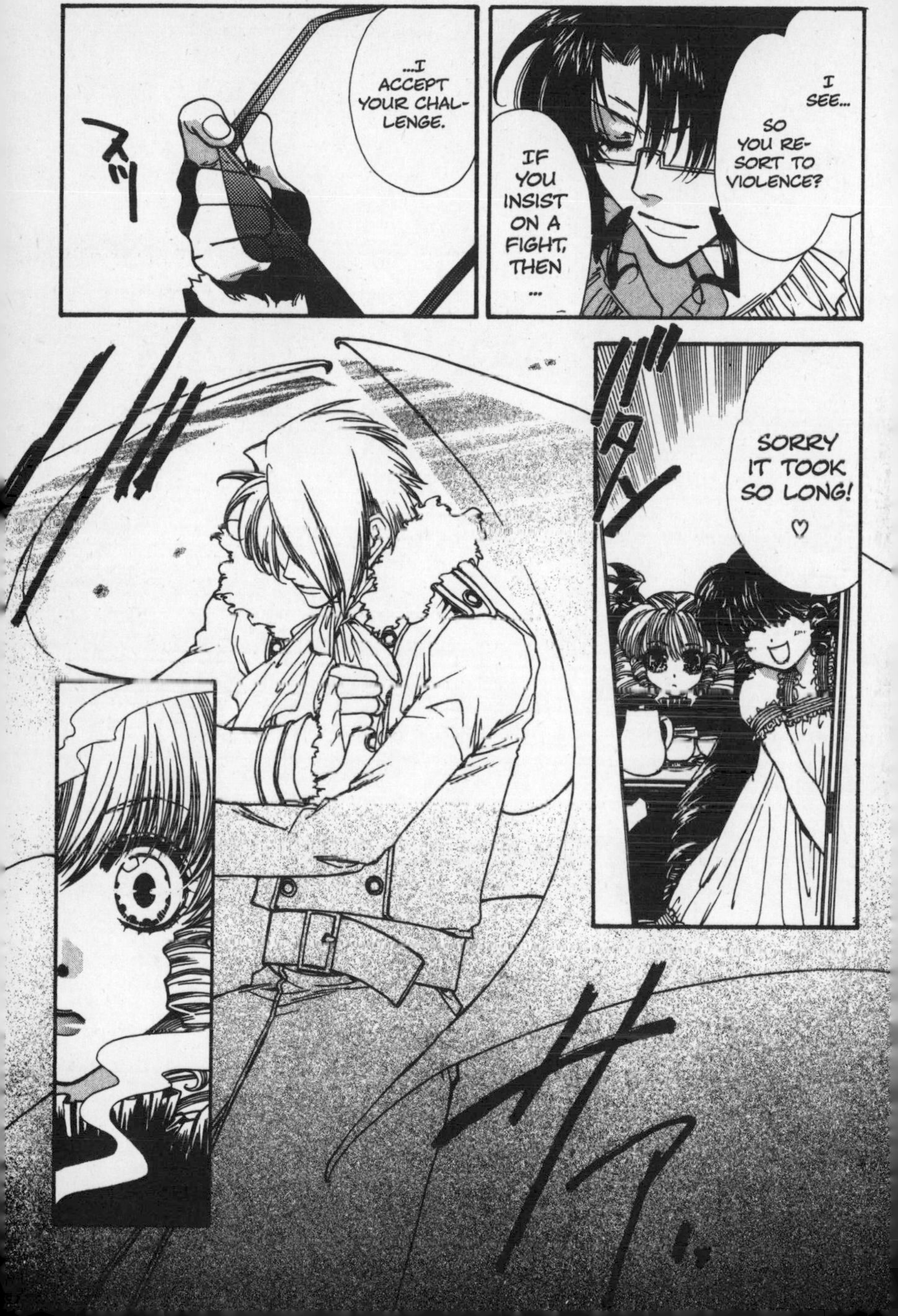
I SEE...
SO YOU RESORT TO VIOLENCE?
IF YOU INSIST ON A FIGHT, THEN ...
...I ACCEPT YOUR CHALLENGE.
SORRY IT TOOK SO LONG! ♡

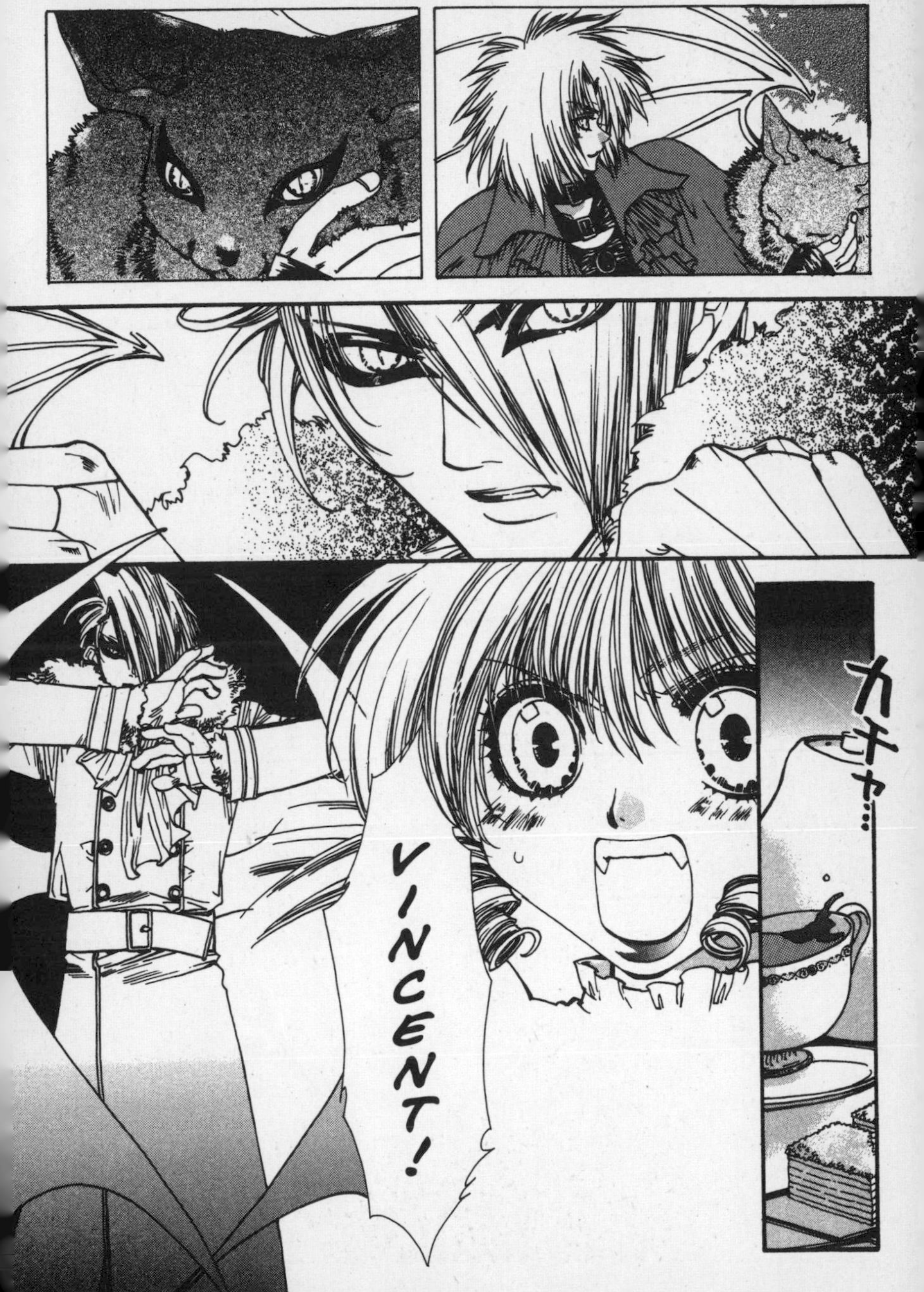
カキャ…
VINCENT!

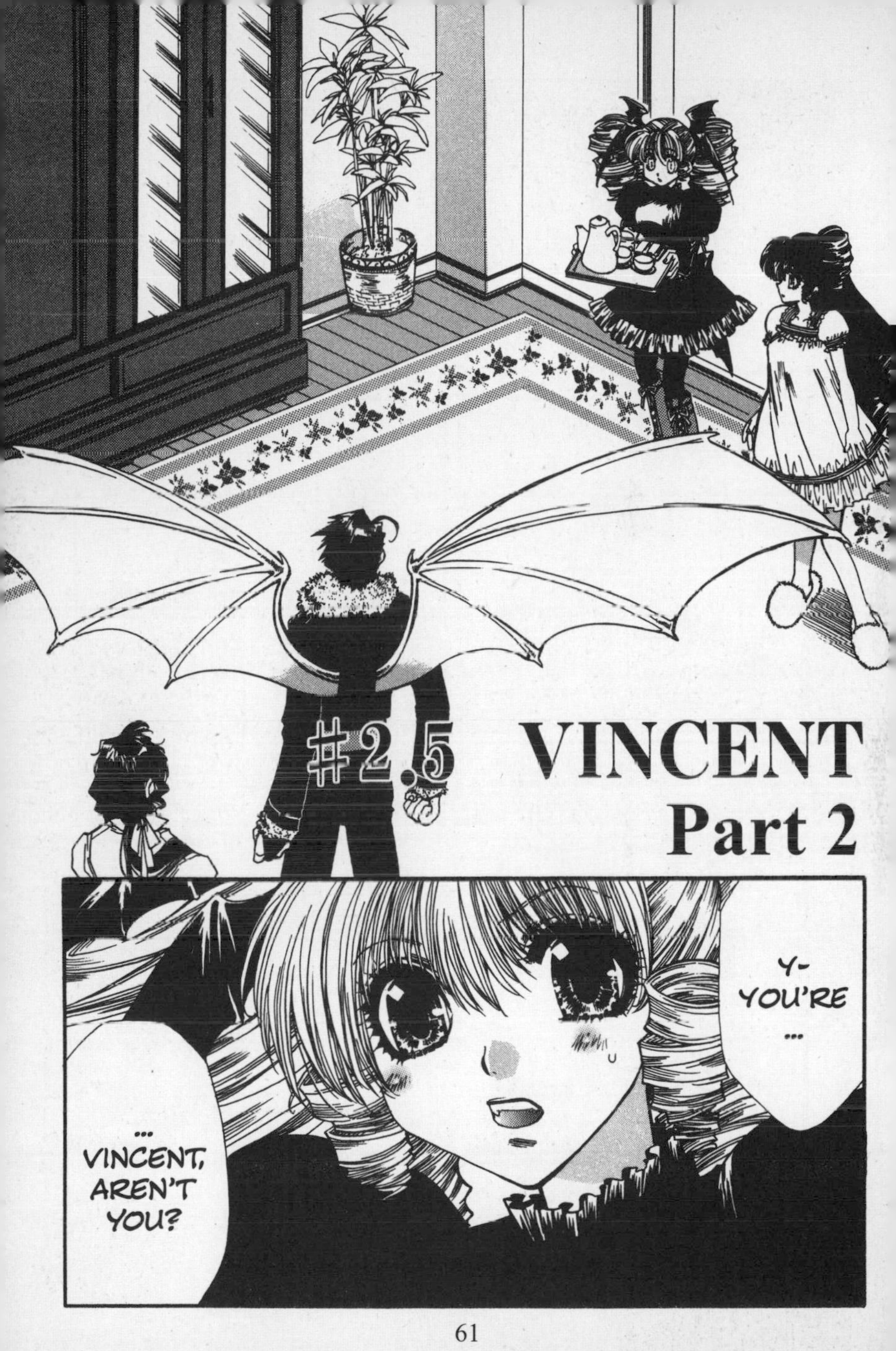

#2.5
VINCENT
Part 2
Y- YOU'RE ...
... VINCENT, AREN'T YOU?

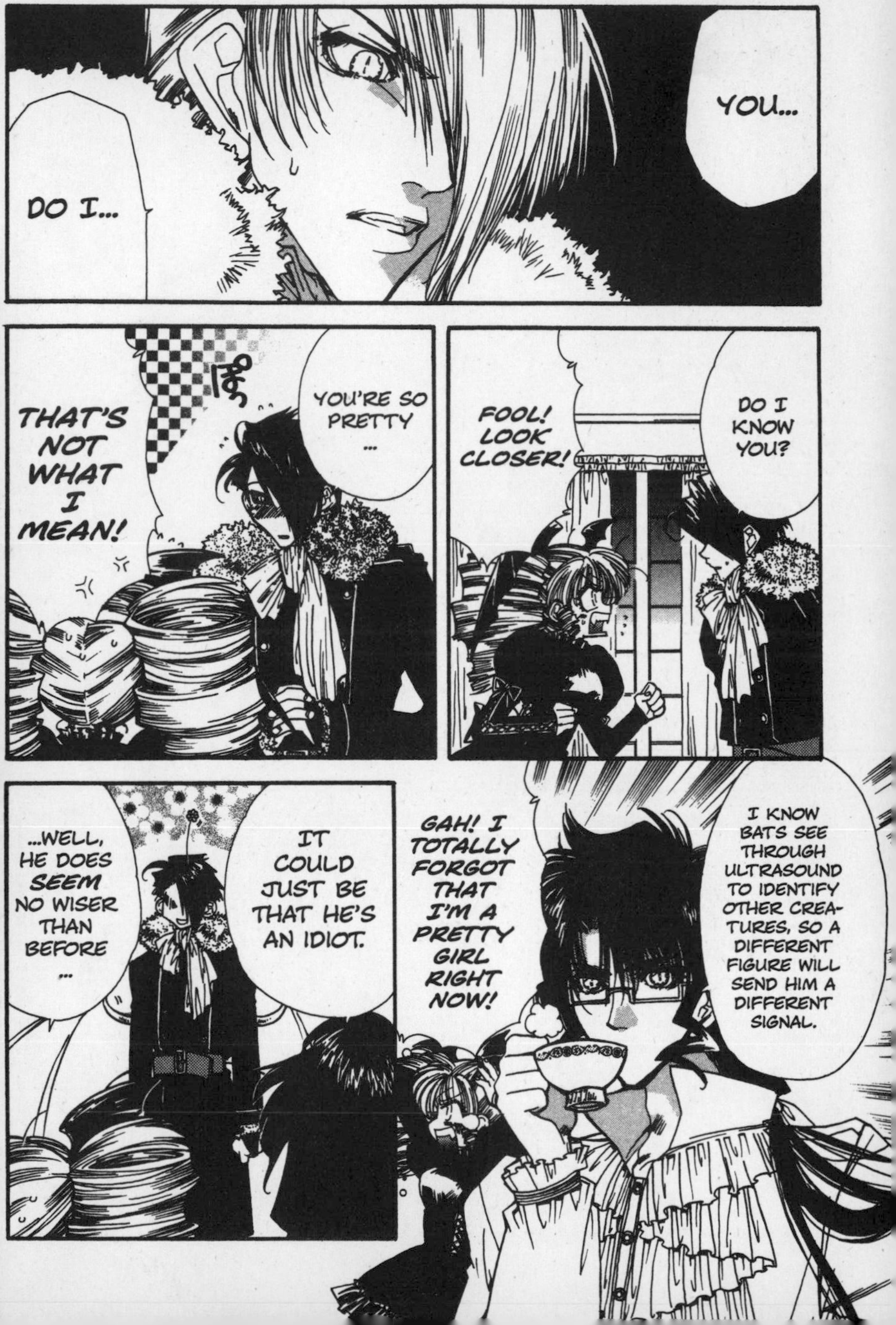
YOU...
DO I...
DO I KNOW YOU?
FOOL! LOOK CLOSER!
YOU'RE SO PRETTY ...
THAT'S NOT WHAT I MEAN!
I KNOW BATS SEE THROUGH ULTRASOUND TO IDENTIFY OTHER CREA-TURES, SO A DIFFERENT FIGURE WILL SEND HIM A DIFFERENT SIGNAL.
GAH! I TOTALLY FORGOT THAT I'M A PRETTY GIRL RIGHT NOW!
IT COULD JUST BE THAT HE'S AN IDIOT.
...WELL, HE DOES SEEM NO WISER THAN BEFORE ...

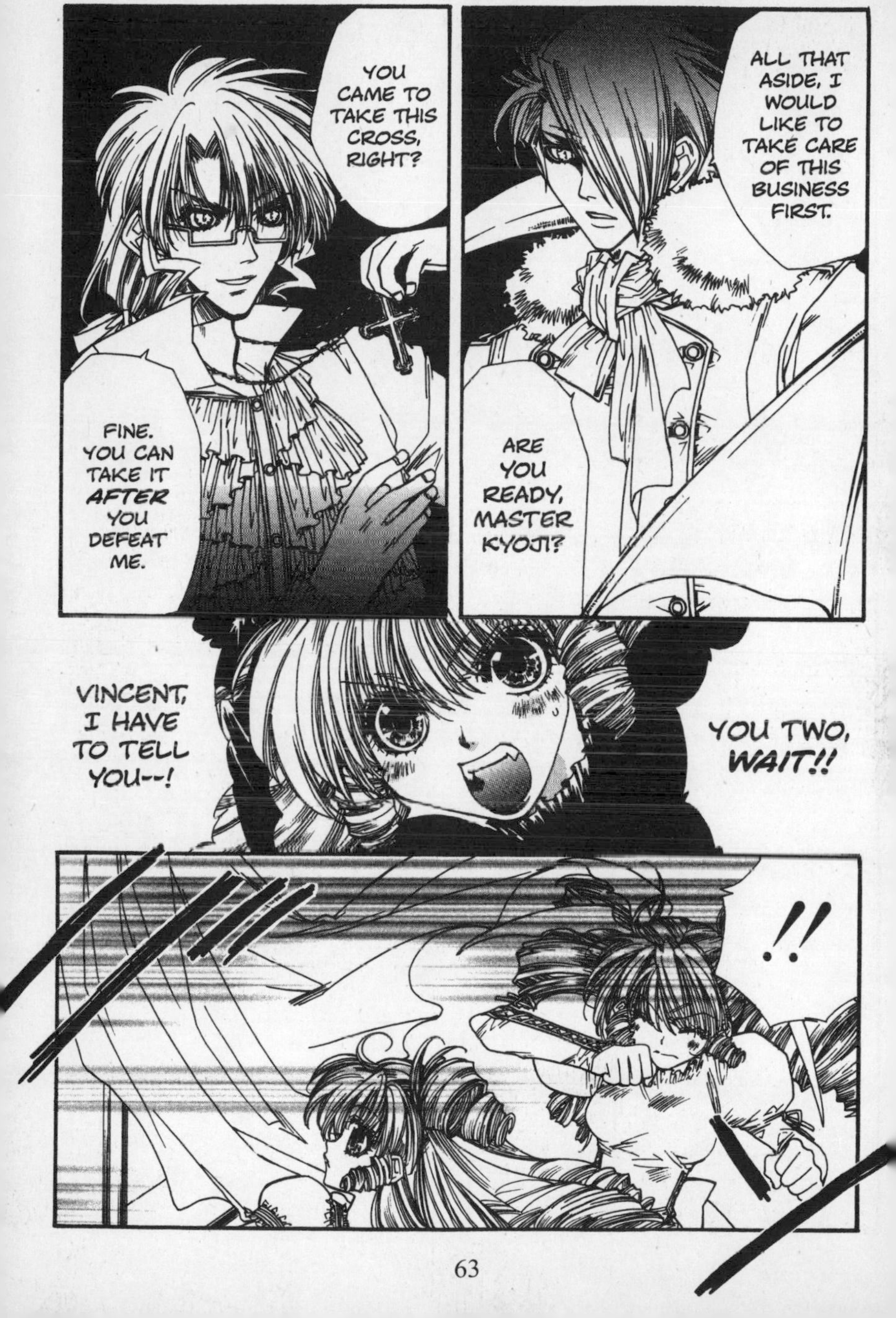
ALL THAT ASIDE, I WOULD LIKE TO TAKE CARE OF THIS BUSINESS FIRST.
ARE YOU READY, MASTER KYOJI?
YOU CAME TO TAKE THIS CROSS, RIGHT?
FINE. YOU CAN TAKE IT *AFTER* YOU DEFEAT ME.
YOU TWO, *WAIT!!*
VINCENT, I HAVE TO TELL YOU--!
!!

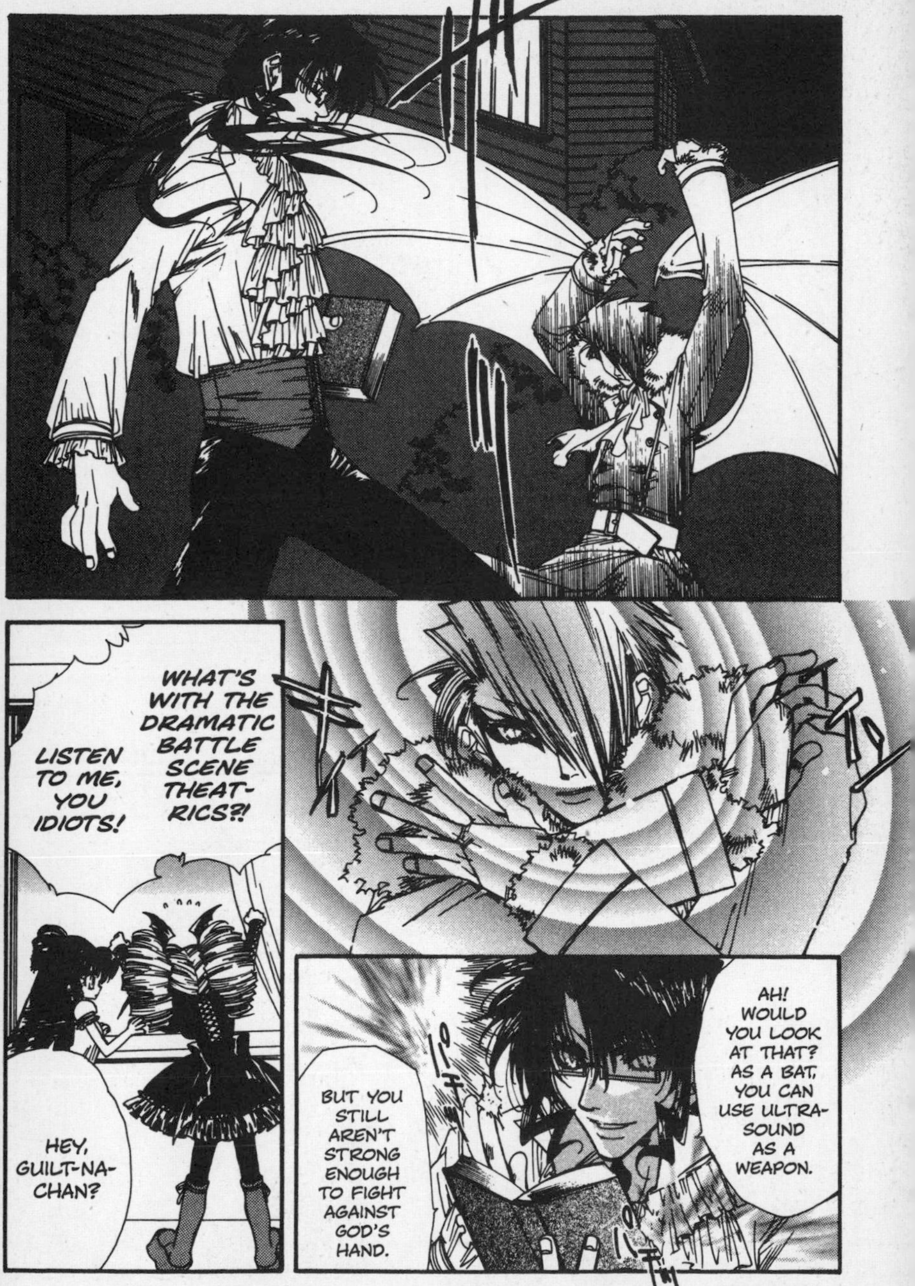
AH! WOULD YOU LOOK AT THAT? AS A BAT, YOU CAN USE ULTRA-SOUND AS A WEAPON.
BUT YOU STILL AREN'T STRONG ENOUGH TO FIGHT AGAINST GOD'S HAND.
WHAT'S WITH THE DRAMATIC BATTLE SCENE THEAT-RICS?!
LISTEN TO ME, YOU IDIOTS!
HEY, GUILT-NA-CHAN?

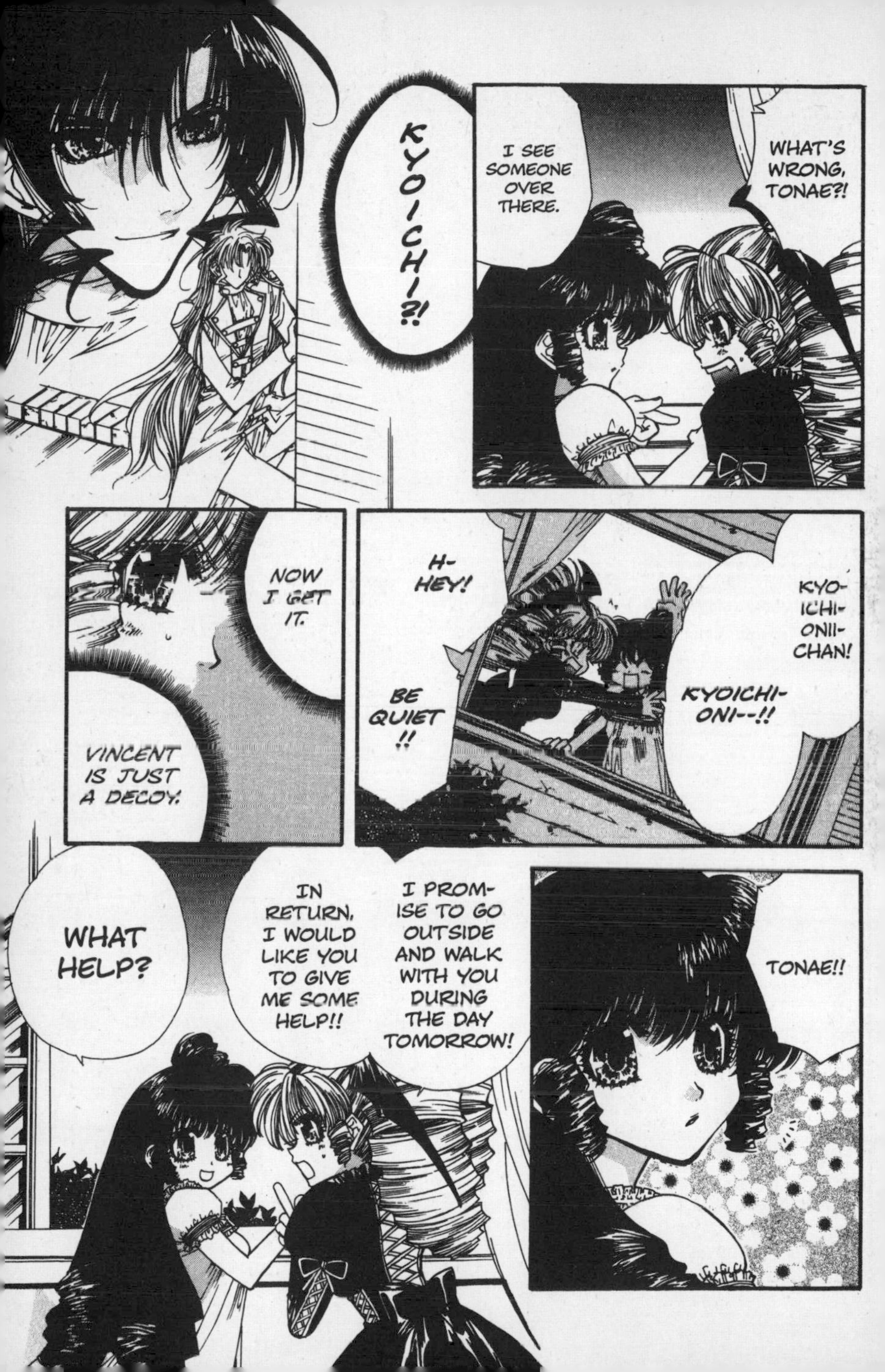
WHAT'S WRONG, TONAE?!
I SEE SOMEONE OVER THERE.
KYOICHI?!
KYO-ICHI-ONII-CHAN!
KYOICHI-ONI--!!
H-HEY!
BE QUIET!!
NOW I GET IT.
VINCENT IS JUST A DECOY.
TONAE!!
I PROM-ISE TO GO OUTSIDE AND WALK WITH YOU DURING THE DAY TOMORROW!
IN RETURN, I WOULD LIKE YOU TO GIVE ME SOME HELP!!
WHAT HELP?

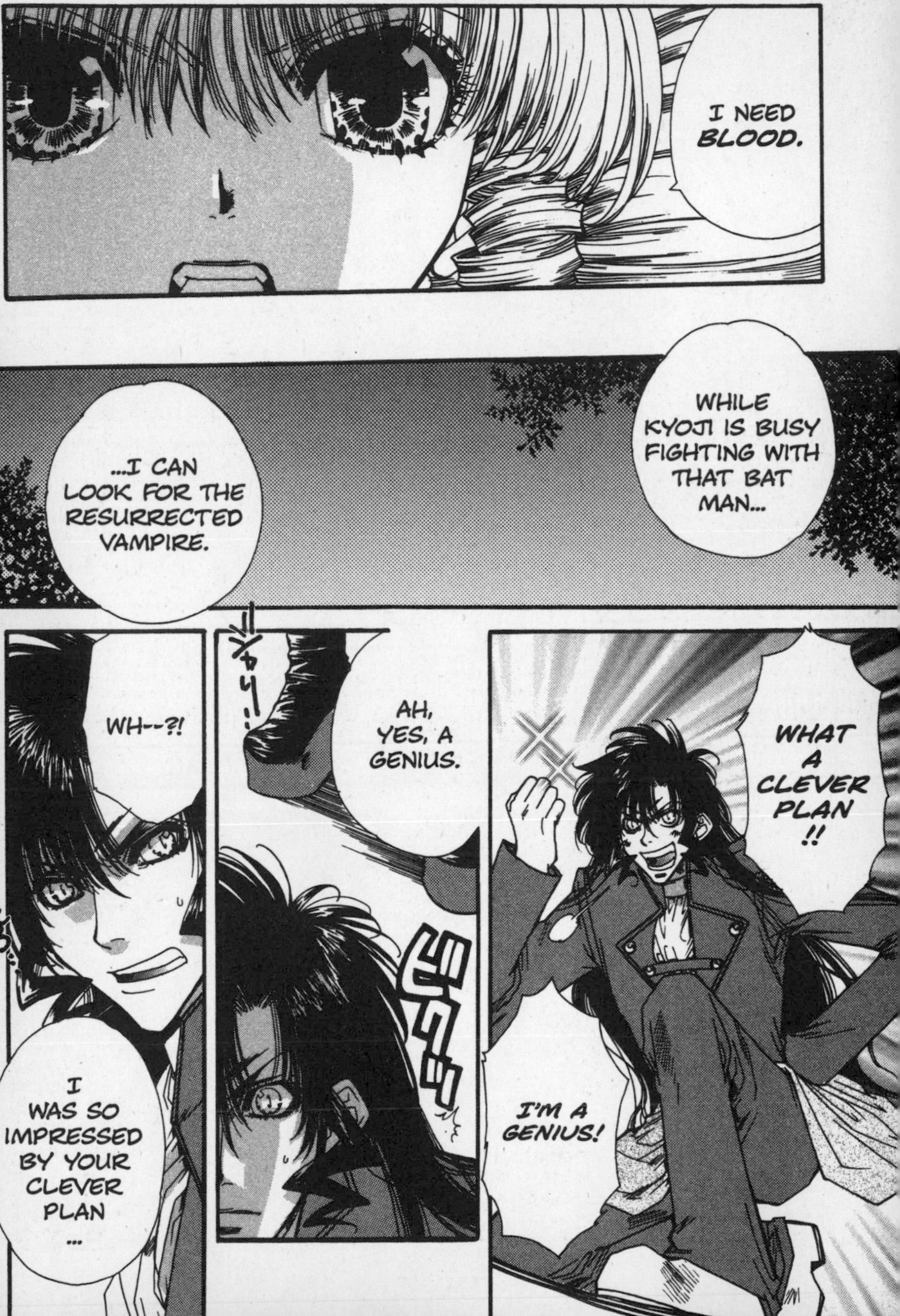
I NEED BLOOD.
WHILE KYOJI IS BUSY FIGHTING WITH THAT BAT MAN...
...I CAN LOOK FOR THE RESURRECTED VAMPIRE.
WHAT A CLEVER PLAN!!
I'M A GENIUS!
AH, YES, A GENIUS.
WH--?!
I WAS SO IMPRESSED BY YOUR CLEVER PLAN ...

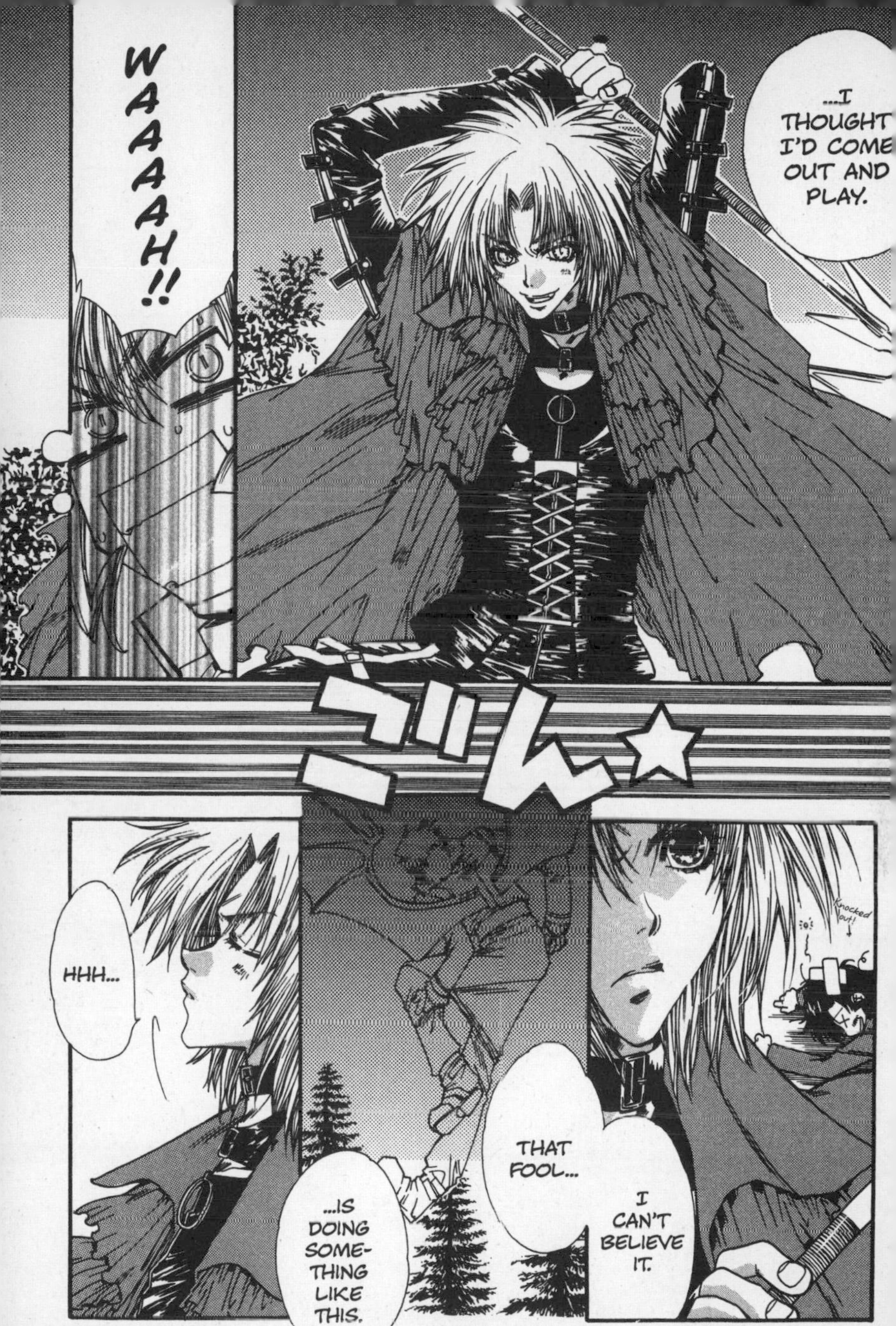
...I THOUGHT I'D COME OUT AND PLAY.
WAAAAAH!!
ごん☆
Knocked out!
THAT FOOL...
I CAN'T BELIEVE IT.
...IS DOING SOME-THING LIKE THIS.
HHH...

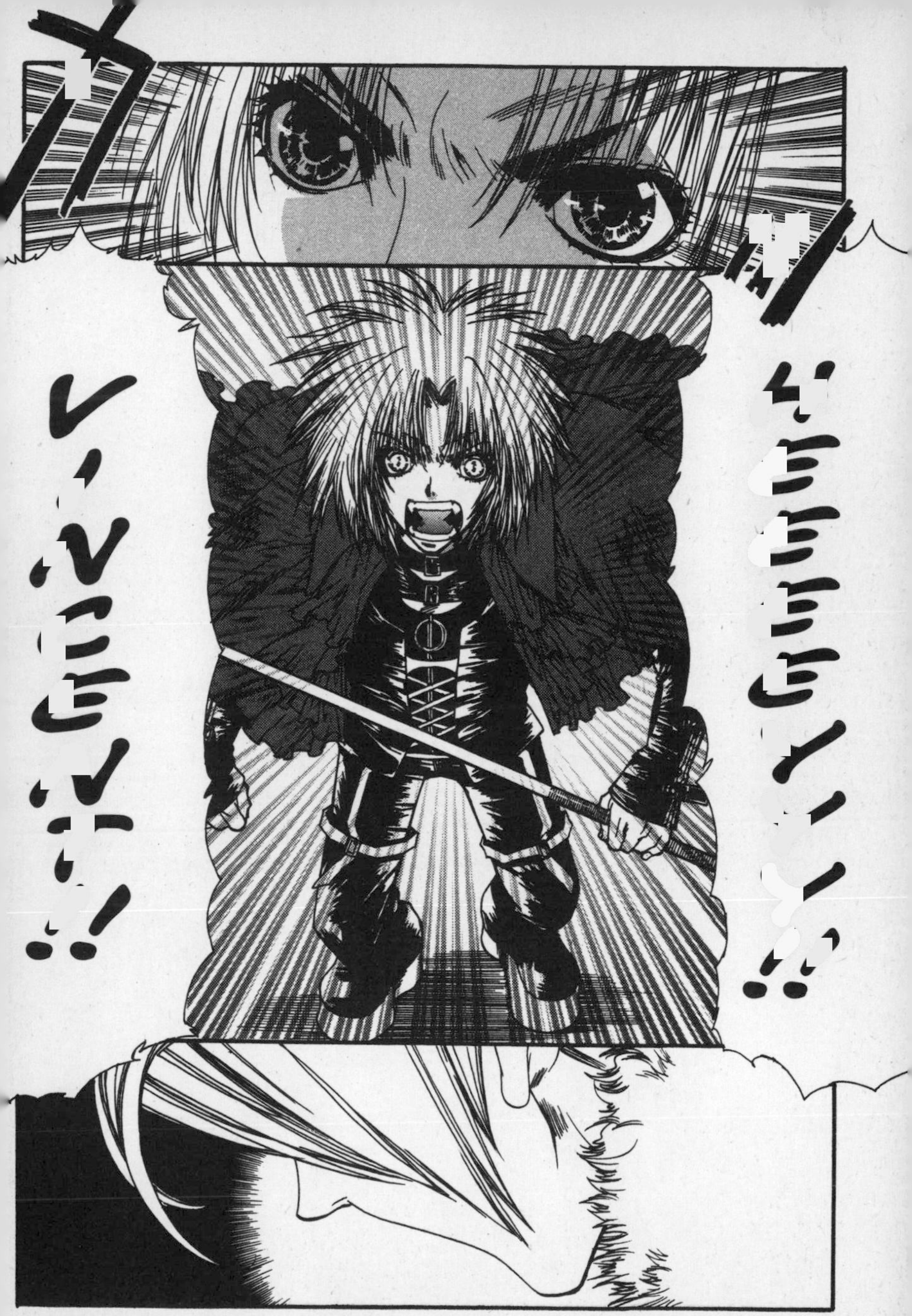

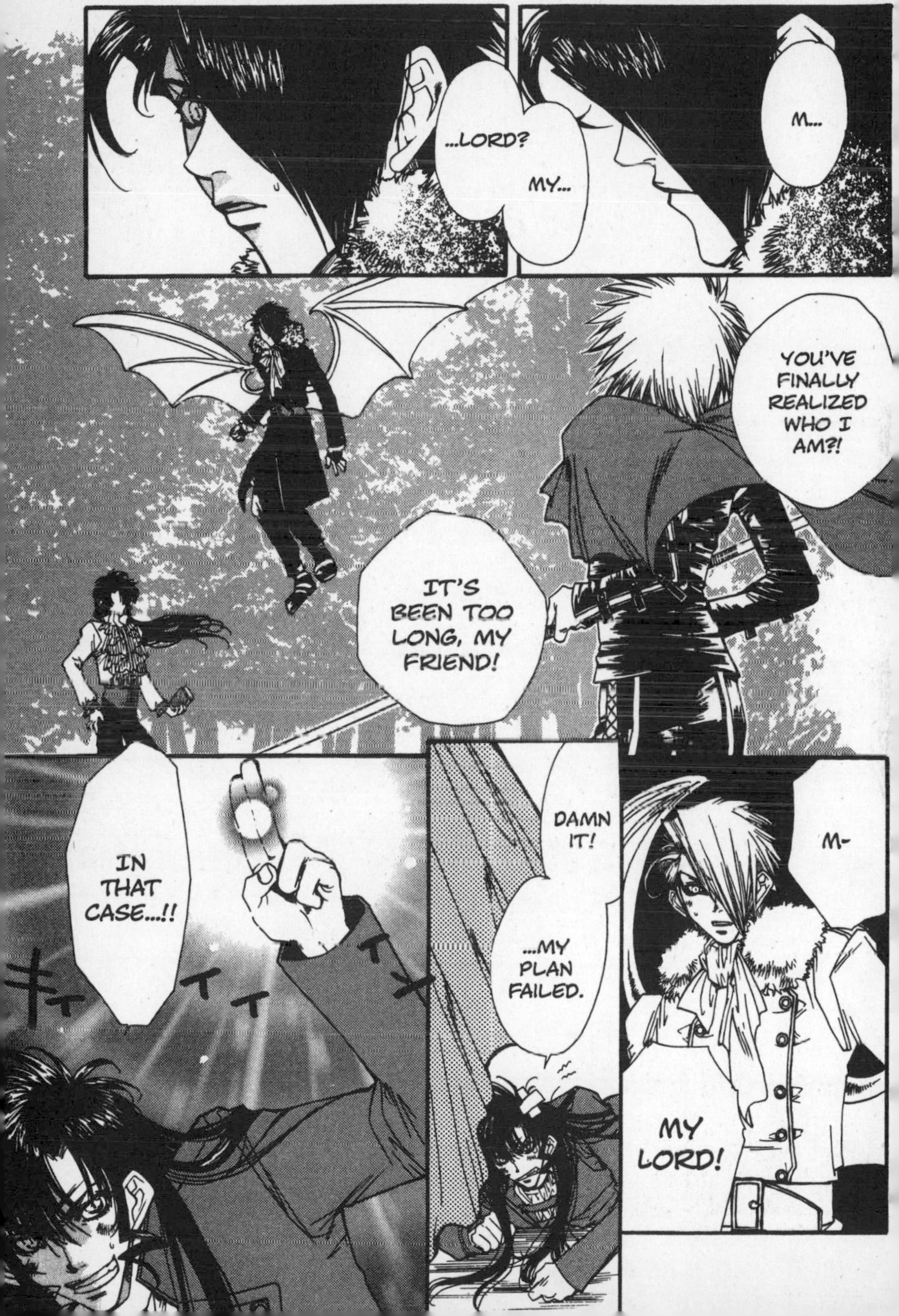
M...
MY...
...LORD?
YOU'VE FINALLY REALIZED WHO I AM?!
IT'S BEEN TOO LONG, MY FRIEND!
M-
MY LORD!
DAMN IT!
...MY PLAN FAILED.
IN THAT CASE...!!

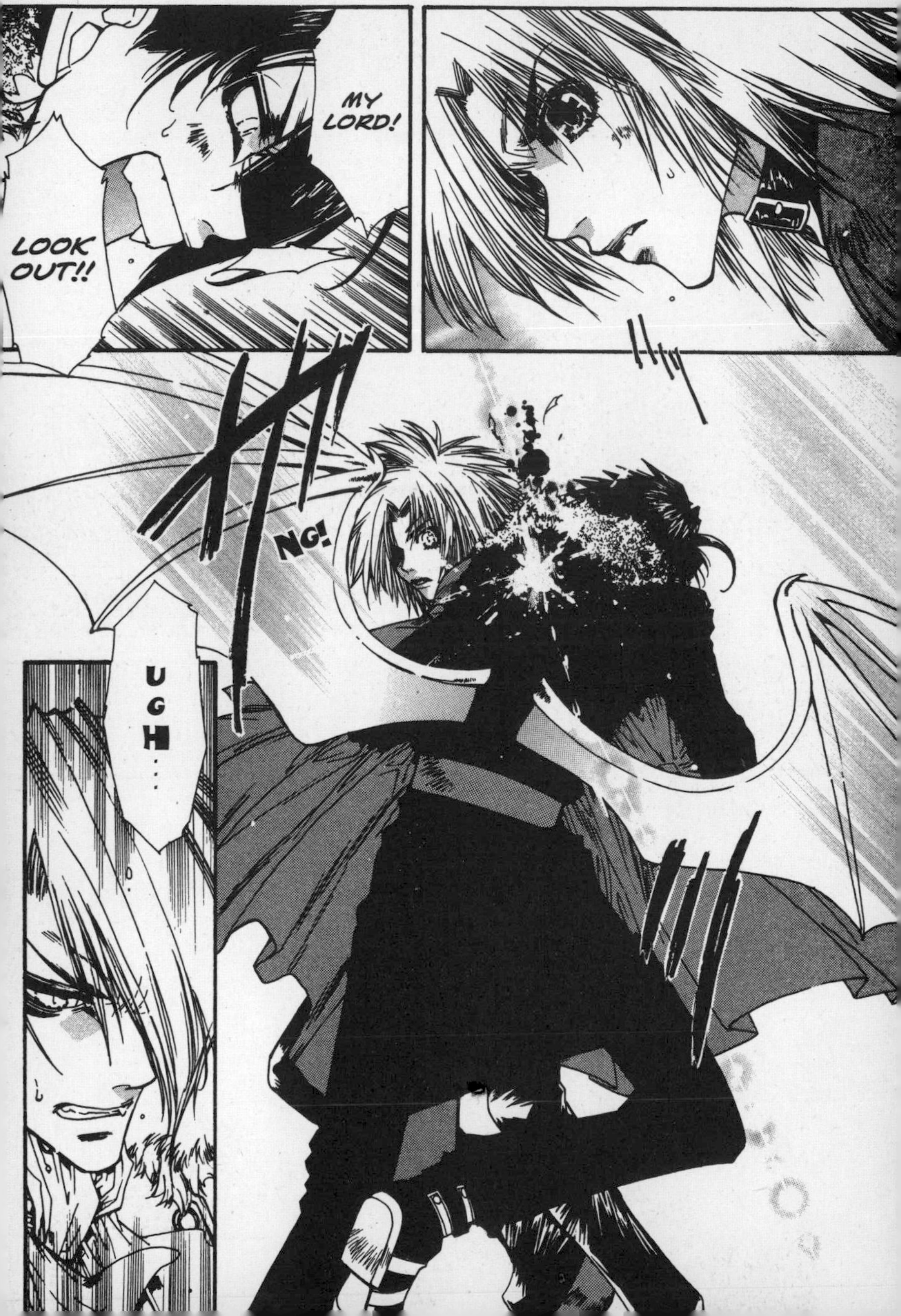
MY LORD!
LOOK OUT!!
NG!
UGH...

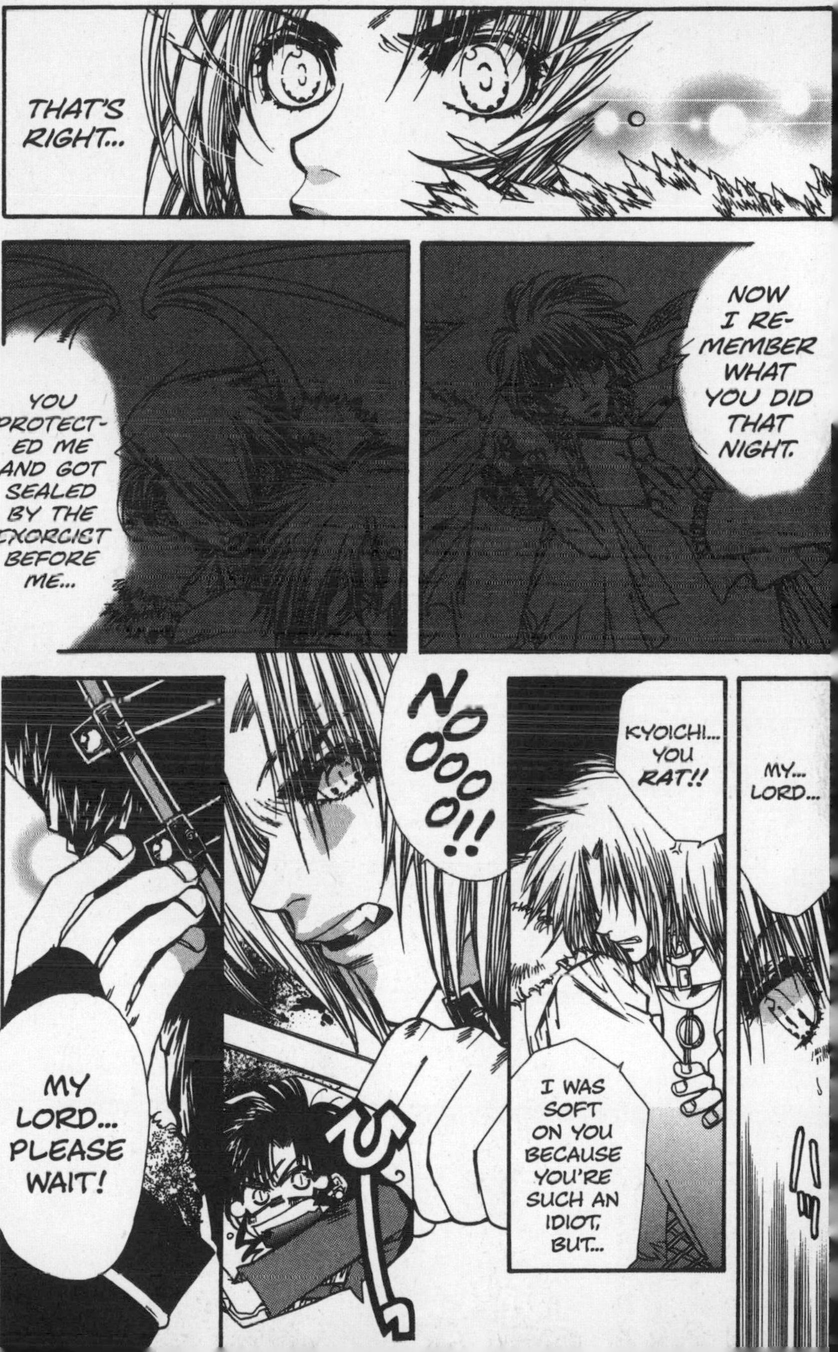
THAT'S RIGHT...
NOW I RE-MEMBER WHAT YOU DID THAT NIGHT.
YOU PROTECT-ED ME AND GOT SEALED BY THE EXORCIST BEFORE ME...
MY... LORD...
KYOICHI... YOU RAT!!
I WAS SOFT ON YOU BECAUSE YOU'RE SUCH AN IDIOT, BUT...
NOOOOOO!!
MY LORD... PLEASE WAIT!

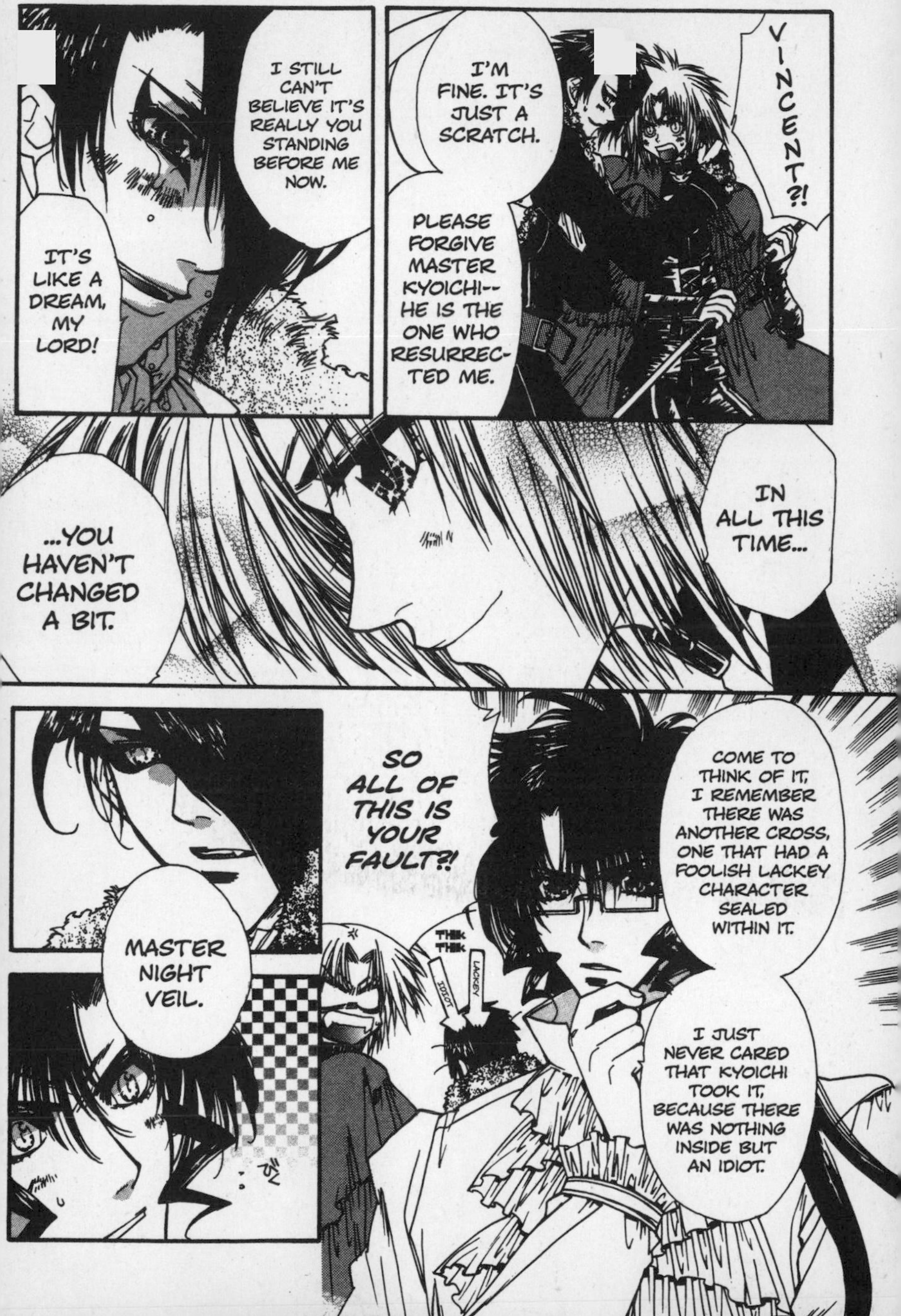
VINCENT?!
I'M FINE. IT'S JUST A SCRATCH.
PLEASE FORGIVE MASTER KYOICHI-- HE IS THE ONE WHO RESURRECTED ME.
I STILL CAN'T BELIEVE IT'S REALLY YOU STANDING BEFORE ME NOW.
IT'S LIKE A DREAM, MY LORD!
IN ALL THIS TIME...
...YOU HAVEN'T CHANGED A BIT.
COME TO THINK OF IT, I REMEMBER THERE WAS ANOTHER CROSS, ONE THAT HAD A FOOLISH LACKEY CHARACTER SEALED WITHIN IT.
I JUST NEVER CARED THAT KYOICHI TOOK IT, BECAUSE THERE WAS NOTHING INSIDE BUT AN IDIOT.
SO ALL OF THIS IS YOUR FAULT?!
THWK THWK
LACKEY
IDIOT
MASTER NIGHT VEIL.

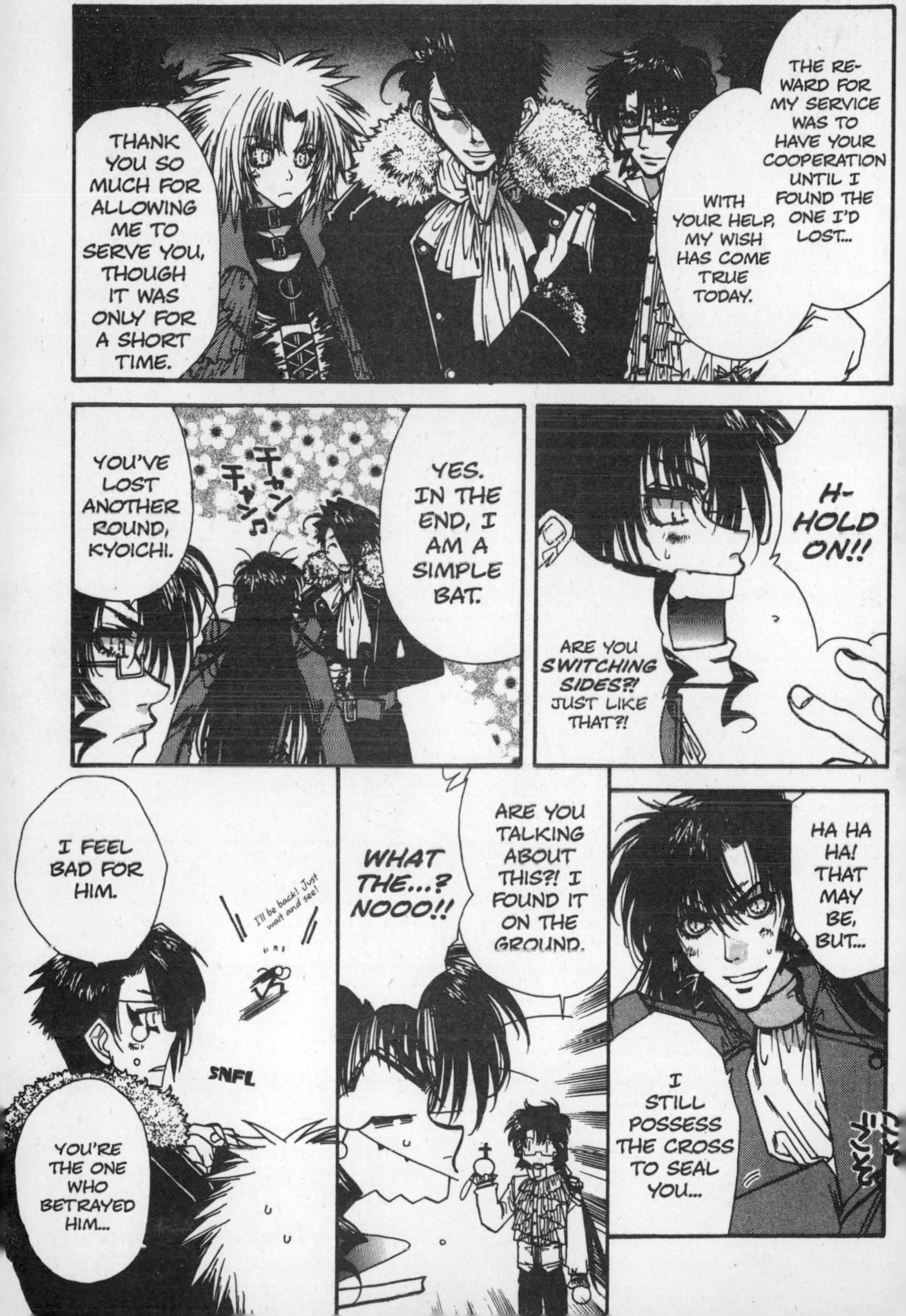
THE RE-WARD FOR MY SERVICE WAS TO HAVE YOUR COOPERATION UNTIL I FOUND THE ONE I'D LOST...
WITH YOUR HELP, MY WISH HAS COME TRUE TODAY.
THANK YOU SO MUCH FOR ALLOWING ME TO SERVE YOU, THOUGH IT WAS ONLY FOR A SHORT TIME.
H-HOLD ON!!
ARE YOU SWITCHING SIDES?! JUST LIKE THAT?!
YES. IN THE END, I AM A SIMPLE BAT.
チャンチャン♫
YOU'VE LOST ANOTHER ROUND, KYOICHI.
HA HA HA! THAT MAY BE, BUT...
I STILL POSSESS THE CROSS TO SEAL YOU...
ARE YOU TALKING ABOUT THIS?! I FOUND IT ON THE GROUND.
WHAT THE...? NOOO!!
I FEEL BAD FOR HIM.
I'll be back! Just wait and see!
SNFL
YOU'RE THE ONE WHO BETRAYED HIM...

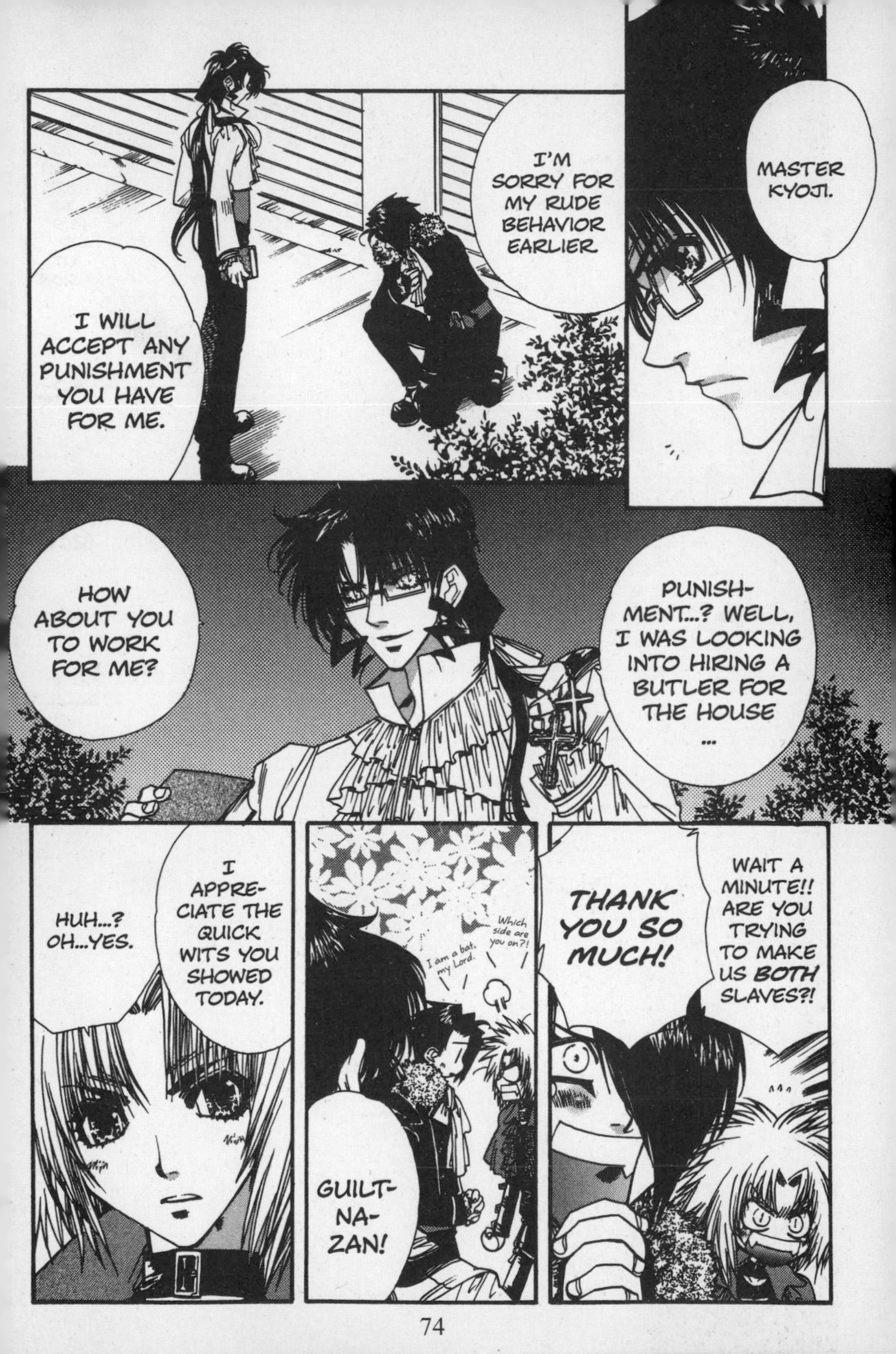
MASTER KYOJI.
I'M SORRY FOR MY RUDE BEHAVIOR EARLIER
I WILL ACCEPT ANY PUNISHMENT YOU HAVE FOR ME.
PUNISH-MENT...? WELL, I WAS LOOKING INTO HIRING A BUTLER FOR THE HOUSE ...
HOW ABOUT YOU TO WORK FOR ME?
WAIT A MINUTE!! ARE YOU TRYING TO MAKE US BOTH SLAVES?!
THANK YOU SO MUCH!
Which side are you on?!
I am a bat, my Lord.
GUILT-NA-ZAN!
I APPRE-CIATE THE QUICK WITS YOU SHOWED TODAY.
HUH...? OH...YES.

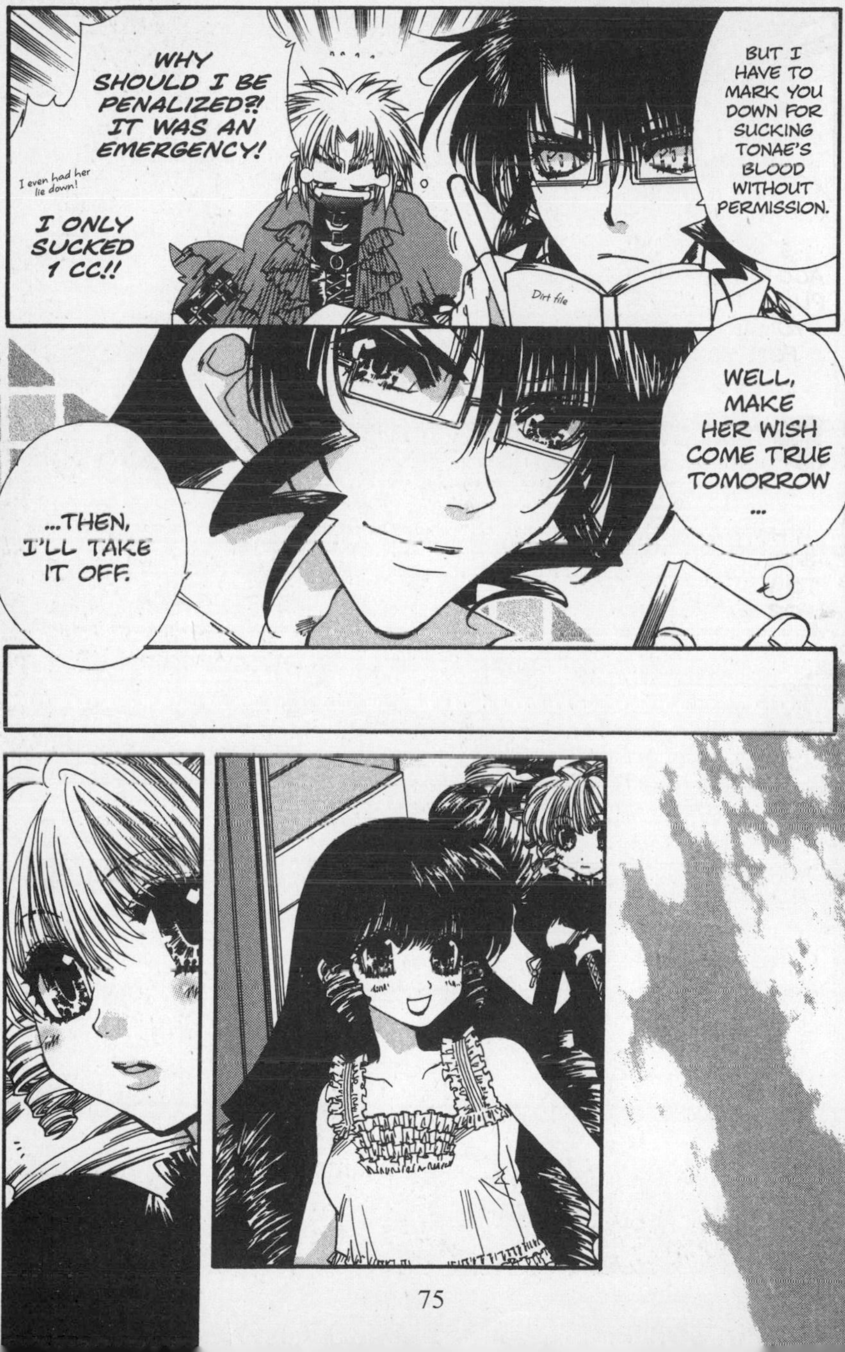
BUT I HAVE TO MARK YOU DOWN FOR SUCKING TONAE'S BLOOD WITHOUT PERMISSION.
Dirt file
WHY SHOULD I BE PENALIZED?! IT WAS AN EMERGENCY!
I even had her lie down!
I ONLY SUCKED 1 CC!!
WELL, MAKE HER WISH COME TRUE TOMORROW ...
...THEN, I'LL TAKE IT OFF.

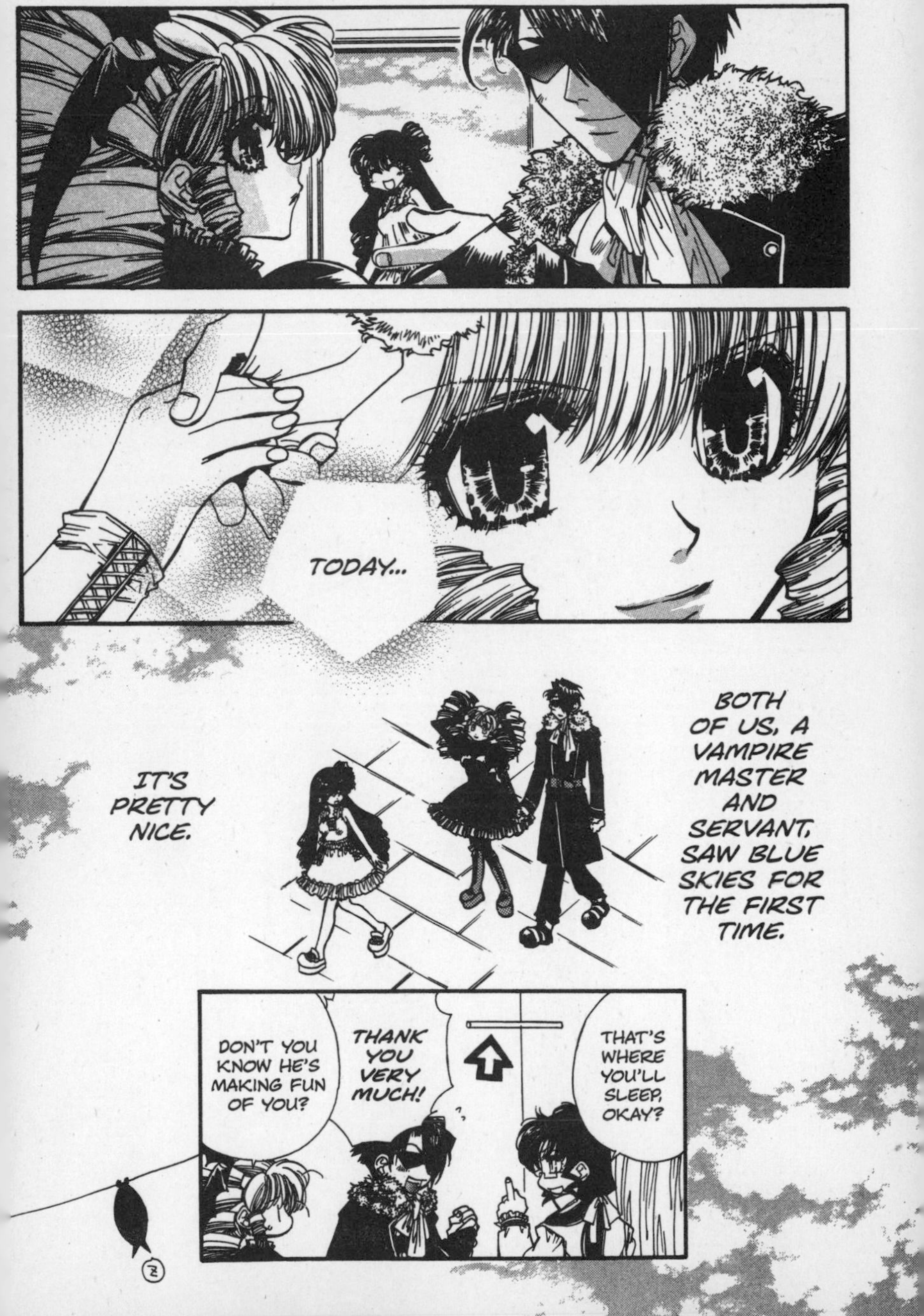
TODAY...
BOTH OF US, A VAMPIRE MASTER AND SERVANT, SAW BLUE SKIES FOR THE FIRST TIME.
IT'S PRETTY NICE.
THAT'S WHERE YOU'LL SLEEP, OKAY?
THANK YOU VERY MUCH!
DON'T YOU KNOW HE'S MAKING FUN OF YOU?

Vincent

BONUS COMIC STRIP

VAMPIRE DOLL

REFLECTIONS

VIN-CHAN, CAN I HANG MY UNIFORM HERE?
OF COURSE YOU CAN!
....
WHY ARE YOU BLUSH-ING?

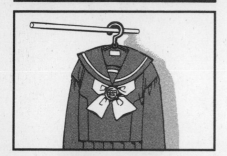

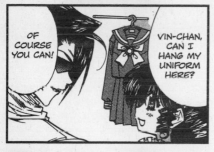

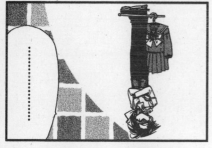

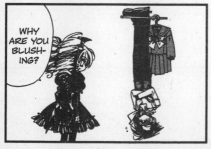

TONAE

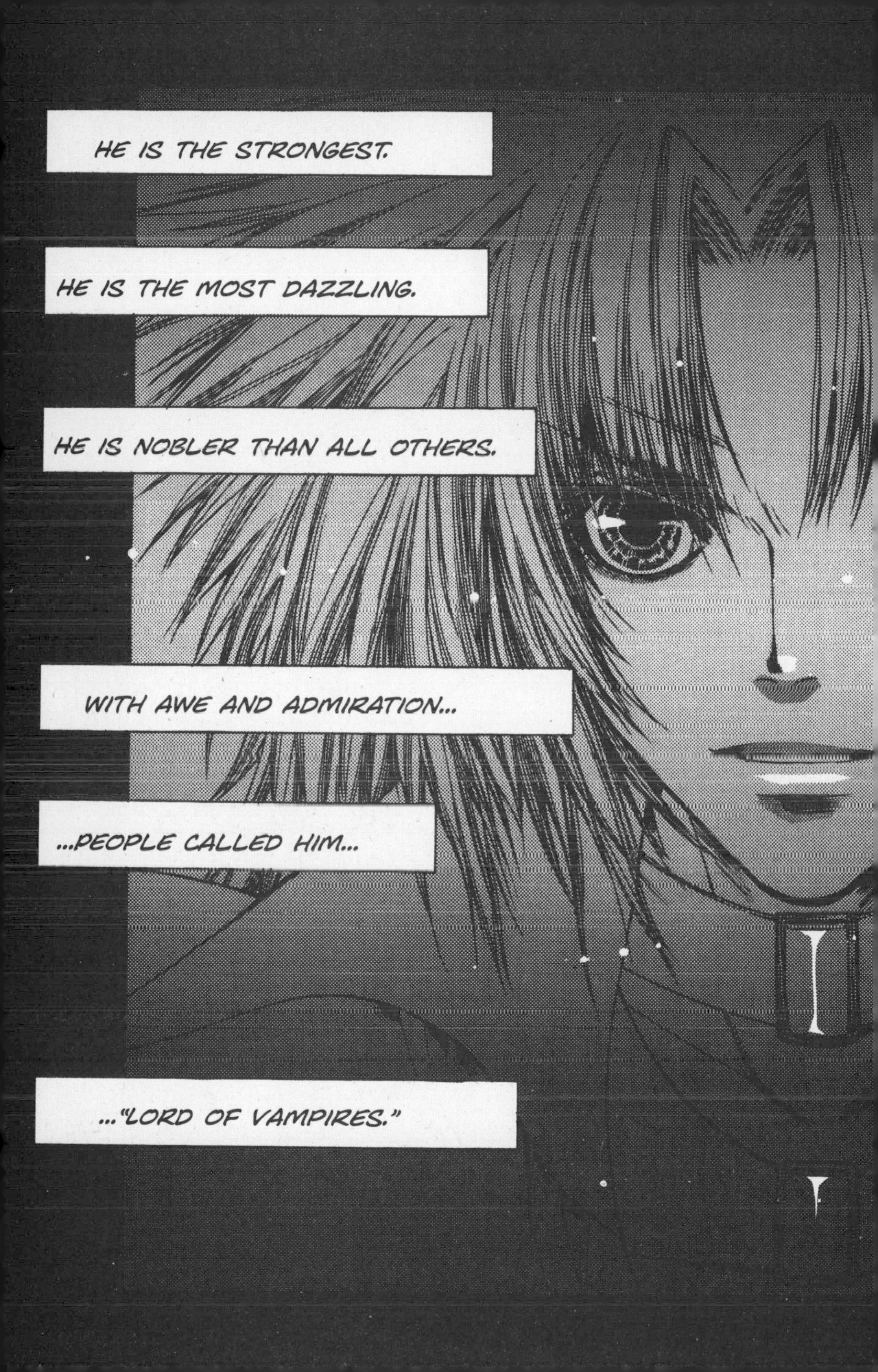
HE IS THE STRONGEST.
HE IS THE MOST DAZZLING.
HE IS NOBLER THAN ALL OTHERS.
WITH AWE AND ADMIRATION...
...PEOPLE CALLED HIM...
..."LORD OF VAMPIRES."

♯3 Mandarin

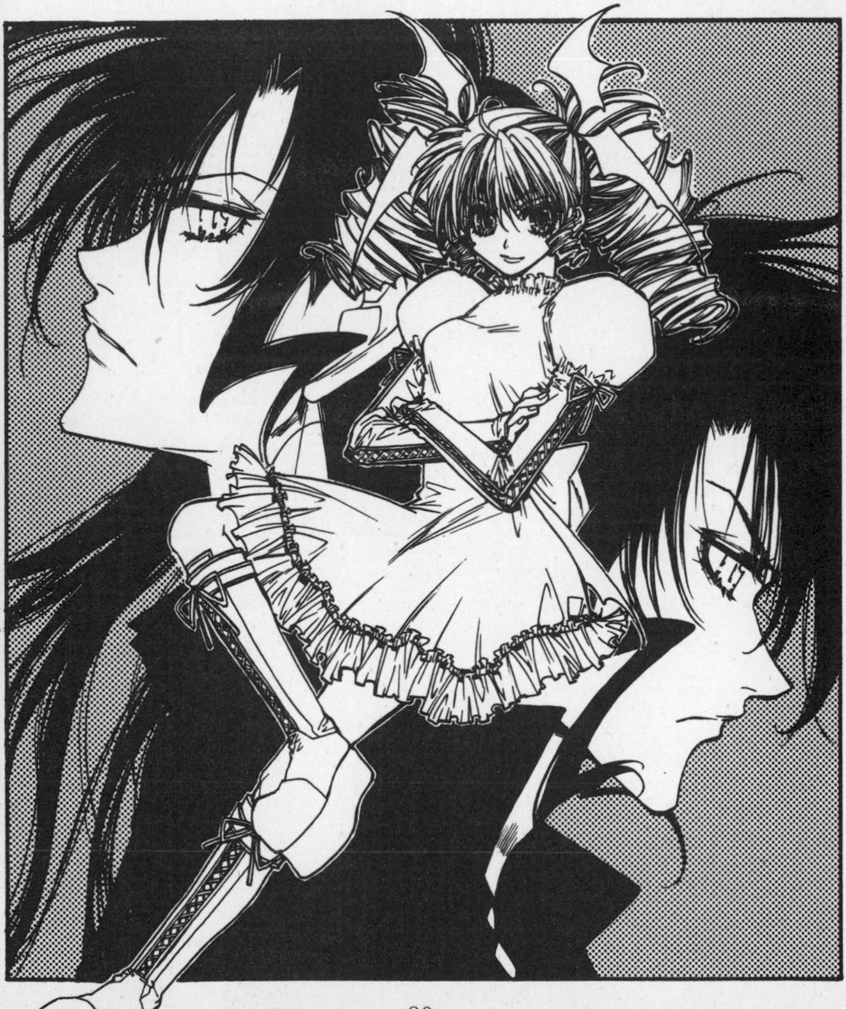

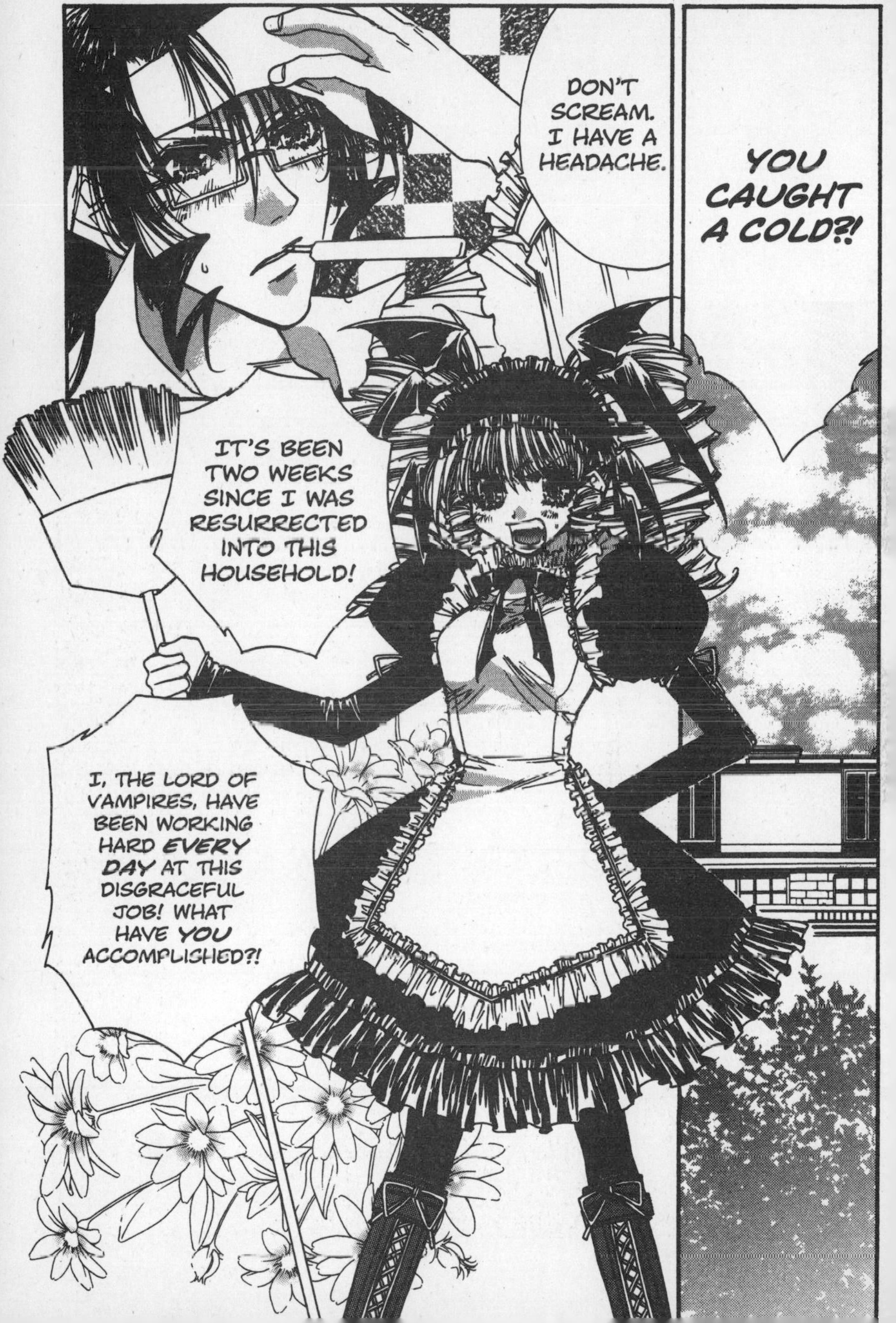
YOU CAUGHT A COLD?!
DON'T SCREAM. I HAVE A HEADACHE.
IT'S BEEN TWO WEEKS SINCE I WAS RESURRECTED INTO THIS HOUSEHOLD!
I, THE LORD OF VAMPIRES, HAVE BEEN WORKING HARD EVERY DAY AT THIS DISGRACEFUL JOB! WHAT HAVE YOU ACCOMPLISHED?!

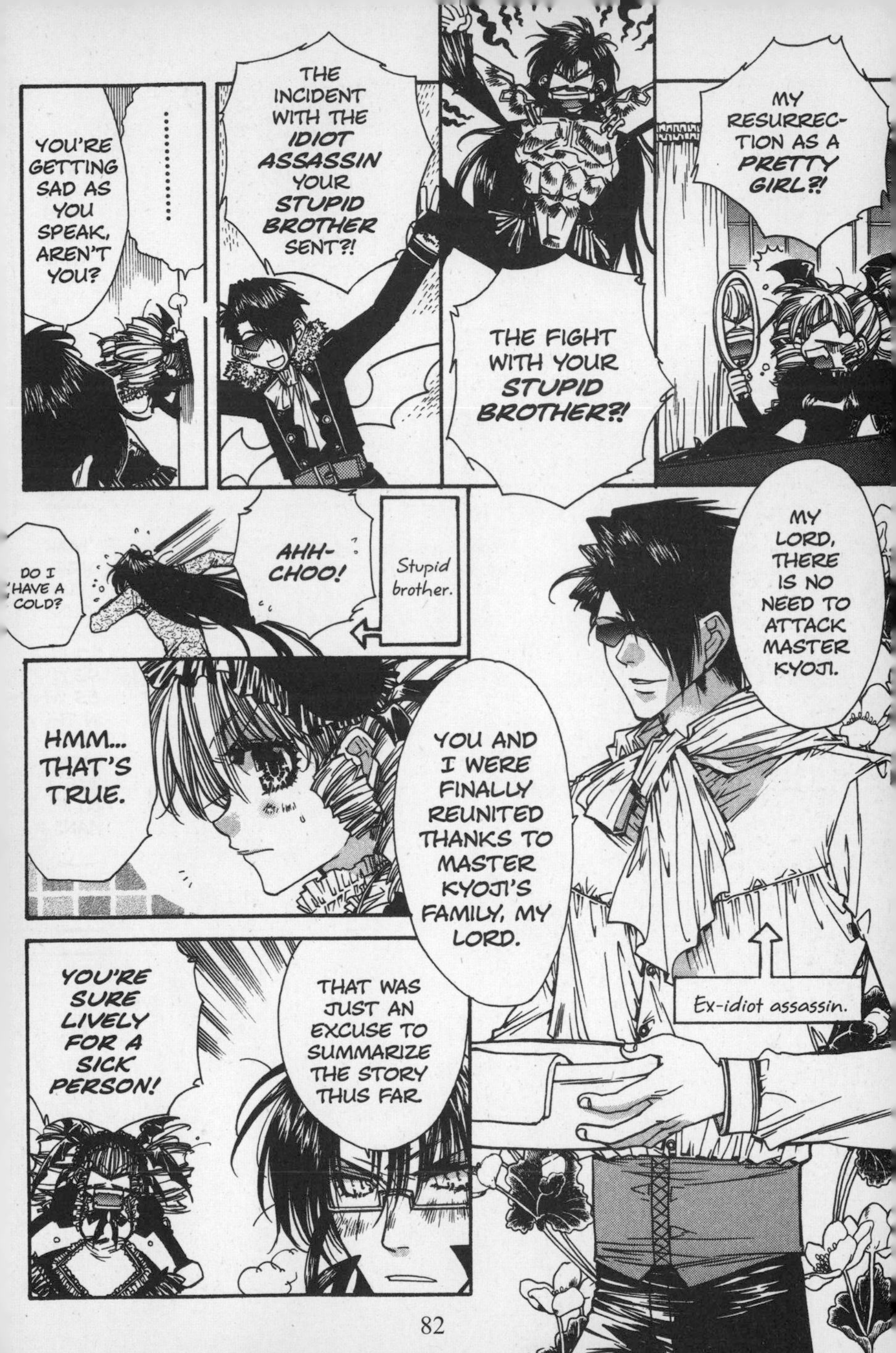

MY RESURRECTION AS A PRETTY GIRL?!
THE FIGHT WITH YOUR STUPID BROTHER?!
THE INCIDENT WITH THE IDIOT ASSASSIN YOUR STUPID BROTHER SENT?!
....
YOU'RE GETTING SAD AS YOU SPEAK, AREN'T YOU?
MY LORD, THERE IS NO NEED TO ATTACK MASTER KYOJI.
YOU AND I WERE FINALLY REUNITED THANKS TO MASTER KYOJI'S FAMILY, MY LORD.
Ex-idiot assassin.
Stupid brother.
AHH-CHOO!
DO I HAVE A COLD?
HMM... THAT'S TRUE.
THAT WAS JUST AN EXCUSE TO SUMMARIZE THE STORY THUS FAR
YOU'RE SURE LIVELY FOR A SICK PERSON!

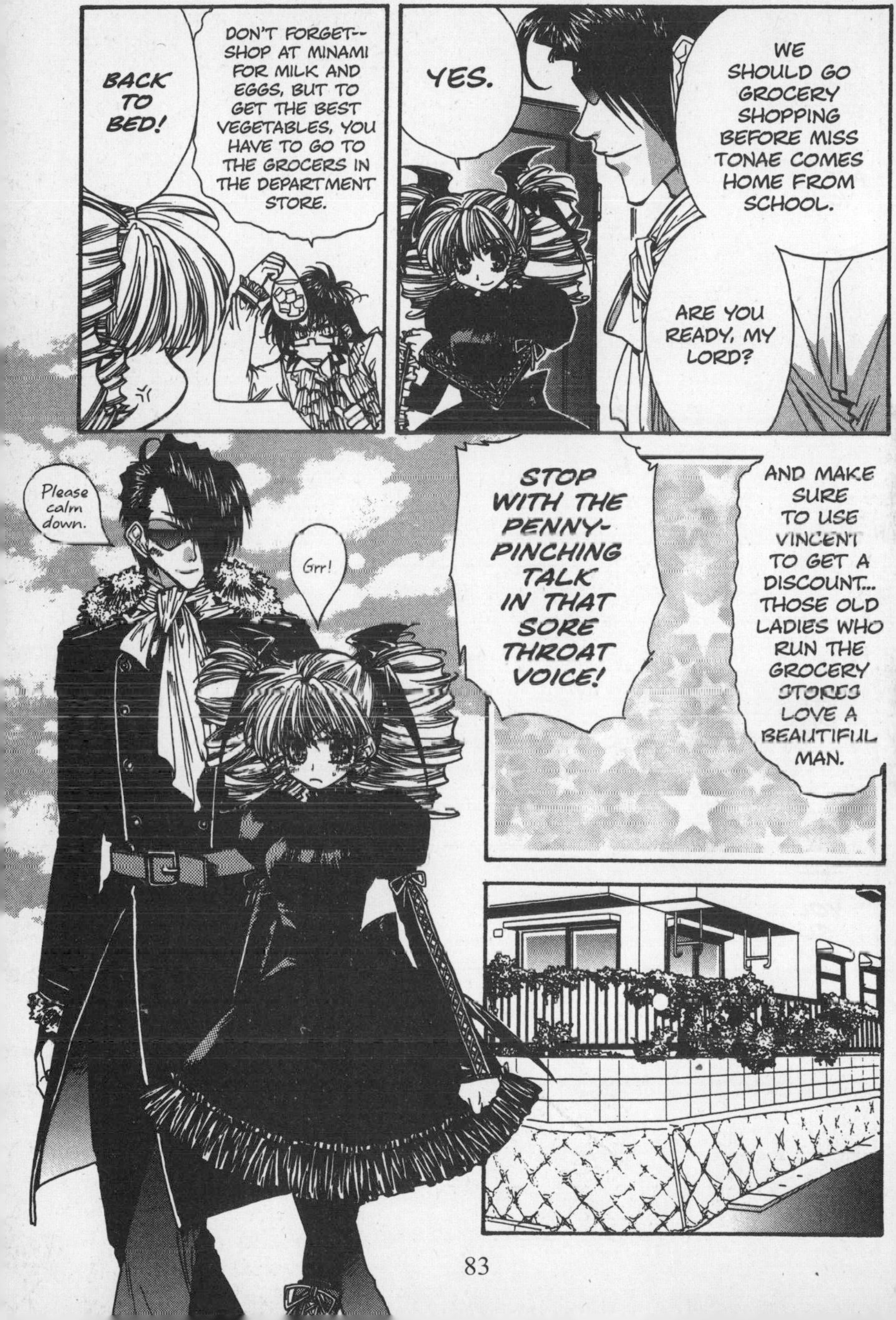
WE SHOULD GO GROCERY SHOPPING BEFORE MISS TONAE COMES HOME FROM SCHOOL.
YES.
ARE YOU READY, MY LORD?
DON'T FORGET-- SHOP AT MINAMI FOR MILK AND EGGS, BUT TO GET THE BEST VEGETABLES, YOU HAVE TO GO TO THE GROCERS IN THE DEPARTMENT STORE.
BACK TO BED!
AND MAKE SURE TO USE VINCENT TO GET A DISCOUNT... THOSE OLD LADIES WHO RUN THE GROCERY STORES LOVE A BEAUTIFUL MAN.
STOP WITH THE PENNY-PINCHING TALK IN THAT SORE THROAT VOICE!
Grr!
Please calm down.

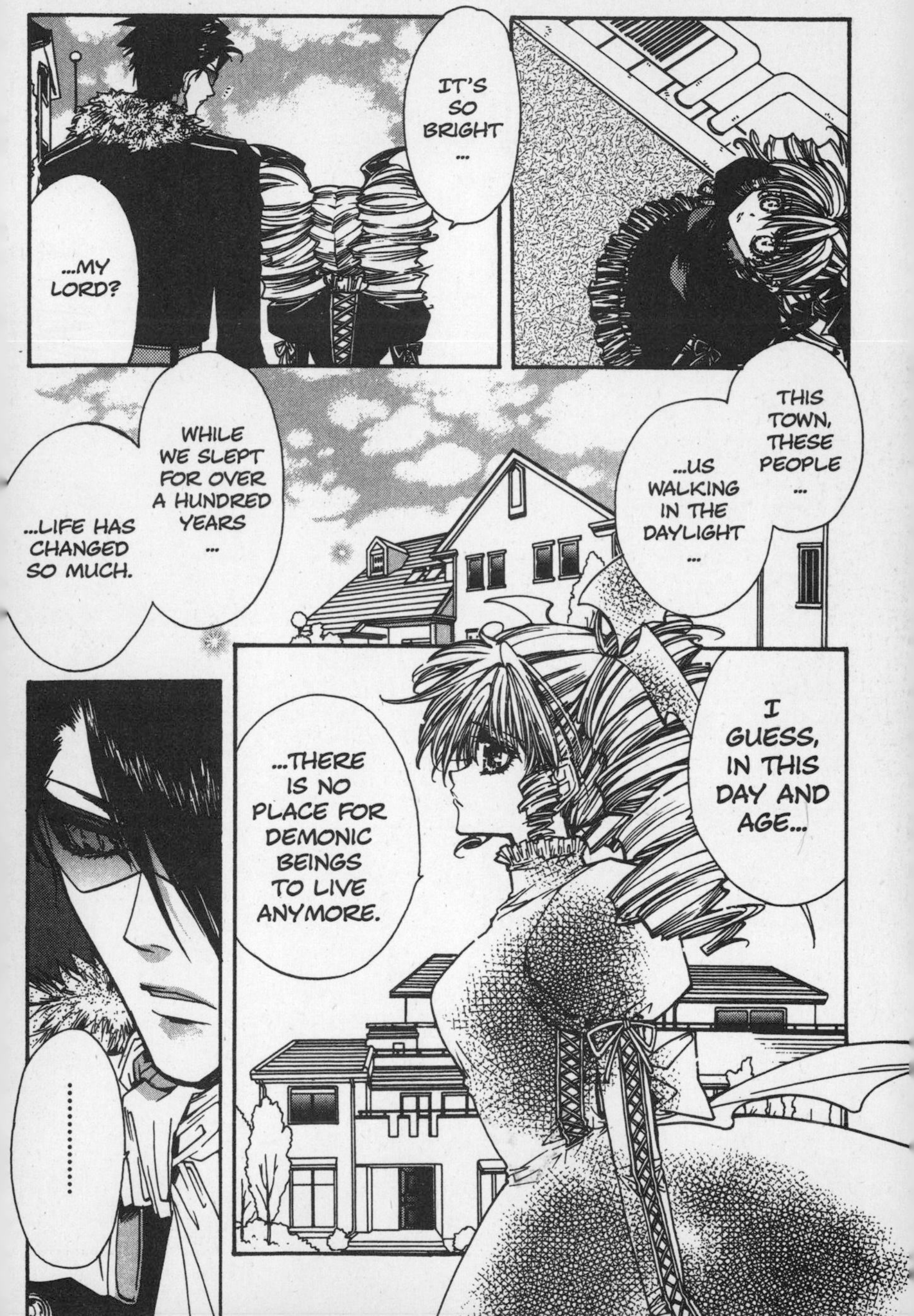
IT'S SO BRIGHT ...
...MY LORD?
THIS TOWN, THESE PEOPLE ...
...US WALKING IN THE DAYLIGHT ...
WHILE WE SLEPT FOR OVER A HUNDRED YEARS ...
...LIFE HAS CHANGED SO MUCH.
I GUESS, IN THIS DAY AND AGE...
...THERE IS NO PLACE FOR DEMONIC BEINGS TO LIVE ANYMORE.
....

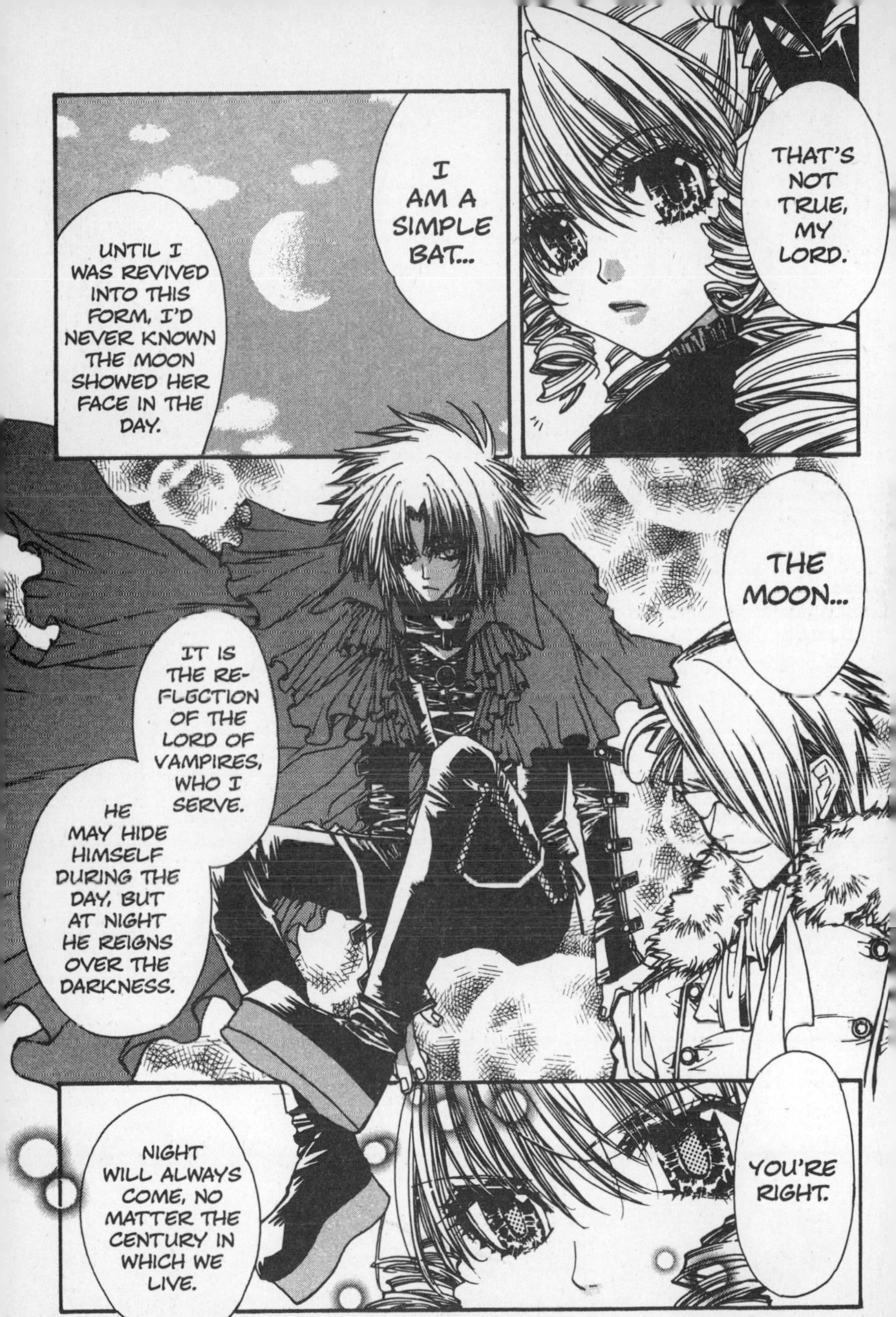
THAT'S NOT TRUE, MY LORD.
I AM A SIMPLE BAT...
UNTIL I WAS REVIVED INTO THIS FORM, I'D NEVER KNOWN THE MOON SHOWED HER FACE IN THE DAY.
THE MOON...
IT IS THE RE-FLECTION OF THE LORD OF VAMPIRES, WHO I SERVE.
HE MAY HIDE HIMSELF DURING THE DAY, BUT AT NIGHT HE REIGNS OVER THE DARKNESS.
YOU'RE RIGHT.
NIGHT WILL ALWAYS COME, NO MATTER THE CENTURY IN WHICH WE LIVE.

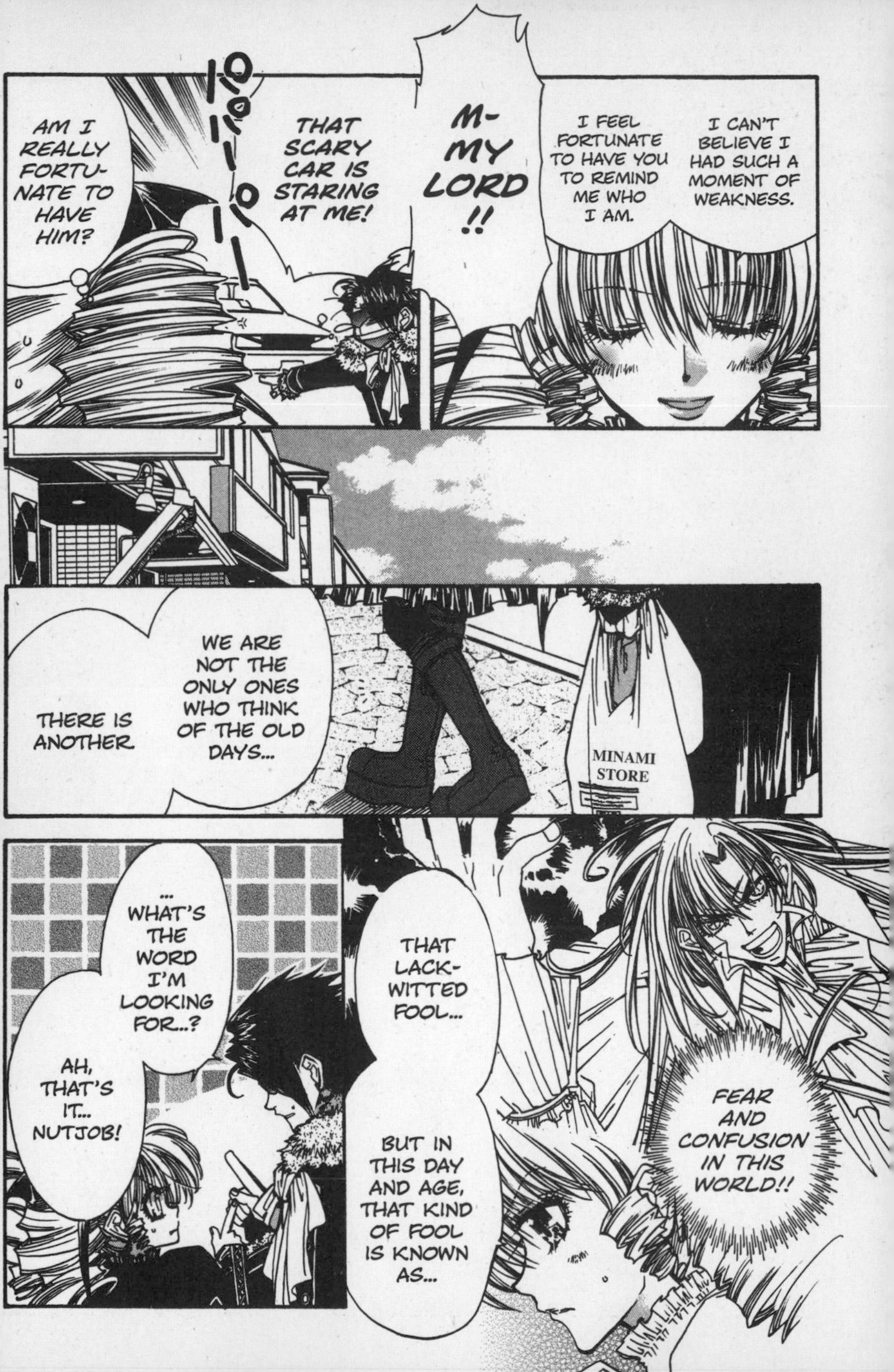

I CAN'T BELIEVE I HAD SUCH A MOMENT OF WEAKNESS.
I FEEL FORTUNATE TO HAVE YOU TO REMIND ME WHO I AM.
M-MY LORD!!
THAT SCARY CAR IS STARING AT ME!
AM I REALLY FORTU-NATE TO HAVE HIM?
WE ARE NOT THE ONLY ONES WHO THINK OF THE OLD DAYS...
THERE IS ANOTHER
MINAMI STORE
THAT LACK-WITTED FOOL...
FEAR AND CONFUSION IN THIS WORLD!!
BUT IN THIS DAY AND AGE, THAT KIND OF FOOL IS KNOWN AS...
...WHAT'S THE WORD I'M LOOKING FOR...?
AH, THAT'S IT... NUTJOB!

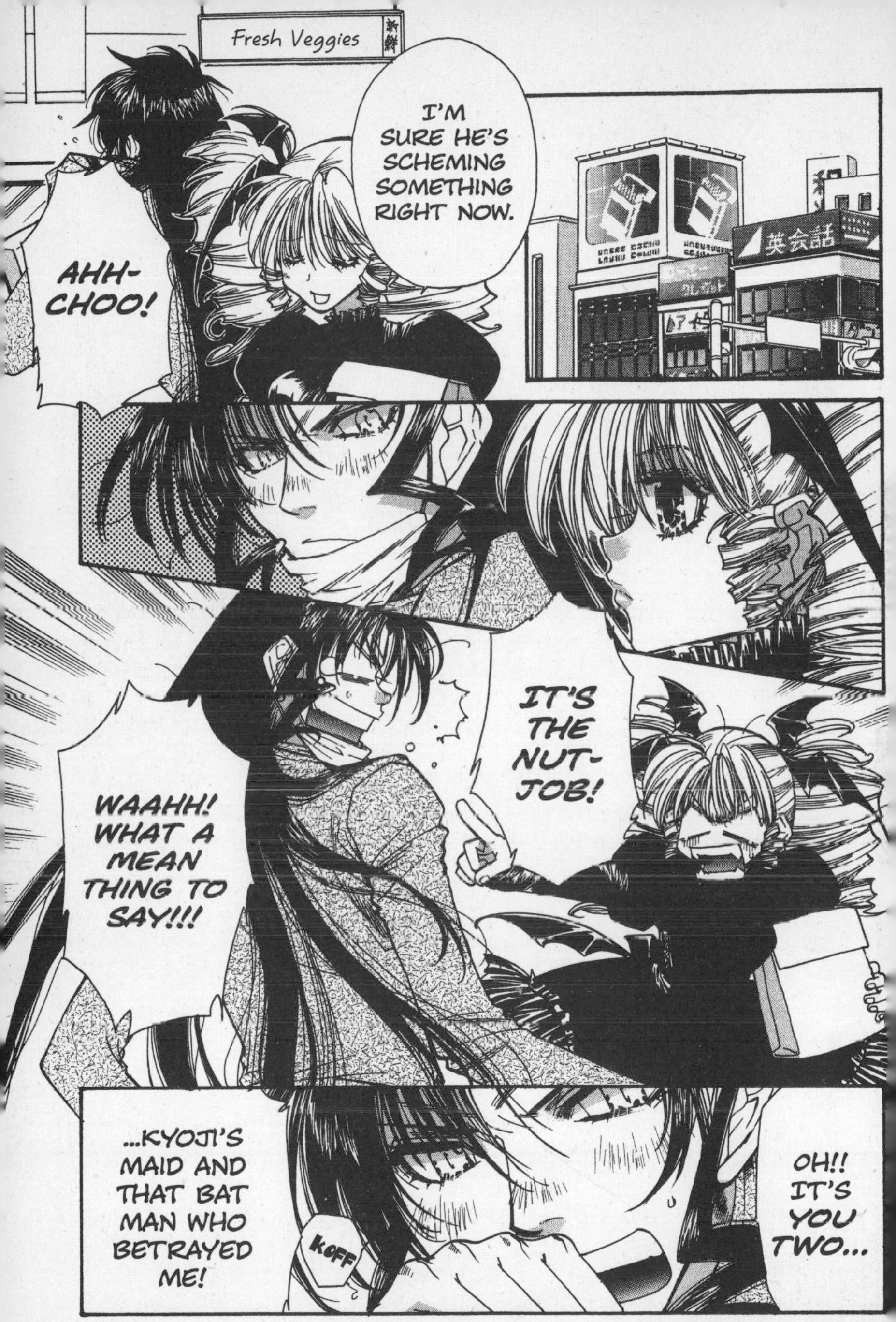
英会話
Fresh Veggies
I'M SURE HE'S SCHEMING SOMETHING RIGHT NOW.
AHH-CHOO!
IT'S THE NUT-JOB!
WAAHH! WHAT A MEAN THING TO SAY!!!
OH!! IT'S YOU TWO...
KOFF
...KYOJI'S MAID AND THAT BAT MAN WHO BETRAYED ME!

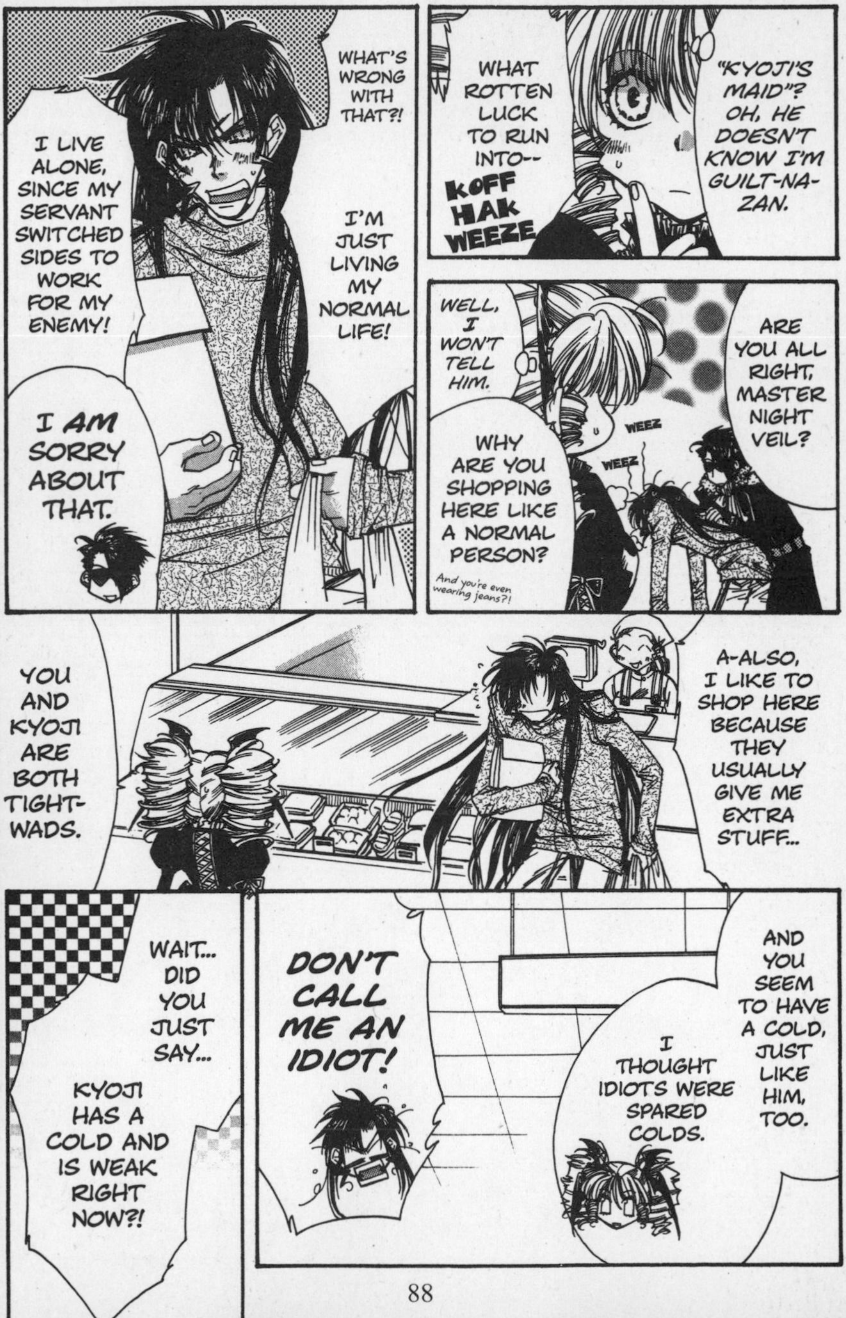
"KYOJI'S MAID"? OH, HE DOESN'T KNOW I'M GUILT-NA-ZAN.
WHAT ROTTEN LUCK TO RUN INTO--
KOFF HAK WEEZE
ARE YOU ALL RIGHT, MASTER NIGHT VEIL?
WEEZ
WEEZ
WELL, I WON'T TELL HIM.
WHY ARE YOU SHOPPING HERE LIKE A NORMAL PERSON?
And you're even wearing jeans?!
WHAT'S WRONG WITH THAT?!
I'M JUST LIVING MY NORMAL LIFE!
I LIVE ALONE, SINCE MY SERVANT SWITCHED SIDES TO WORK FOR MY ENEMY!
I AM SORRY ABOUT THAT.
A-ALSO, I LIKE TO SHOP HERE BECAUSE THEY USUALLY GIVE ME EXTRA STUFF...
YOU AND KYOJI ARE BOTH TIGHT-WADS.
AND YOU SEEM TO HAVE A COLD, JUST LIKE HIM, TOO.
I THOUGHT IDIOTS WERE SPARED COLDS.
DON'T CALL ME AN IDIOT!
WAIT... DID YOU JUST SAY...
KYOJI HAS A COLD AND IS WEAK RIGHT NOW?!

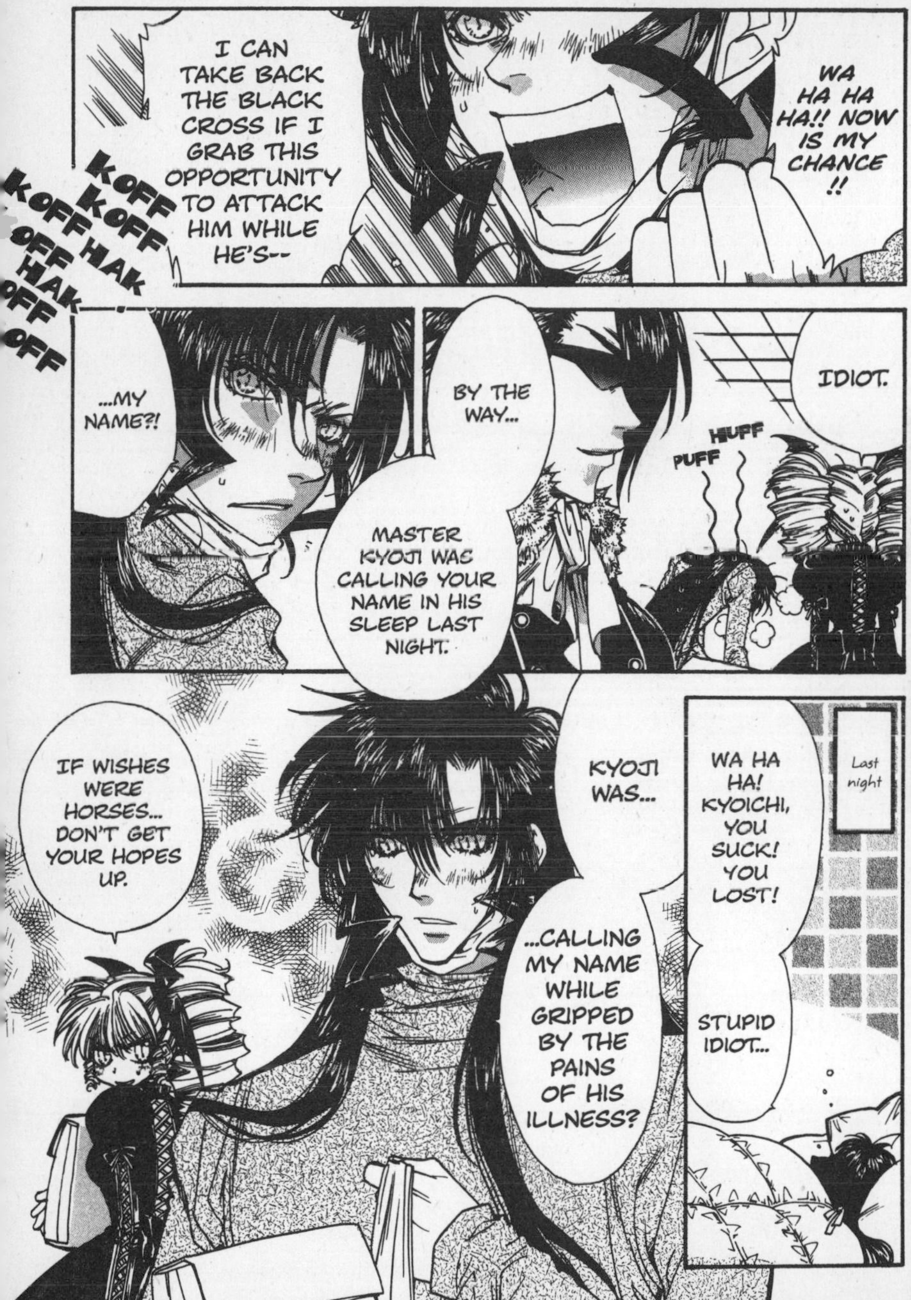
WA HA HA!! NOW IS MY CHANCE !!
I CAN TAKE BACK THE BLACK CROSS IF I GRAB THIS OPPORTUNITY TO ATTACK HIM WHILE HE'S--
KOFF KOFF KOFF HAK OFF HAK OFF OFF
IDIOT.
HUFF
PUFF
BY THE WAY...
MASTER KYOJI WAS CALLING YOUR NAME IN HIS SLEEP LAST NIGHT.
...MY NAME?!
Last night
WA HA HA! KYOICHI, YOU SUCK! YOU LOST!
STUPID IDIOT...
KYOJI WAS...
...CALLING MY NAME WHILE GRIPPED BY THE PAINS OF HIS ILLNESS?
IF WISHES WERE HORSES... DON'T GET YOUR HOPES UP.

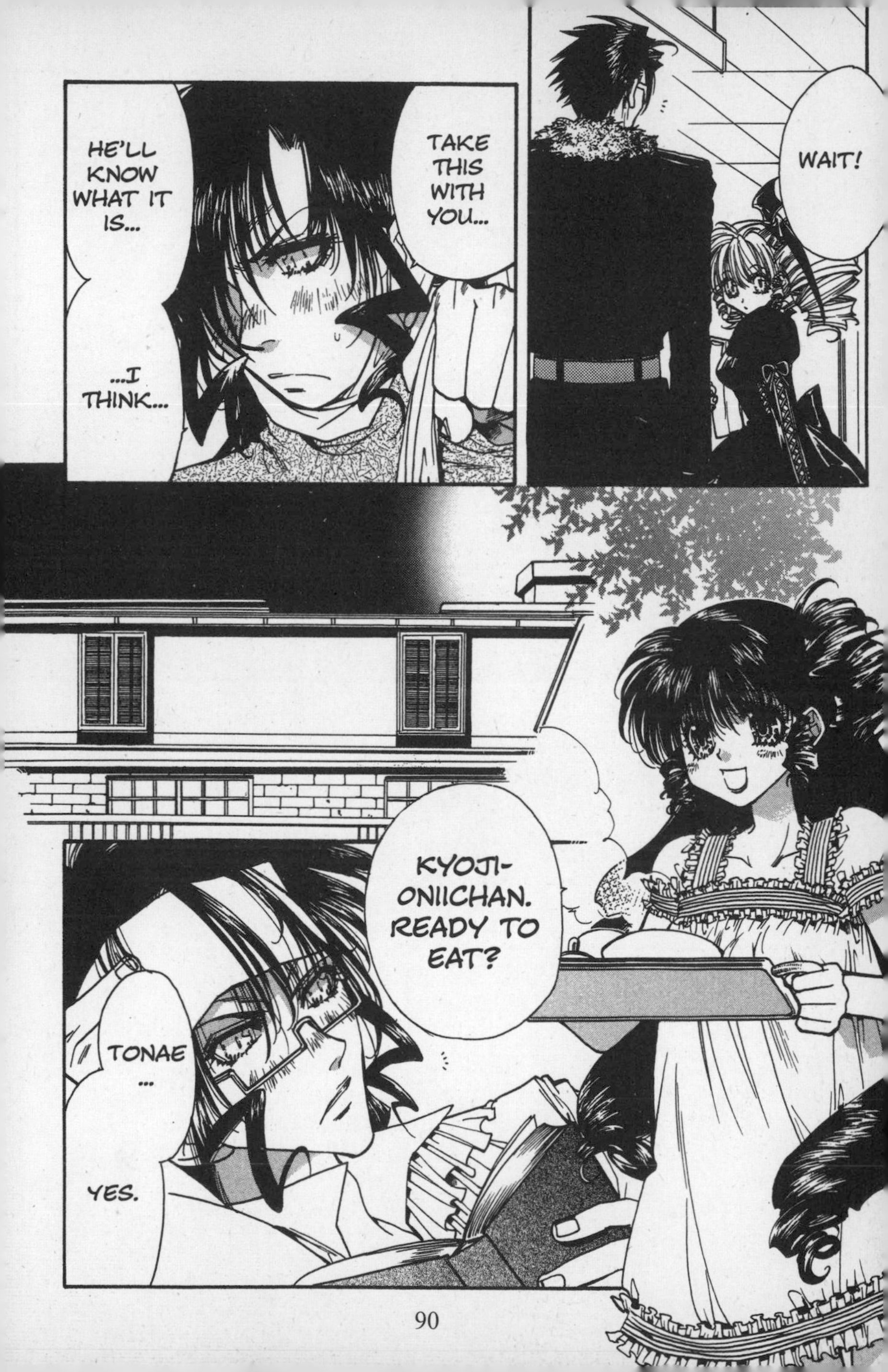
WAIT!
TAKE THIS WITH YOU...
HE'LL KNOW WHAT IT IS...
...I THINK...
KYOJI-ONIICHAN. READY TO EAT?
TONAE ...
YES.

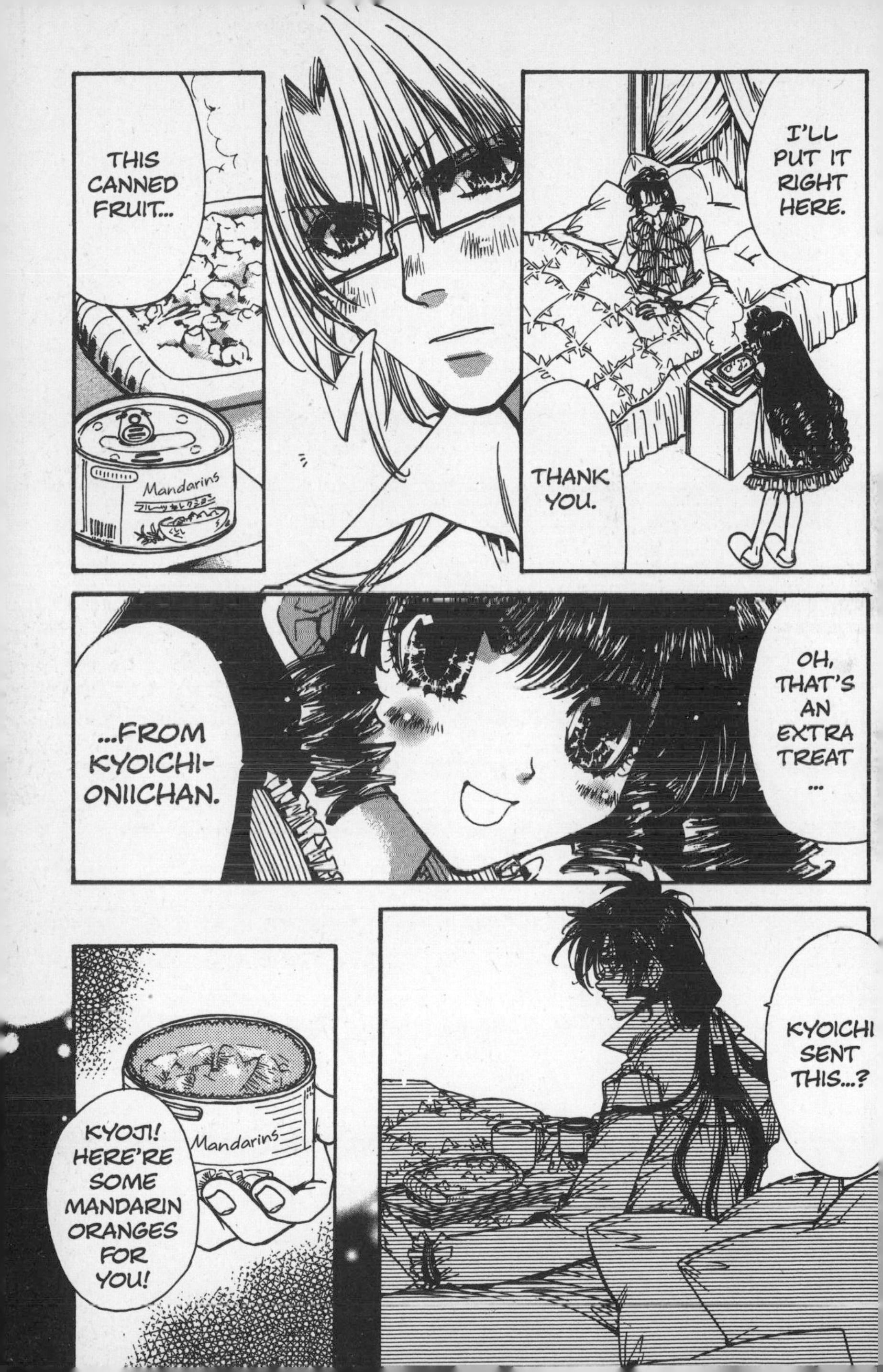
I'LL PUT IT RIGHT HERE.
THANK YOU.
THIS CANNED FRUIT...
Mandarins
OH, THAT'S AN EXTRA TREAT ...
...FROM KYOICHI-ONIICHAN.
KYOICHI SENT THIS...?
KYOJI! HERE'RE SOME MANDARIN ORANGES FOR YOU!
Mandarins

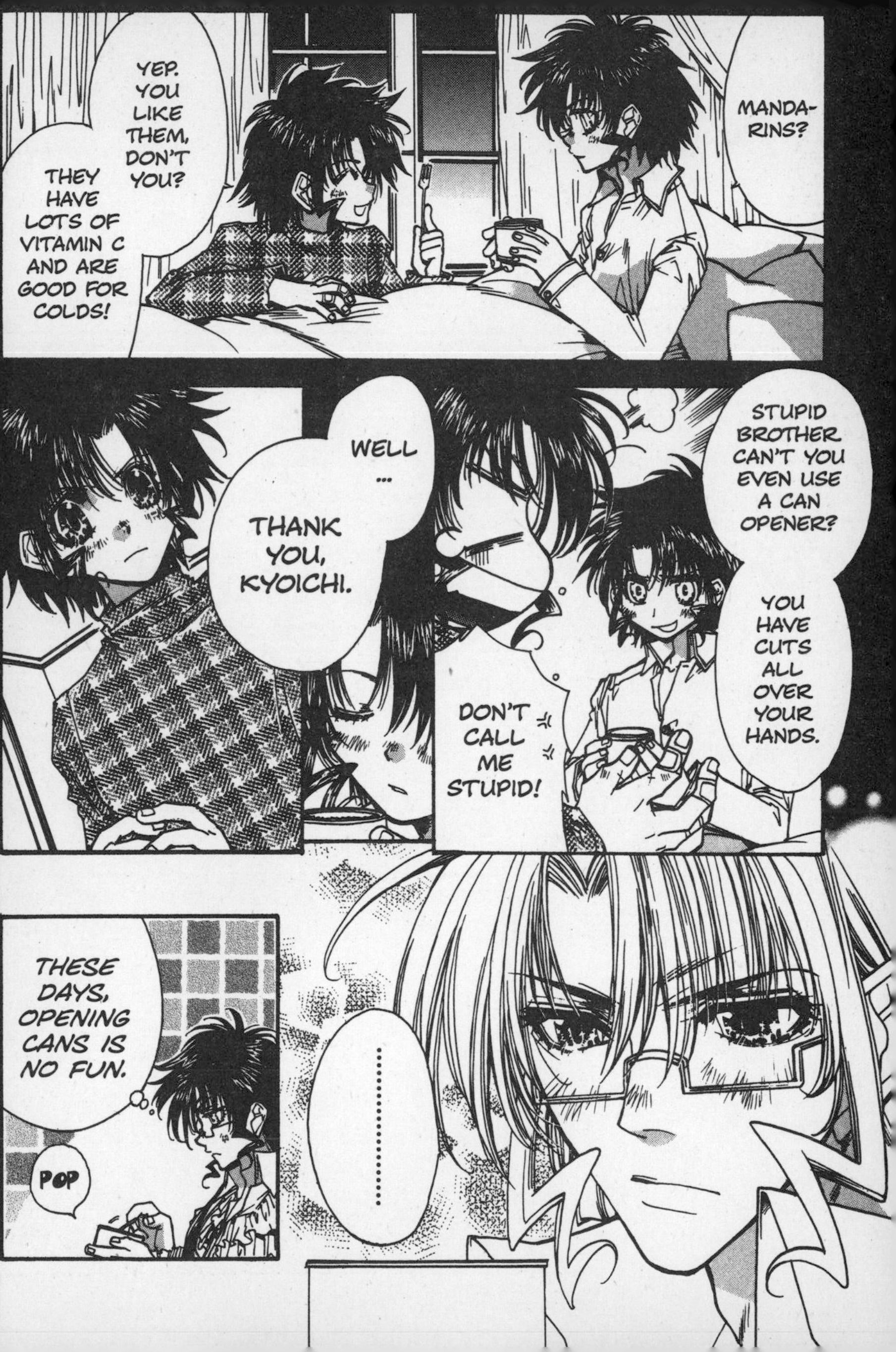
MANDA-RINS?
YEP. YOU LIKE THEM, DON'T YOU?
THEY HAVE LOTS OF VITAMIN C AND ARE GOOD FOR COLDS!
STUPID BROTHER CAN'T YOU EVEN USE A CAN OPENER?
YOU HAVE CUTS ALL OVER YOUR HANDS.
DON'T CALL ME STUPID!
WELL ...
THANK YOU, KYOICHI.
......
THESE DAYS, OPENING CANS IS NO FUN.
POP

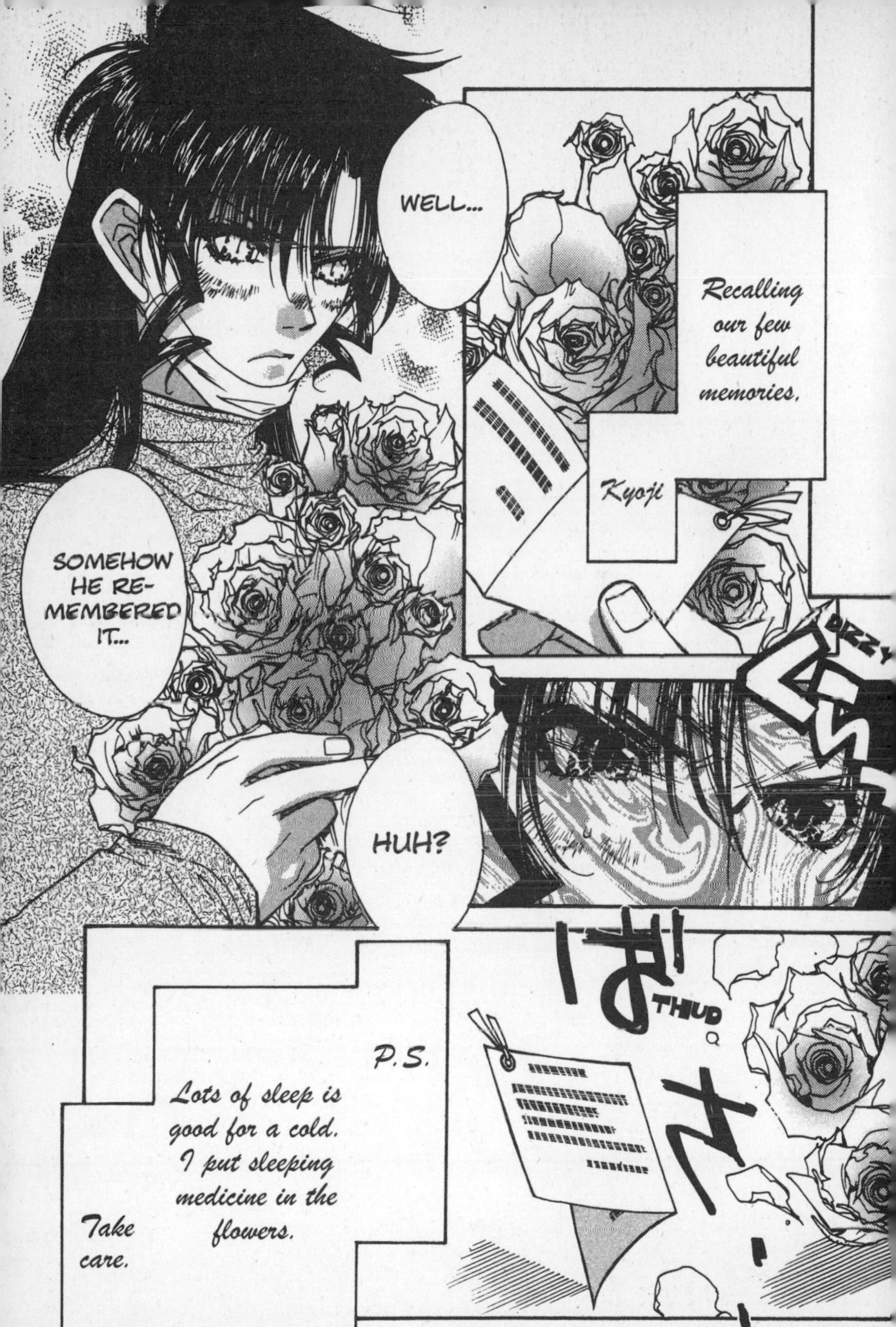
Recalling our few beautiful memories.
Kyoji
DIZZY
WELL...
SOMEHOW HE RE-MEMBERED IT...
HUH?
THUD
P.S.
Lots of sleep is good for a cold. I put sleeping medicine in the flowers.
Take care.

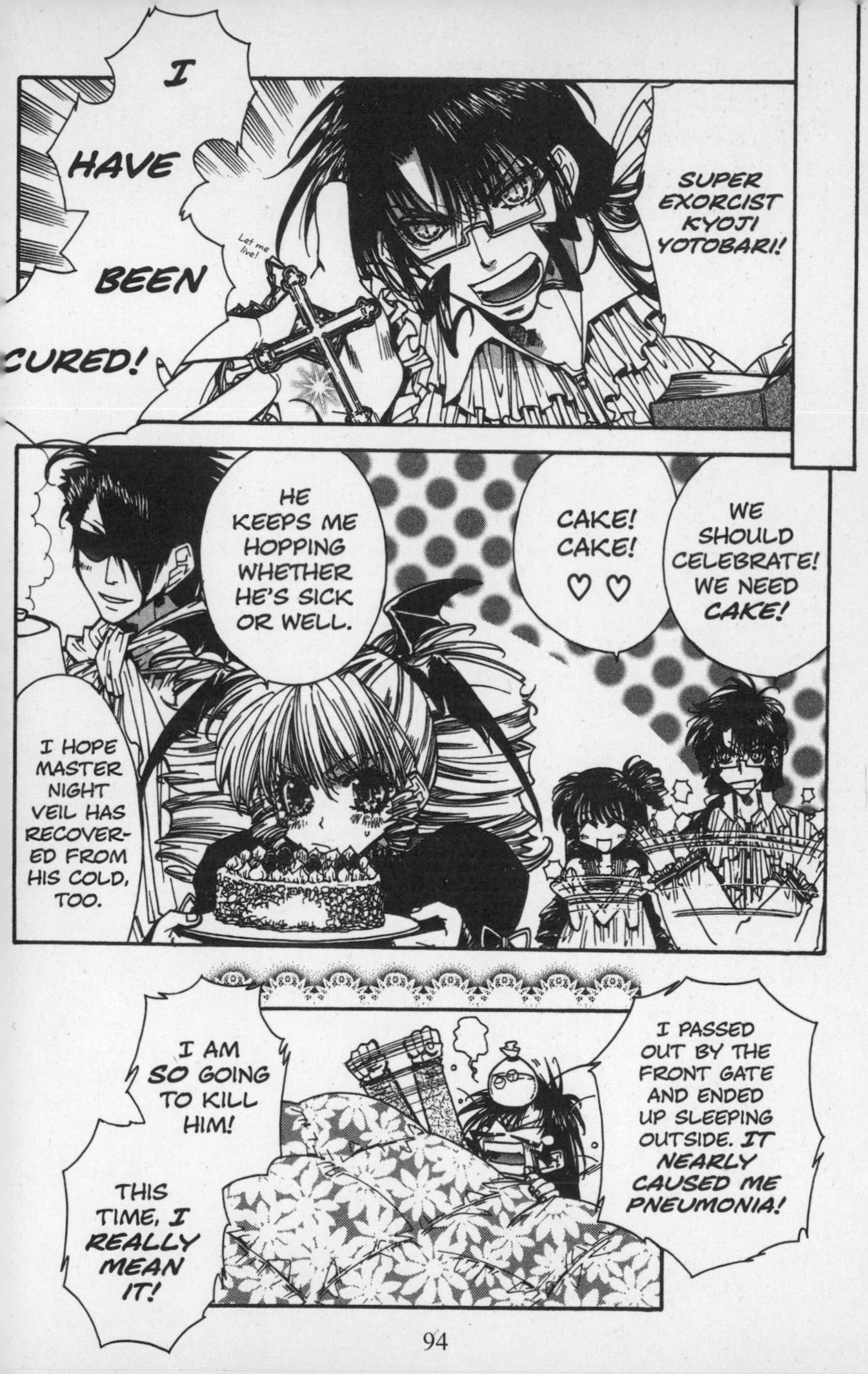
SUPER EXORCIST KYOJI YOTOBARI!
Let me live!
I HAVE BEEN CURED!
WE SHOULD CELEBRATE! WE NEED CAKE!
CAKE! CAKE! ♡ ♡
HE KEEPS ME HOPPING WHETHER HE'S SICK OR WELL.
I HOPE MASTER NIGHT VEIL HAS RECOVERED FROM HIS COLD, TOO.
I PASSED OUT BY THE FRONT GATE AND ENDED UP SLEEPING OUTSIDE. IT NEARLY CAUSED ME PNEUMONIA!
I AM SO GOING TO KILL HIM!
THIS TIME, I REALLY MEAN IT!

Mandarin

BONUS COMIC STRIP

TAKE THIS WITH YOU...
HE'LL KNOW WHAT IT IS...
ISN'T IT SOMETHING THE IDIOT BROTHER ORIGINALLY BOUGHT FOR HIMSELF?
NO, I FOUND OTHER STUFF.
LET'S SEE...
...JUST A CAN OF MANDARIN ORANGES IN THERE?
APPLES AND GAUZE.
WAS HE TRYING TO MAKE APPLE JUICE...
...BY HIM-SELF?
HONEY AND HARD CANDY.
HE CAN'T HANDLE BITTER MEDICINE, HUH?
POOR GUY.

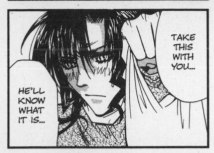

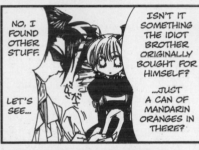

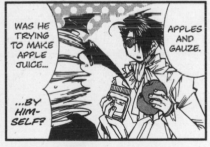

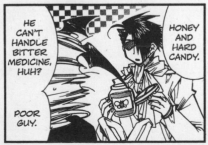

VAMPIRE DOLL
REFLECTIONS

KYOICHI

♯4 PRESENT

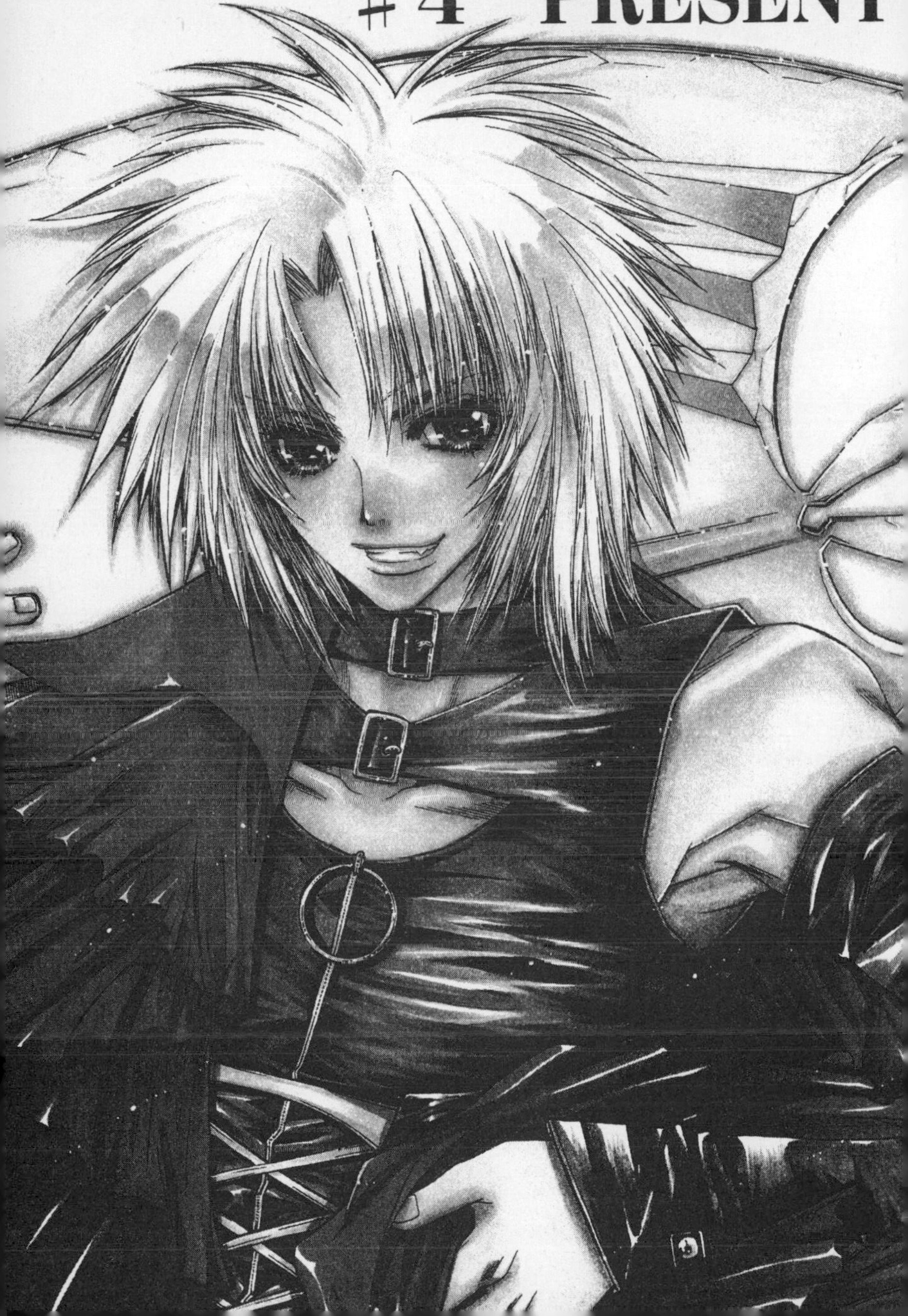

CONCEPT DRAWING

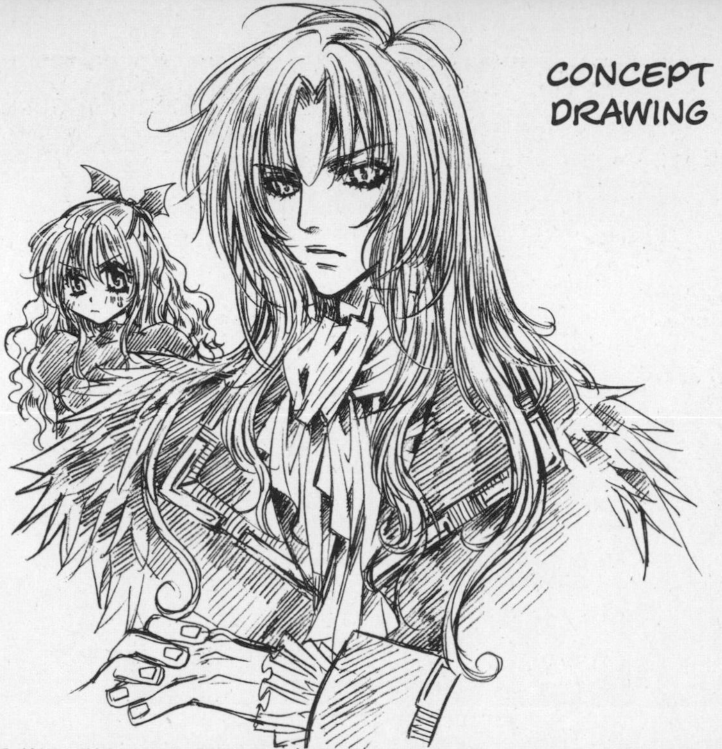

I'VE HAD THE NAME "GUILT-NA-ZAN" IN MY HEAD SINCE JUNIOR HIGH. THE CHARACTER WAS TOTALLY DIFFERENT BACK THEN, BUT THE NAME HAS REMAINED WITH ME ALL THIS TIME. RIGHT BEFORE I TURNED TWENTY, THIS IS THE DESIGN I CAME UP WITH FOR HIM. ORIGINALLY, HE USED TO HAVE AN EXTRAVAGANT OUTFIT AND HIS HAIR WAS BLOND. HE ALSO LOOKED OLDER, MORE MATURE AND MORE VAMPIRIC.

THE GIRL TO THE LEFT IS MY DESIGN FOR GUILT-NA FROM BACK THEN. YOU CAN TELL FROM THIS SKETCH THAT I DIDN'T CHANGE MUCH, MOSTLY JUST HER HAIRSTYLE. SHE'S STILL WEARING THE SAME CLOTHES AND BAT HAIRCLIP.

LET ME SHARE WITH YOU THE STORY OF HOW I CAME UP WITH THE FINAL DESIGN FOR GUILT-NA-ZAN. EVER SINCE I STARTED DRAWING MANGA FOR *ZERO-SUM* MAGAZINE, I'VE HAD THIS FRIEND WHO WILL GIVE ME HER OPINIONS ON THE NEW CHARACTERS I DRAW. SHE SAID, "THIS SKETCH OF GUILT-NA-ZAN LOOKS JUST LIKE THE YOTOBARI BROTHERS (KYOJI AND KYOICHI). WHY DON'T YOU MAKE HIM YOUNG AND NAUGHTY, INSTEAD?" "WHY DON'T YOU MAKE HIS HAIR SHORT?" "I LIKE SILVER HAIR." AS SHE GRADUALLY SHARED THESE THOUGHTS WITH ME, SHE INSPIRED NEW IDEAS. IT GOT ME THINKING, "I LIKE HIS UNPREDICTABLE QUALITY." SO I LET GO OF THE ORIGINAL IDEA OF GUILT-NA-ZAN BEING A NOBLE-LOOKING PERSON. IN ADDITION, I THOUGHT, "I WANT HIM TO FEEL MORE LIKE A TRANSFORMING HERO. SINCE I'VE MADE SO MANY CHANGES TO HIS LOOKS, I SHOULD CHANGE HIS CLOTHES, TOO." SO NOW HE HAS A TIGHT COSTUME WITH A RED CLOAK. I REALLY DON'T MIND ALL THESE CHANGES TO MY LEADING MAN BECAUSE THEY BETTER ACCOMMODATE MY TASTES.

FOR GUILT-NA, I'VE ALWAYS LIKED THE CONTRAST OF HER BLONDE HAIR AGAINST THE BLACK DRESS, SO I STUCK WITH THAT COMBINATION. SINCE I WANTED HER TO HAVE A STRONG WITCH-GIRLISH FEEL, I GAVE HER CURLY PIGTAILS. AND BOY DO THEY CURL AND CURL AND CURL...

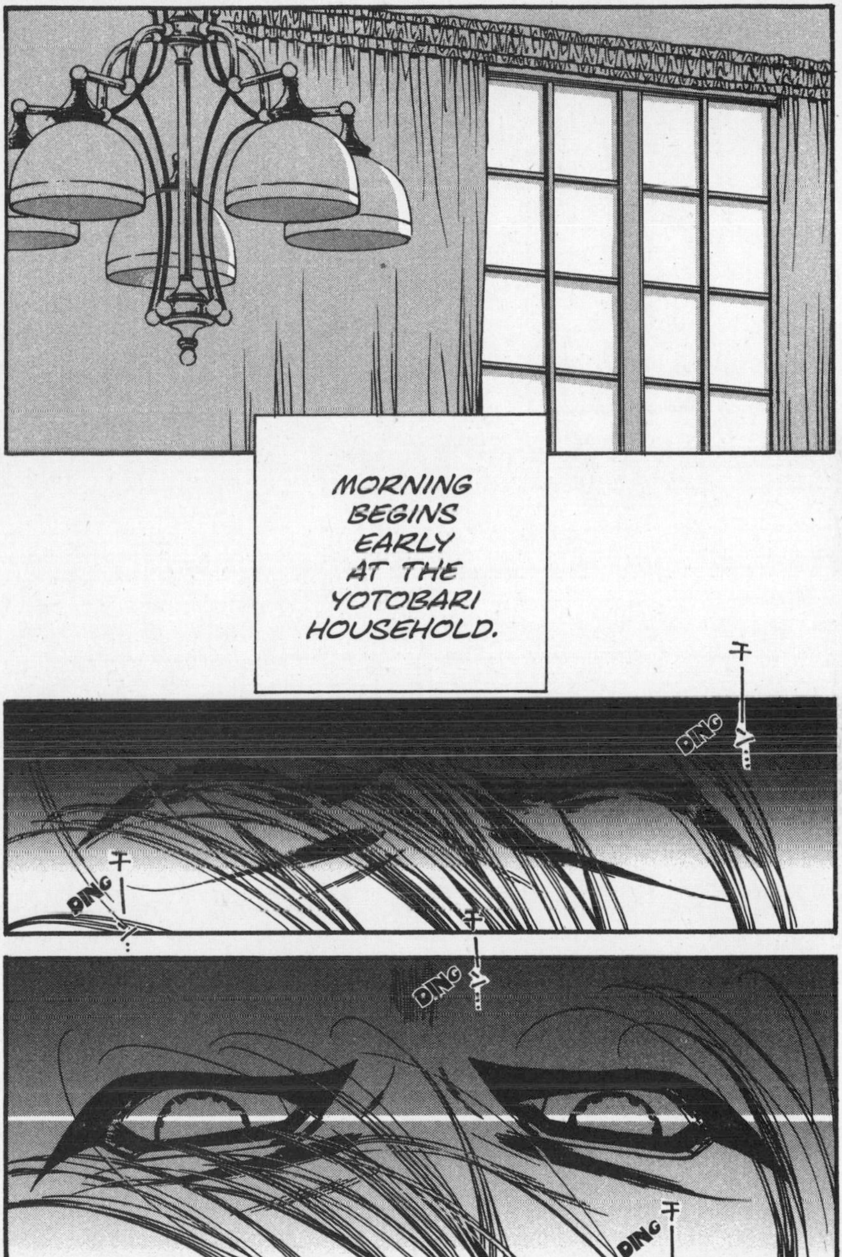
MORNING BEGINS EARLY AT THE YOTOBARI HOUSEHOLD.
チーン…
DING
チーン…
DING
チーン…
DING
チーン…
DING

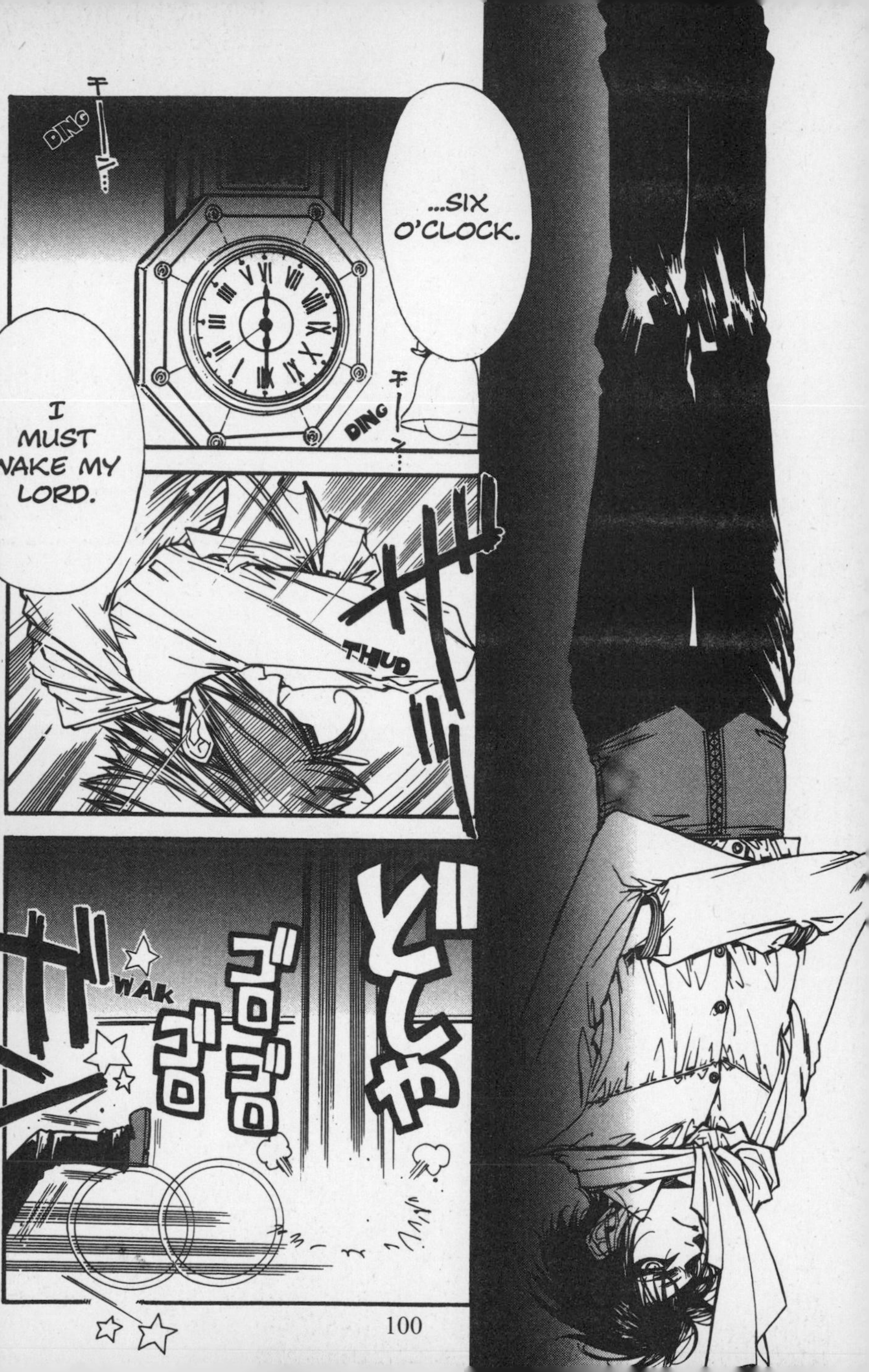
...SIX O'CLOCK.
DING
DING
I MUST WAKE MY LORD.
THUD
どしゃ
ゴロゴロ
WAK
ガッ

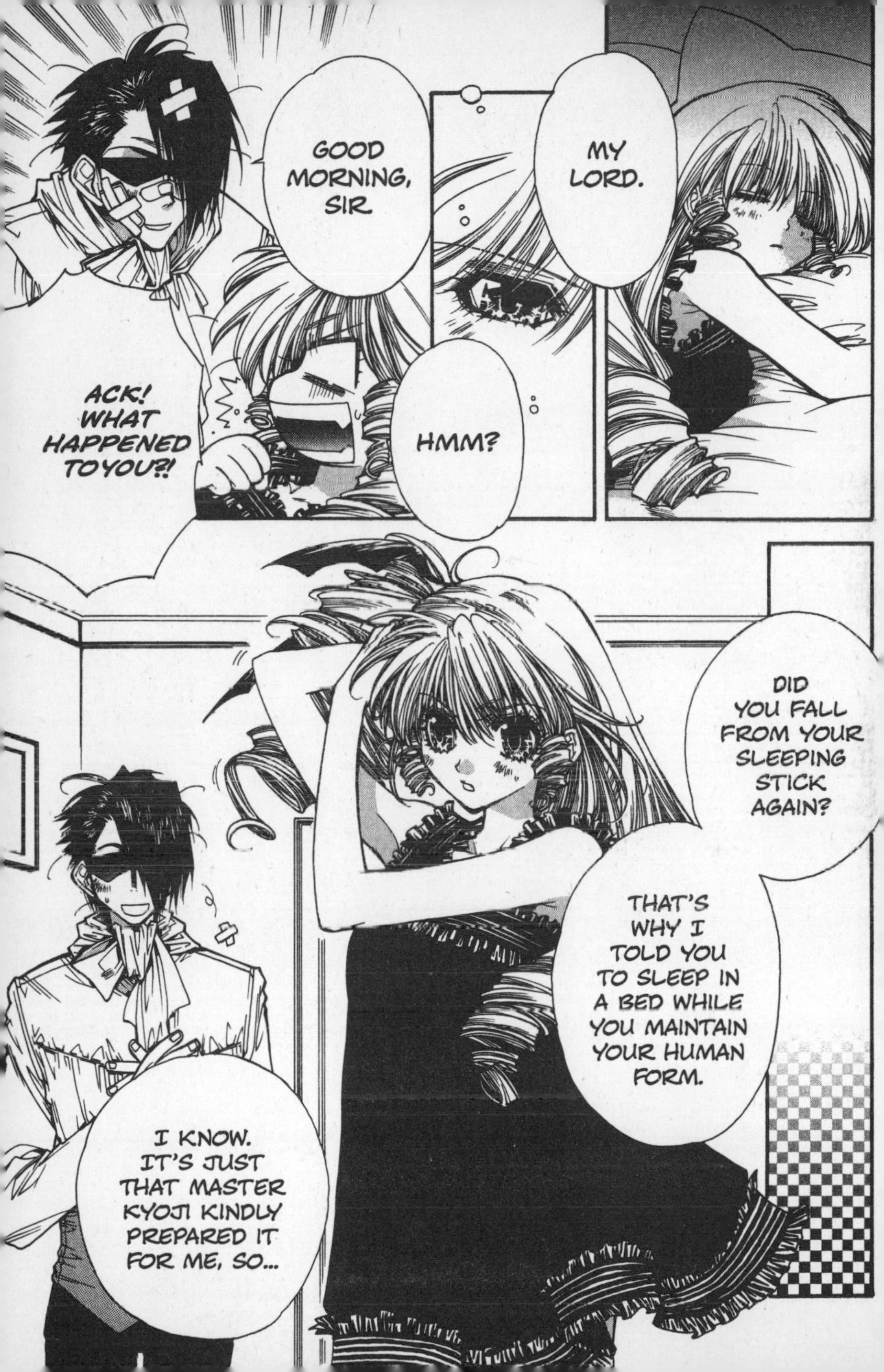
MY LORD.
HMM?
GOOD MORNING, SIR
ACK! WHAT HAPPENED TO YOU?!
DID YOU FALL FROM YOUR SLEEPING STICK AGAIN?
THAT'S WHY I TOLD YOU TO SLEEP IN A BED WHILE YOU MAINTAIN YOUR HUMAN FORM.
I KNOW. IT'S JUST THAT MASTER KYOJI KINDLY PREPARED IT FOR ME, SO...

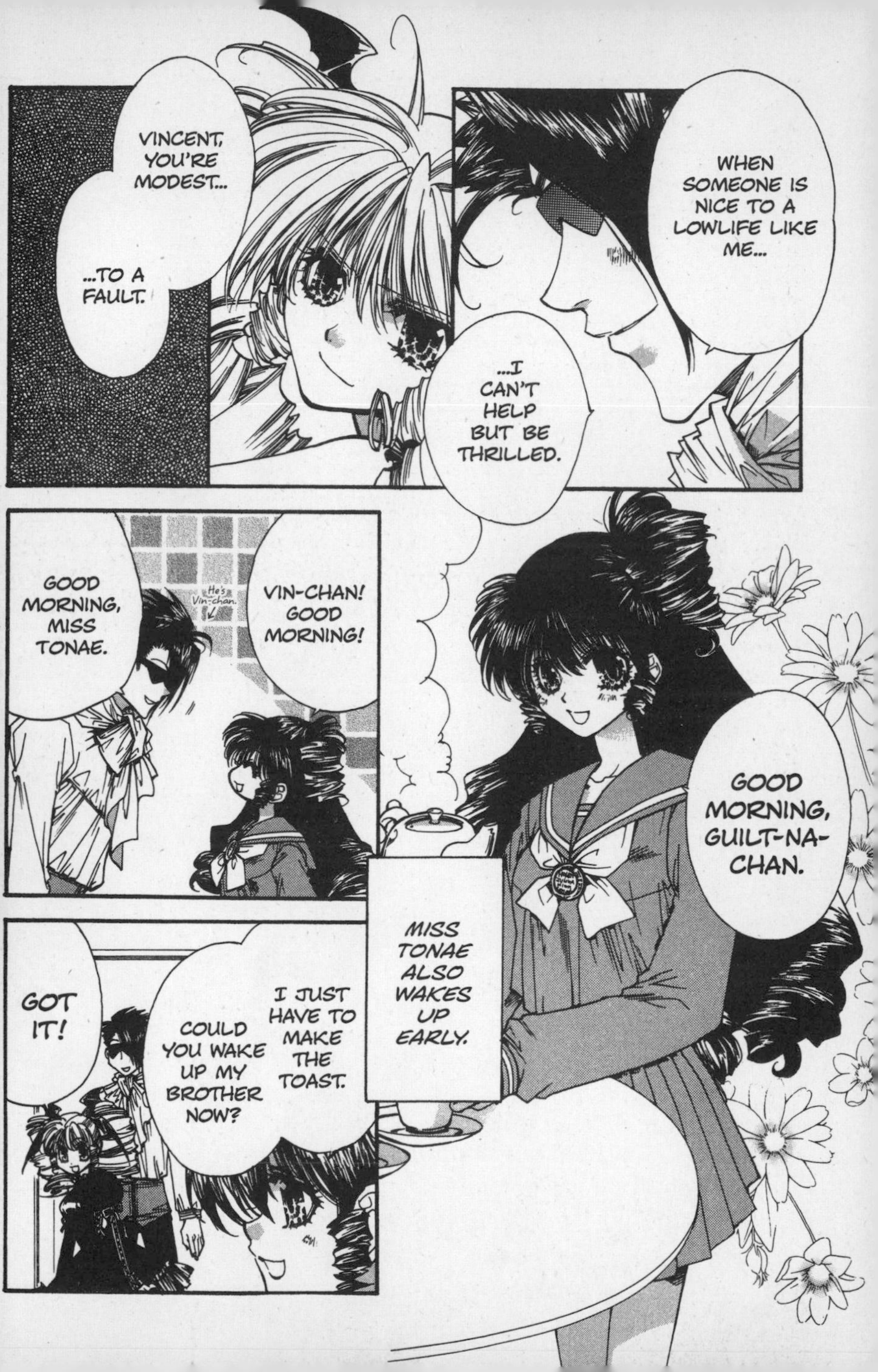
WHEN SOMEONE IS NICE TO A LOWLIFE LIKE ME...
...I CAN'T HELP BUT BE THRILLED.
VINCENT, YOU'RE MODEST...
...TO A FAULT.
GOOD MORNING, GUILT-NA-CHAN.
MISS TONAE ALSO WAKES UP EARLY.
VIN-CHAN! GOOD MORNING!
He's Vin-chan.
GOOD MORNING, MISS TONAE.
I JUST HAVE TO MAKE THE TOAST.
COULD YOU WAKE UP MY BROTHER NOW?
GOT IT!

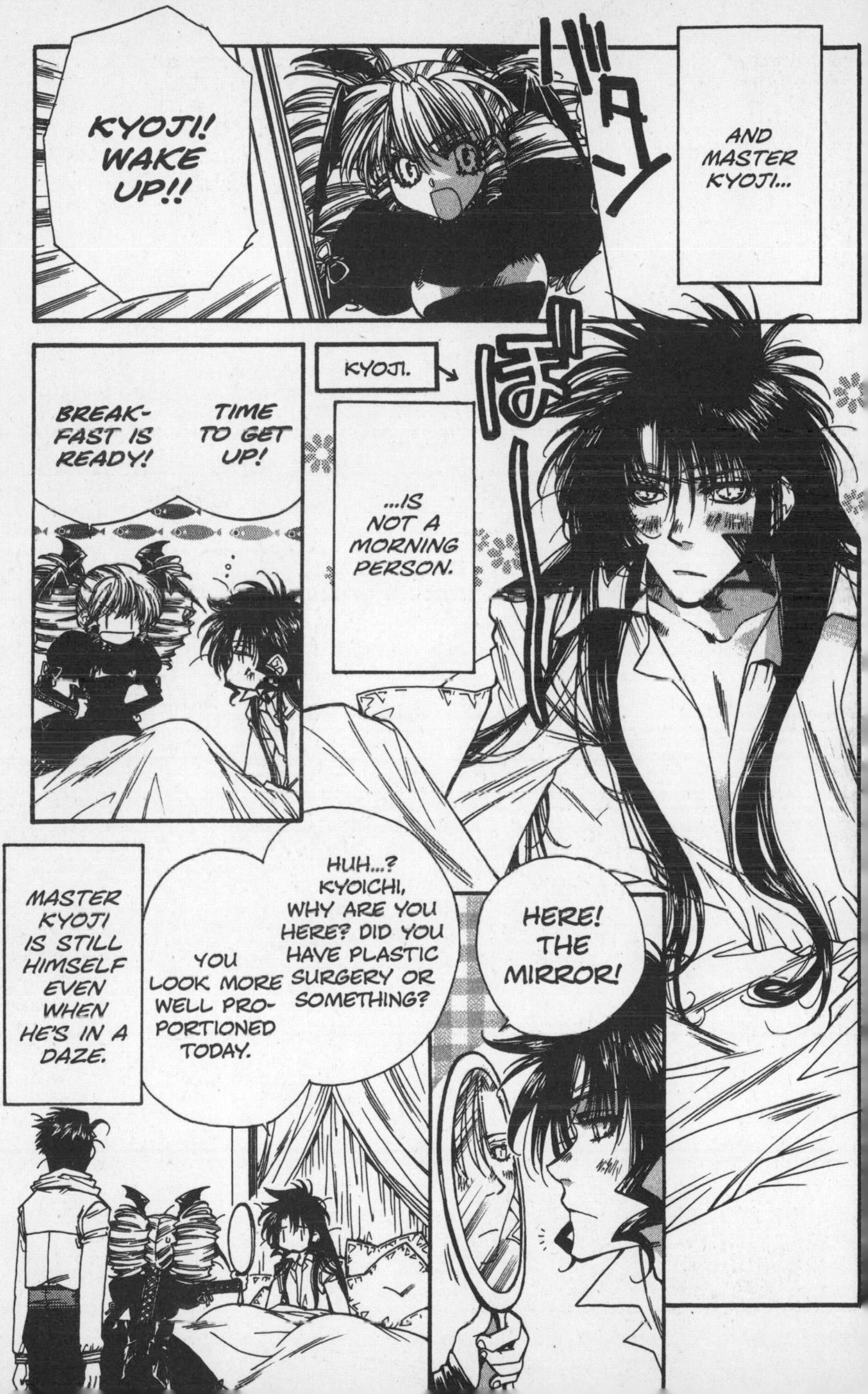
AND MASTER KYOJI...
バタン
KYOJI! WAKE UP!!
KYOJI.
ぼ
...IS NOT A MORNING PERSON.
TIME TO GET UP!
BREAK-FAST IS READY!
HERE! THE MIRROR!
HUH...? KYOICHI, WHY ARE YOU HERE? DID YOU HAVE PLASTIC SURGERY OR SOMETHING?
YOU LOOK MORE WELL PRO-PORTIONED TODAY.
MASTER KYOJI IS STILL HIMSELF EVEN WHEN HE'S IN A DAZE.

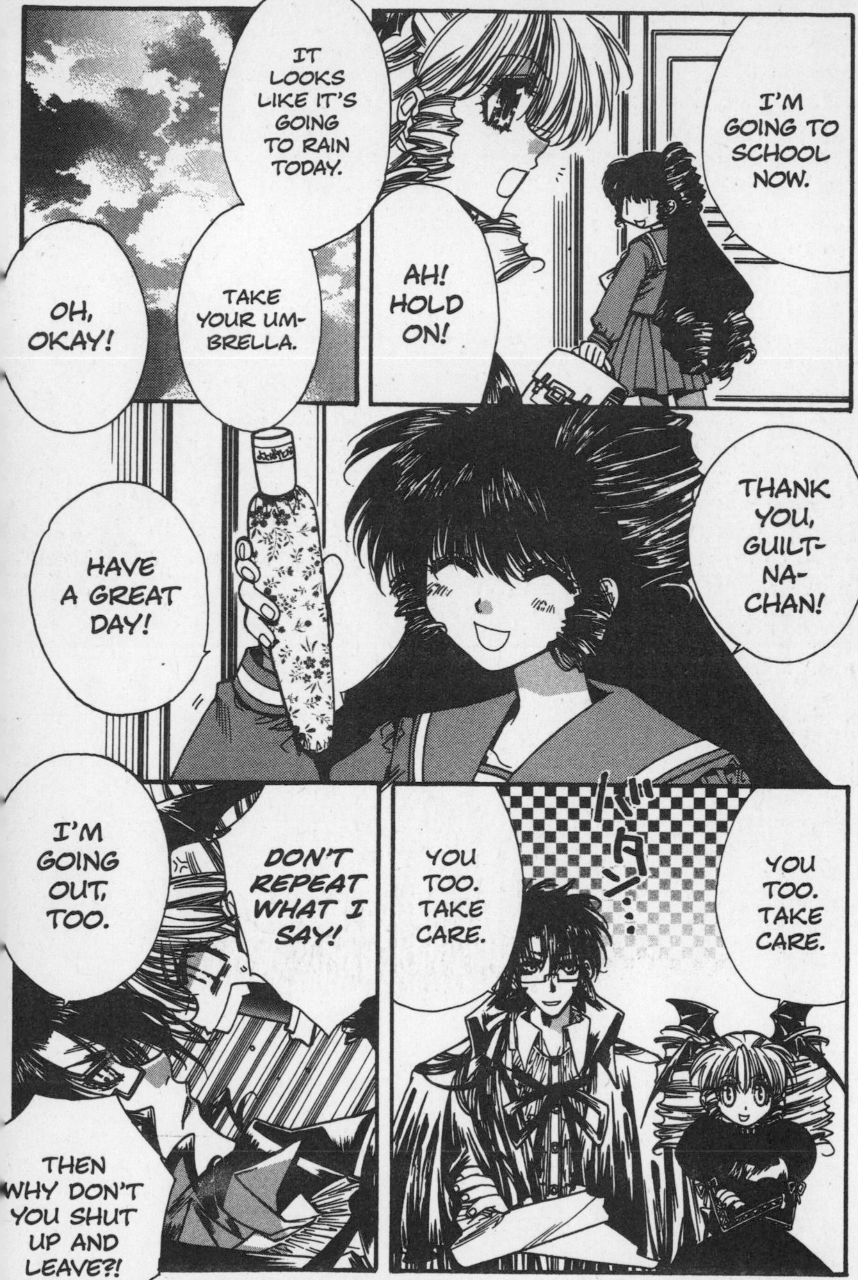

I'M GOING TO SCHOOL NOW.
AH! HOLD ON!
IT LOOKS LIKE IT'S GOING TO RAIN TODAY.
TAKE YOUR UM-BRELLA.
OH, OKAY!
THANK YOU, GUILT-NA-CHAN!
HAVE A GREAT DAY!
YOU TOO. TAKE CARE.
バタン…
YOU TOO. TAKE CARE.
DON'T REPEAT WHAT I SAY!
I'M GOING OUT, TOO.
THEN WHY DON'T YOU SHUT UP AND LEAVE?!

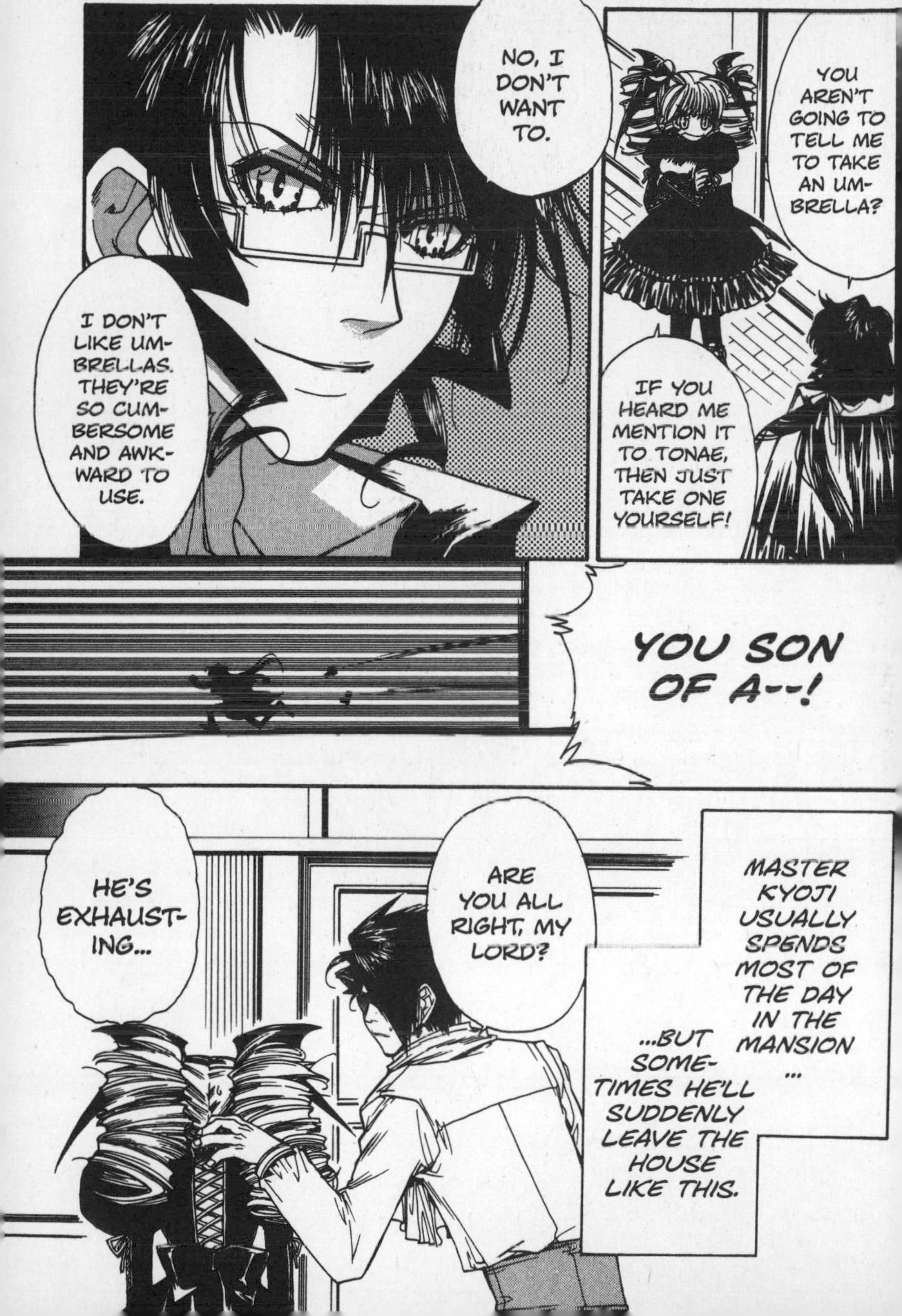

YOU AREN'T GOING TO TELL ME TO TAKE AN UM-BRELLA?
IF YOU HEARD ME MENTION IT TO TONAE, THEN JUST TAKE ONE YOURSELF!
NO, I DON'T WANT TO.
I DON'T LIKE UM-BRELLAS. THEY'RE SO CUM-BERSOME AND AWK-WARD TO USE.
YOU SON OF A--!
MASTER KYOJI USUALLY SPENDS MOST OF THE DAY IN THE MANSION...
...BUT SOME-TIMES HE'LL SUDDENLY LEAVE THE HOUSE LIKE THIS.
ARE YOU ALL RIGHT, MY LORD?
HE'S EXHAUST-ING...

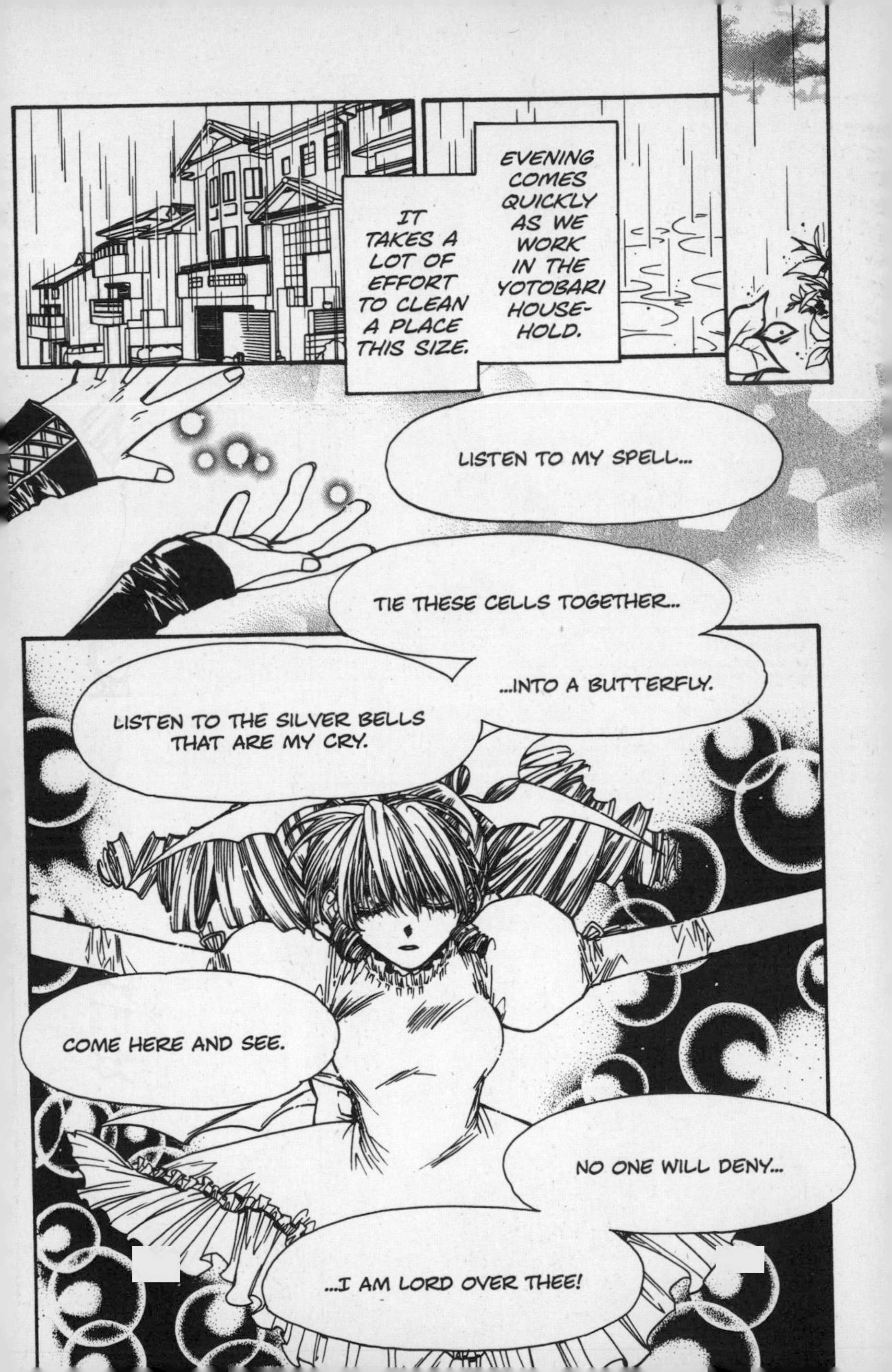
EVENING COMES QUICKLY AS WE WORK IN THE YOTOBARI HOUSE-HOLD.
IT TAKES A LOT OF EFFORT TO CLEAN A PLACE THIS SIZE.
LISTEN TO MY SPELL...
TIE THESE CELLS TOGETHER...
...INTO A BUTTERFLY.
LISTEN TO THE SILVER BELLS THAT ARE MY CRY.
COME HERE AND SEE.
NO ONE WILL DENY...
...I AM LORD OVER THEE!

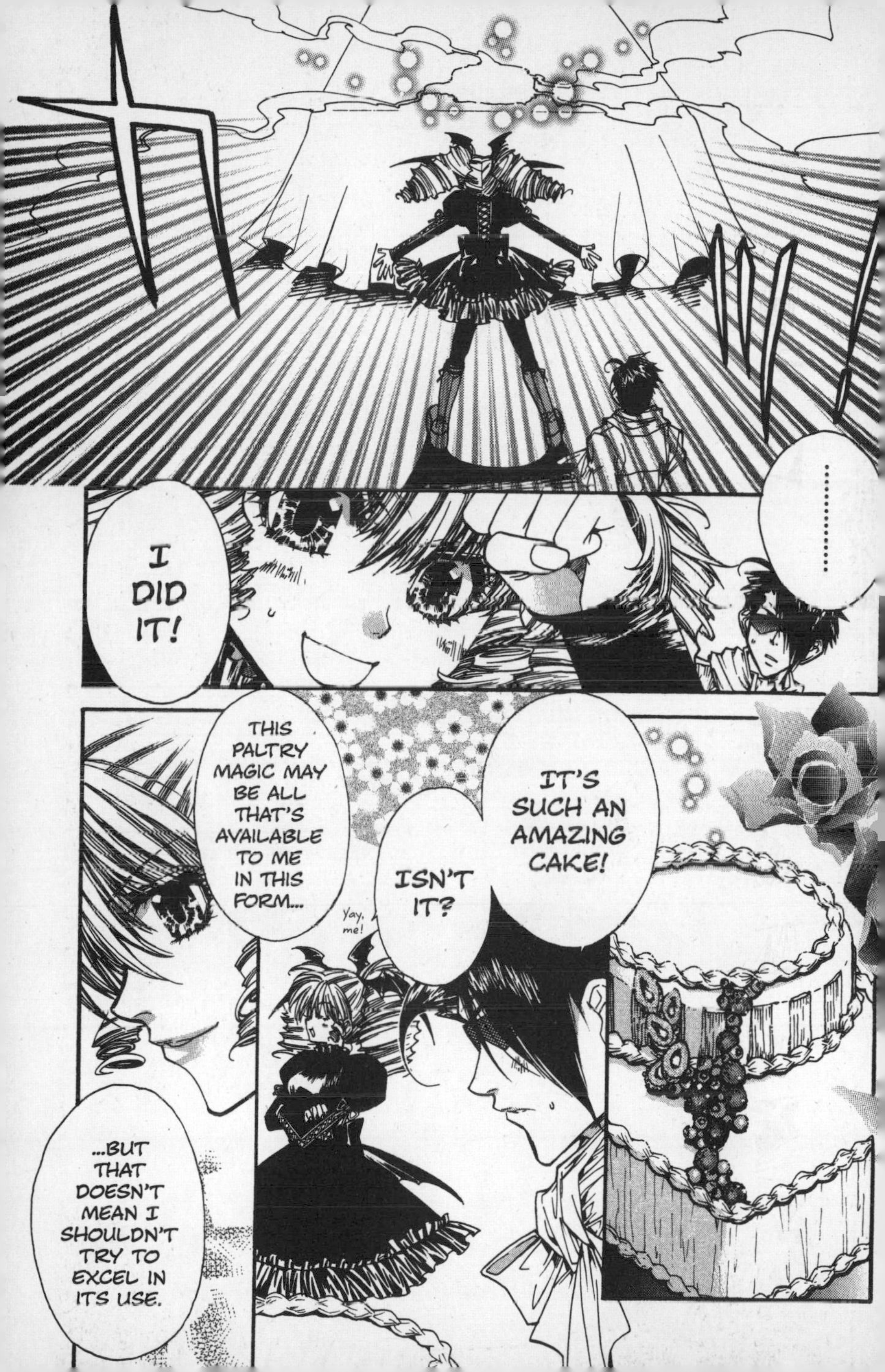
……
I DID IT!
IT'S SUCH AN AMAZING CAKE!
ISN'T IT?
Yay, me!
THIS PALTRY MAGIC MAY BE ALL THAT'S AVAILABLE TO ME IN THIS FORM...
...BUT THAT DOESN'T MEAN I SHOULDN'T TRY TO EXCEL IN ITS USE.

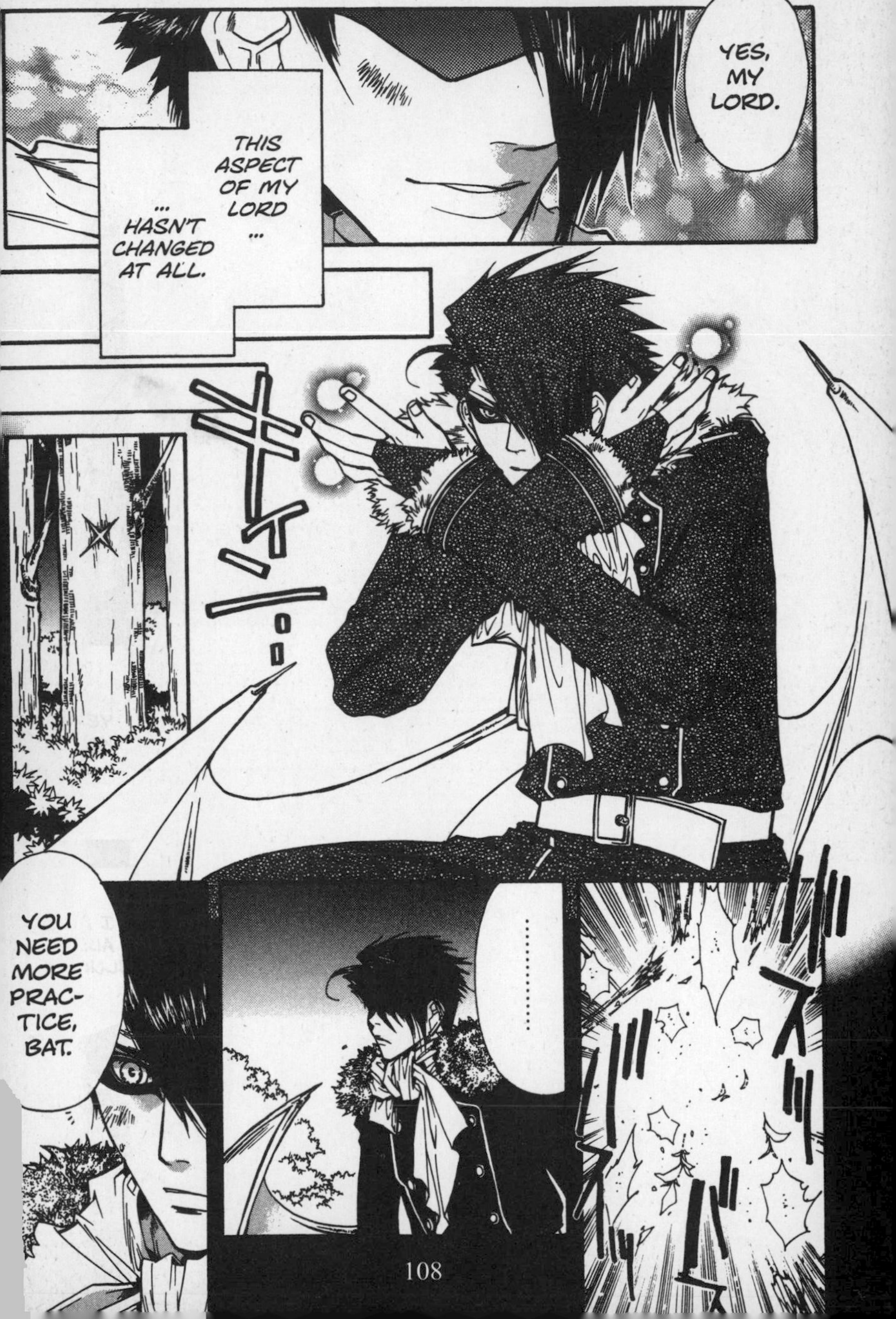
YES, MY LORD.
THIS ASPECT OF MY LORD ...
... HASN'T CHANGED AT ALL.
....
YOU NEED MORE PRAC-TICE, BAT.

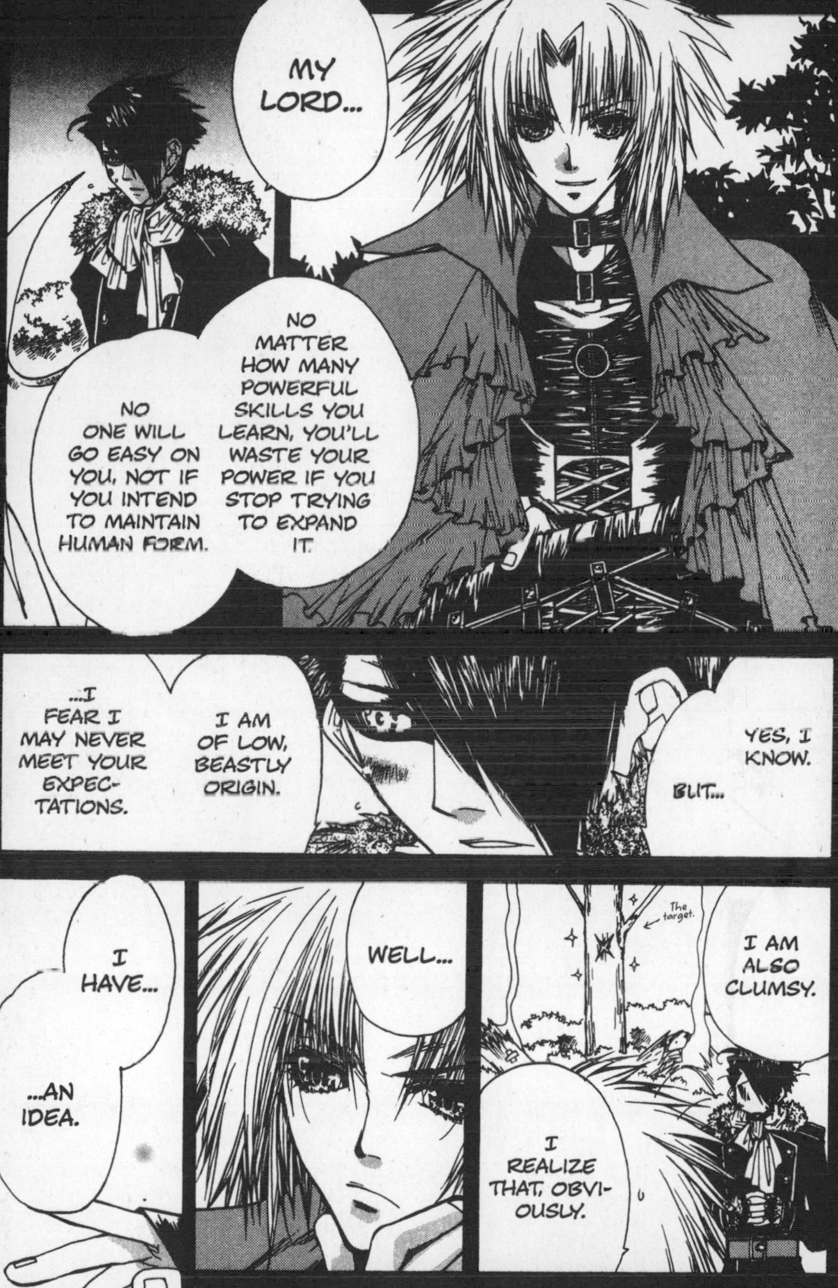
MY LORD...
NO MATTER HOW MANY POWERFUL SKILLS YOU LEARN, YOU'LL WASTE YOUR POWER IF YOU STOP TRYING TO EXPAND IT.
NO ONE WILL GO EASY ON YOU, NOT IF YOU INTEND TO MAINTAIN HUMAN FORM.
YES, I KNOW.
BUT...
I AM OF LOW, BEASTLY ORIGIN.
...I FEAR I MAY NEVER MEET YOUR EXPEC-TATIONS.
The target.
I AM ALSO CLUMSY.
I REALIZE THAT, OBVI-OUSLY.
WELL...
I HAVE...
...AN IDEA.

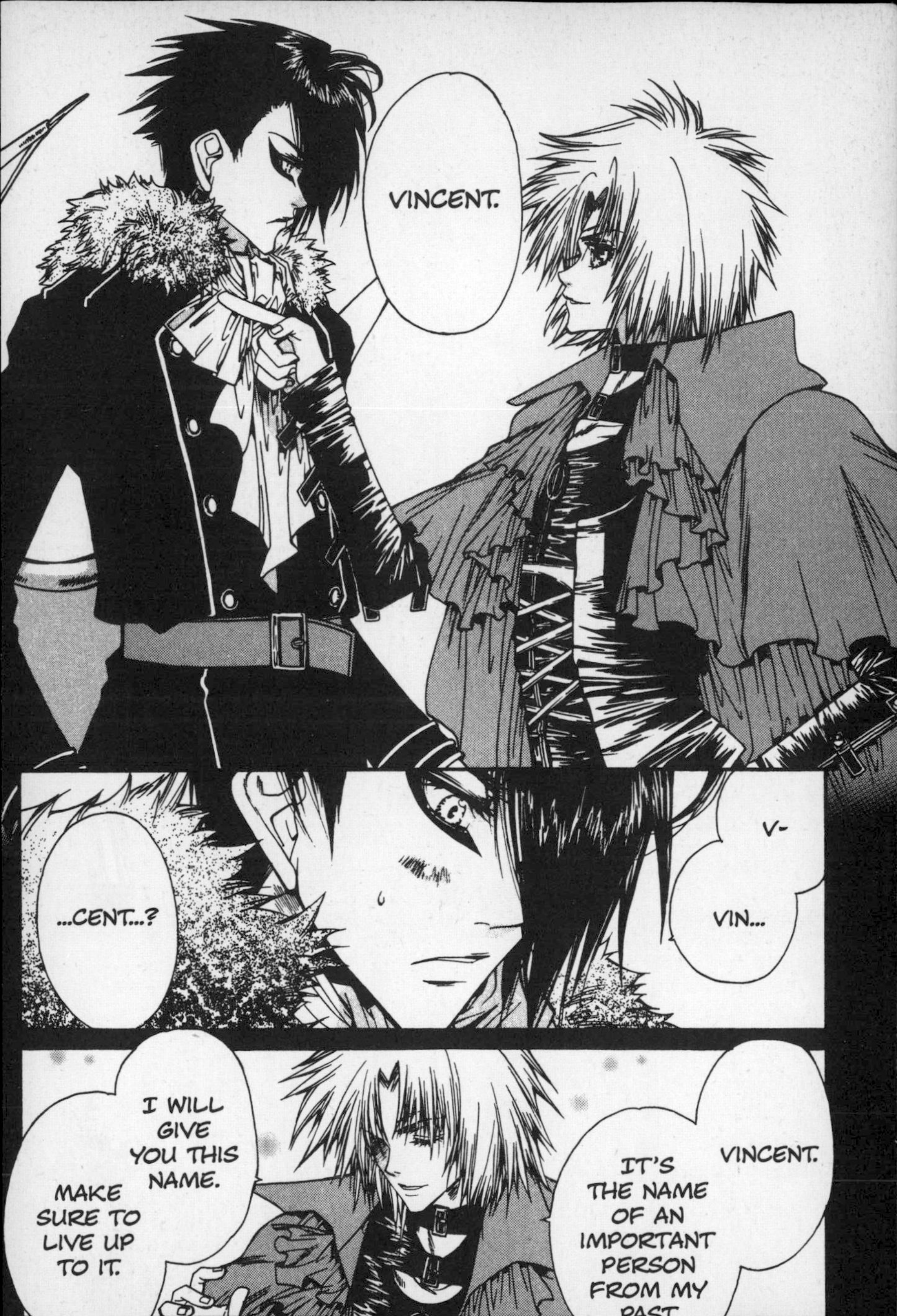
VINCENT.
V-
VIN...
...CENT...?
VINCENT.
IT'S THE NAME OF AN IMPORTANT PERSON FROM MY PAST.
I WILL GIVE YOU THIS NAME.
MAKE SURE TO LIVE UP TO IT.

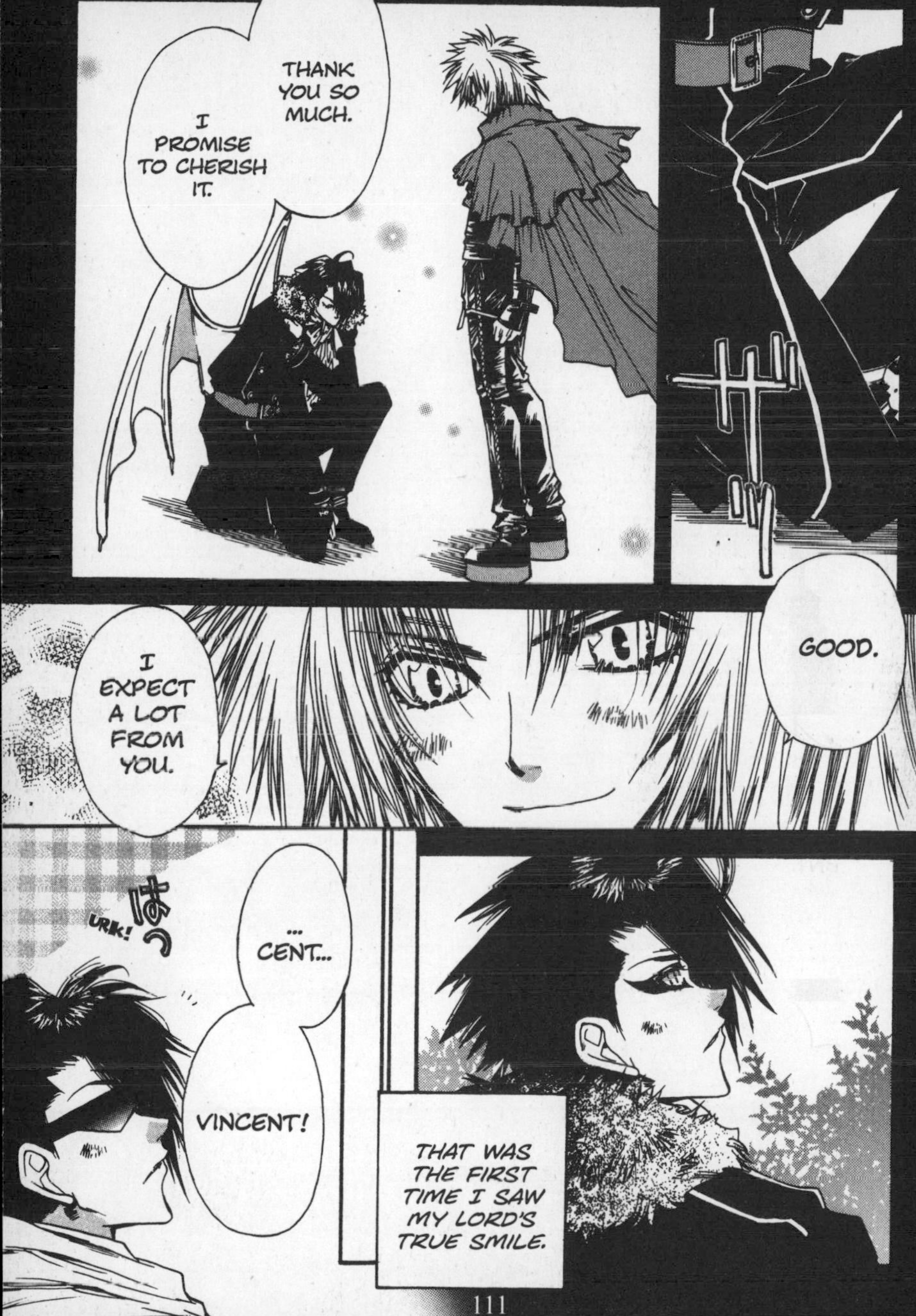
THANK YOU SO MUCH.
I PROMISE TO CHERISH IT.
GOOD.
I EXPECT A LOT FROM YOU.
THAT WAS THE FIRST TIME I SAW MY LORD'S TRUE SMILE.
... CENT...
VINCENT!
はっ
URK!

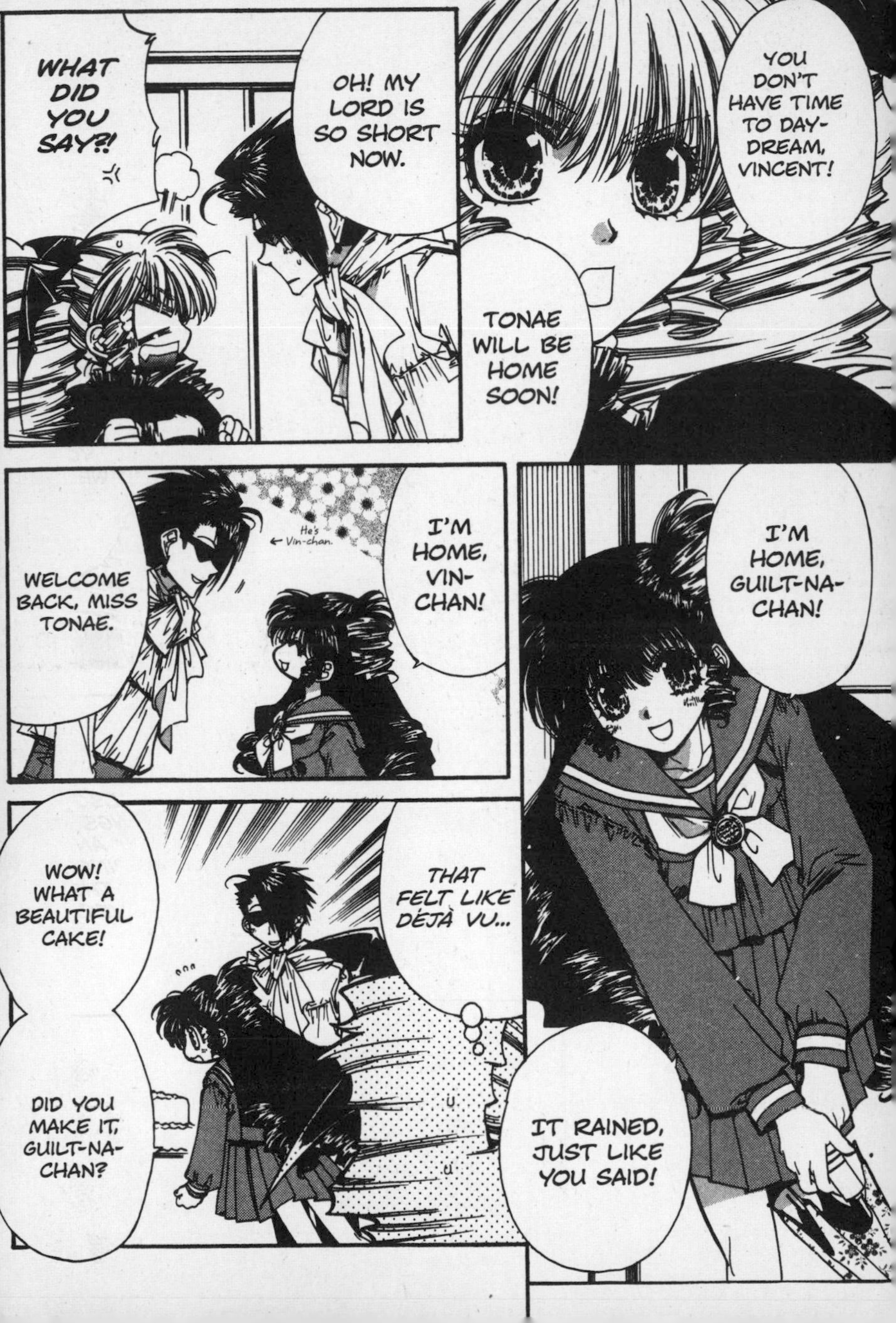
YOU DON'T HAVE TIME TO DAY-DREAM, VINCENT!
TONAE WILL BE HOME SOON!
OH! MY LORD IS SO SHORT NOW.
WHAT DID YOU SAY?!
I'M HOME, GUILT-NA-CHAN!
IT RAINED, JUST LIKE YOU SAID!
I'M HOME, VIN-CHAN!
He's ← Vin-chan.
WELCOME BACK, MISS TONAE.
THAT FELT LIKE DÉJÀ VU...
WOW! WHAT A BEAUTIFUL CAKE!
DID YOU MAKE IT, GUILT-NA-CHAN?

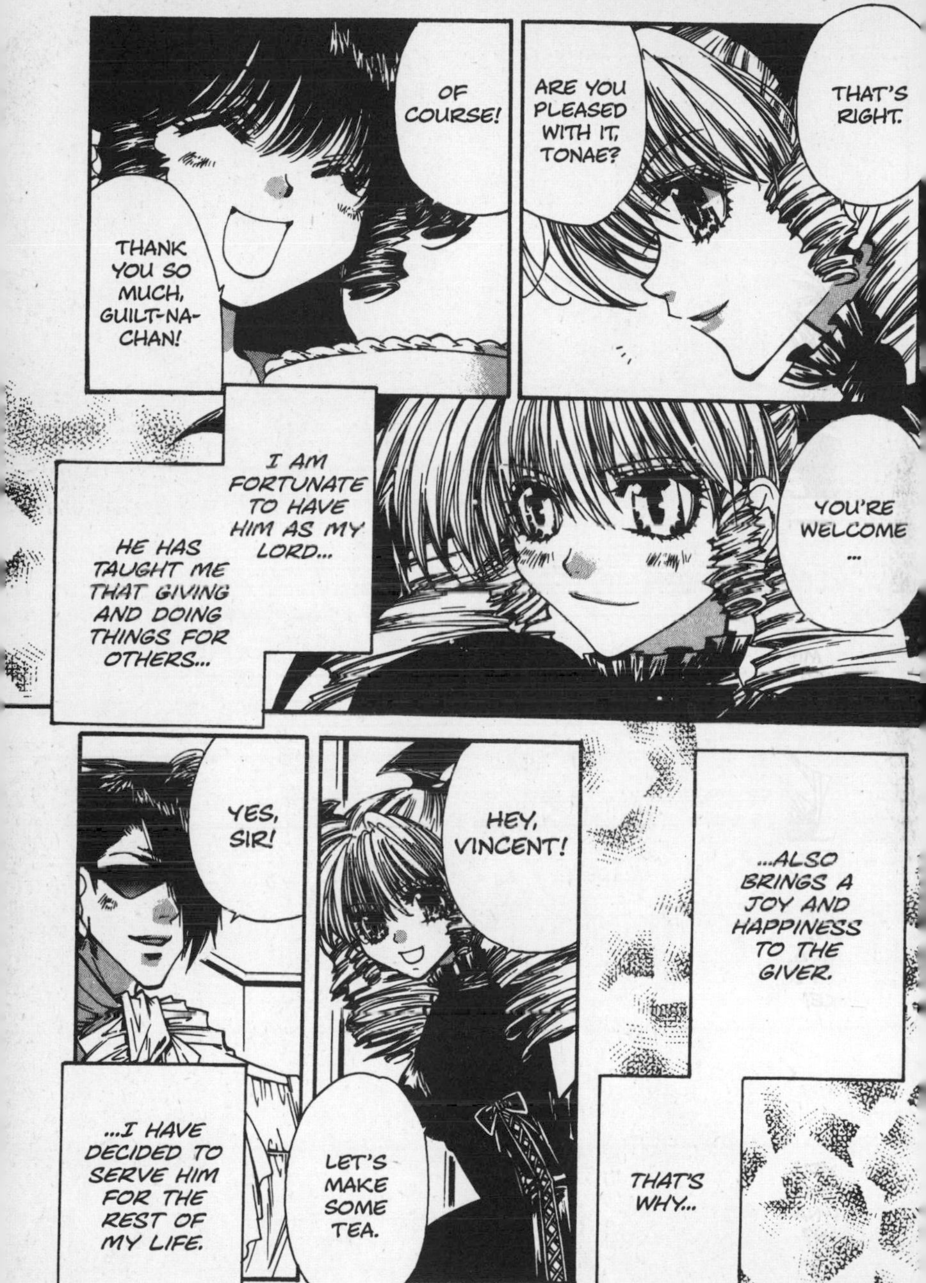
THAT'S RIGHT.
ARE YOU PLEASED WITH IT, TONAE?
OF COURSE!
THANK YOU SO MUCH, GUILT-NA-CHAN!
YOU'RE WELCOME ...
I AM FORTUNATE TO HAVE HIM AS MY LORD...
HE HAS TAUGHT ME THAT GIVING AND DOING THINGS FOR OTHERS...
...ALSO BRINGS A JOY AND HAPPINESS TO THE GIVER.
THAT'S WHY...
HEY, VINCENT!
LET'S MAKE SOME TEA.
YES, SIR!
...I HAVE DECIDED TO SERVE HIM FOR THE REST OF MY LIFE.

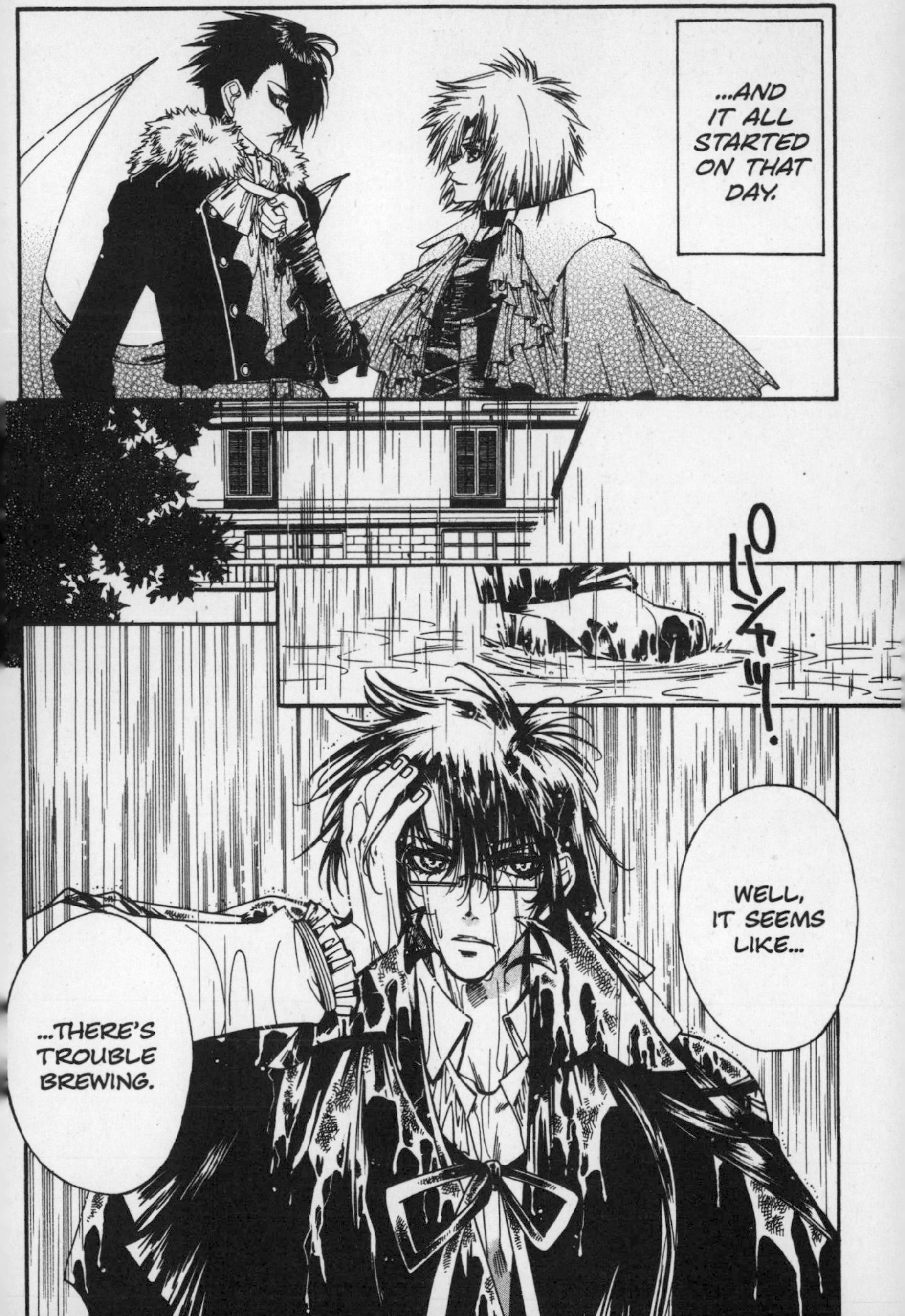
...AND IT ALL STARTED ON THAT DAY.
ぴシャッ!
WELL, IT SEEMS LIKE...
...THERE'S TROUBLE BREWING.

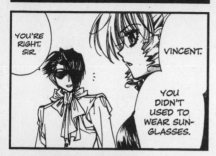

Vampire Doll Reflections

Bonus Comic Strip

Present

VINCENT.
YOU DIDN'T USED TO WEAR SUN-GLASSES.
YOU'RE RIGHT, SIR
AS A BAT, I'M UNUSED TO SEEING IN SUNLIGHT AND ARTIFICIAL LIGHT. WORKING DURING THE DAY HAS MADE THESE A NECESSITY.
...BUT THERE IS ONE OTHER REASON.
I WAS TOLD, "YOUR FACE SCARES ME. YOU SHOULD HIDE IT."
TONAE SAID THAT?
NO, SIR. IT WAS MASTER NIGHT VEIL.
....

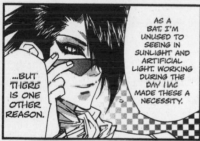

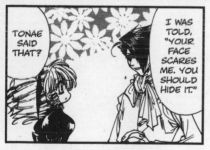

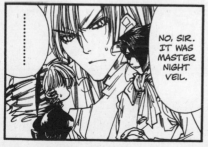

VINCENT

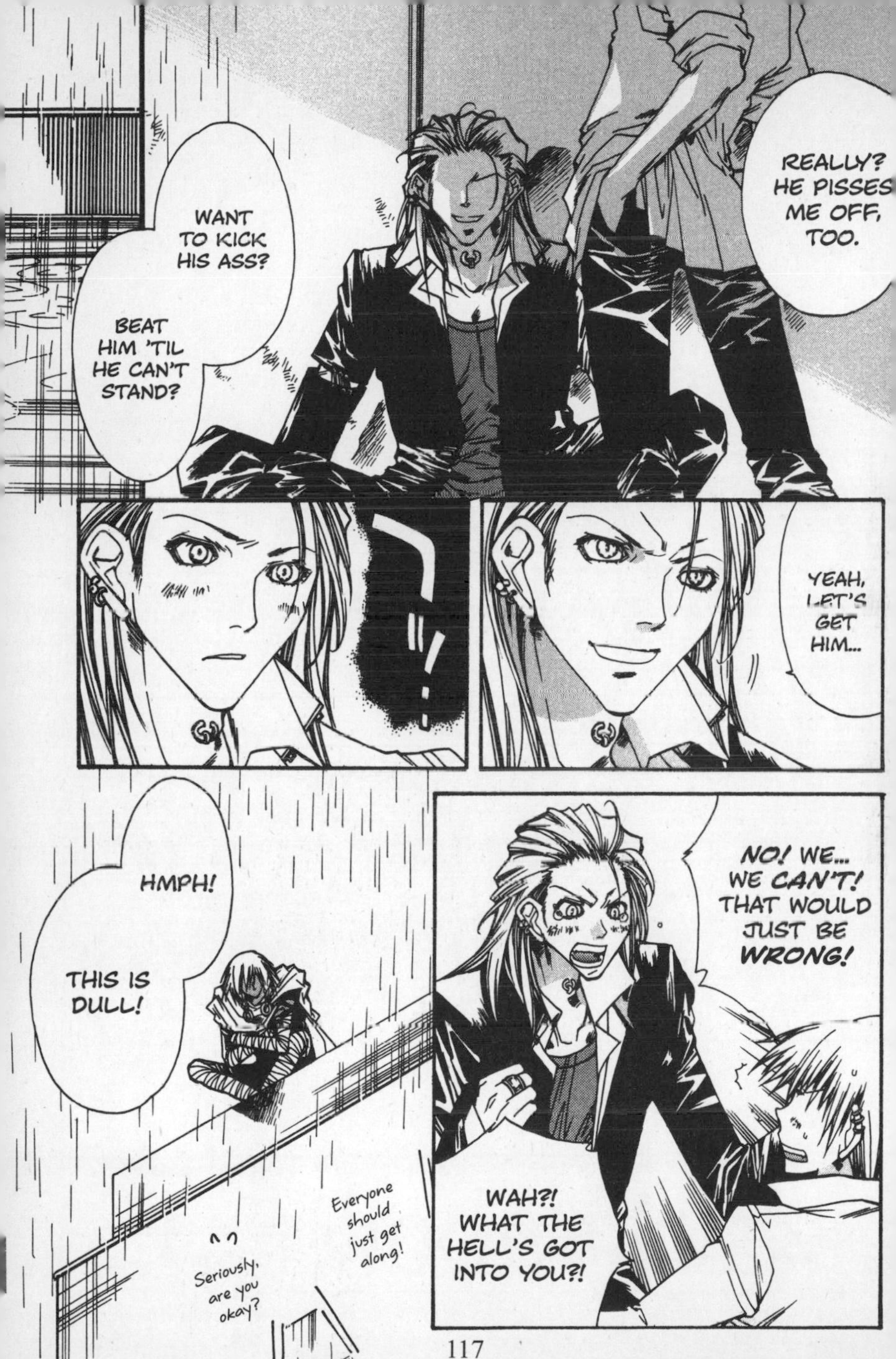
REALLY? HE PISSES ME OFF, TOO.
WANT TO KICK HIS ASS?
BEAT HIM 'TIL HE CAN'T STAND?
YEAH, LET'S GET HIM...
NO! WE... WE CAN'T! THAT WOULD JUST BE WRONG!
WAH?! WHAT THE HELL'S GOT INTO YOU?!
HMPH!
THIS IS DULL!
Everyone should just get along!
Seriously, are you okay?

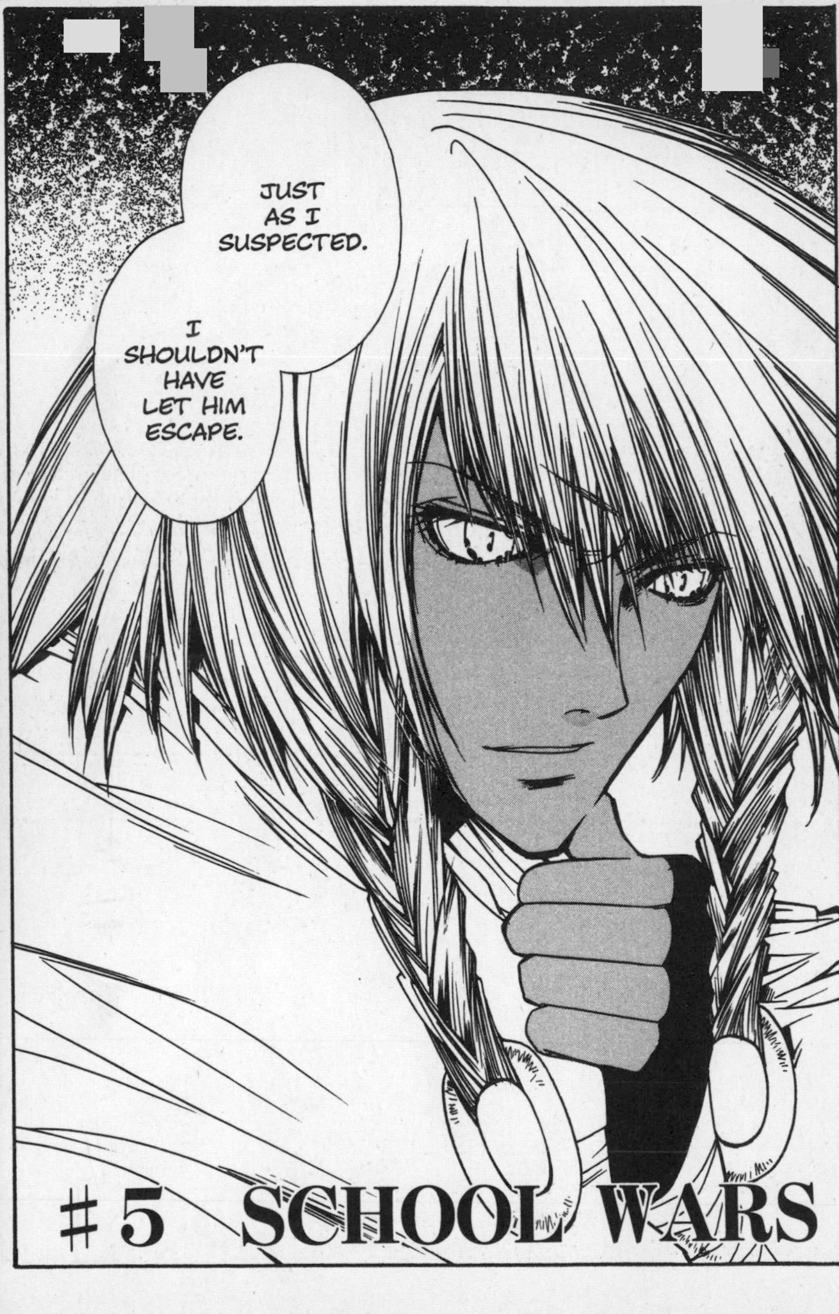
JUST AS I SUSPECTED.
I SHOULDN'T HAVE LET HIM ESCAPE.
♯5 SCHOOL WARS

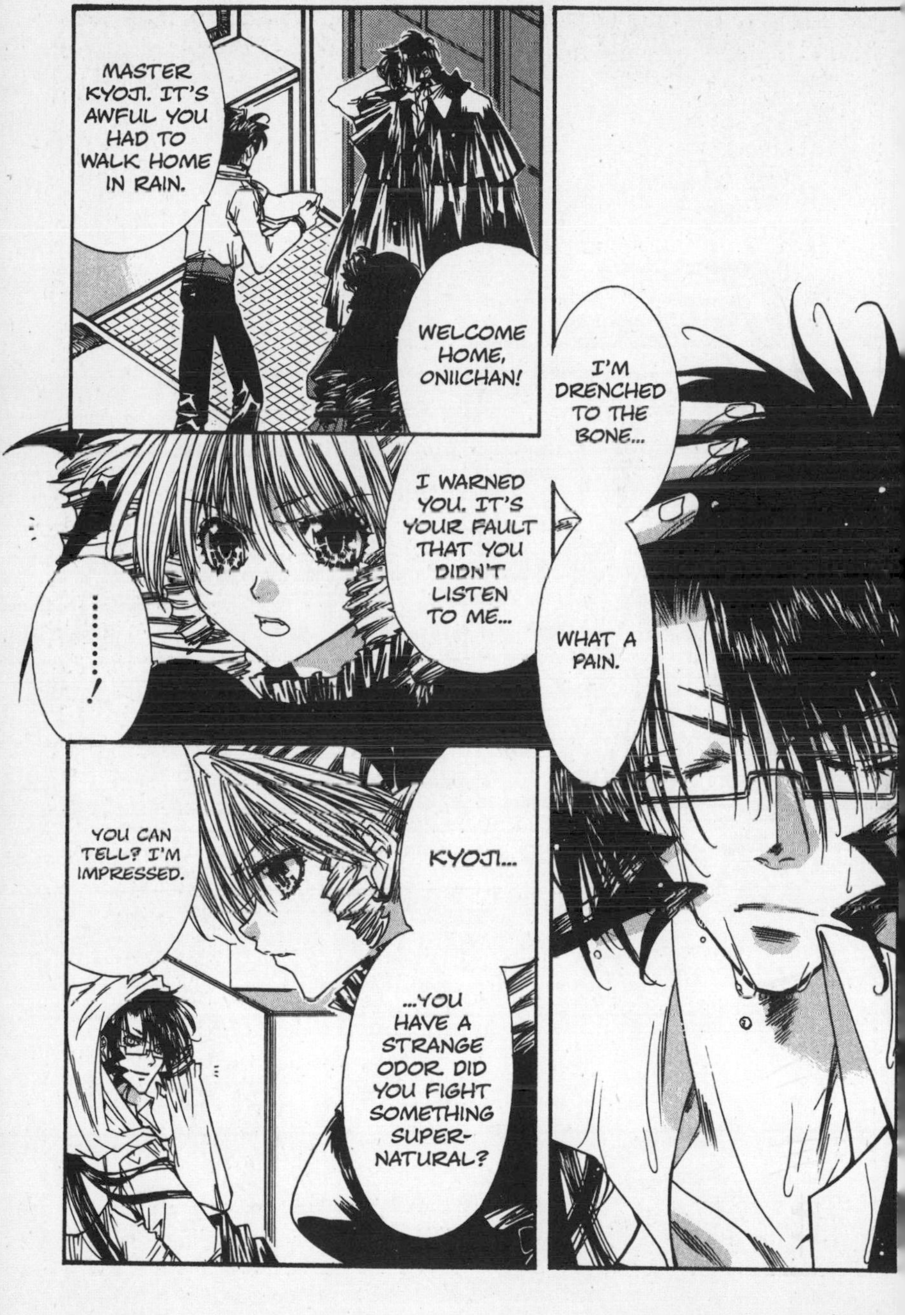
I'M DRENCHED TO THE BONE...
WHAT A PAIN.
MASTER KYOJI. IT'S AWFUL YOU HAD TO WALK HOME IN RAIN.
WELCOME HOME, ONIICHAN!
I WARNED YOU. IT'S YOUR FAULT THAT YOU DIDN'T LISTEN TO ME...
......!
KYOJI...
...YOU HAVE A STRANGE ODOR. DID YOU FIGHT SOMETHING SUPER-NATURAL?
YOU CAN TELL? I'M IMPRESSED.

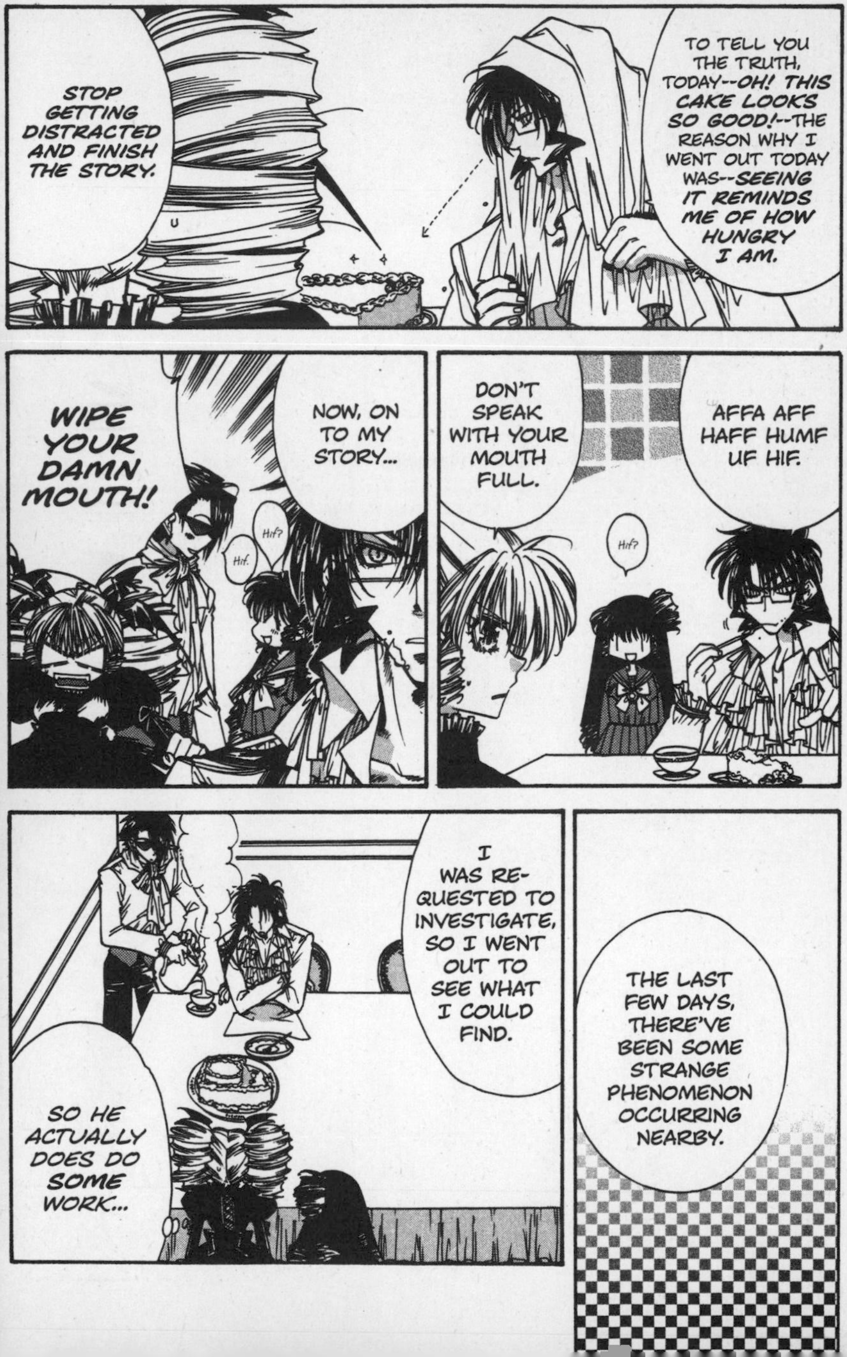
TO TELL YOU THE TRUTH, TODAY--OH! THIS CAKE LOOKS SO GOOD!--THE REASON WHY I WENT OUT TODAY WAS--SEEING IT REMINDS ME OF HOW HUNGRY I AM.
STOP GETTING DISTRACTED AND FINISH THE STORY.
AFFA AFF HAFF HUMF UF HIF.
DON'T SPEAK WITH YOUR MOUTH FULL.
Hif?
NOW, ON TO MY STORY...
WIPE YOUR DAMN MOUTH!
Hif?
Hif.
THE LAST FEW DAYS, THERE'VE BEEN SOME STRANGE PHENOMENON OCCURRING NEARBY.
I WAS RE-QUESTED TO INVESTIGATE, SO I WENT OUT TO SEE WHAT I COULD FIND.
SO HE ACTUALLY DOES DO SOME WORK...

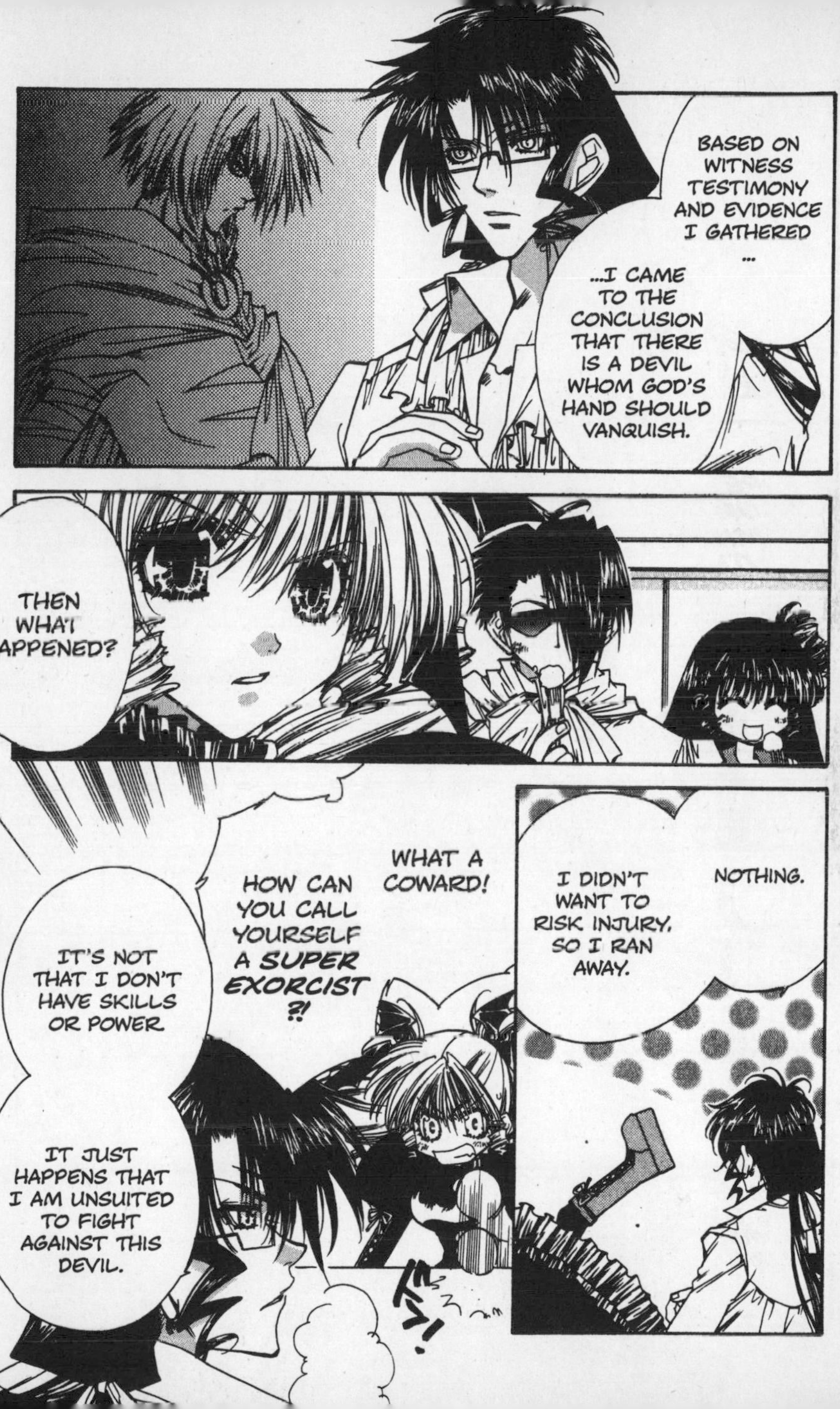
BASED ON WITNESS TESTIMONY AND EVIDENCE I GATHERED ...
...I CAME TO THE CONCLUSION THAT THERE IS A DEVIL WHOM GOD'S HAND SHOULD VANQUISH.
THEN WHAT HAPPENED?
NOTHING.
I DIDN'T WANT TO RISK INJURY, SO I RAN AWAY.
WHAT A COWARD!
HOW CAN YOU CALL YOURSELF A *SUPER EXORCIST* ?!
IT'S NOT THAT I DON'T HAVE SKILLS OR POWER
IT JUST HAPPENS THAT I AM UNSUITED TO FIGHT AGAINST THIS DEVIL.

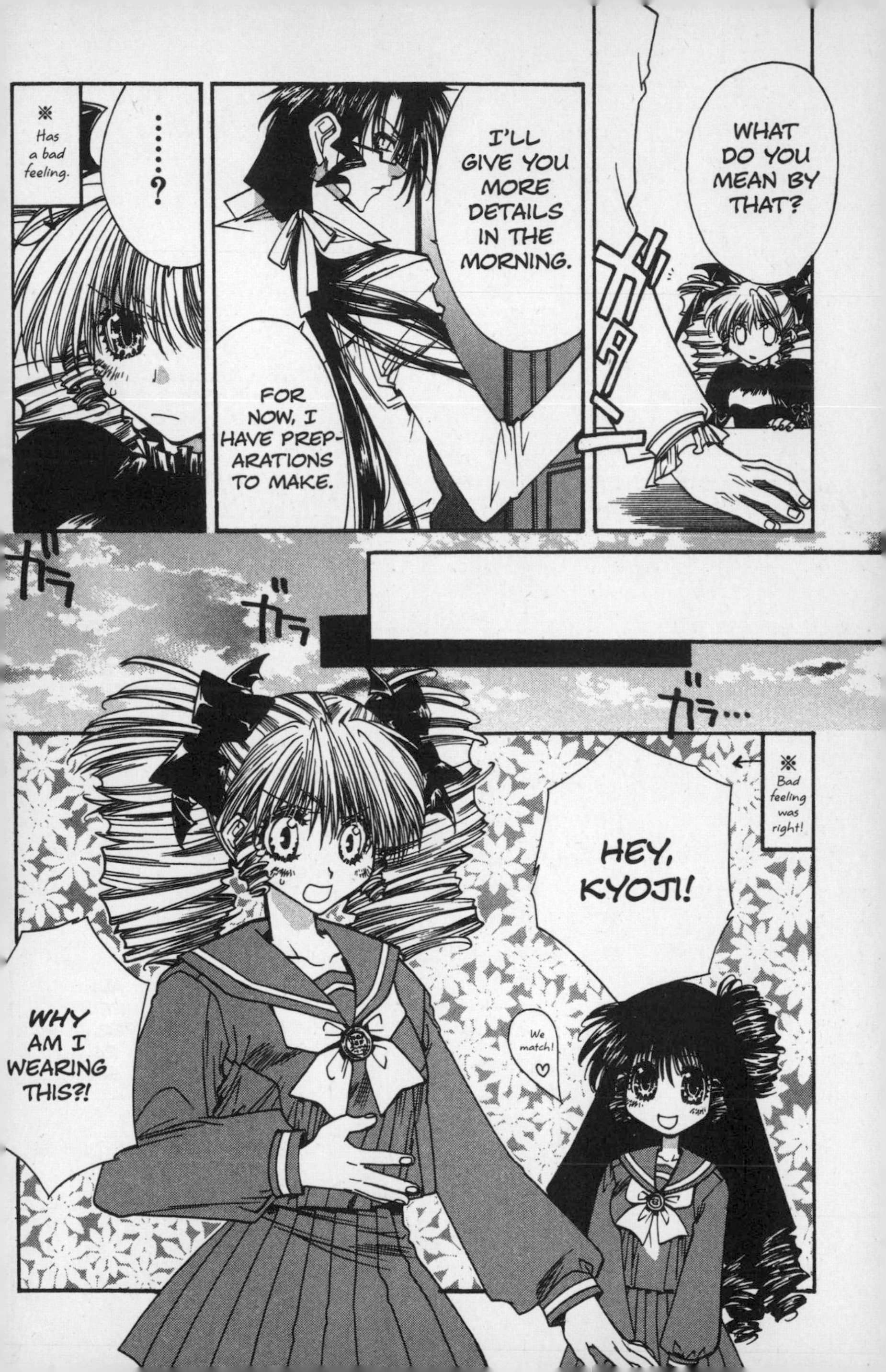

WHAT DO YOU MEAN BY THAT?
I'LL GIVE YOU MORE DETAILS IN THE MORNING.
FOR NOW, I HAVE PREPARATIONS TO MAKE.
※ Has a bad feeling.
......?
ガラ
ガラ
ガラ…
※ Bad feeling was right!
HEY, KYOJI!
We match! ♡
WHY AM I WEARING THIS?!

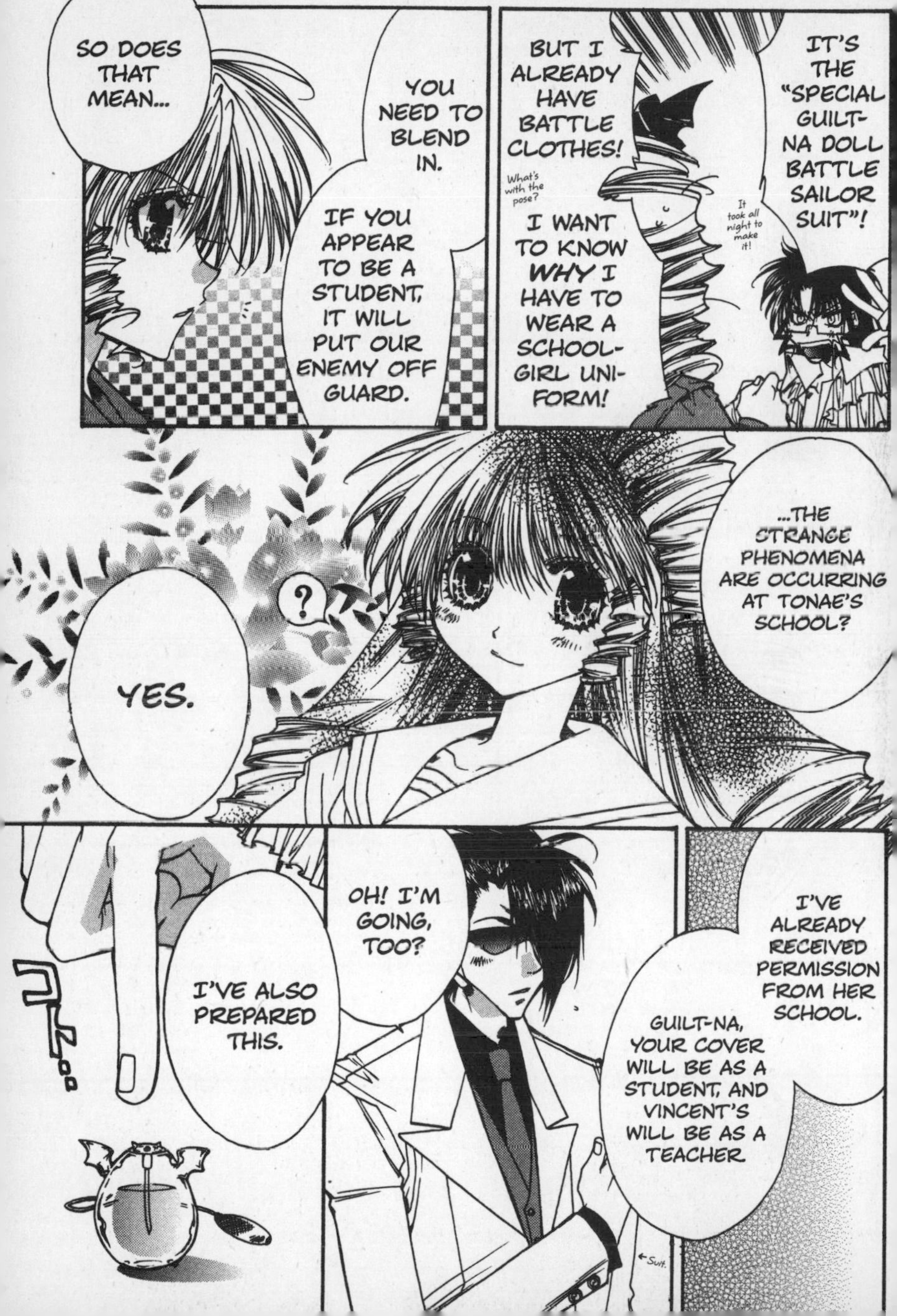
IT'S THE "SPECIAL GUILT-NA DOLL BATTLE SAILOR SUIT"!
It took all night to make it!
BUT I ALREADY HAVE BATTLE CLOTHES!
What's with the pose?
I WANT TO KNOW WHY I HAVE TO WEAR A SCHOOL-GIRL UNI-FORM!
YOU NEED TO BLEND IN.
IF YOU APPEAR TO BE A STUDENT, IT WILL PUT OUR ENEMY OFF GUARD.
SO DOES THAT MEAN...
...THE STRANGE PHENOMENA ARE OCCURRING AT TONAE'S SCHOOL?
?
YES.
I'VE ALREADY RECEIVED PERMISSION FROM HER SCHOOL.
GUILT-NA, YOUR COVER WILL BE AS A STUDENT, AND VINCENT'S WILL BE AS A TEACHER
← Suit.
OH! I'M GOING, TOO?
I'VE ALSO PREPARED THIS.

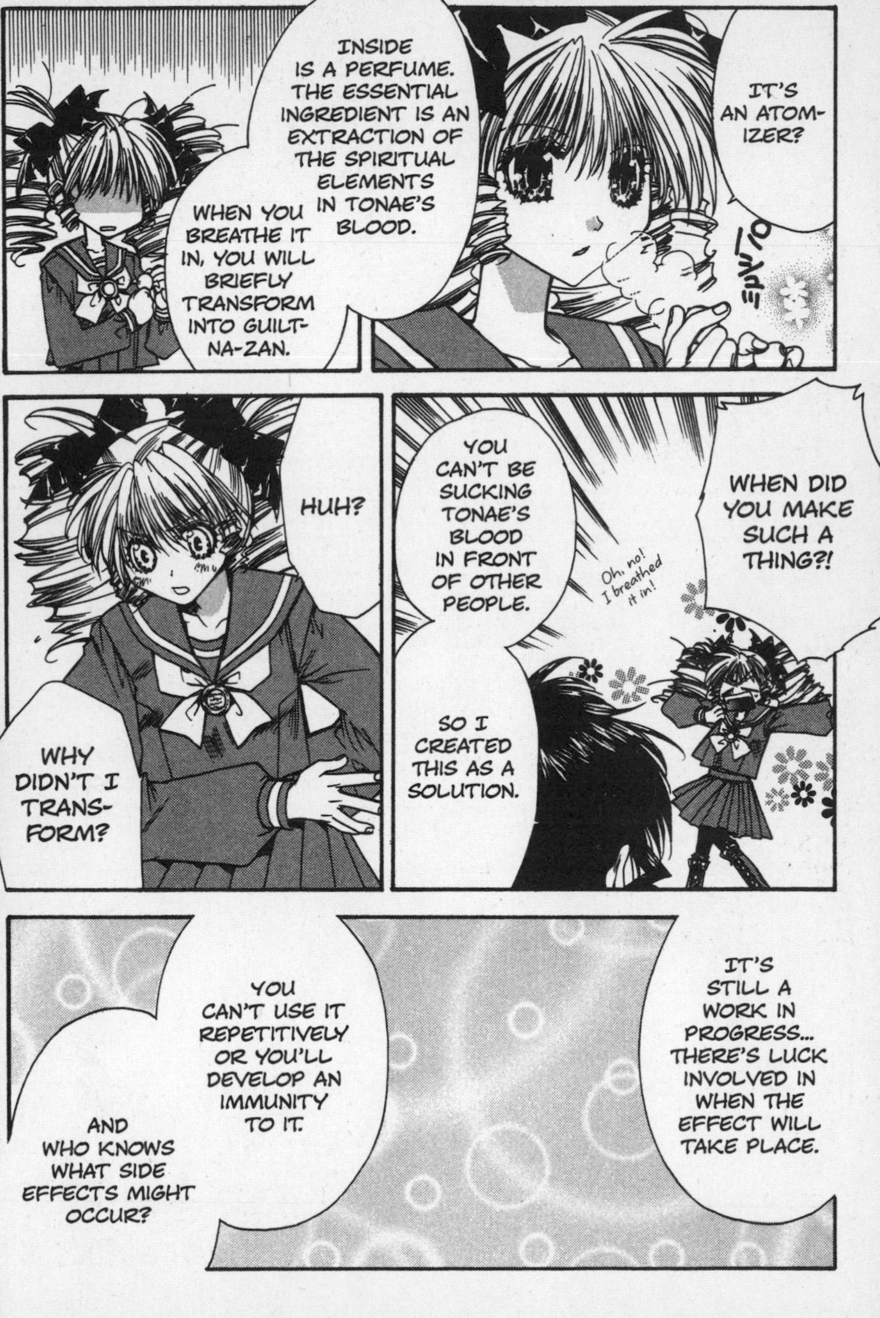
IT'S AN ATOMIZER?
INSIDE IS A PERFUME. THE ESSENTIAL INGREDIENT IS AN EXTRACTION OF THE SPIRITUAL ELEMENTS IN TONAE'S BLOOD.
WHEN YOU BREATHE IT IN, YOU WILL BRIEFLY TRANSFORM INTO GUILT-NA-ZAN.
WHEN DID YOU MAKE SUCH A THING?!
Oh, no! I breathed it in!
YOU CAN'T BE SUCKING TONAE'S BLOOD IN FRONT OF OTHER PEOPLE.
SO I CREATED THIS AS A SOLUTION.
HUH?
WHY DIDN'T I TRANS-FORM?
IT'S STILL A WORK IN PROGRESS... THERE'S LUCK INVOLVED IN WHEN THE EFFECT WILL TAKE PLACE.
YOU CAN'T USE IT REPETITIVELY OR YOU'LL DEVELOP AN IMMUNITY TO IT.
AND WHO KNOWS WHAT SIDE EFFECTS MIGHT OCCUR?

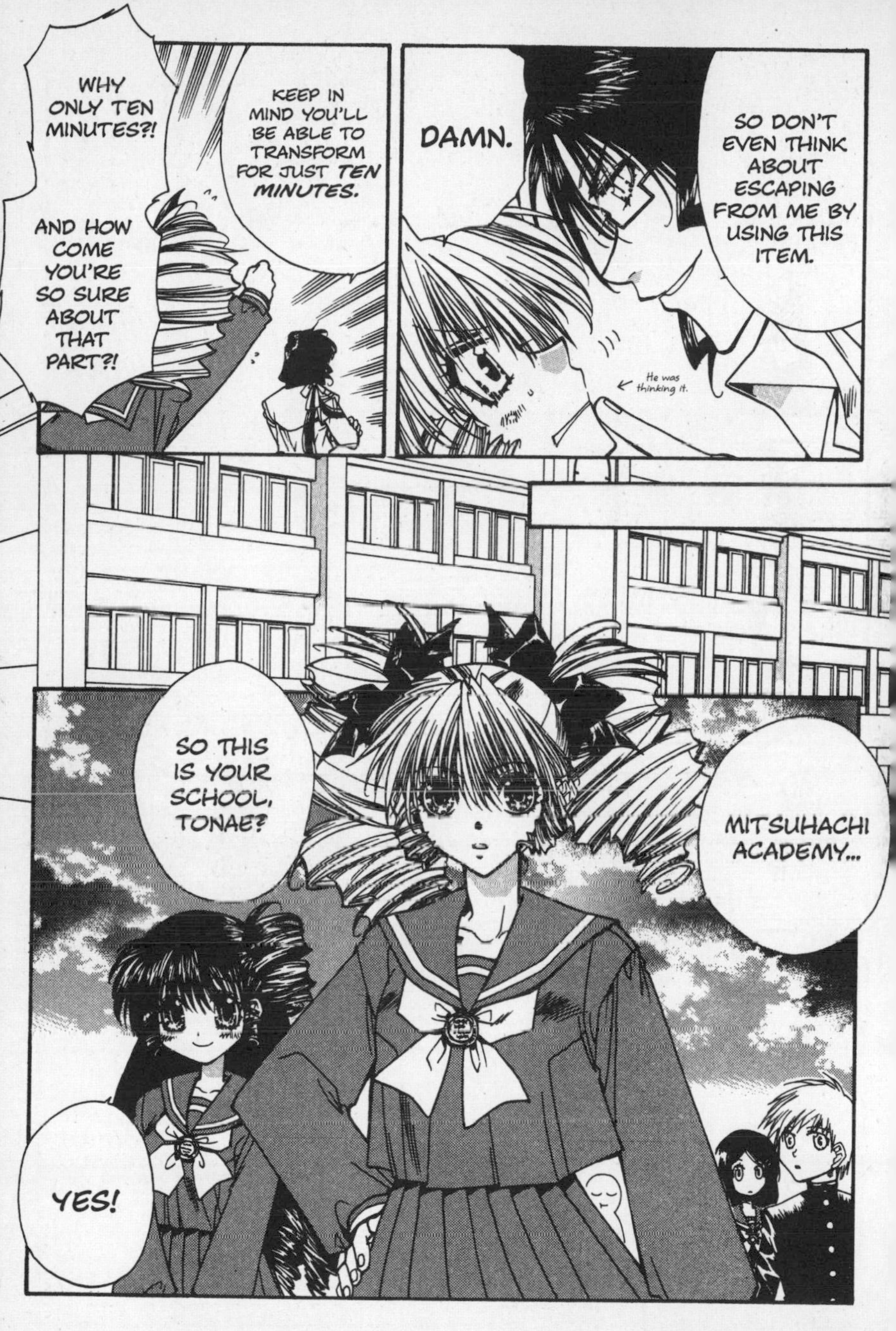
SO DON'T EVEN THINK ABOUT ESCAPING FROM ME BY USING THIS ITEM.
DAMN.
He was thinking it.
KEEP IN MIND YOU'LL BE ABLE TO TRANSFORM FOR JUST *TEN MINUTES.*
WHY ONLY TEN MINUTES?!
AND HOW COME YOU'RE SO SURE ABOUT THAT PART?!
MITSUHACHI ACADEMY...
SO THIS IS YOUR SCHOOL, TONAE?
YES!

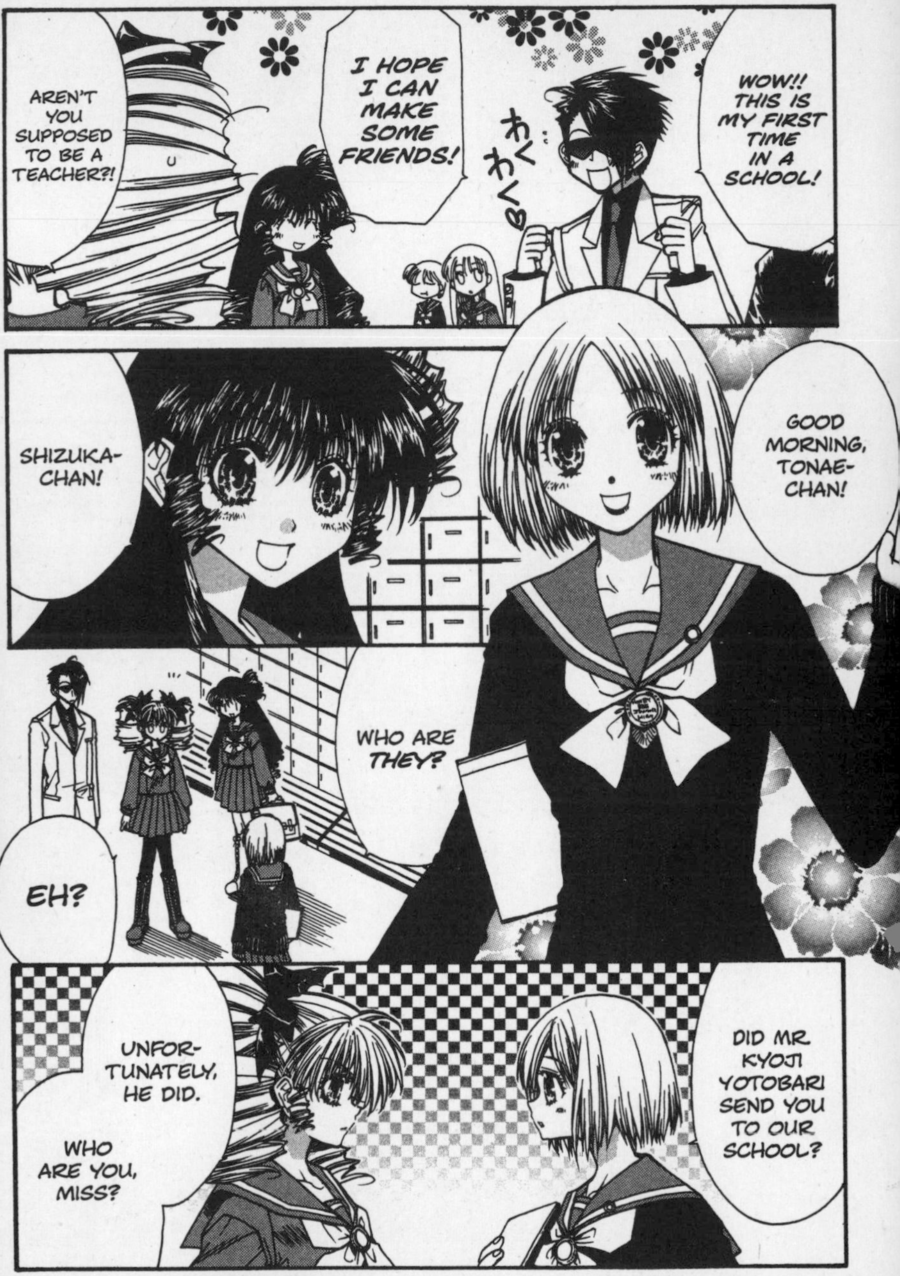
WOW!! THIS IS MY FIRST TIME IN A SCHOOL!
わくわく
I HOPE I CAN MAKE SOME FRIENDS!
AREN'T YOU SUPPOSED TO BE A TEACHER?!
GOOD MORNING, TONAE-CHAN!
SHIZUKA-CHAN!
WHO ARE THEY?
EH?
DID MR KYOJI YOTOBARI SEND YOU TO OUR SCHOOL?
UNFORTUNATELY, HE DID.
WHO ARE YOU, MISS?

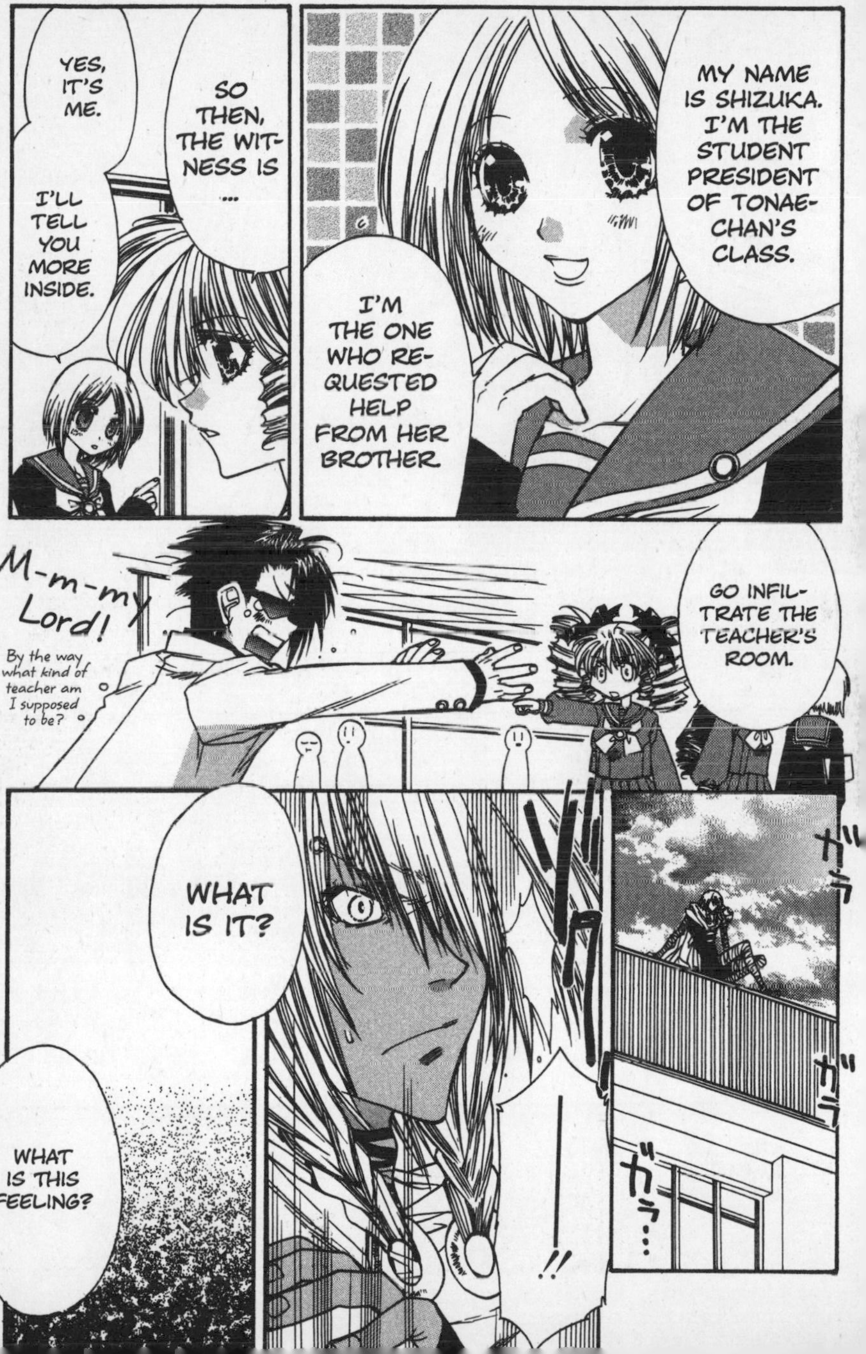
MY NAME IS SHIZUKA. I'M THE STUDENT PRESIDENT OF TONAE-CHAN'S CLASS.
I'M THE ONE WHO RE-QUESTED HELP FROM HER BROTHER
SO THEN, THE WIT-NESS IS ...
YES, IT'S ME.
I'LL TELL YOU MORE INSIDE.
GO INFIL-TRATE THE TEACHER'S ROOM.
M-m-my Lord!
By the way what kind of teacher am I supposed to be?
ガラ
ガラ
ガラ…
!!
WHAT IS IT?
WHAT IS THIS FEELING?

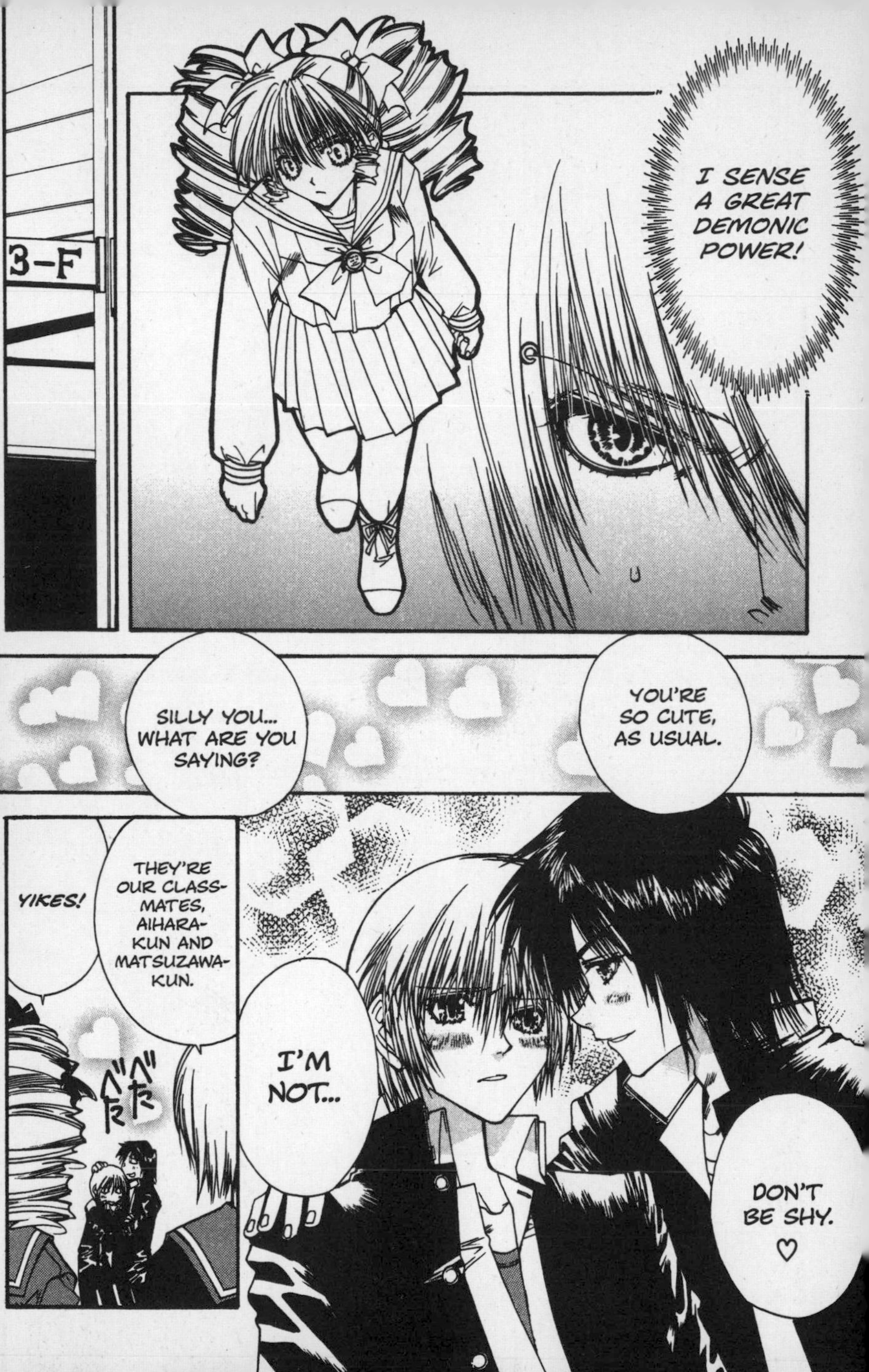
I SENSE A GREAT DEMONIC POWER!
YOU'RE SO CUTE, AS USUAL.
SILLY YOU... WHAT ARE YOU SAYING?
DON'T BE SHY. ♡
I'M NOT...
THEY'RE OUR CLASSMATES, AIHARA-KUN AND MATSUZAWA-KUN.
YIKES!
べたべた

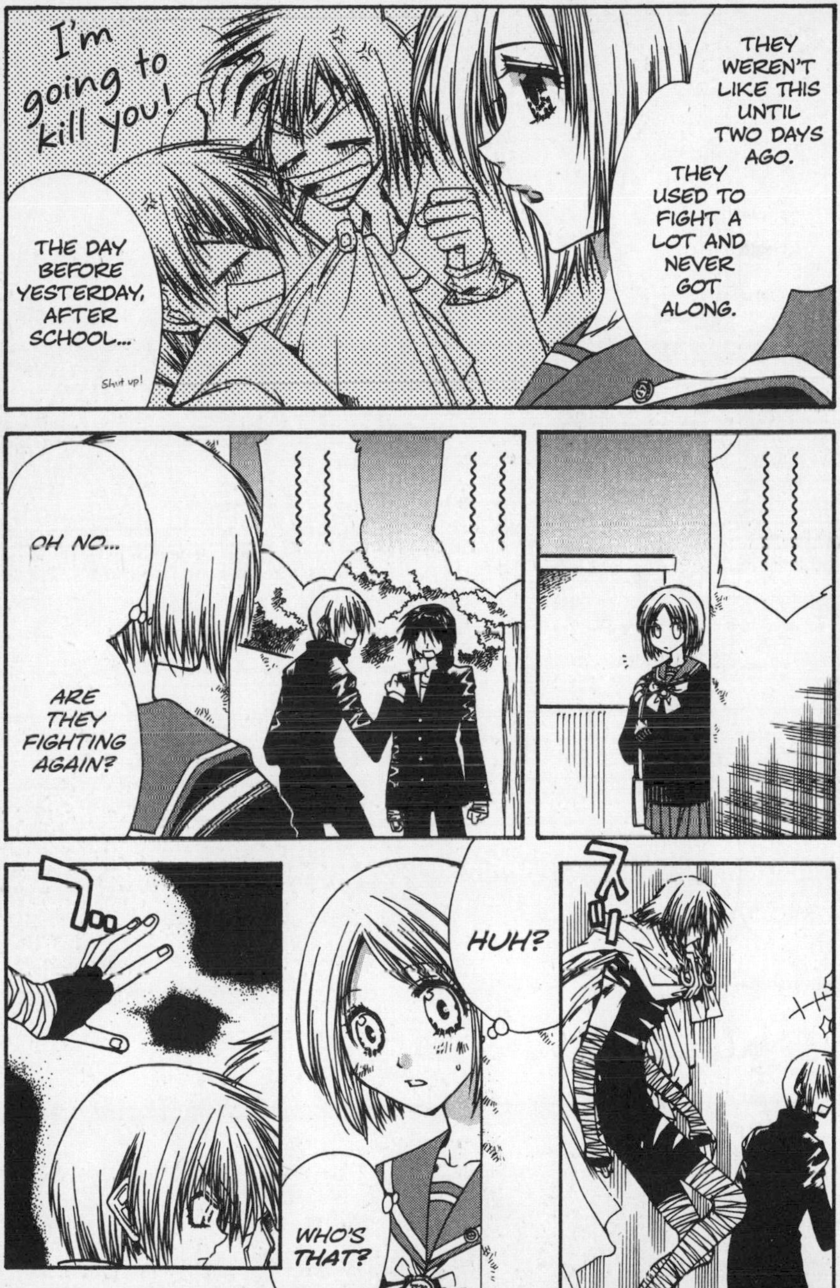
THEY WEREN'T LIKE THIS UNTIL TWO DAYS AGO.
THEY USED TO FIGHT A LOT AND NEVER GOT ALONG.
I'm going to kill you!
THE DAY BEFORE YESTERDAY, AFTER SCHOOL...
Shut up!
OH NO...
ARE THEY FIGHTING AGAIN?
HUH?
WHO'S THAT?

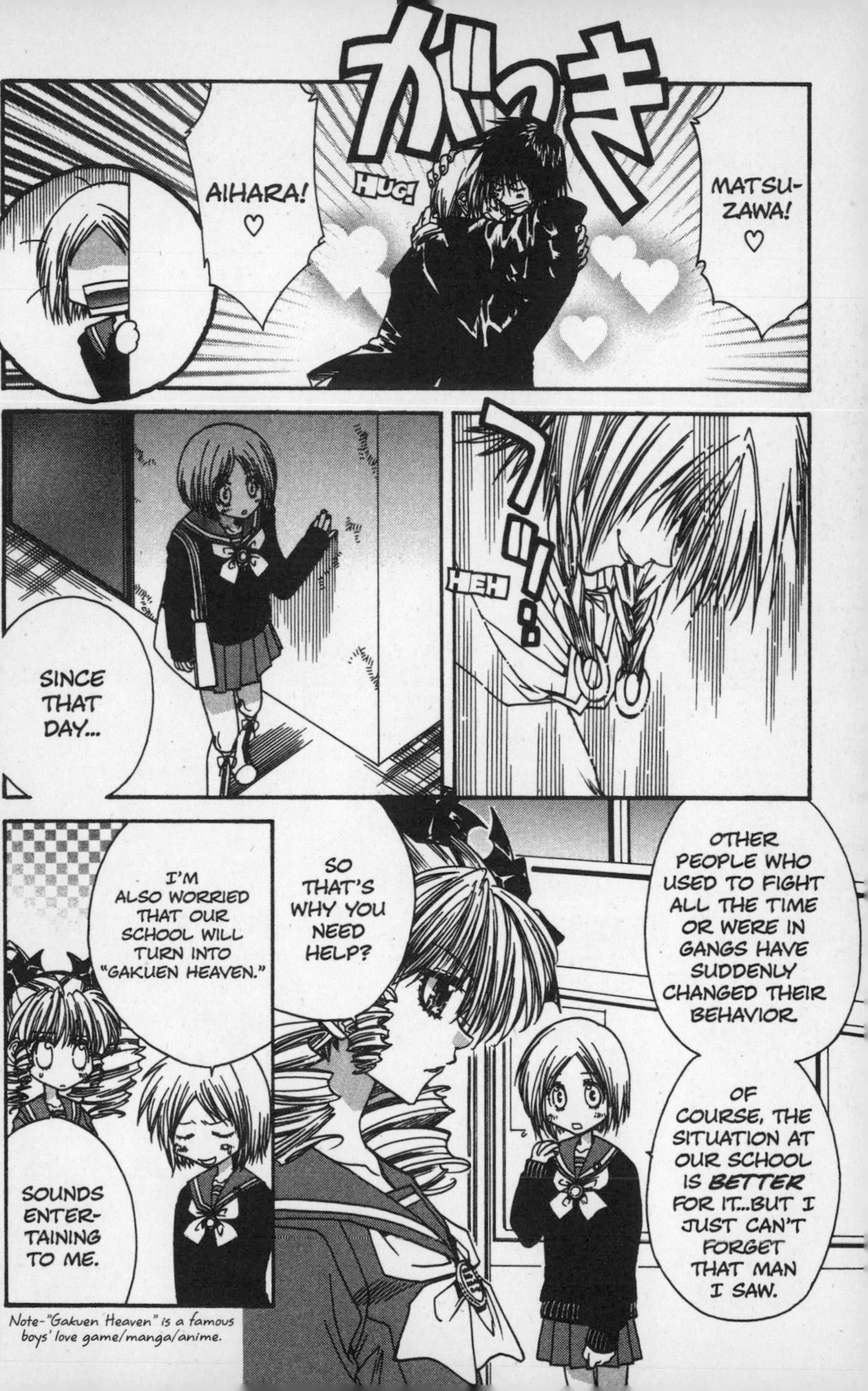
がっき
MATSU-ZAWA! ♡
HUG!
AIHARA! ♡
HEH
SINCE THAT DAY...
OTHER PEOPLE WHO USED TO FIGHT ALL THE TIME OR WERE IN GANGS HAVE SUDDENLY CHANGED THEIR BEHAVIOR
OF COURSE, THE SITUATION AT OUR SCHOOL IS *BETTER* FOR IT...BUT I JUST CAN'T FORGET THAT MAN I SAW.
SO THAT'S WHY YOU NEED HELP?
I'M ALSO WORRIED THAT OUR SCHOOL WILL TURN INTO "GAKUEN HEAVEN."
SOUNDS ENTER-TAINING TO ME.

Note-"Gakuen Heaven" is a famous boys' love game/manga/anime.

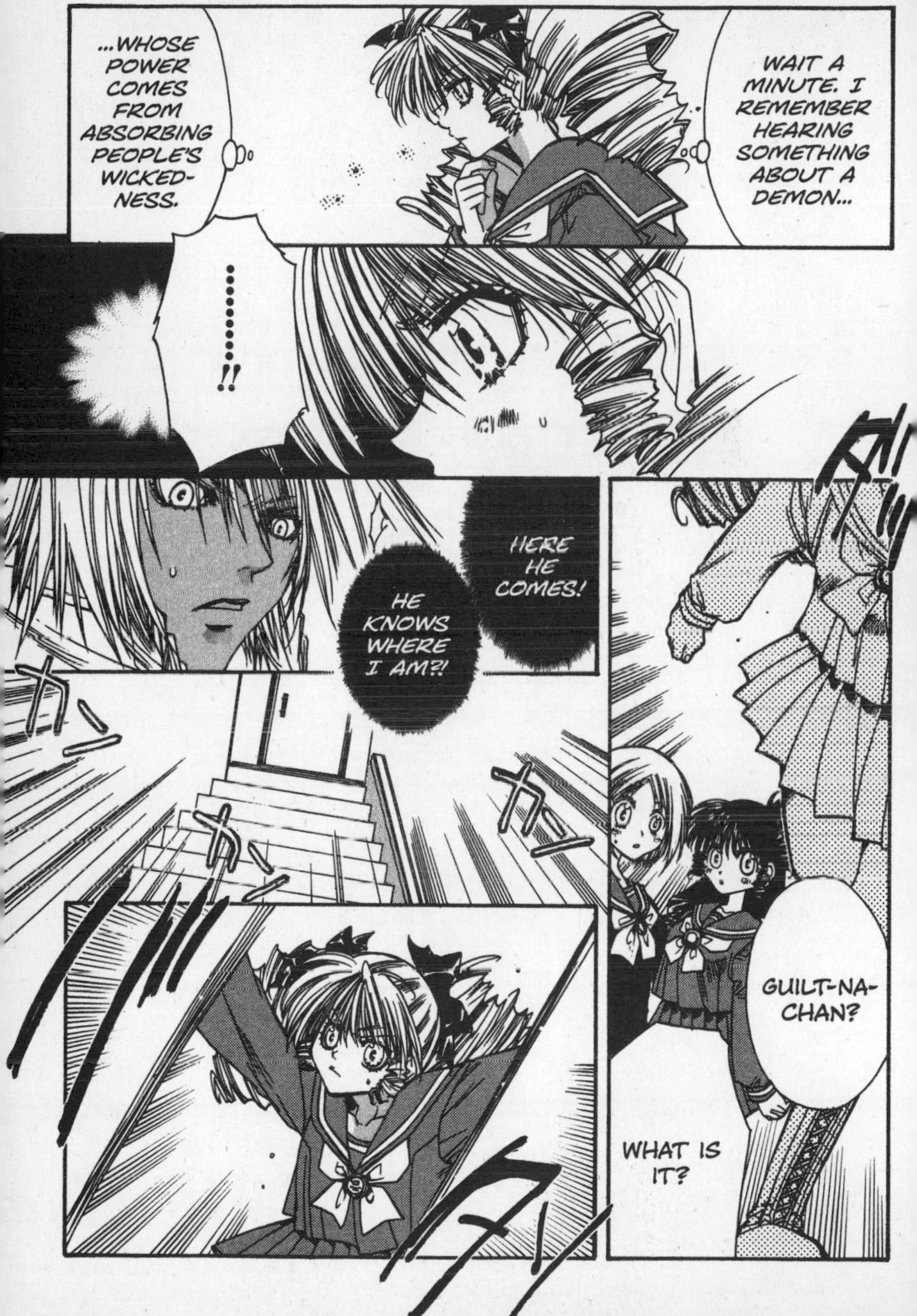
WAIT A MINUTE. I REMEMBER HEARING SOMETHING ABOUT A DEMON...
...WHOSE POWER COMES FROM ABSORBING PEOPLE'S WICKED-NESS.
......!!
GUILT-NA-CHAN?
WHAT IS IT?
HERE HE COMES!
HE KNOWS WHERE I AM?!

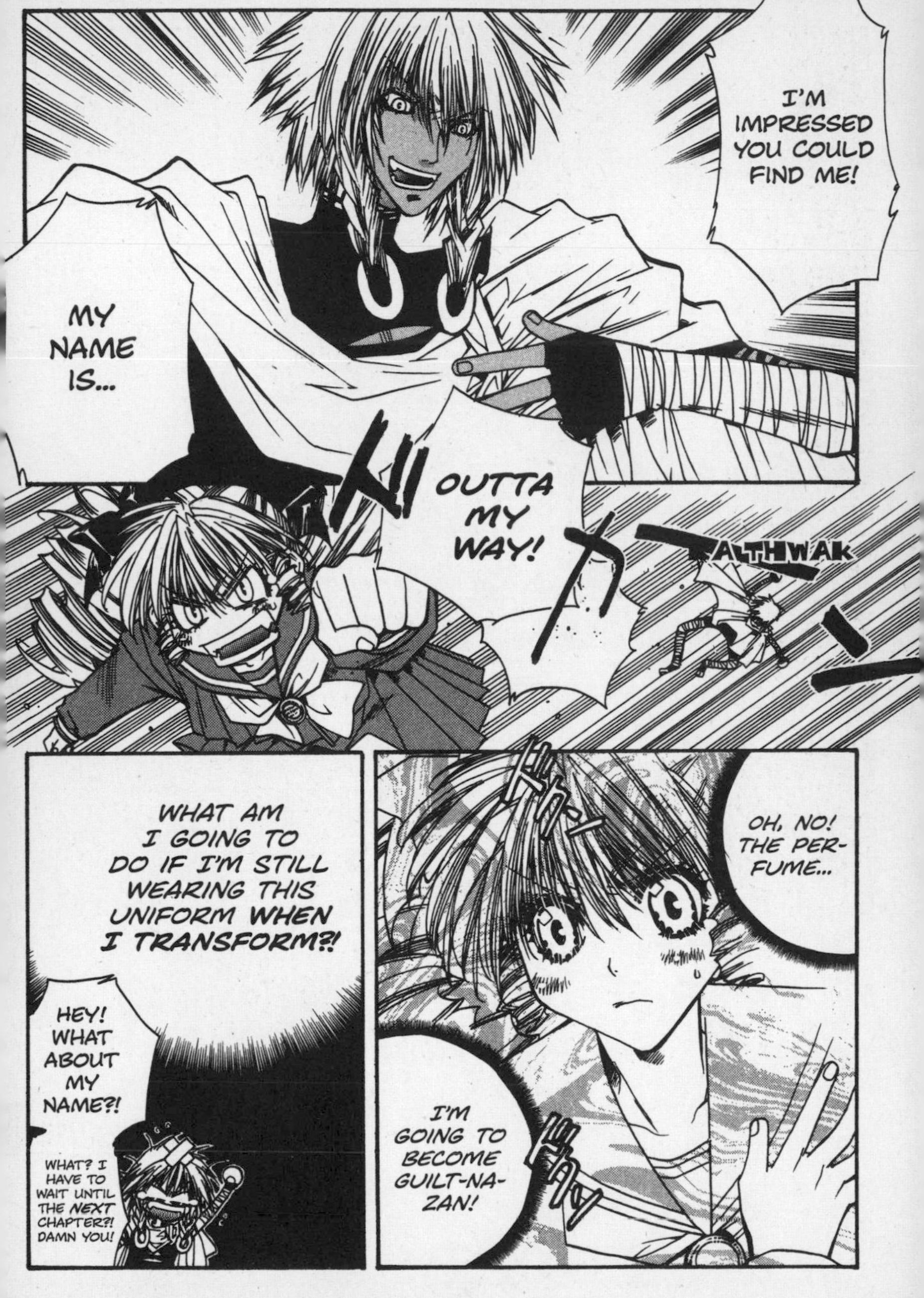
I'M IMPRESSED YOU COULD FIND ME!
MY NAME IS...
OUTTA MY WAY!
ALTHWAK
OH, NO! THE PER-FUME...
I'M GOING TO BECOME GUILT-NA-ZAN!
WHAT AM I GOING TO DO IF I'M STILL WEARING THIS UNIFORM WHEN I TRANSFORM?!
HEY! WHAT ABOUT MY NAME?!
WHAT? I HAVE TO WAIT UNTIL THE NEXT CHAPTER?! DAMN YOU!

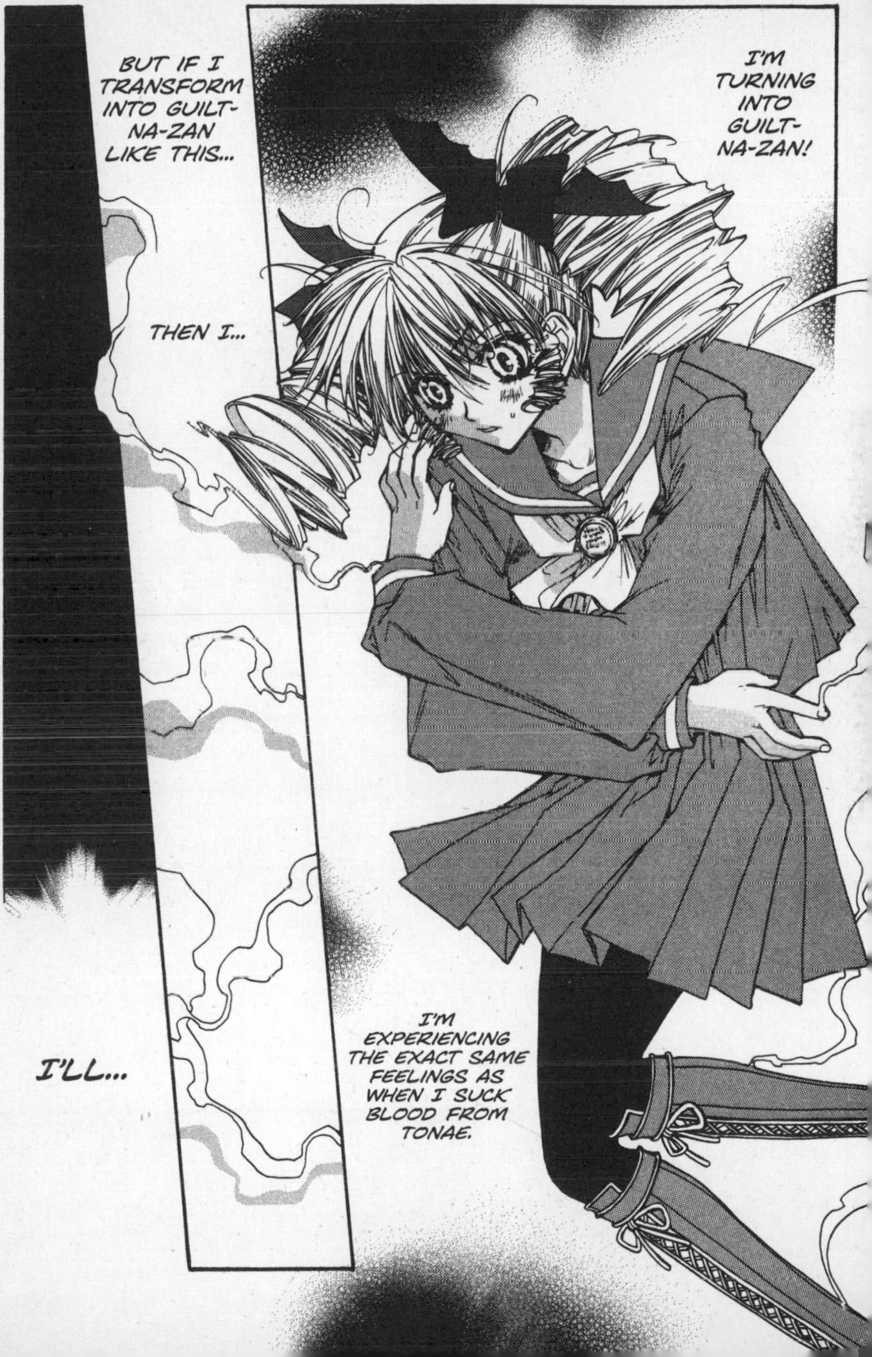
I'M TURNING INTO GUILT-NA-ZAN!
I'M EXPERIENCING THE EXACT SAME FEELINGS AS WHEN I SUCK BLOOD FROM TONAE.
BUT IF I TRANSFORM INTO GUILT-NA-ZAN LIKE THIS...
THEN I...
I'LL...

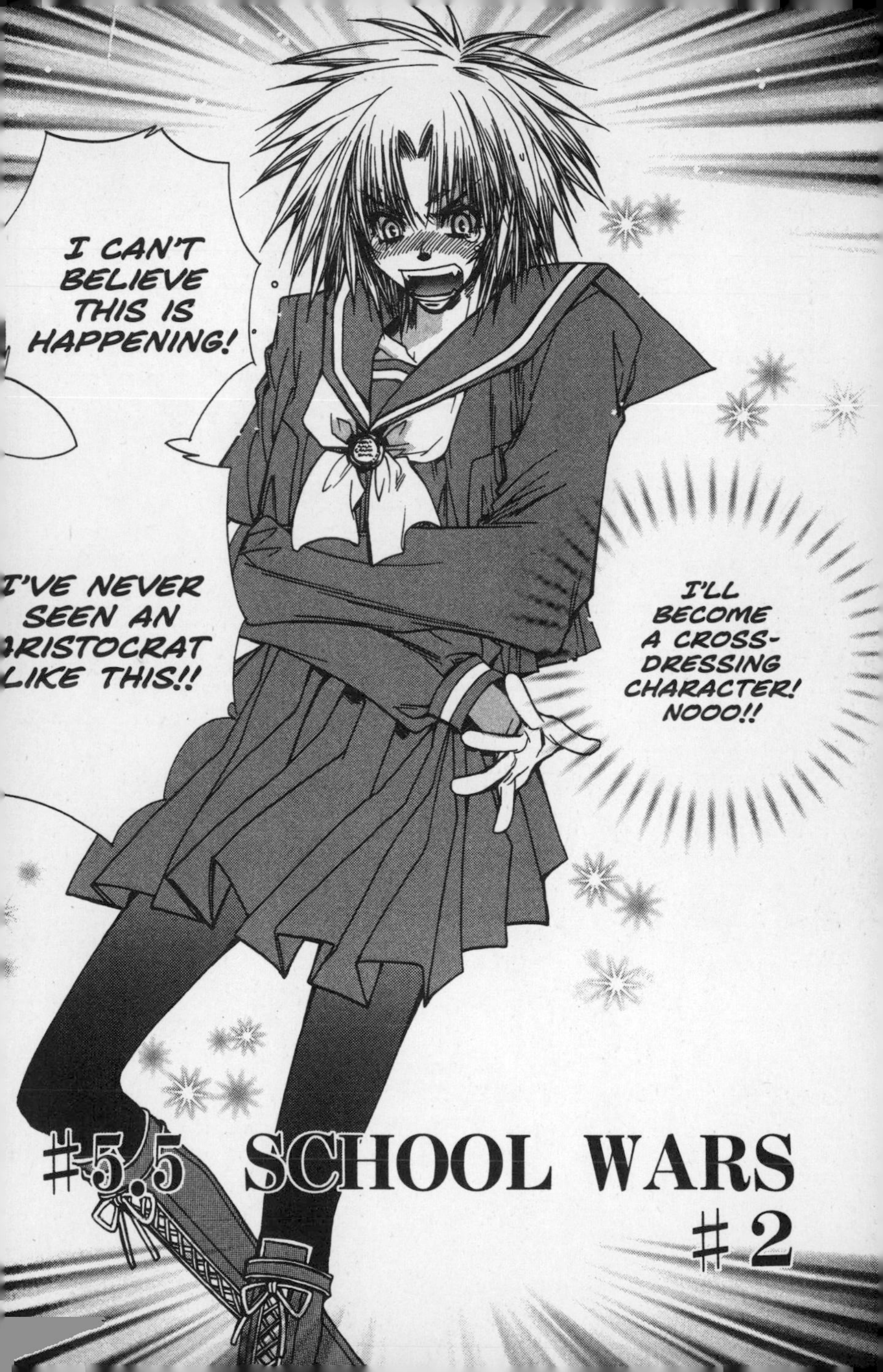
I CAN'T BELIEVE THIS IS HAPPENING!
I'LL BECOME A CROSS-DRESSING CHARACTER! NOOO!!
I'VE NEVER SEEN AN ARISTOCRAT LIKE THIS!!
♯5.5 SCHOOL WARS ♯2

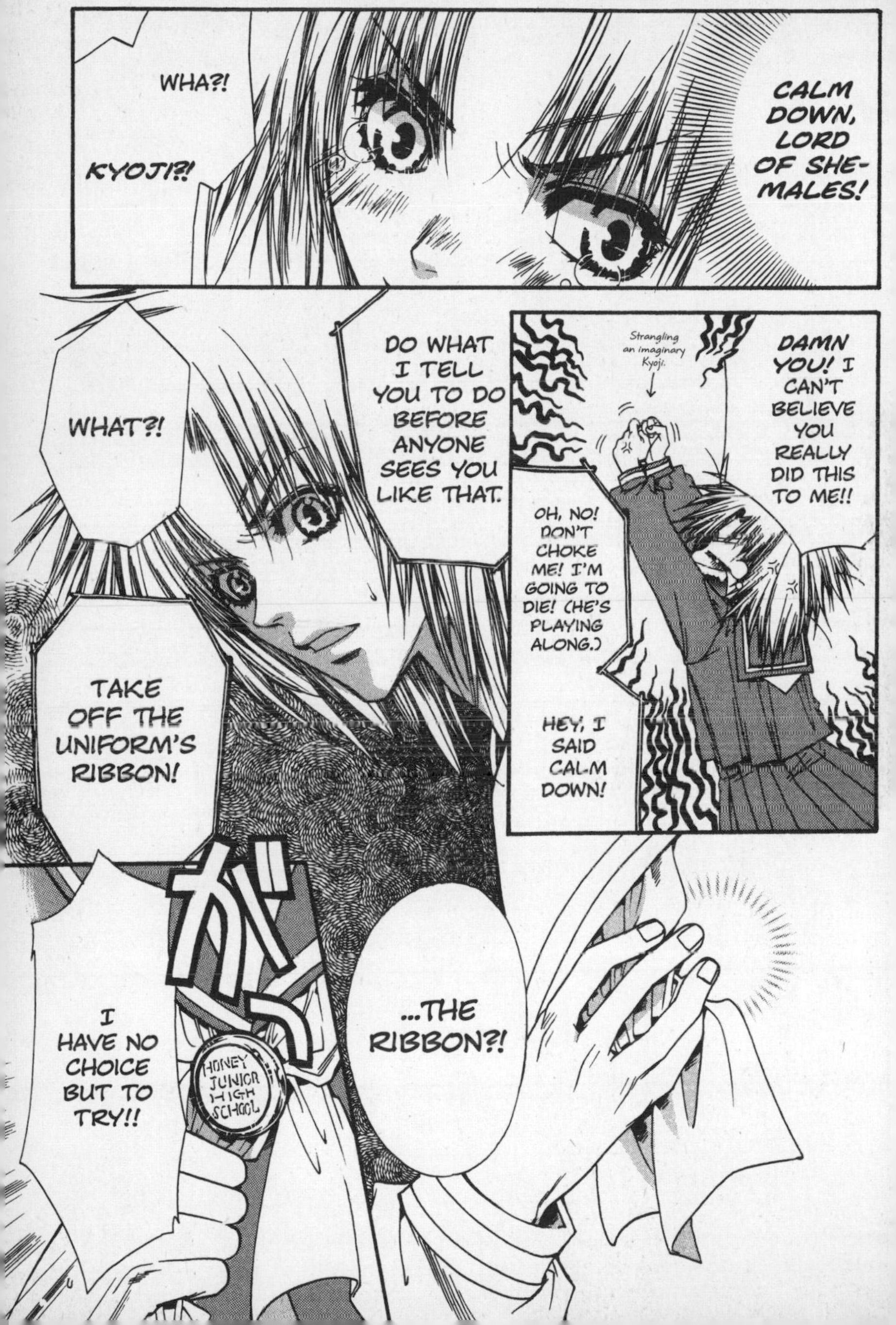
CALM DOWN, LORD OF SHE-MALES!
WHA?!
KYOJI?!
DAMN YOU! I CAN'T BELIEVE YOU REALLY DID THIS TO ME!!
Strangling an imaginary Kyoji.
OH, NO! DON'T CHOKE ME! I'M GOING TO DIE! (HE'S PLAYING ALONG.)
HEY, I SAID CALM DOWN!
DO WHAT I TELL YOU TO DO BEFORE ANYONE SEES YOU LIKE THAT.
WHAT?!
TAKE OFF THE UNIFORM'S RIBBON!
...THE RIBBON?!
HONEY JUNIOR HIGH SCHOOL
I HAVE NO CHOICE BUT TO TRY!!

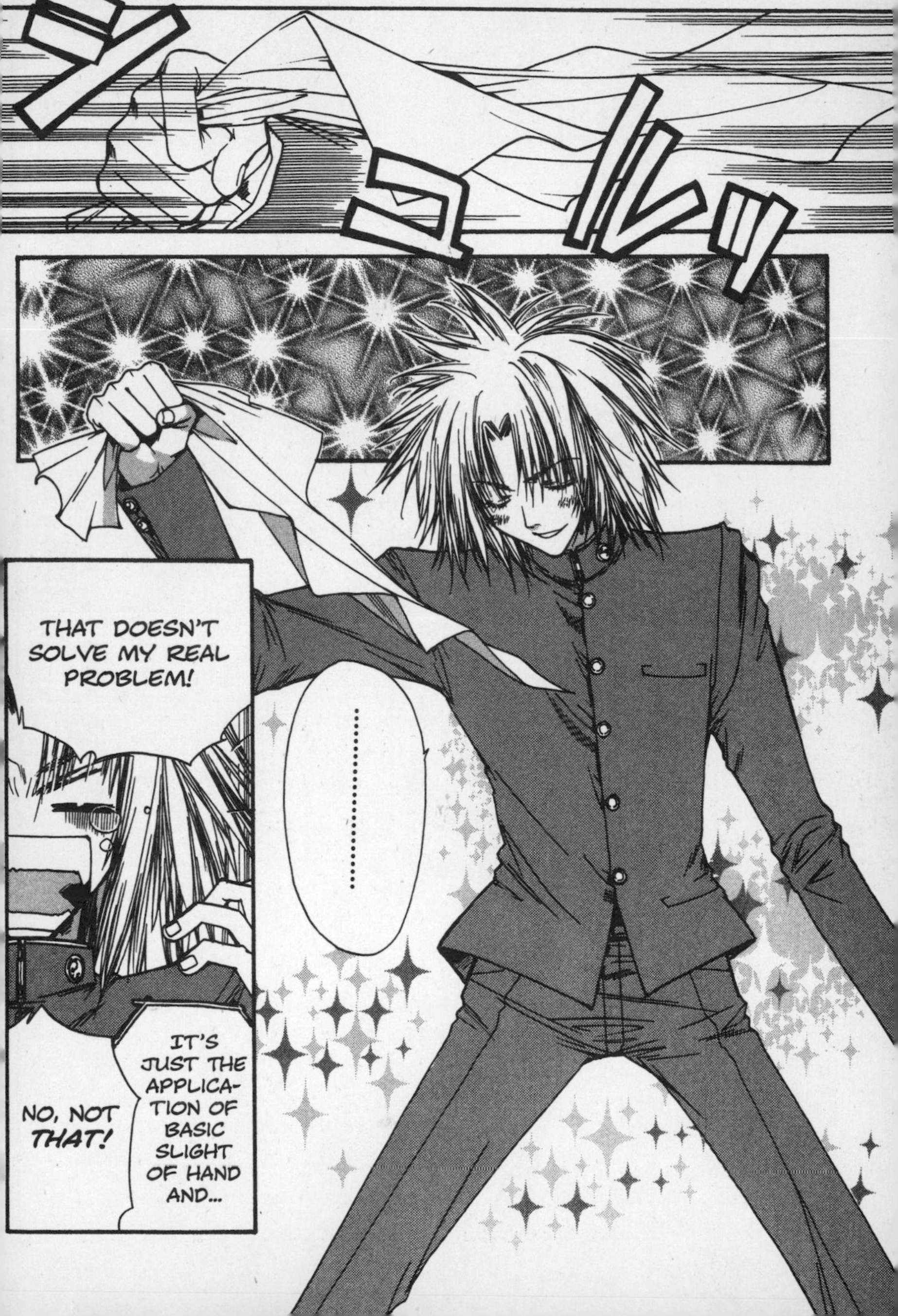
シュルッ
......
IT'S JUST THE APPLICATION OF BASIC SLIGHT OF HAND AND...
NO, NOT *THAT!*
THAT DOESN'T SOLVE MY REAL PROBLEM!

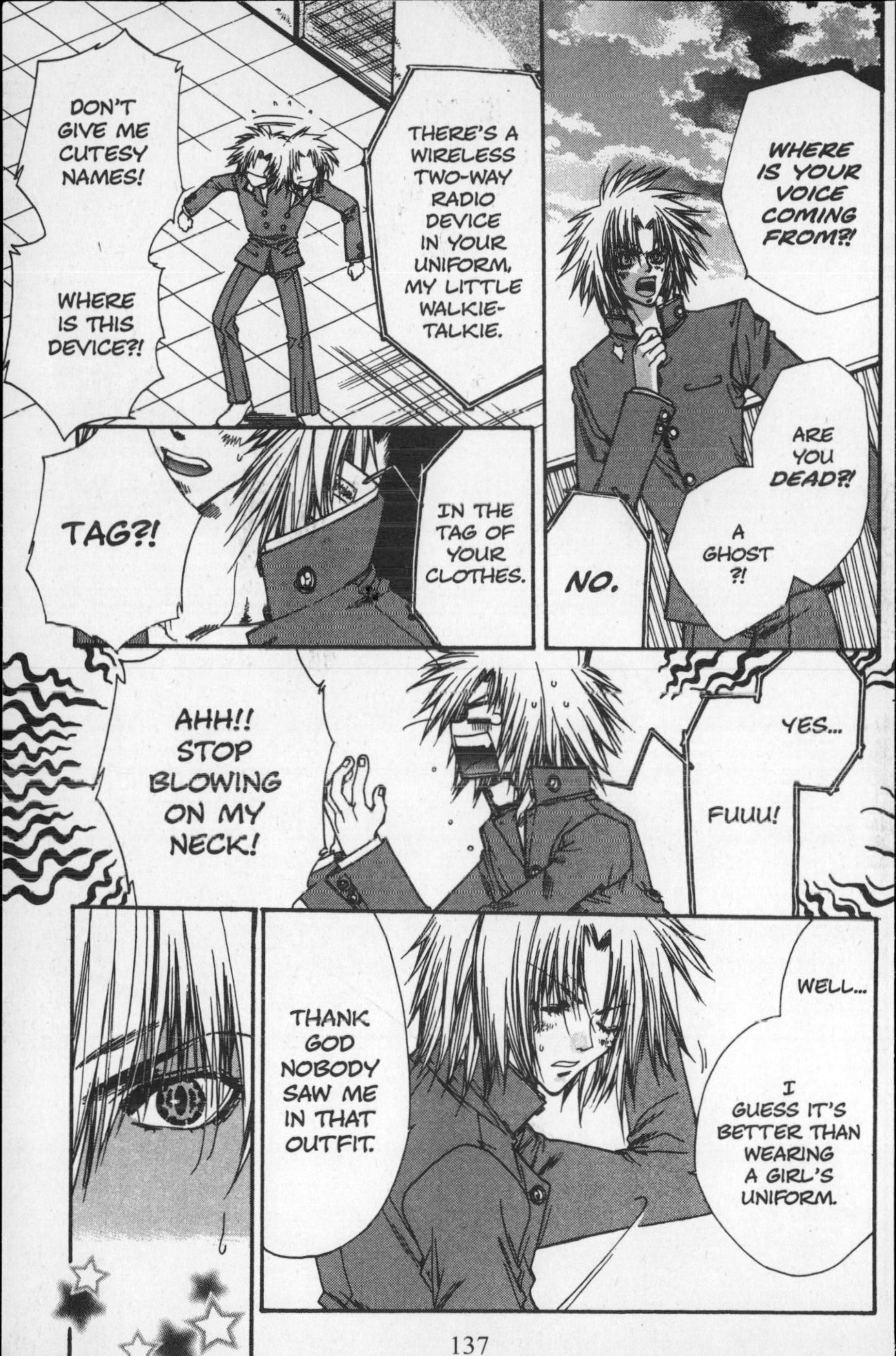
WHERE IS YOUR VOICE COMING FROM?!
ARE YOU DEAD?!
A GHOST ?!
NO.
THERE'S A WIRELESS TWO-WAY RADIO DEVICE IN YOUR UNIFORM, MY LITTLE WALKIE-TALKIE.
DON'T GIVE ME CUTESY NAMES!
WHERE IS THIS DEVICE?!
IN THE TAG OF YOUR CLOTHES.
TAG?!
YES...
FUUU!
AHH!! STOP BLOWING ON MY NECK!
WELL...
I GUESS IT'S BETTER THAN WEARING A GIRL'S UNIFORM.
THANK GOD NOBODY SAW ME IN THAT OUTFIT.

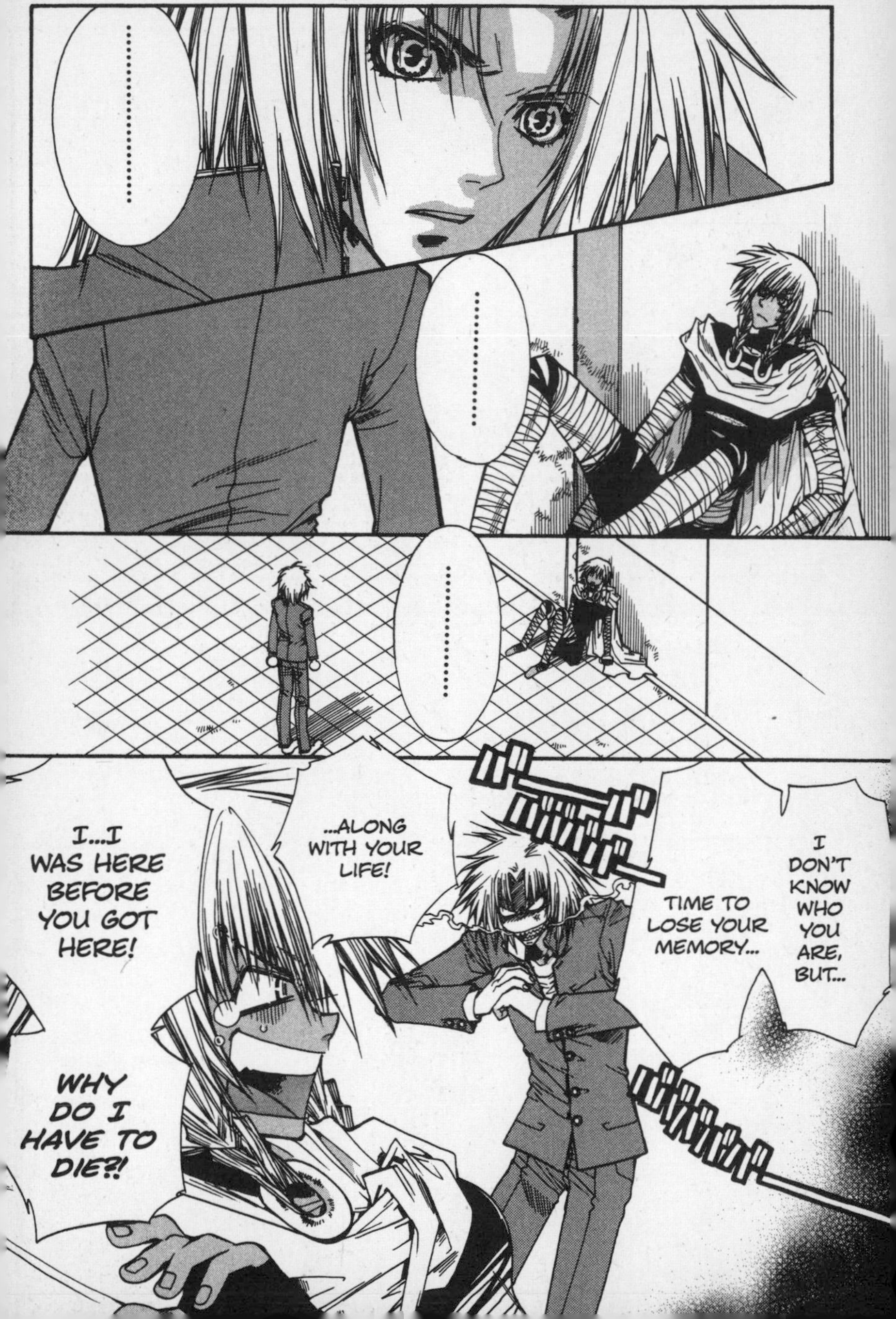
……
……
……
I DON'T KNOW WHO YOU ARE, BUT...
TIME TO LOSE YOUR MEMORY...
...ALONG WITH YOUR LIFE!
I...I WAS HERE BEFORE YOU GOT HERE!
WHY DO I HAVE TO DIE?!

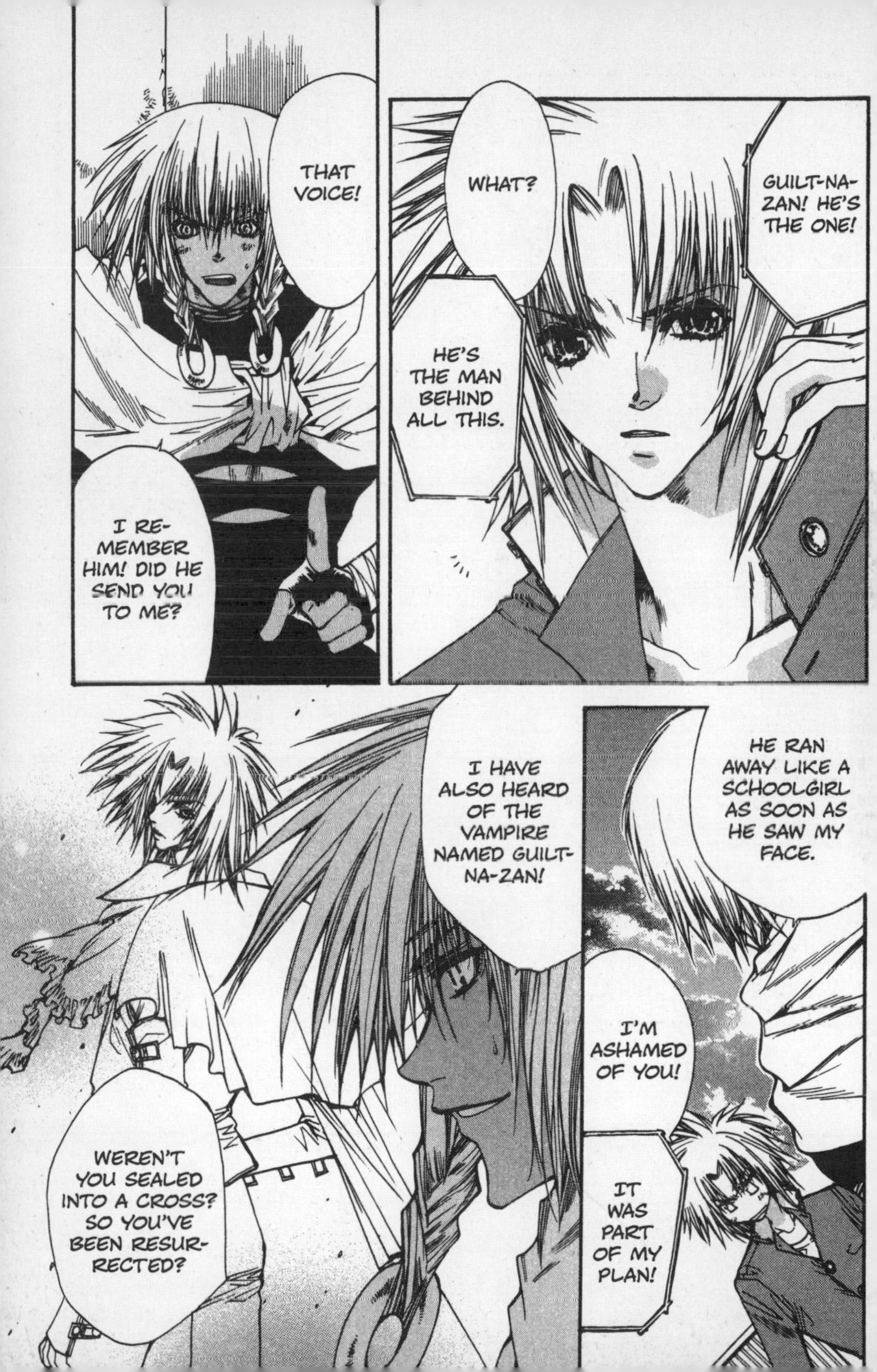
GUILT-NA-ZAN! HE'S THE ONE!
WHAT?
HE'S THE MAN BEHIND ALL THIS.
THAT VOICE!
I RE-MEMBER HIM! DID HE SEND YOU TO ME?
HE RAN AWAY LIKE A SCHOOLGIRL AS SOON AS HE SAW MY FACE.
I'M ASHAMED OF YOU!
IT WAS PART OF MY PLAN!
I HAVE ALSO HEARD OF THE VAMPIRE NAMED GUILT-NA-ZAN!
WEREN'T YOU SEALED INTO A CROSS? SO YOU'VE BEEN RESUR-RECTED?

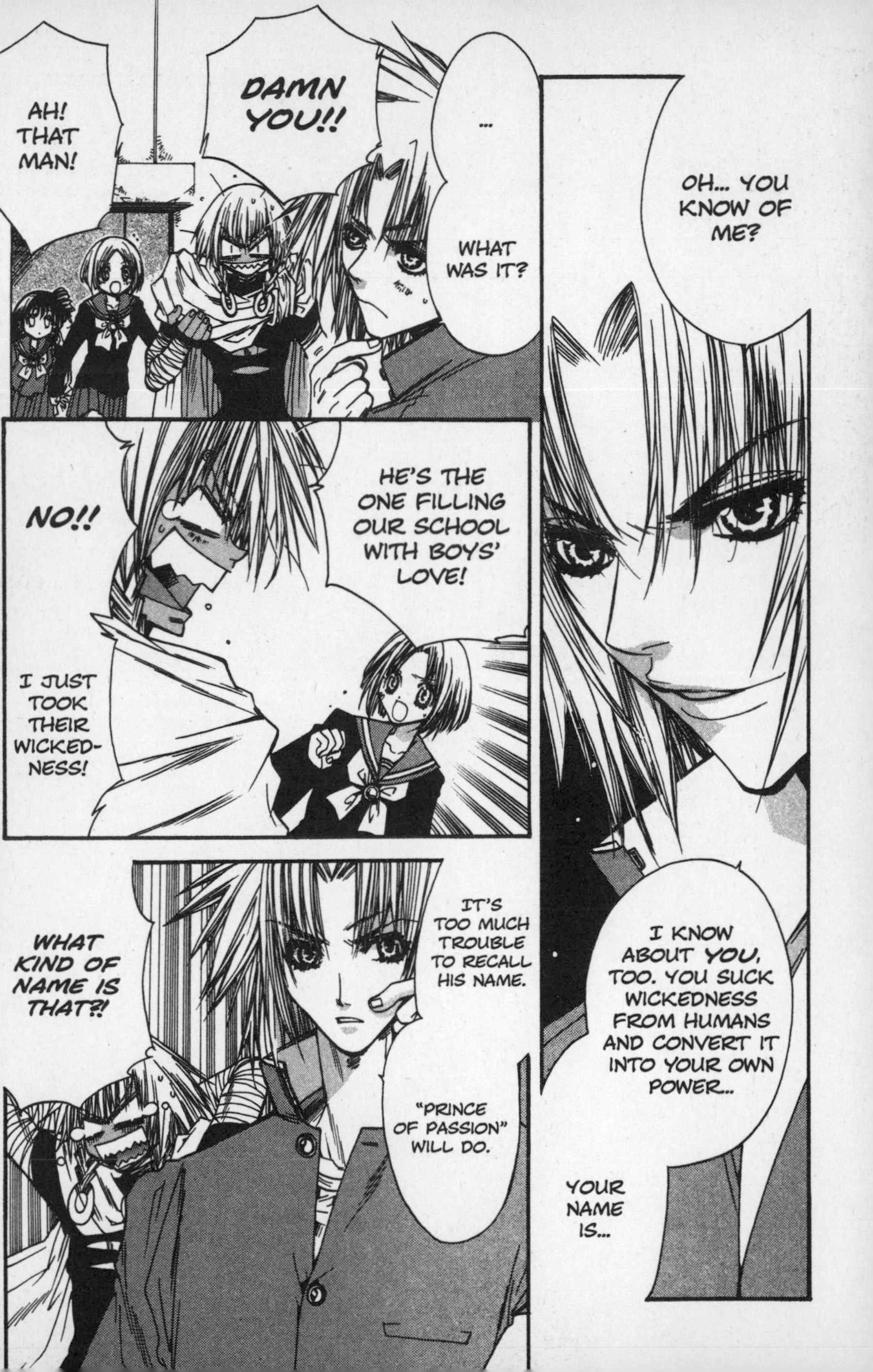
OH... YOU KNOW OF ME?
I KNOW ABOUT YOU, TOO. YOU SUCK WICKEDNESS FROM HUMANS AND CONVERT IT INTO YOUR OWN POWER...
YOUR NAME IS...
...
WHAT WAS IT?
DAMN YOU!!
AH! THAT MAN!
HE'S THE ONE FILLING OUR SCHOOL WITH BOYS' LOVE!
NO!!
I JUST TOOK THEIR WICKEDNESS!
IT'S TOO MUCH TROUBLE TO RECALL HIS NAME.
"PRINCE OF PASSION" WILL DO.
WHAT KIND OF NAME IS THAT?!

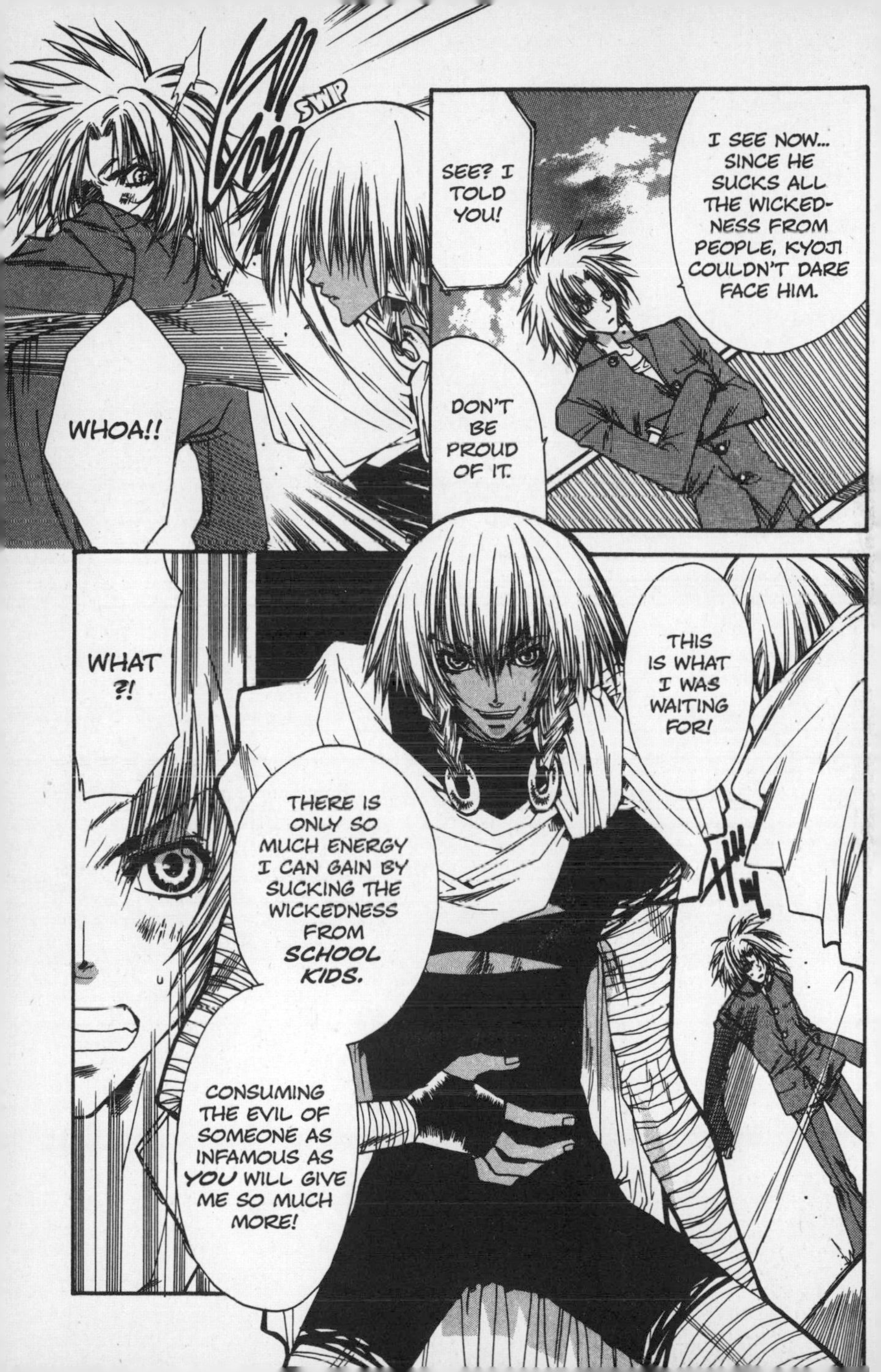
I SEE NOW... SINCE HE SUCKS ALL THE WICKEDNESS FROM PEOPLE, KYOJI COULDN'T DARE FACE HIM.
SEE? I TOLD YOU!
DON'T BE PROUD OF IT.
SWIP
WHOA!!
THIS IS WHAT I WAS WAITING FOR!
WHAT ?!
THERE IS ONLY SO MUCH ENERGY I CAN GAIN BY SUCKING THE WICKEDNESS FROM SCHOOL KIDS.
CONSUMING THE EVIL OF SOMEONE AS INFAMOUS AS YOU WILL GIVE ME SO MUCH MORE!

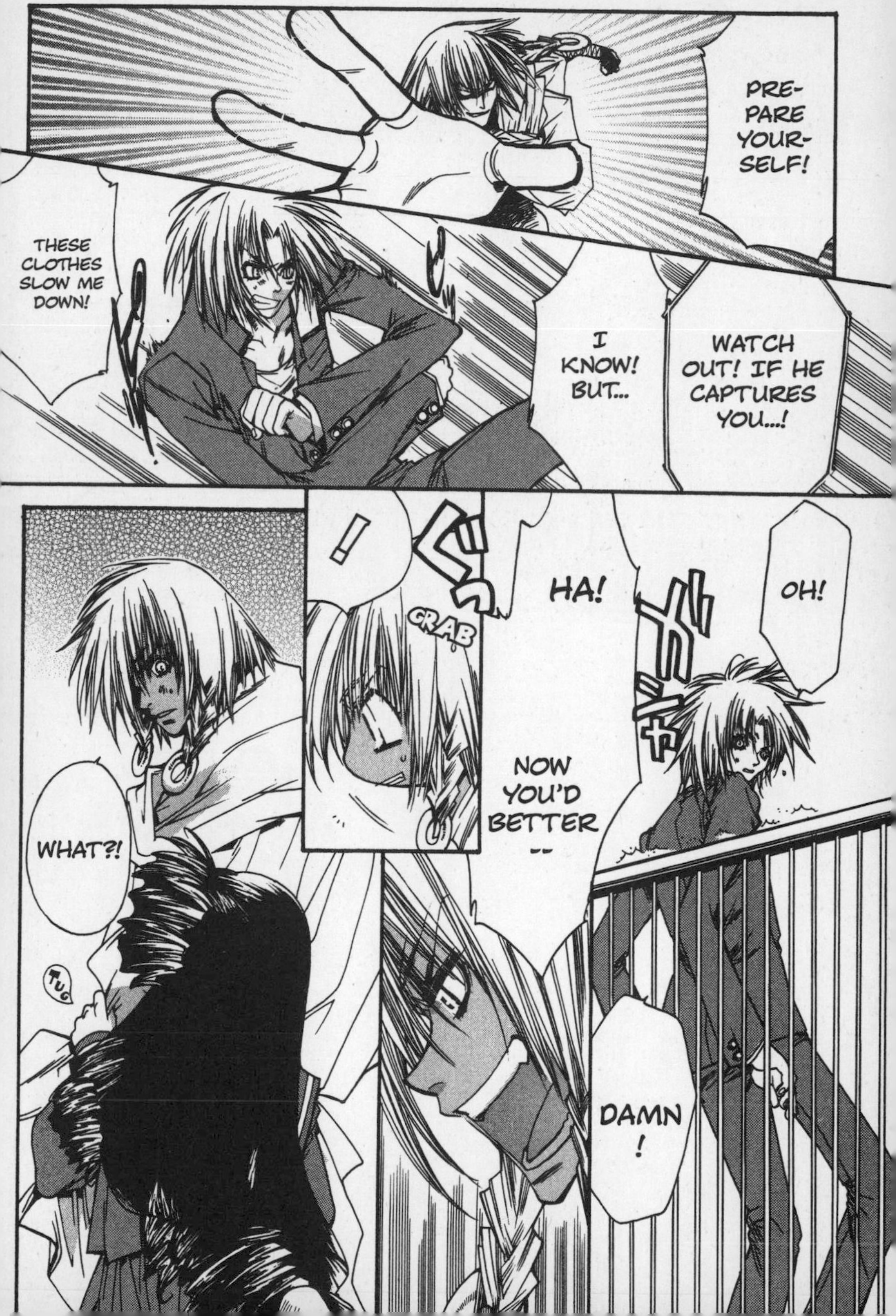
PRE-
PARE
YOUR-
SELF!
WATCH OUT! IF HE CAPTURES YOU...!
I KNOW! BUT...
THESE CLOTHES SLOW ME DOWN!
OH!
HA!
!
CRAB
NOW YOU'D BETTER --
DAMN !
WHAT?!
TUG

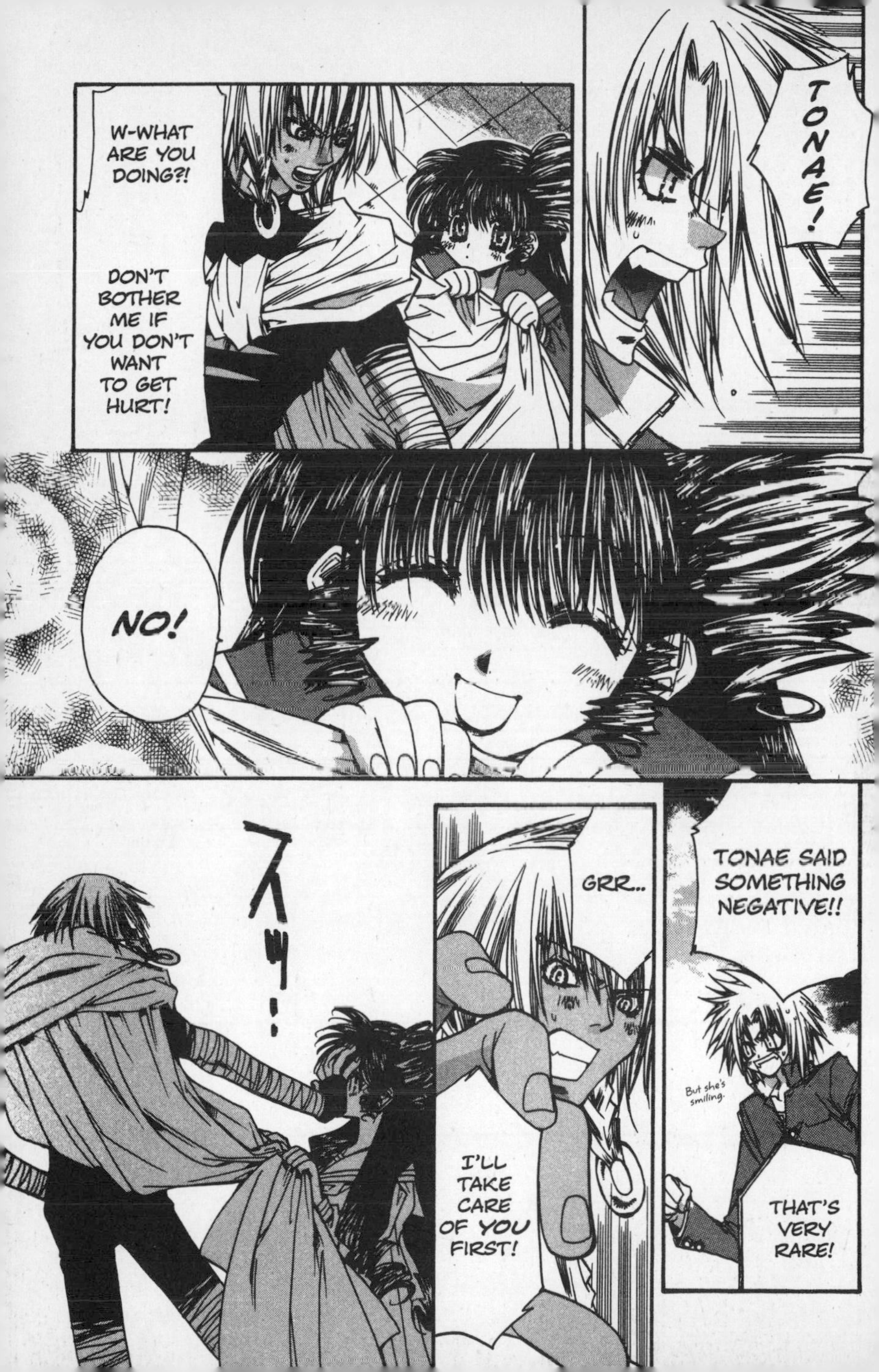
TONAE!
W-WHAT ARE YOU DOING?!
DON'T BOTHER ME IF YOU DON'T WANT TO GET HURT!
NO!
TONAE SAID SOMETHING NEGATIVE!!
But she's smiling.
THAT'S VERY RARE!
GRR...
I'LL TAKE CARE OF YOU FIRST!
スッ!!

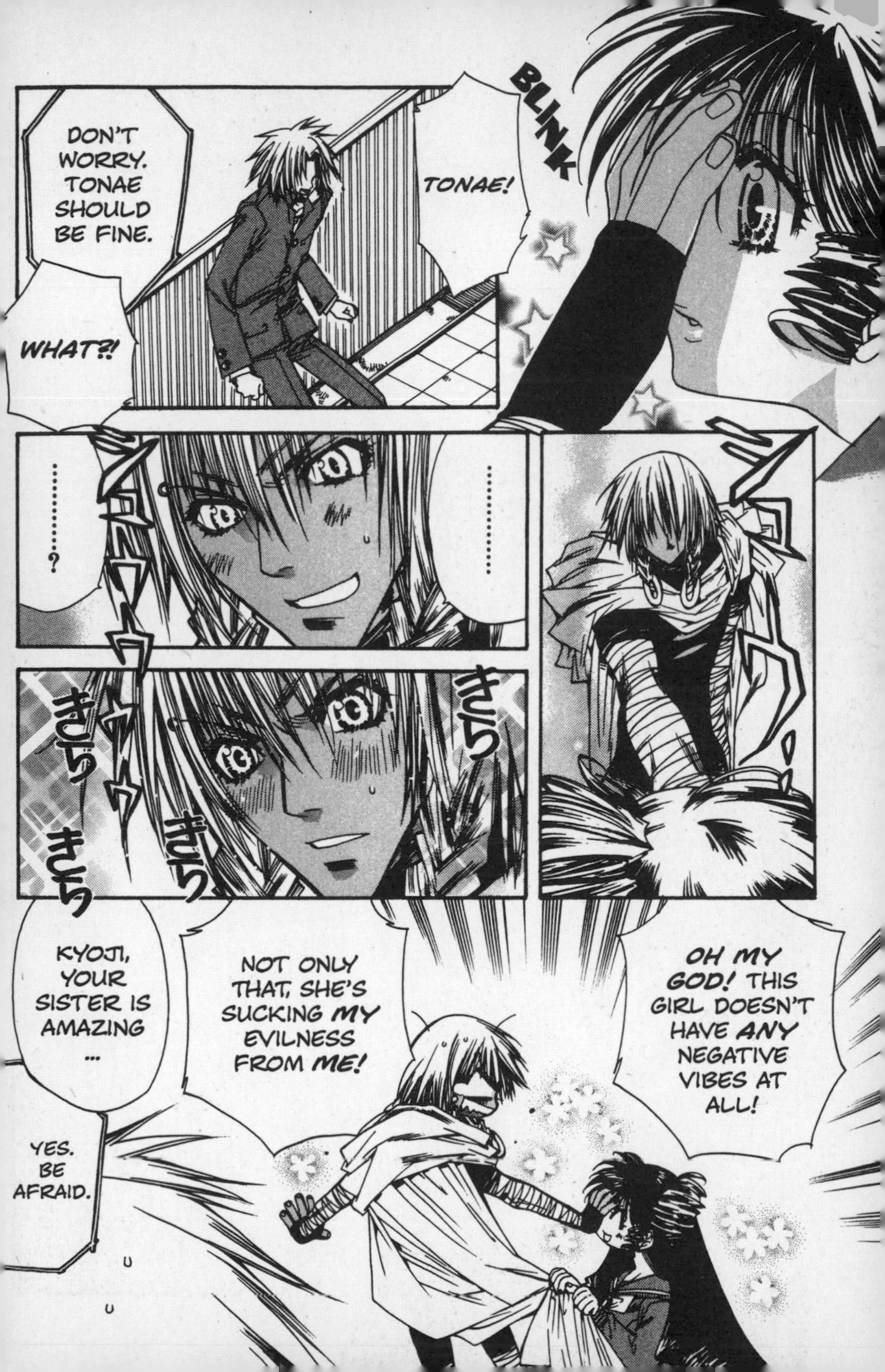
BLINK
TONAE!
DON'T WORRY. TONAE SHOULD BE FINE.
WHAT?!
......
......?
きら
きら
きら
きら
OH MY GOD! THIS GIRL DOESN'T HAVE ANY NEGATIVE VIBES AT ALL!
NOT ONLY THAT, SHE'S SUCKING MY EVILNESS FROM ME!
KYOJI, YOUR SISTER IS AMAZING ...
YES. BE AFRAID.

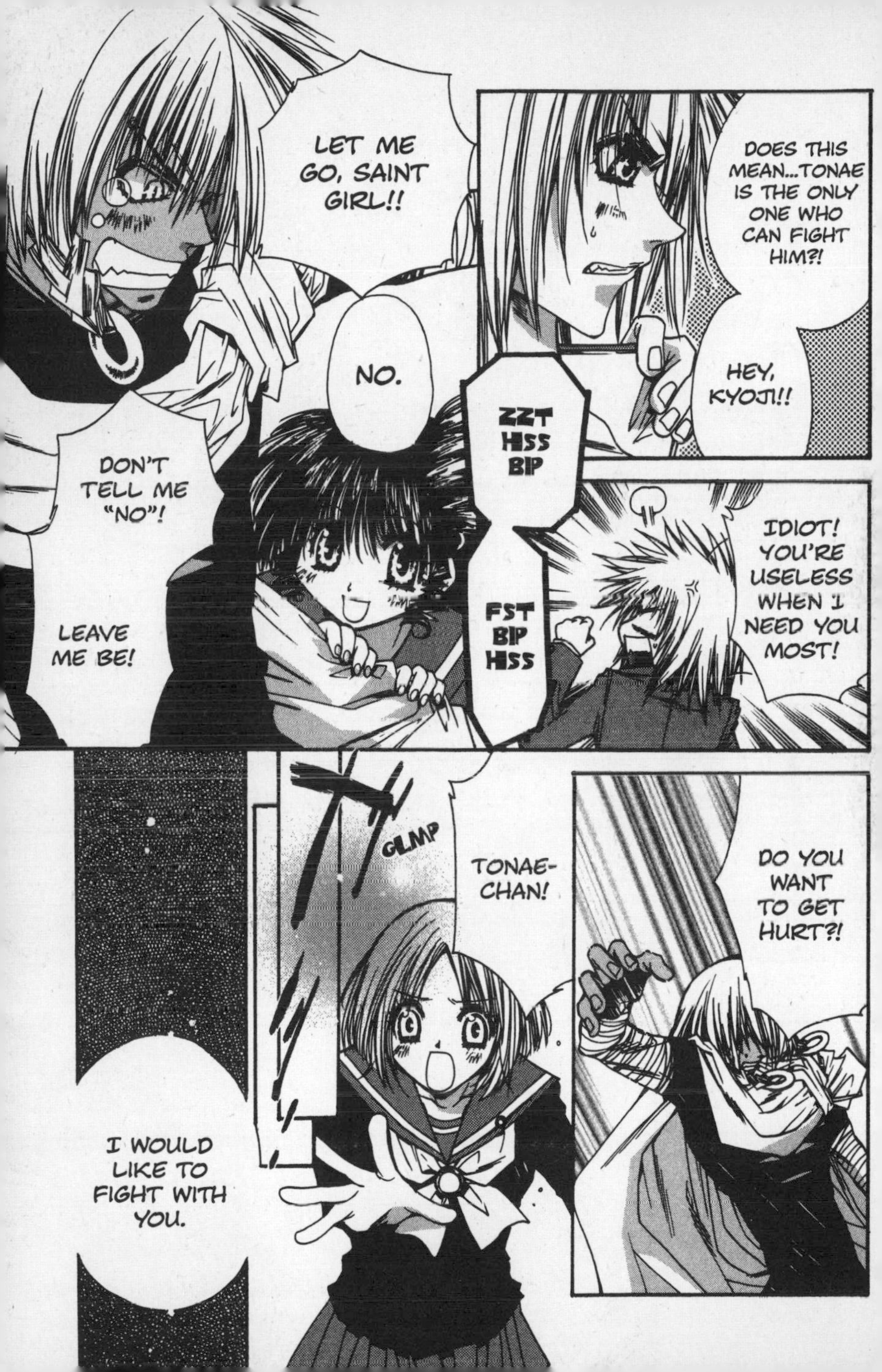
DOES THIS MEAN...TONAE IS THE ONLY ONE WHO CAN FIGHT HIM?!
HEY, KYOJI!!
IDIOT! YOU'RE USELESS WHEN I NEED YOU MOST!
LET ME GO, SAINT GIRL!!
NO.
ZZT HISS BIP
FST BIP HISS
DON'T TELL ME "NO"!
LEAVE ME BE!
DO YOU WANT TO GET HURT?!
GLMP
TONAE-CHAN!
I WOULD LIKE TO FIGHT WITH YOU.

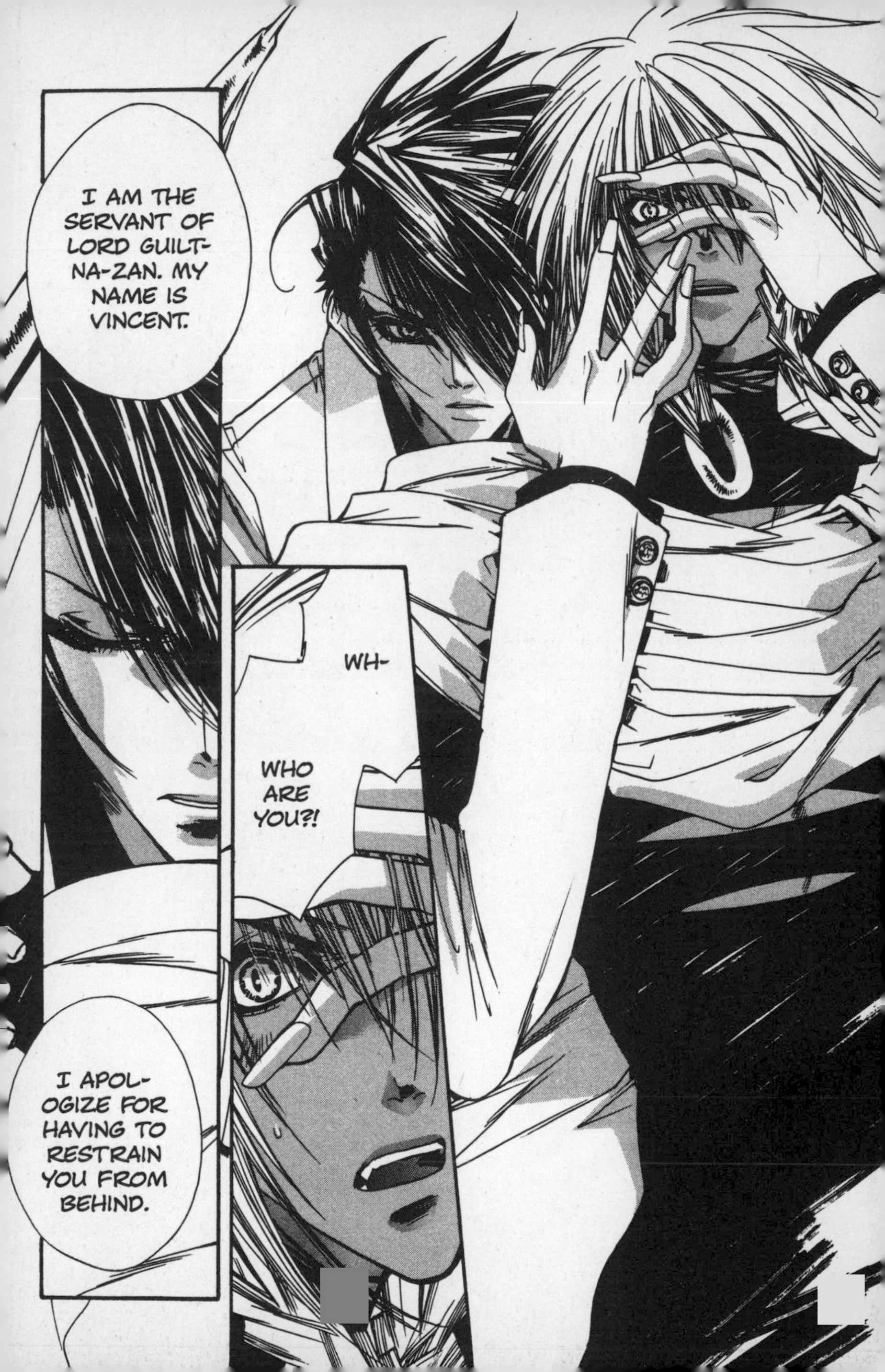
WH-
WHO ARE YOU?!
I AM THE SERVANT OF LORD GUILT-NA-ZAN. MY NAME IS VINCENT.
I APOLOGIZE FOR HAVING TO RESTRAIN YOU FROM BEHIND.

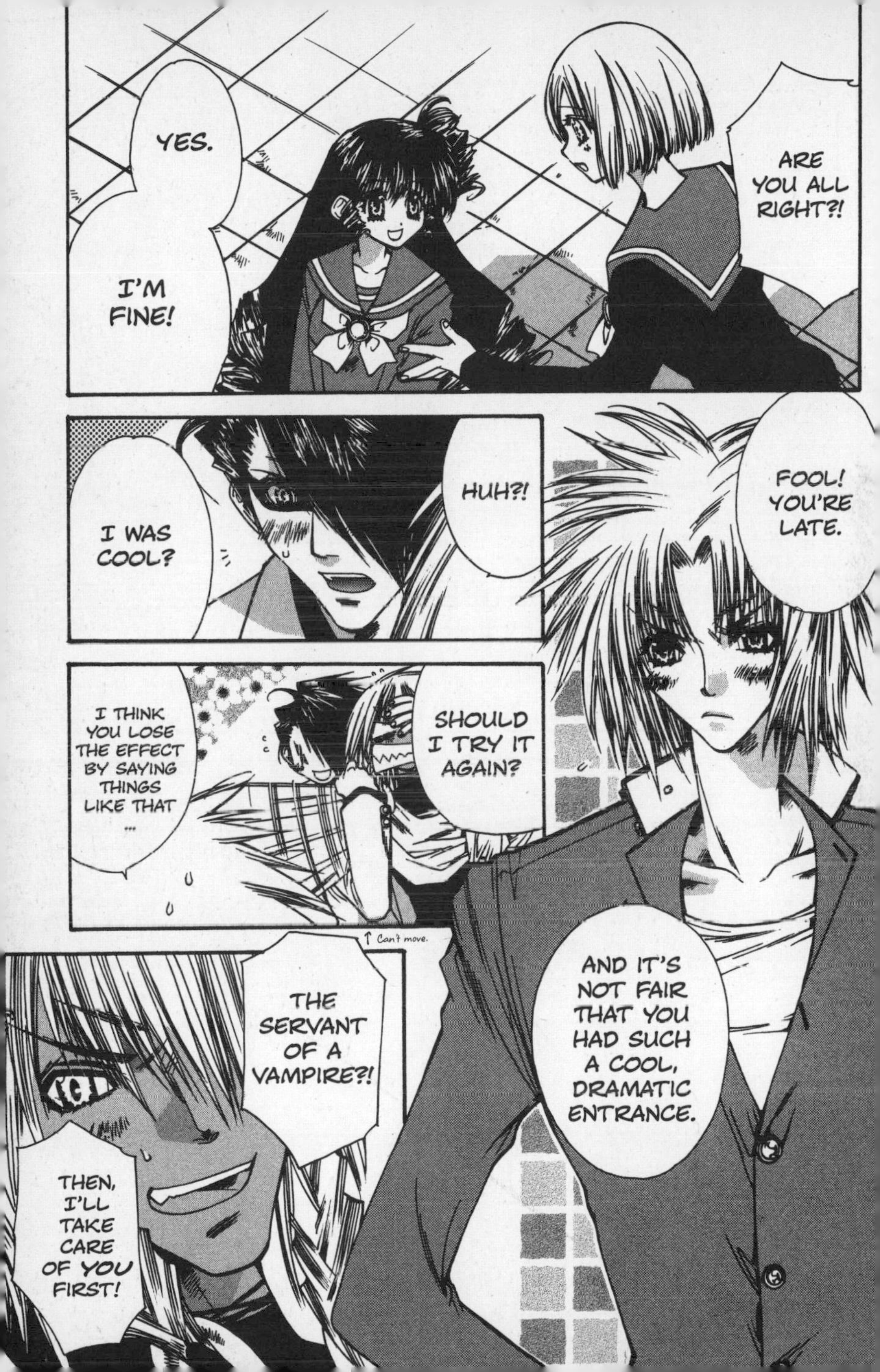
ARE YOU ALL RIGHT?!
YES.
I'M FINE!
FOOL! YOU'RE LATE.
AND IT'S NOT FAIR THAT YOU HAD SUCH A COOL, DRAMATIC ENTRANCE.
HUH?!
I WAS COOL?
SHOULD I TRY IT AGAIN?
I THINK YOU LOSE THE EFFECT BY SAYING THINGS LIKE THAT ...
↑ Can't move.
THE SERVANT OF A VAMPIRE?!
THEN, I'LL TAKE CARE OF YOU FIRST!

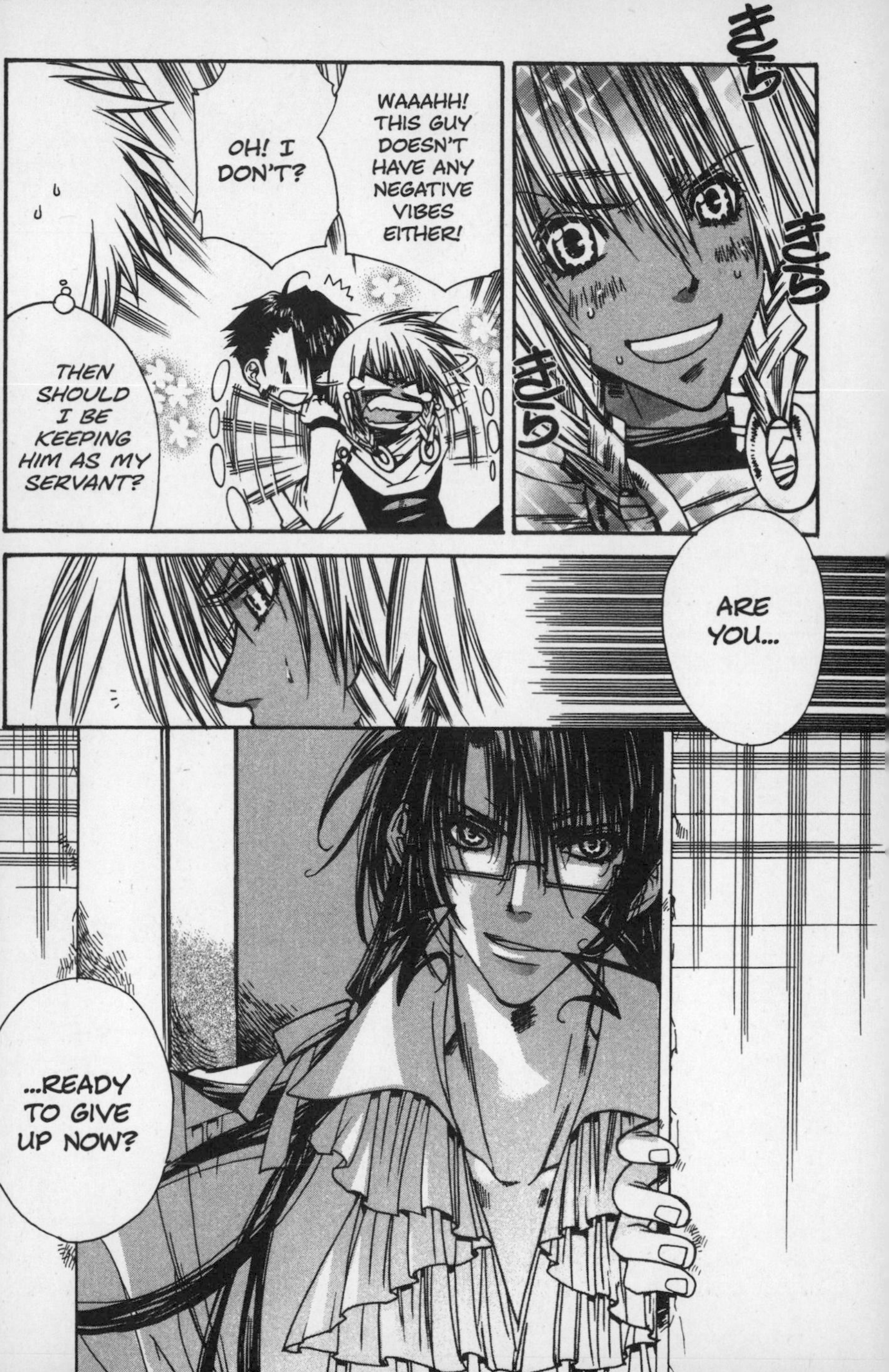
きら
きら
きら
WAAAHH! THIS GUY DOESN'T HAVE ANY NEGATIVE VIBES EITHER!
OH! I DON'T?
THEN SHOULD I BE KEEPING HIM AS MY SERVANT?
ARE YOU...
...READY TO GIVE UP NOW?

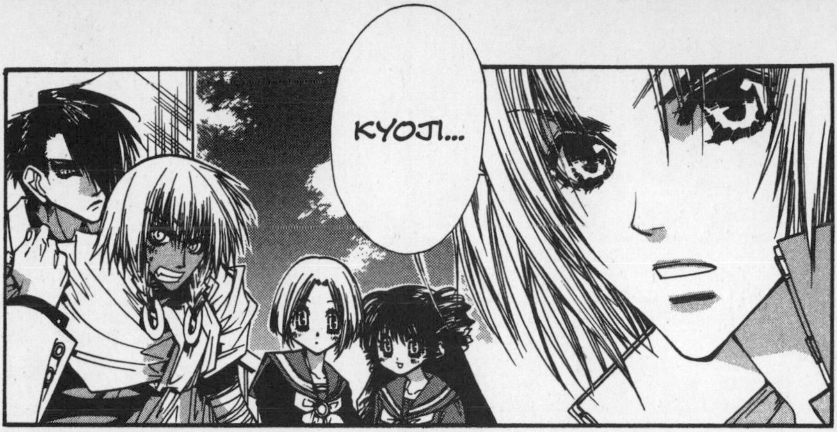
KYOJI...

#5.9 SCHOOL WARS FINAL

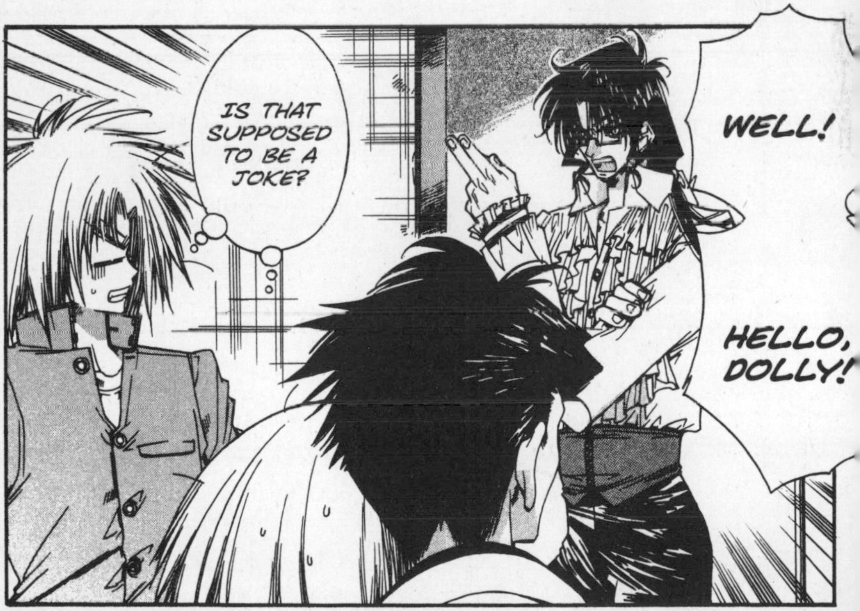
WELL!
HELLO, DOLLY!
IS THAT SUPPOSED TO BE A JOKE?

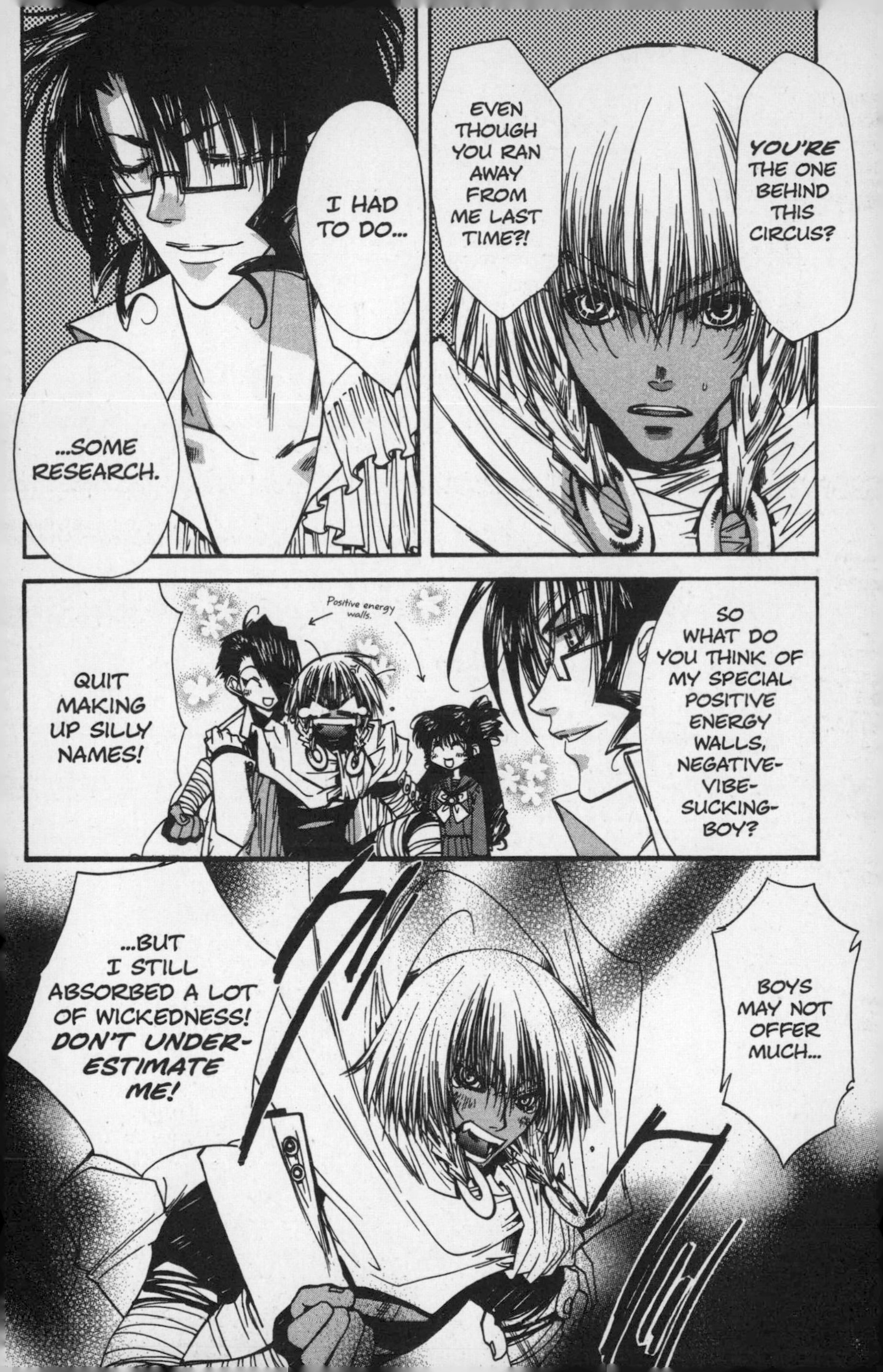
YOU'RE THE ONE BEHIND THIS CIRCUS?
EVEN THOUGH YOU RAN AWAY FROM ME LAST TIME?!
I HAD TO DO...
...SOME RESEARCH.
SO WHAT DO YOU THINK OF MY SPECIAL POSITIVE ENERGY WALLS, NEGATIVE-VIBE-SUCKING-BOY?
Positive energy walls.
QUIT MAKING UP SILLY NAMES!
BOYS MAY NOT OFFER MUCH...
...BUT I STILL ABSORBED A LOT OF WICKEDNESS! DON'T UNDER-ESTIMATE ME!

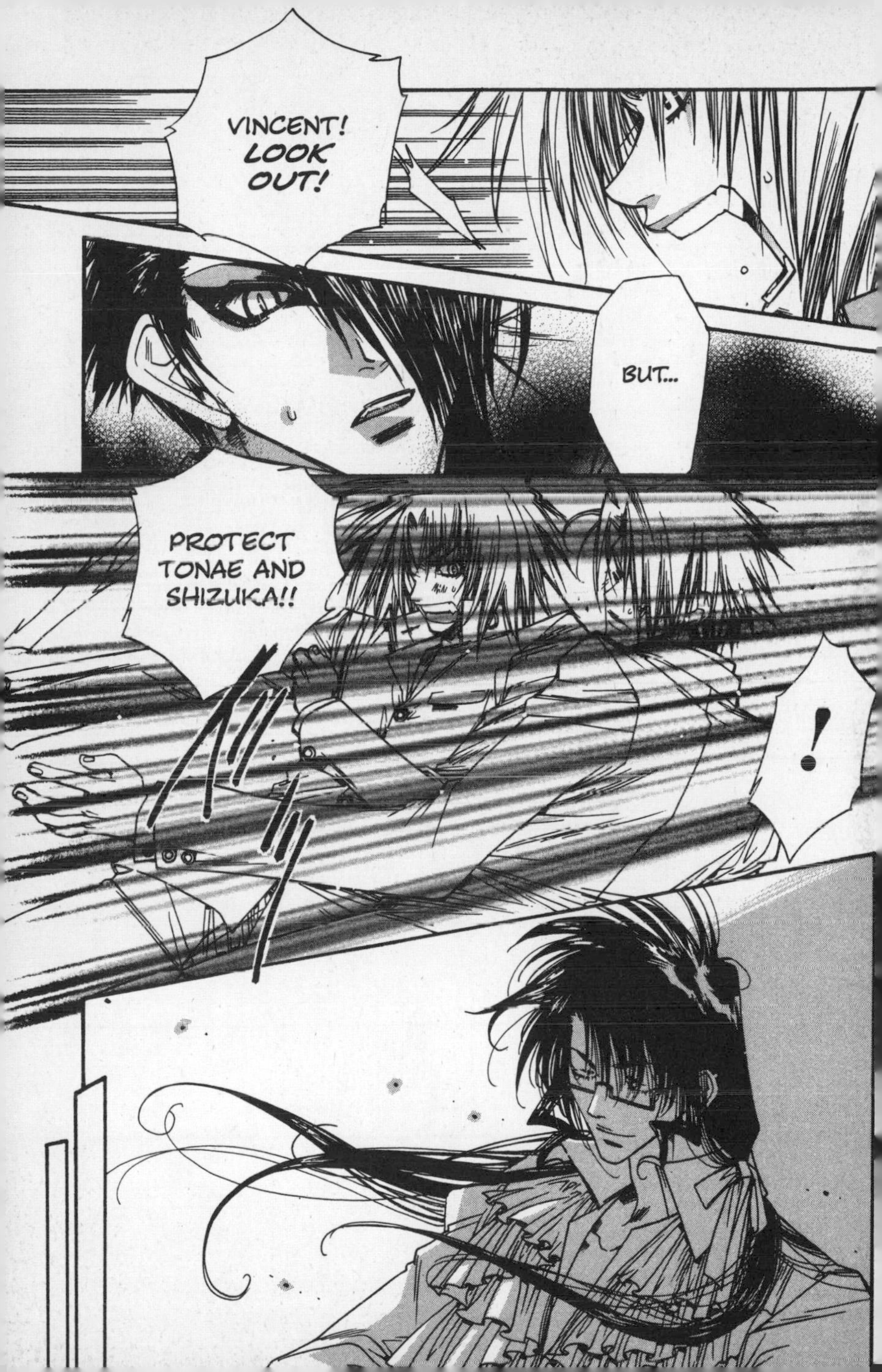
VINCENT! LOOK OUT!
BUT...
PROTECT TONAE AND SHIZUKA!!
!

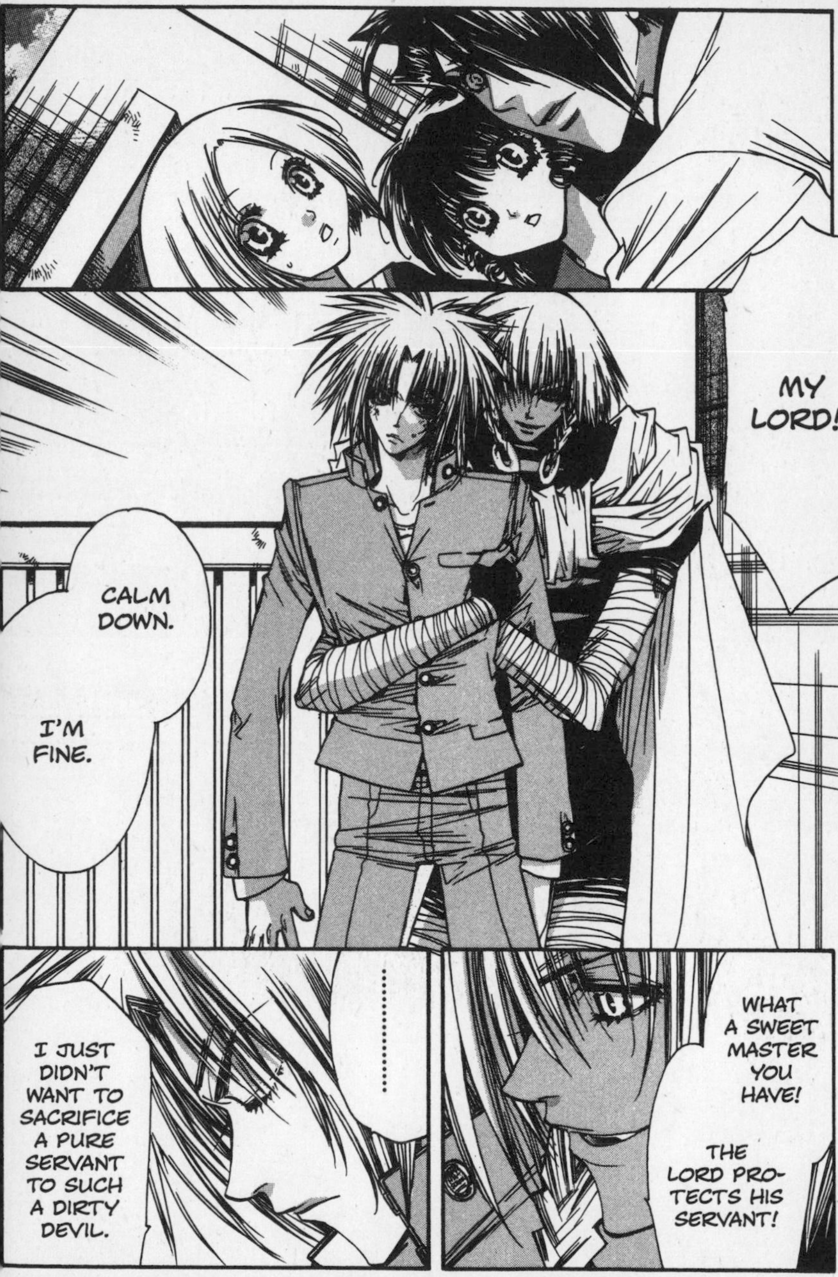
MY LORD!!
CALM DOWN.
I'M FINE.
WHAT A SWEET MASTER YOU HAVE!
THE LORD PROTECTS HIS SERVANT!
......
I JUST DIDN'T WANT TO SACRIFICE A PURE SERVANT TO SUCH A DIRTY DEVIL.

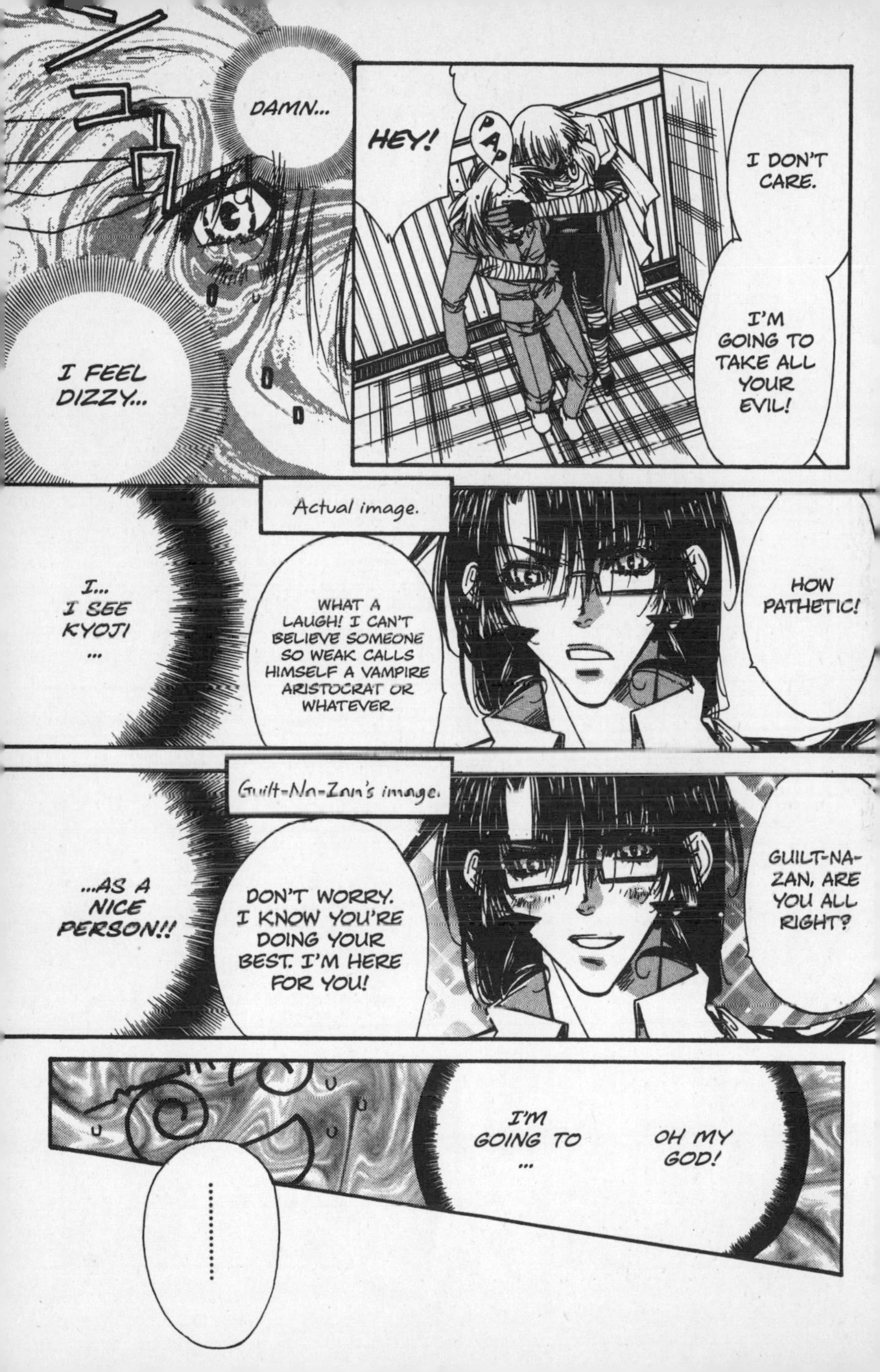
I DON'T CARE.
I'M GOING TO TAKE ALL YOUR EVIL!
PAP
HEY!
DAMN...
I FEEL DIZZY...
Actual image.
HOW PATHETIC!
WHAT A LAUGH! I CAN'T BELIEVE SOMEONE SO WEAK CALLS HIMSELF A VAMPIRE ARISTOCRAT OR WHATEVER.
I... I SEE KYOJI ...
Guilt-Na-Zan's image.
GUILT-NA-ZAN, ARE YOU ALL RIGHT?
DON'T WORRY. I KNOW YOU'RE DOING YOUR BEST. I'M HERE FOR YOU!
...AS A NICE PERSON!!
OH MY GOD!
I'M GOING TO ...
....

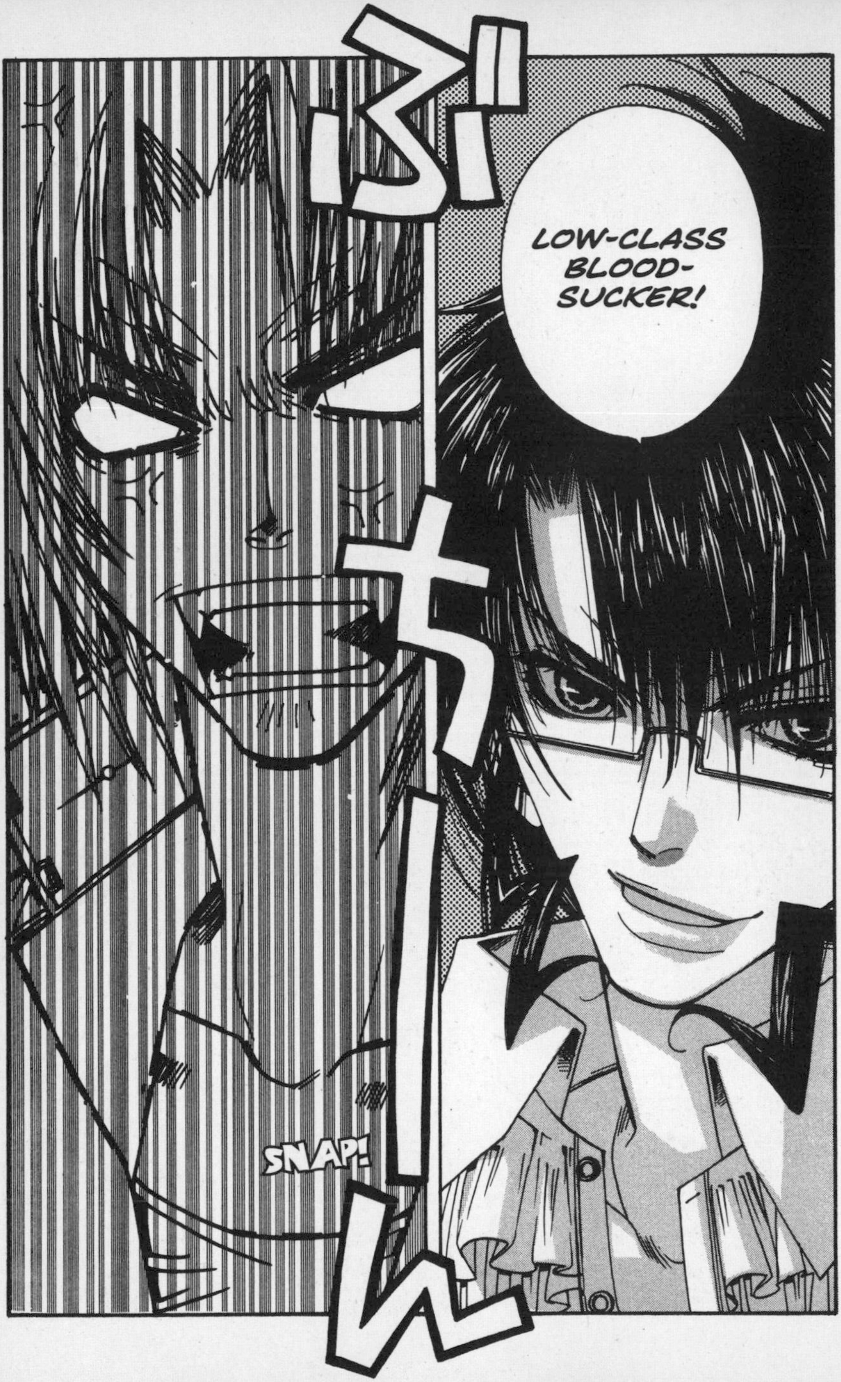
LOW-CLASS BLOOD-SUCKER!
ぶちーん
SNAP!

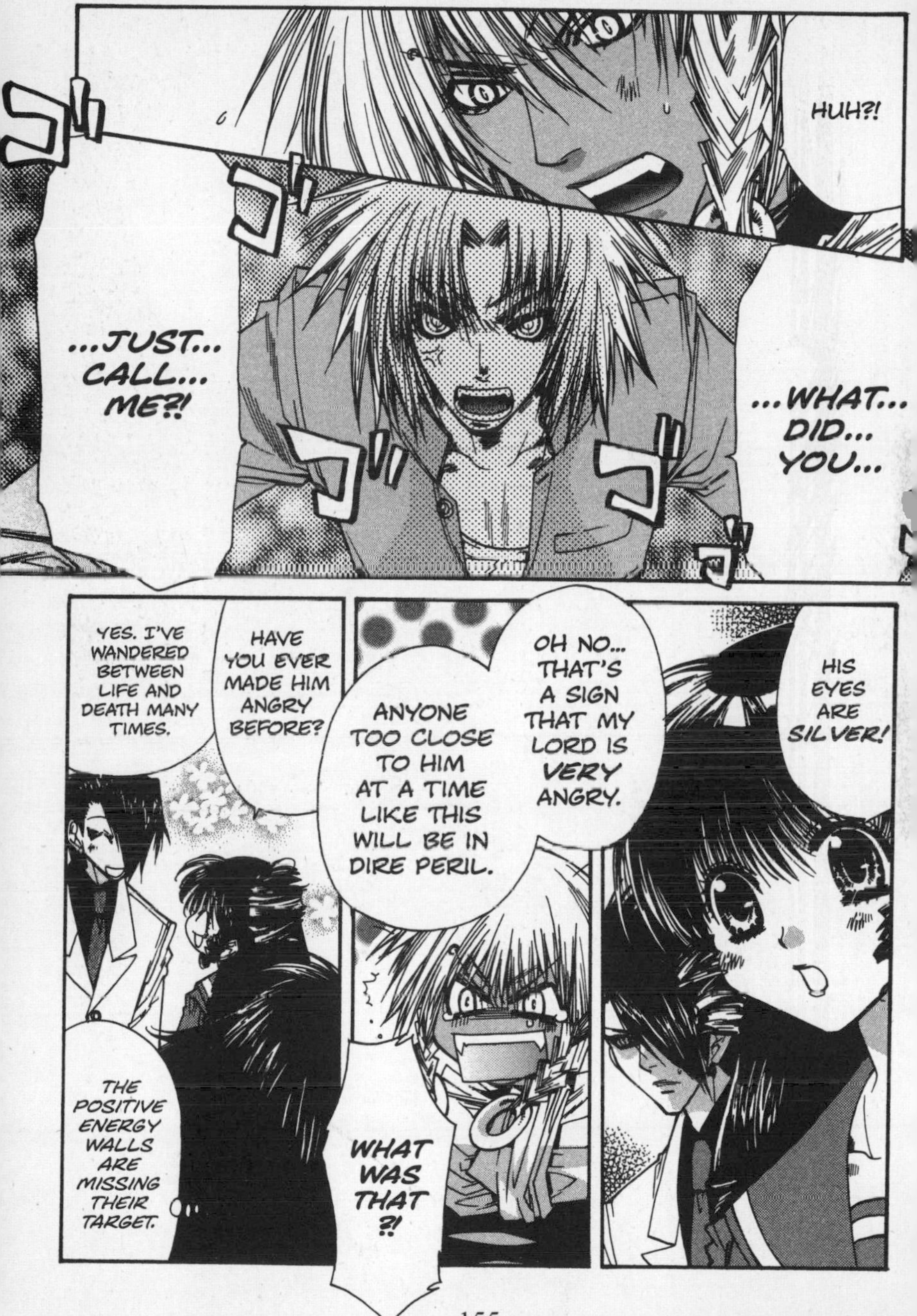
HUH?!
...WHAT... DID... YOU...
...JUST... CALL... ME?!
HIS EYES ARE SILVER!
OH NO... THAT'S A SIGN THAT MY LORD IS VERY ANGRY.
ANYONE TOO CLOSE TO HIM AT A TIME LIKE THIS WILL BE IN DIRE PERIL.
WHAT WAS THAT ?!
HAVE YOU EVER MADE HIM ANGRY BEFORE?
YES. I'VE WANDERED BETWEEN LIFE AND DEATH MANY TIMES.
THE POSITIVE ENERGY WALLS ARE MISSING THEIR TARGET.

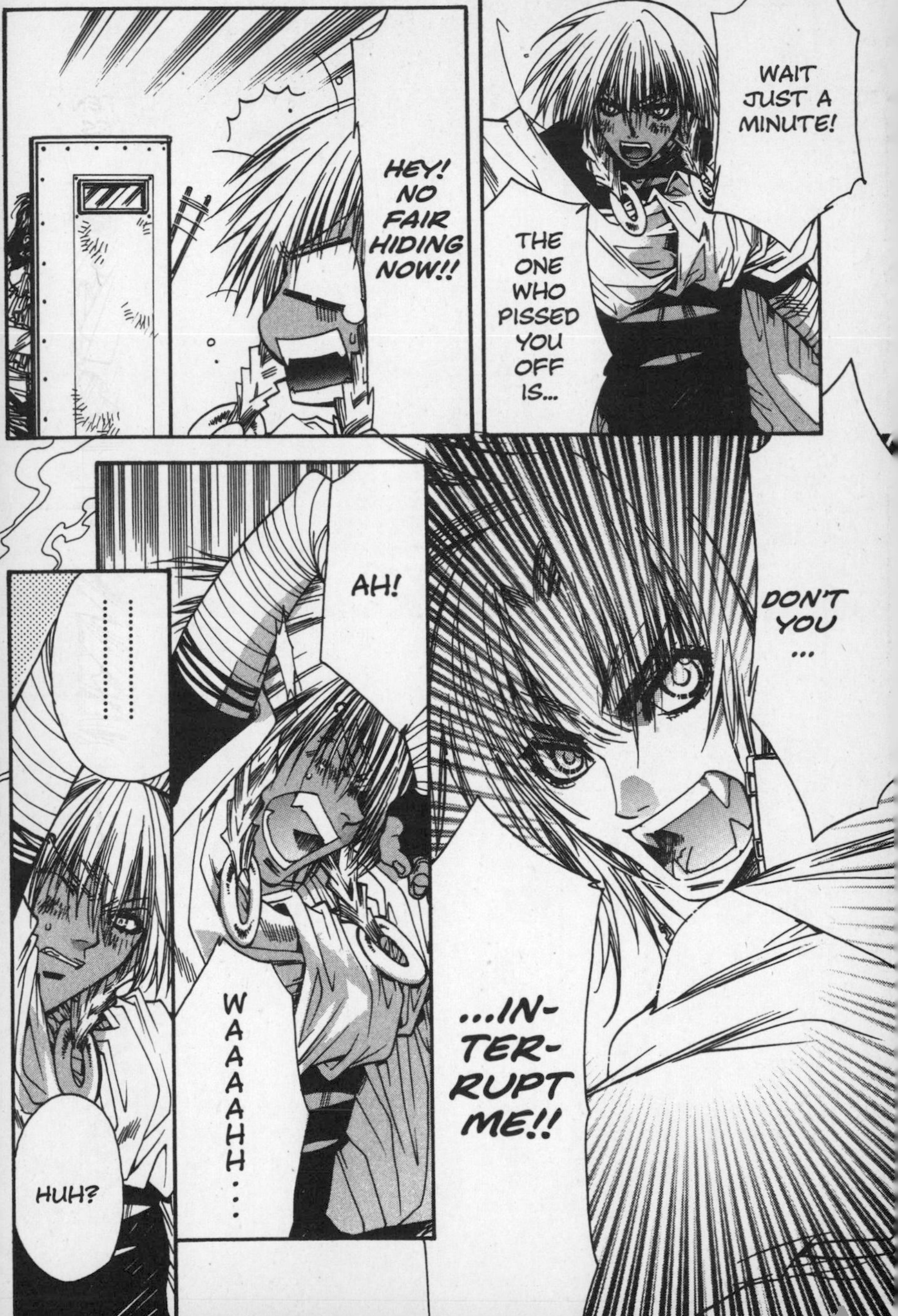
WAIT JUST A MINUTE!
THE ONE WHO PISSED YOU OFF IS...
HEY! NO FAIR HIDING NOW!!
DON'T YOU ...
...IN-TER-RUPT ME!!
AH!
WAAAAAHH...
......
HUH?

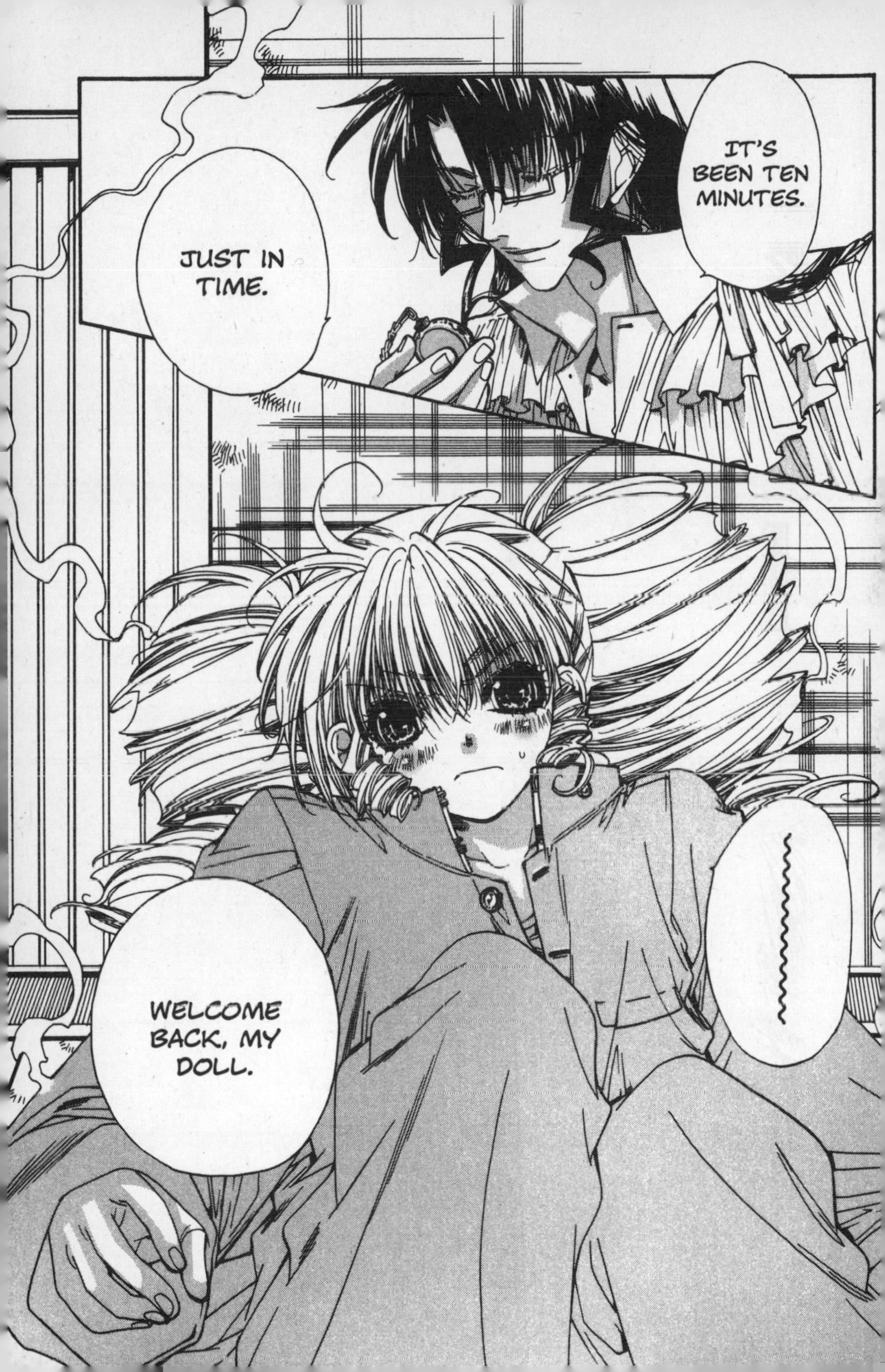
IT'S BEEN TEN MINUTES.
JUST IN TIME.
WELCOME BACK, MY DOLL.

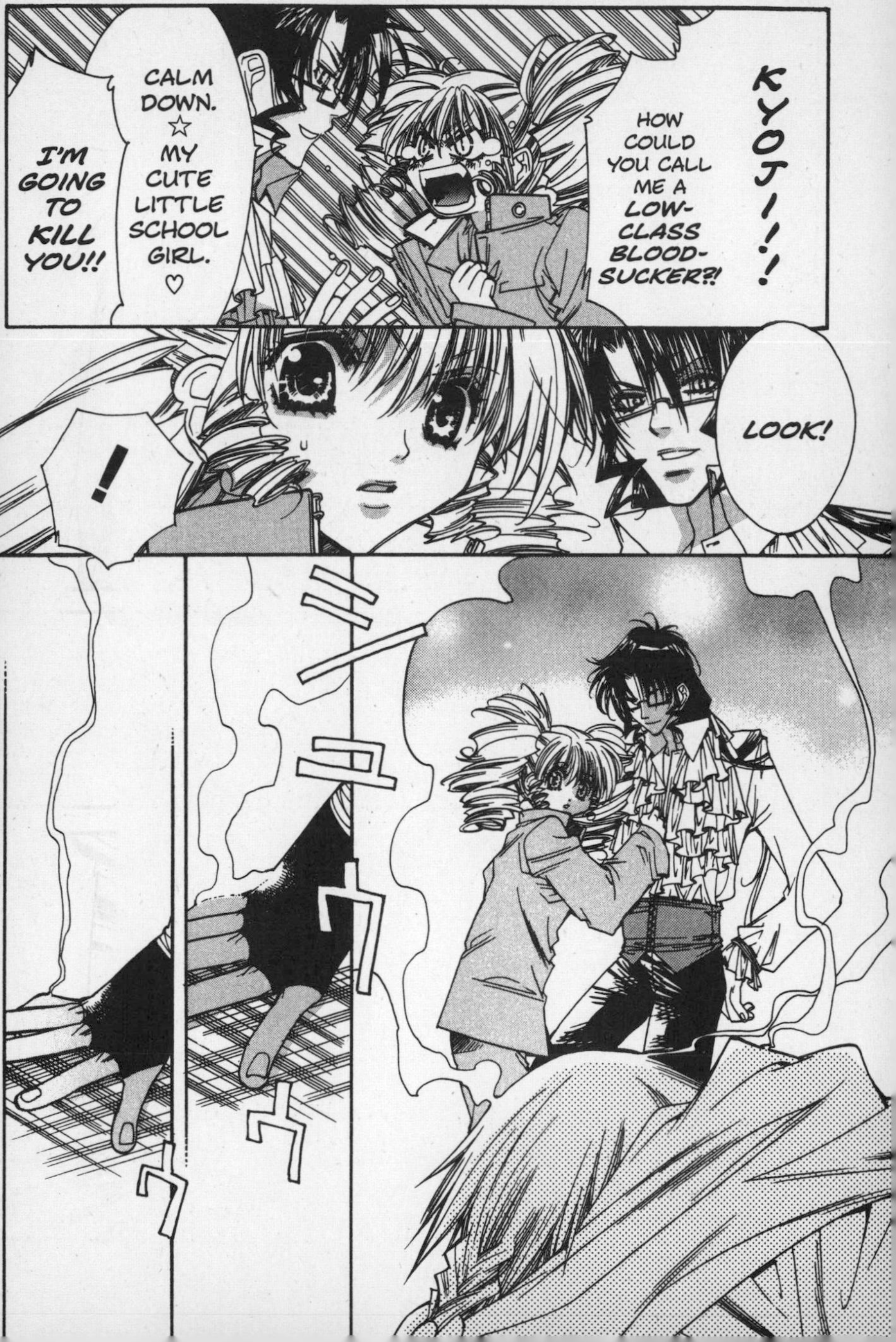
KYOJI!!
HOW COULD YOU CALL ME A LOW-CLASS BLOOD-SUCKER?!
CALM DOWN. ☆ MY CUTE LITTLE SCHOOL GIRL. ♡
I'M GOING TO KILL YOU!!
LOOK!
!

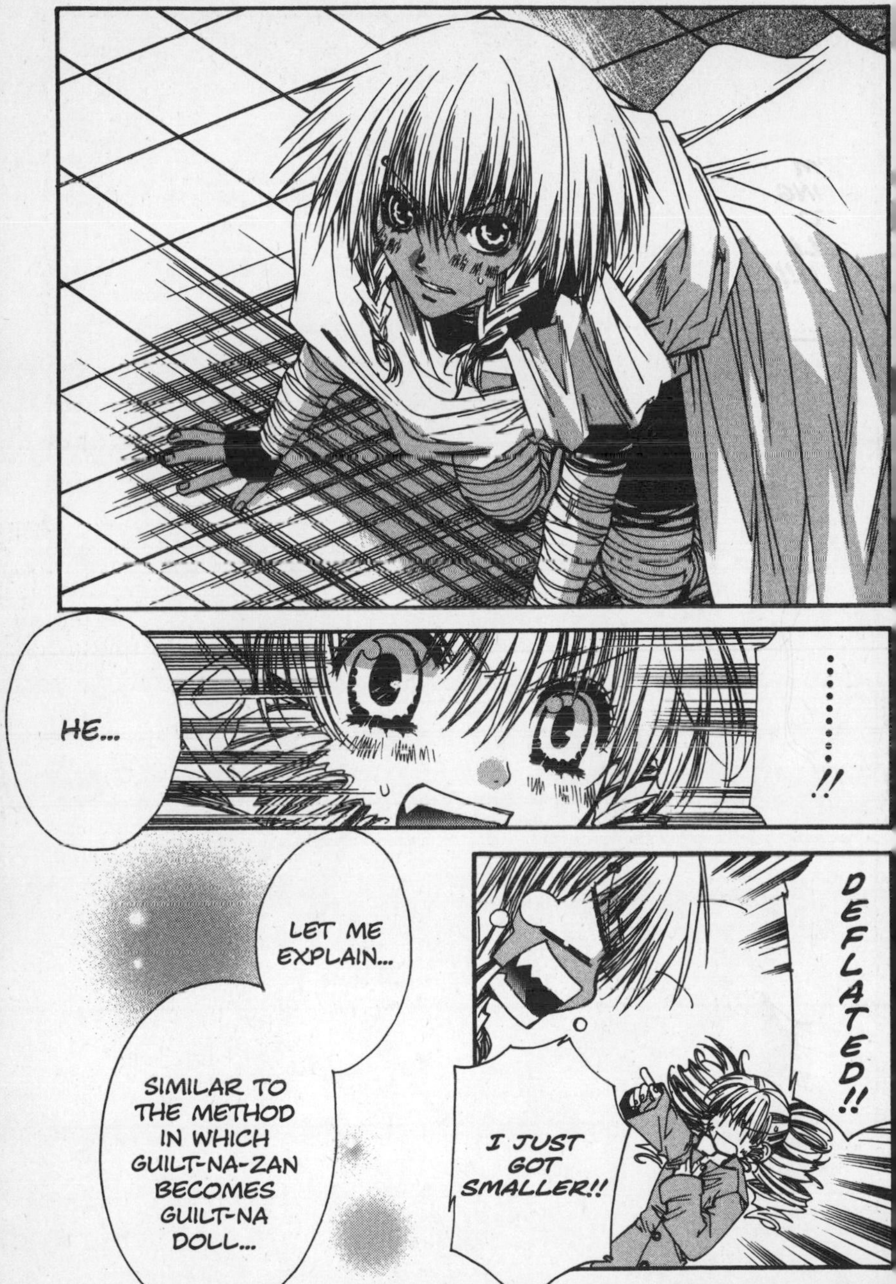

........!!
HE...
DEFLATED!!
I JUST GOT SMALLER!!
LET ME EXPLAIN...
SIMILAR TO THE METHOD IN WHICH GUILT-NA-ZAN BECOMES GUILT-NA DOLL...

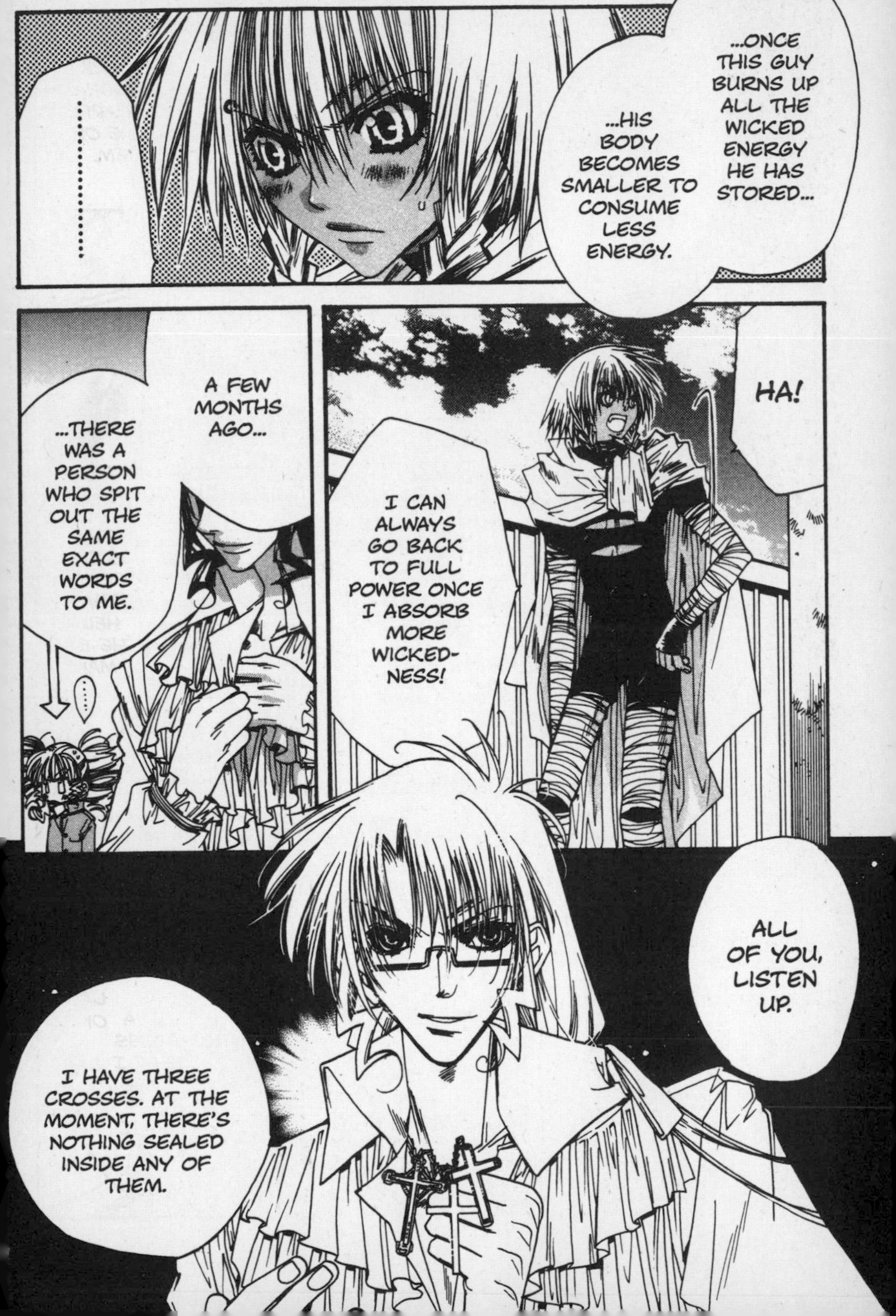
...ONCE THIS GUY BURNS UP ALL THE WICKED ENERGY HE HAS STORED...
...HIS BODY BECOMES SMALLER TO CONSUME LESS ENERGY.
......
HA!
I CAN ALWAYS GO BACK TO FULL POWER ONCE I ABSORB MORE WICKED-NESS!
A FEW MONTHS AGO...
...THERE WAS A PERSON WHO SPIT OUT THE SAME EXACT WORDS TO ME.
......
ALL OF YOU, LISTEN UP.
I HAVE THREE CROSSES. AT THE MOMENT, THERE'S NOTHING SEALED INSIDE ANY OF THEM.

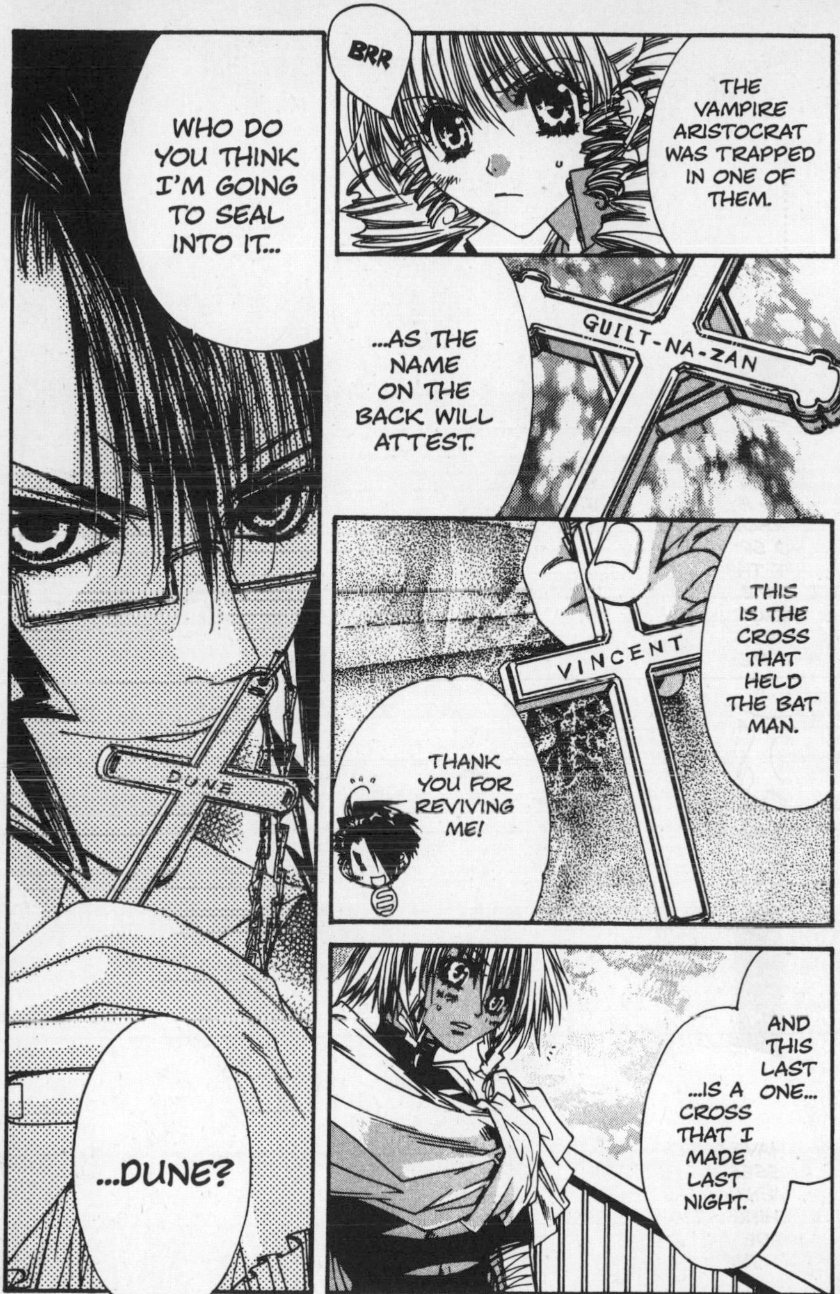

BRR
THE VAMPIRE ARISTOCRAT WAS TRAPPED IN ONE OF THEM.
GUILT-NA-ZAN
...AS THE NAME ON THE BACK WILL ATTEST.
VINCENT
THIS IS THE CROSS THAT HELD THE BAT MAN.
THANK YOU FOR REVIVING ME!
AND THIS LAST ONE...
...IS A CROSS THAT I MADE LAST NIGHT.
WHO DO YOU THINK I'M GOING TO SEAL INTO IT...
DUNE
...DUNE?

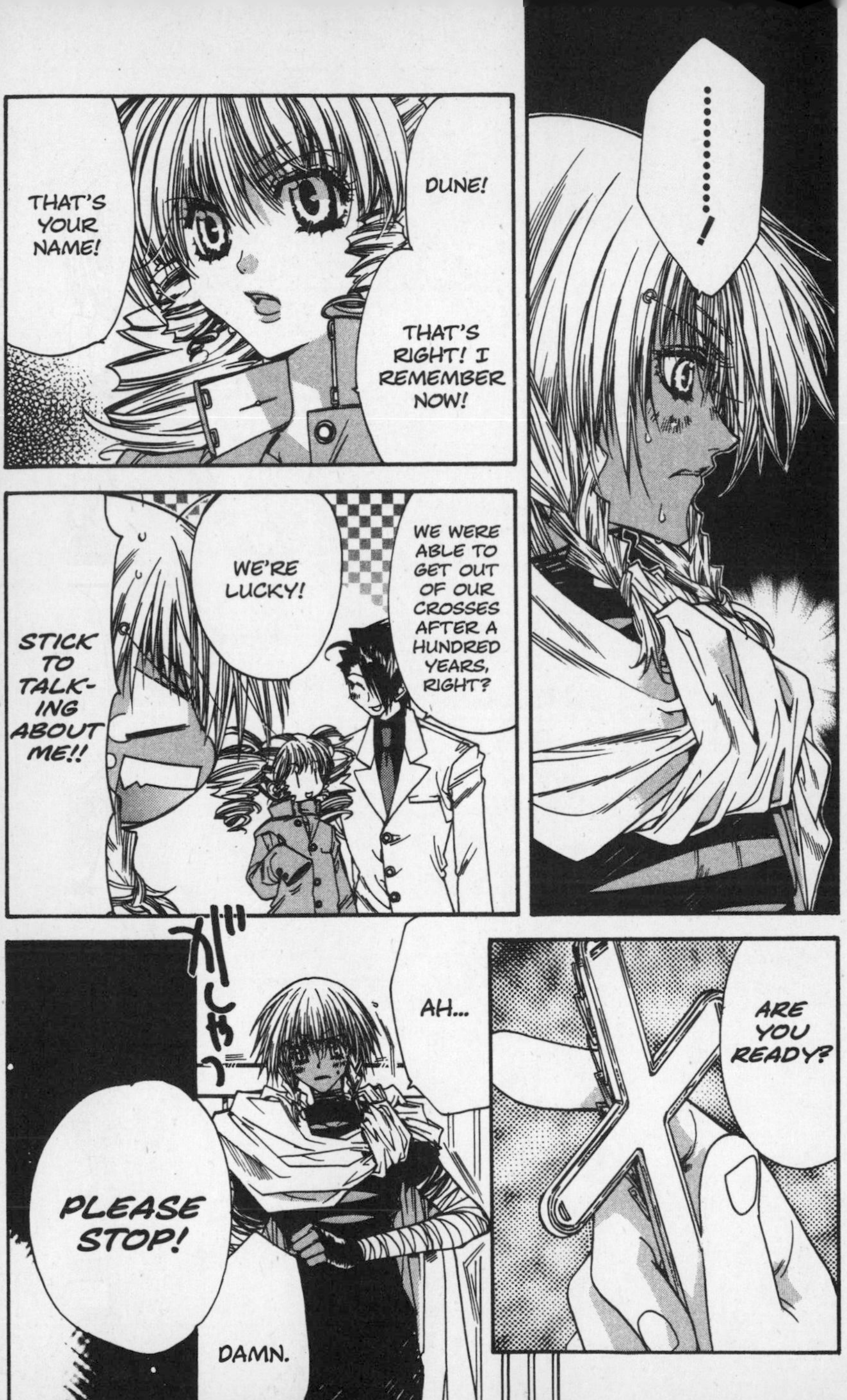
......!
DUNE!
THAT'S RIGHT! I REMEMBER NOW!
THAT'S YOUR NAME!
WE WERE ABLE TO GET OUT OF OUR CROSSES AFTER A HUNDRED YEARS, RIGHT?
WE'RE LUCKY!
STICK TO TALKING ABOUT ME!!
ARE YOU READY?
AH...
PLEASE STOP!
DAMN.

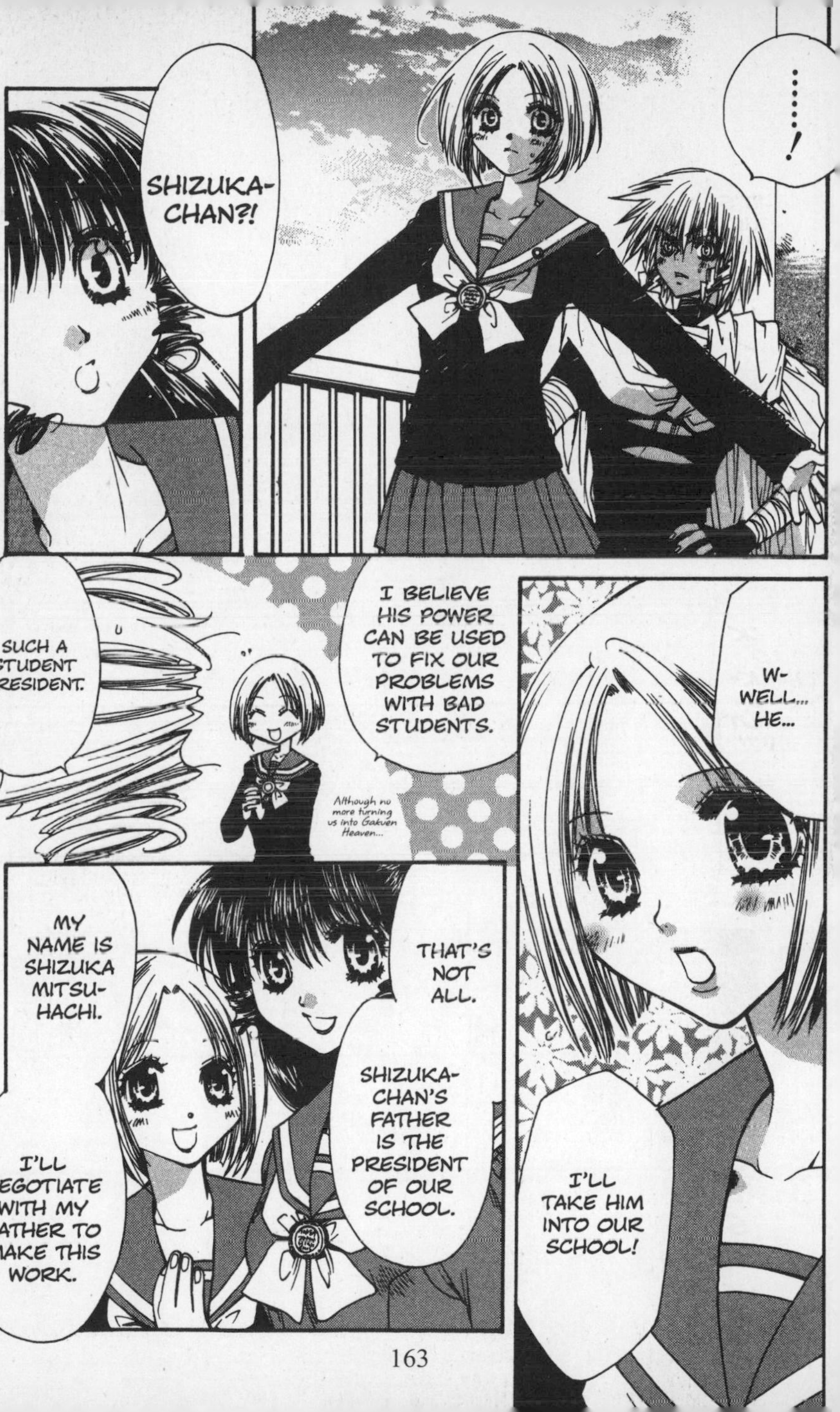
......!
SHIZUKA-CHAN?!
W-WELL... HE...
I'LL TAKE HIM INTO OUR SCHOOL!
I BELIEVE HIS POWER CAN BE USED TO FIX OUR PROBLEMS WITH BAD STUDENTS.
SUCH A STUDENT PRESIDENT.
Although no more turning us into Gakuen Heaven...
THAT'S NOT ALL.
SHIZUKA-CHAN'S FATHER IS THE PRESIDENT OF OUR SCHOOL.
MY NAME IS SHIZUKA MITSUHACHI.
I'LL NEGOTIATE WITH MY FATHER TO MAKE THIS WORK.

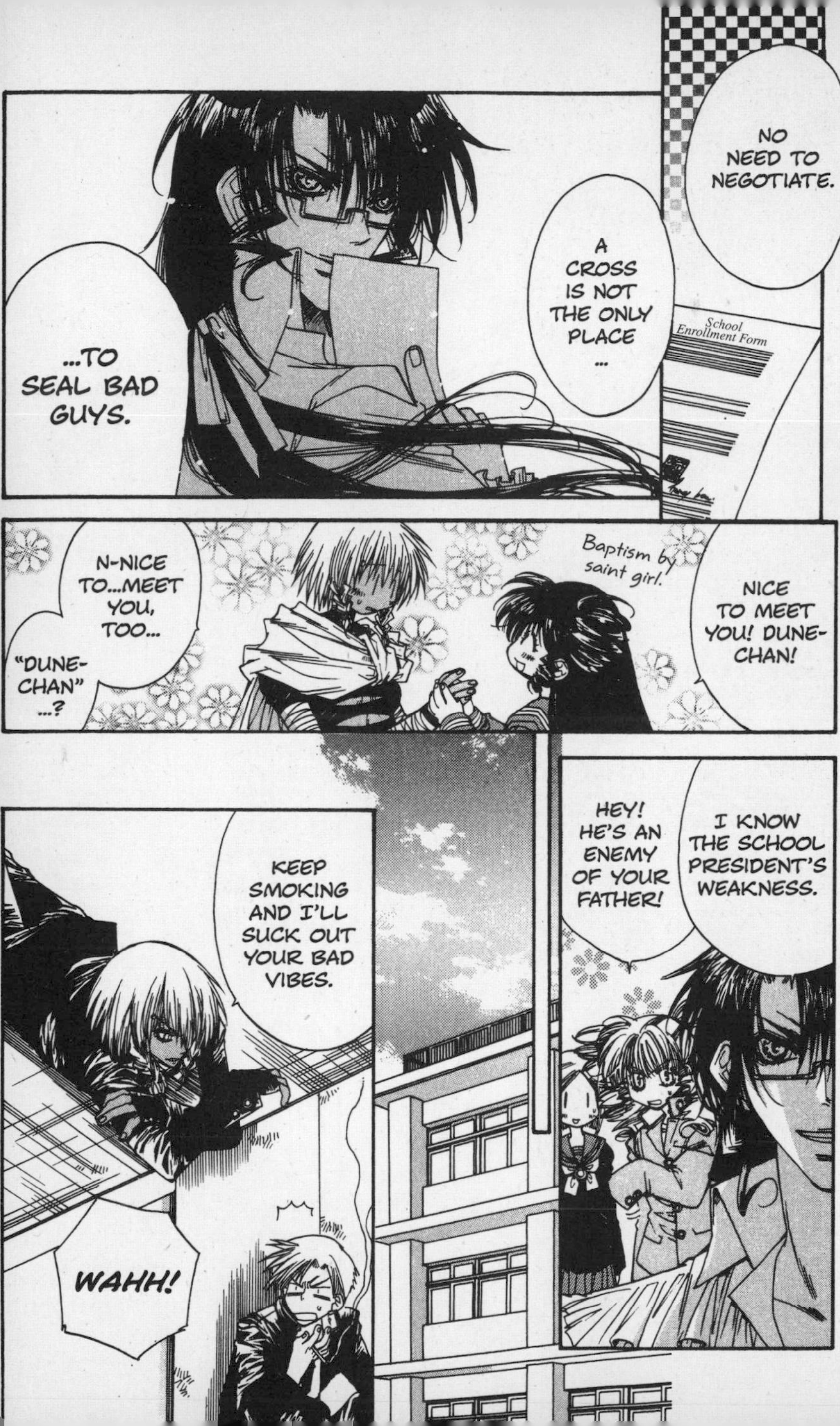
NO NEED TO NEGOTIATE.
A CROSS IS NOT THE ONLY PLACE ...
School Enrollment Form
...TO SEAL BAD GUYS.
NICE TO MEET YOU! DUNE-CHAN!
Baptism by saint girl.
N-NICE TO...MEET YOU, TOO...
"DUNE-CHAN" ...?
I KNOW THE SCHOOL PRESIDENT'S WEAKNESS.
HEY! HE'S AN ENEMY OF YOUR FATHER!
KEEP SMOKING AND I'LL SUCK OUT YOUR BAD VIBES.
WAHH!

School wars

Bonus Comic Strip

Vampire Doll Reflections

WELL!
HELLO, DOLLY!
BAD PUNS WITH THAT SERIOUS FACE...
WHAT? THEY'RE GOOD.
NICE TO TREAT YOU!
HAVE A NICE DAISY!
ENOUGH ALREADY!

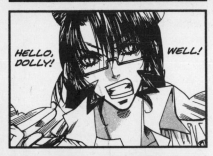

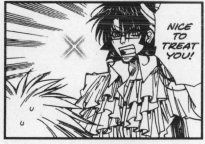

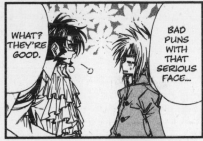

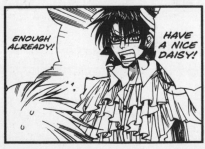

DUNE

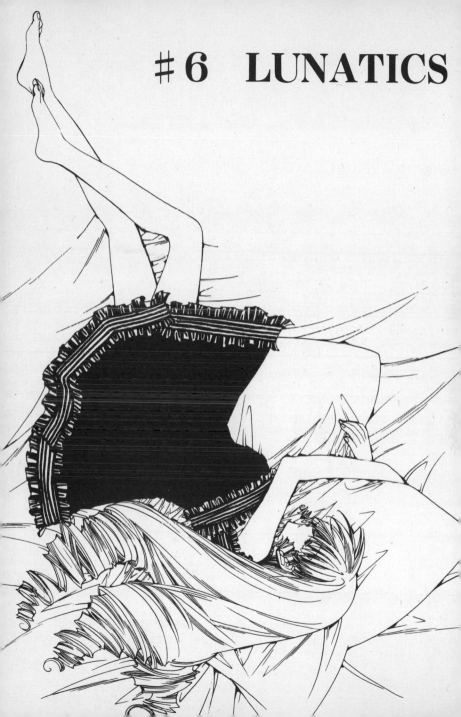

#6 LUNATICS

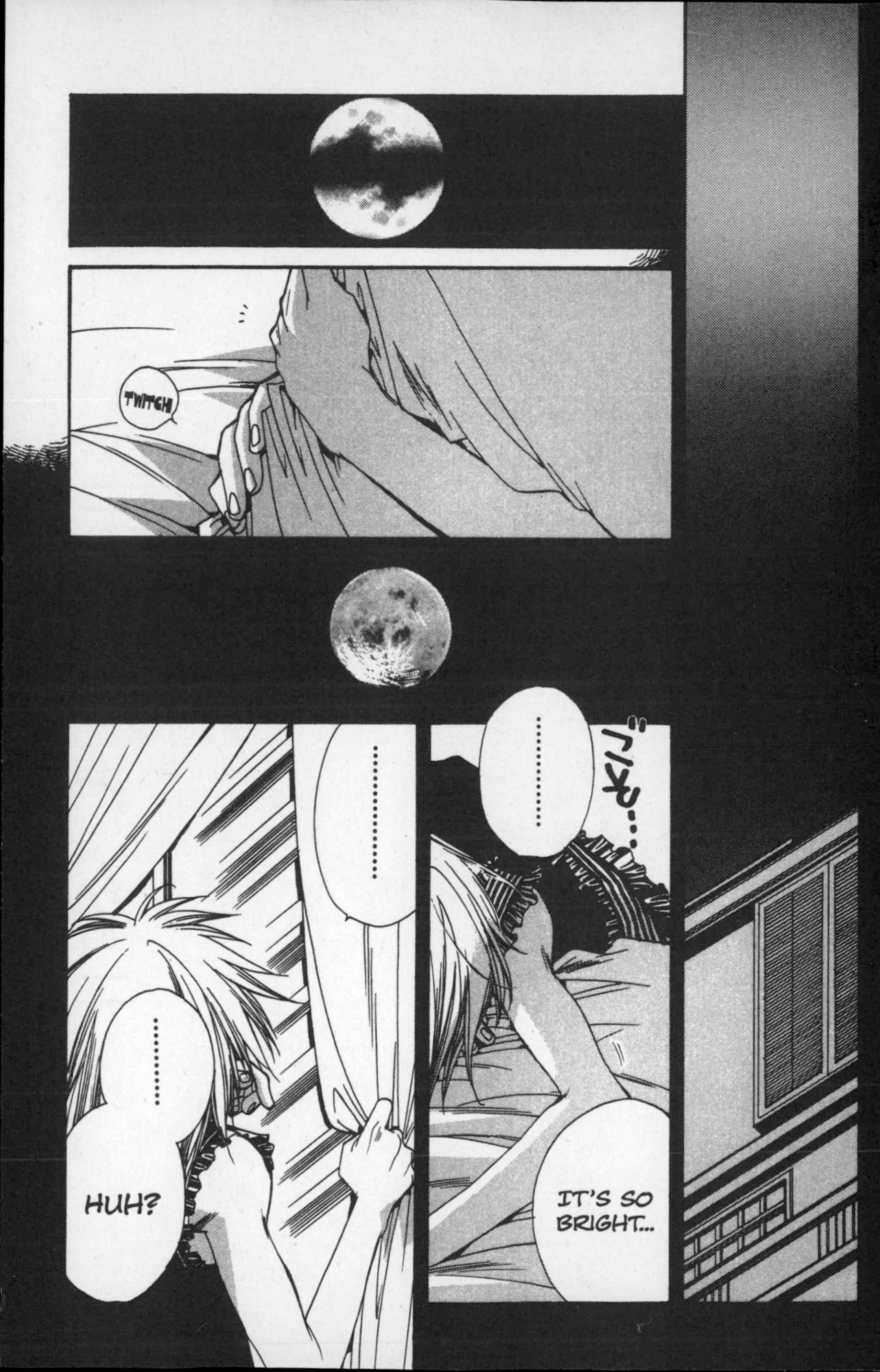
TWITCH
....
IT'S SO BRIGHT...
....
....
HUH?

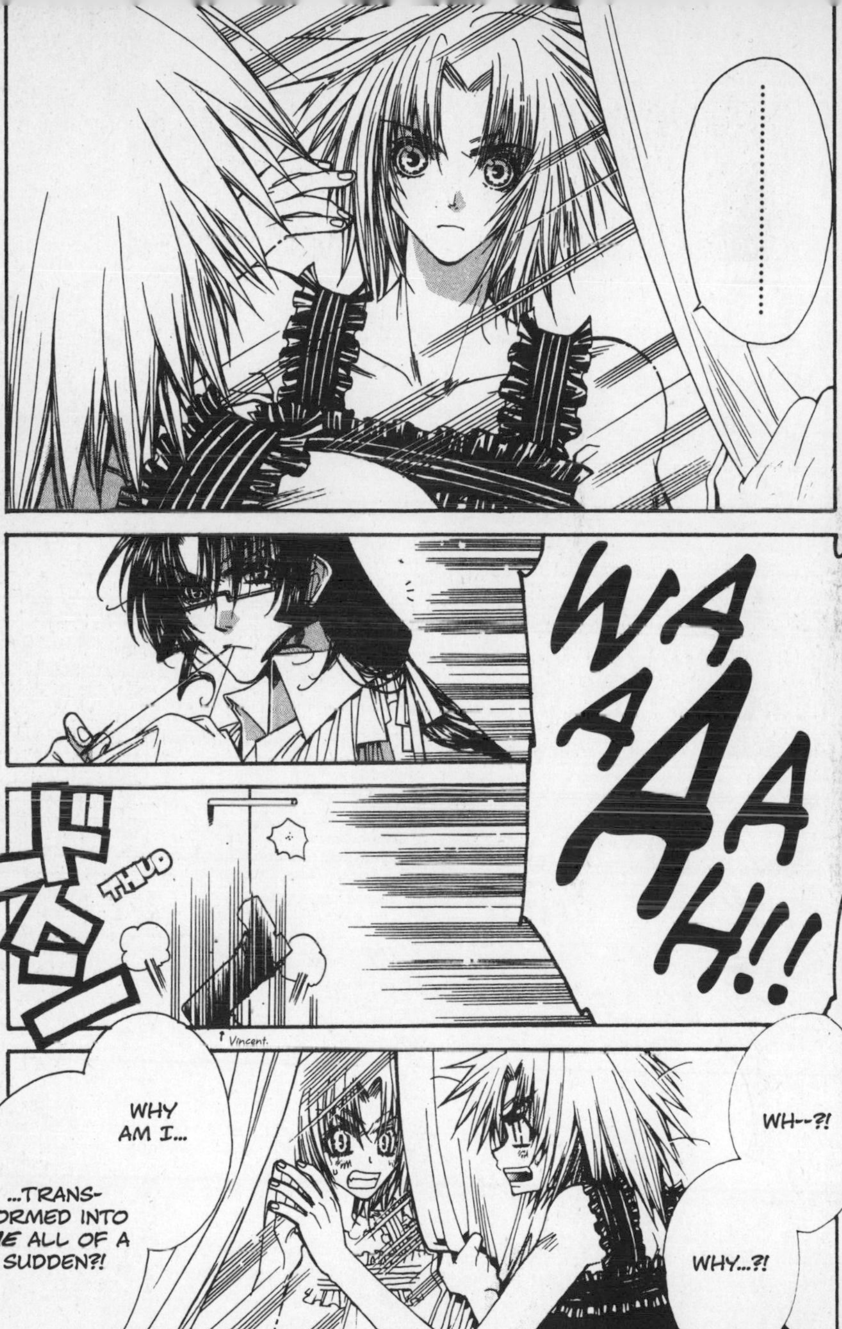
......
WAAAAAH!!
THUD
Vincent.
WH--?!
WHY...?!
WHY AM I...
...TRANS-FORMED INTO *ME* ALL OF A SUDDEN?!

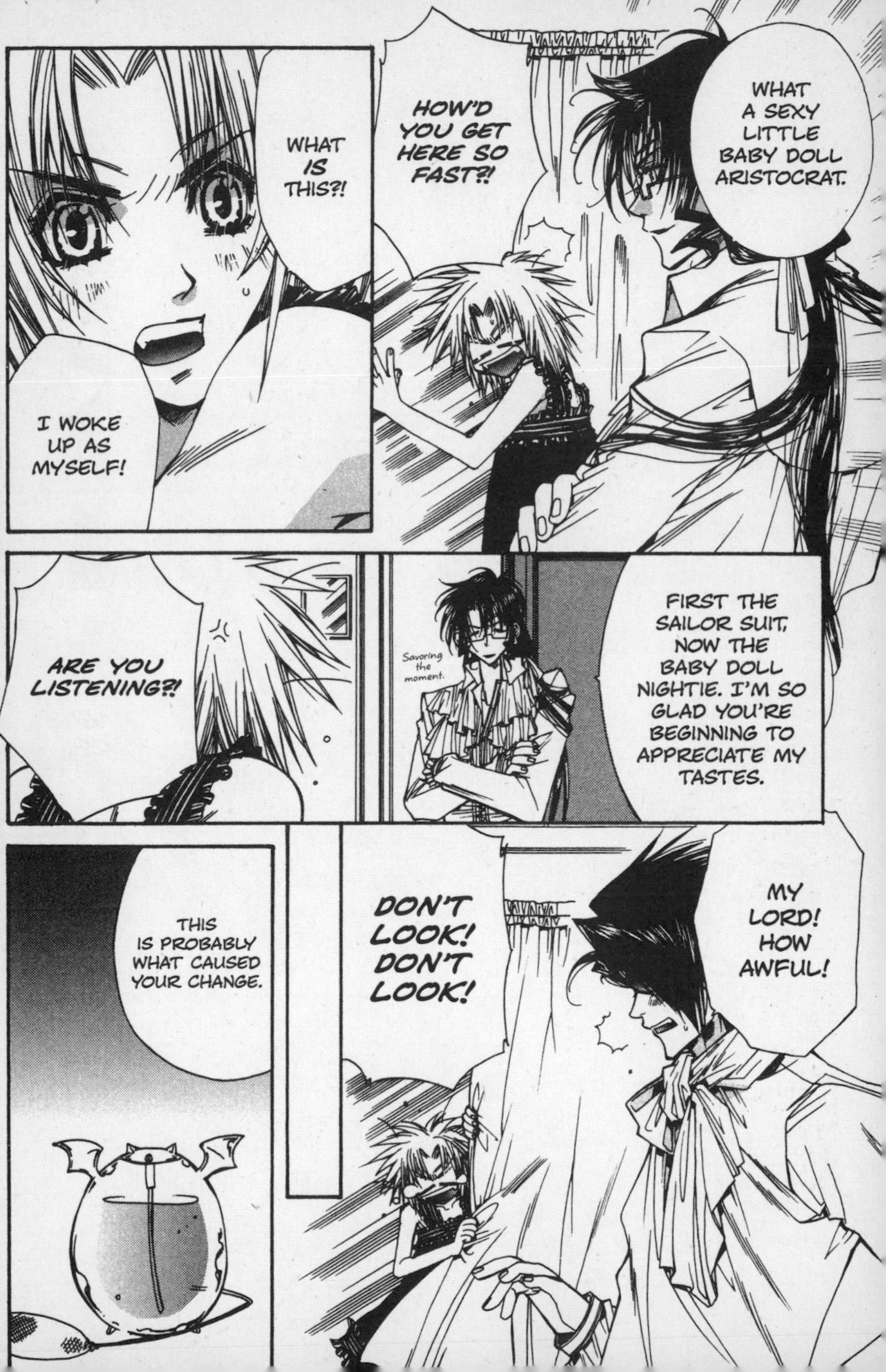
WHAT A SEXY LITTLE BABY DOLL ARISTOCRAT.
HOW'D YOU GET HERE SO FAST?!
WHAT IS THIS?!
I WOKE UP AS MYSELF!
FIRST THE SAILOR SUIT, NOW THE BABY DOLL NIGHTIE. I'M SO GLAD YOU'RE BEGINNING TO APPRECIATE MY TASTES.
Savoring the moment.
ARE YOU LISTENING?!
MY LORD! HOW AWFUL!
DON'T LOOK! DON'T LOOK!
THIS IS PROBABLY WHAT CAUSED YOUR CHANGE.

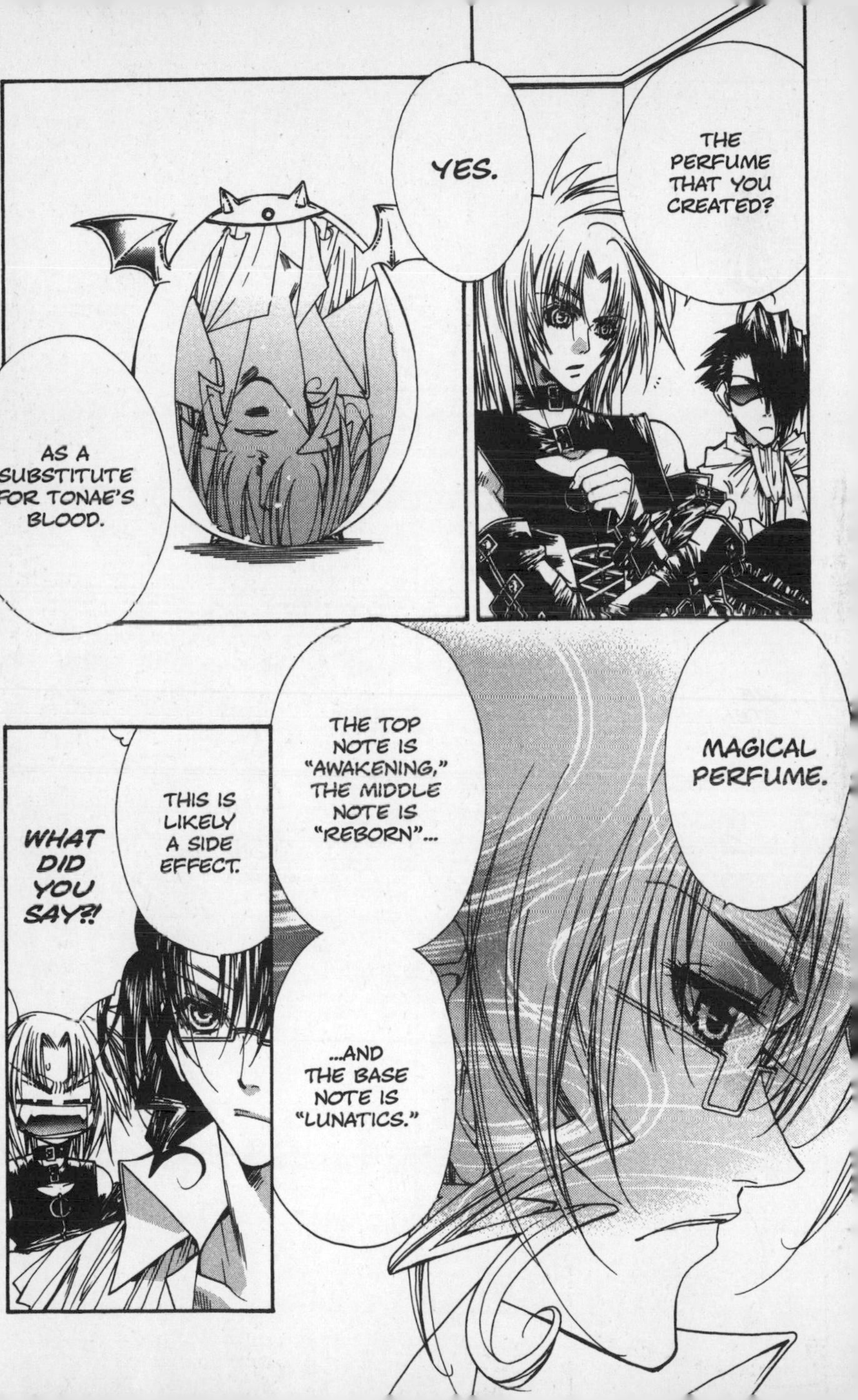
THE PERFUME THAT YOU CREATED?
YES.
AS A SUBSTITUTE FOR TONAE'S BLOOD.
MAGICAL PERFUME.
THE TOP NOTE IS "AWAKENING," THE MIDDLE NOTE IS "REBORN"...
...AND THE BASE NOTE IS "LUNATICS."
THIS IS LIKELY A SIDE EFFECT.
WHAT DID YOU SAY?!

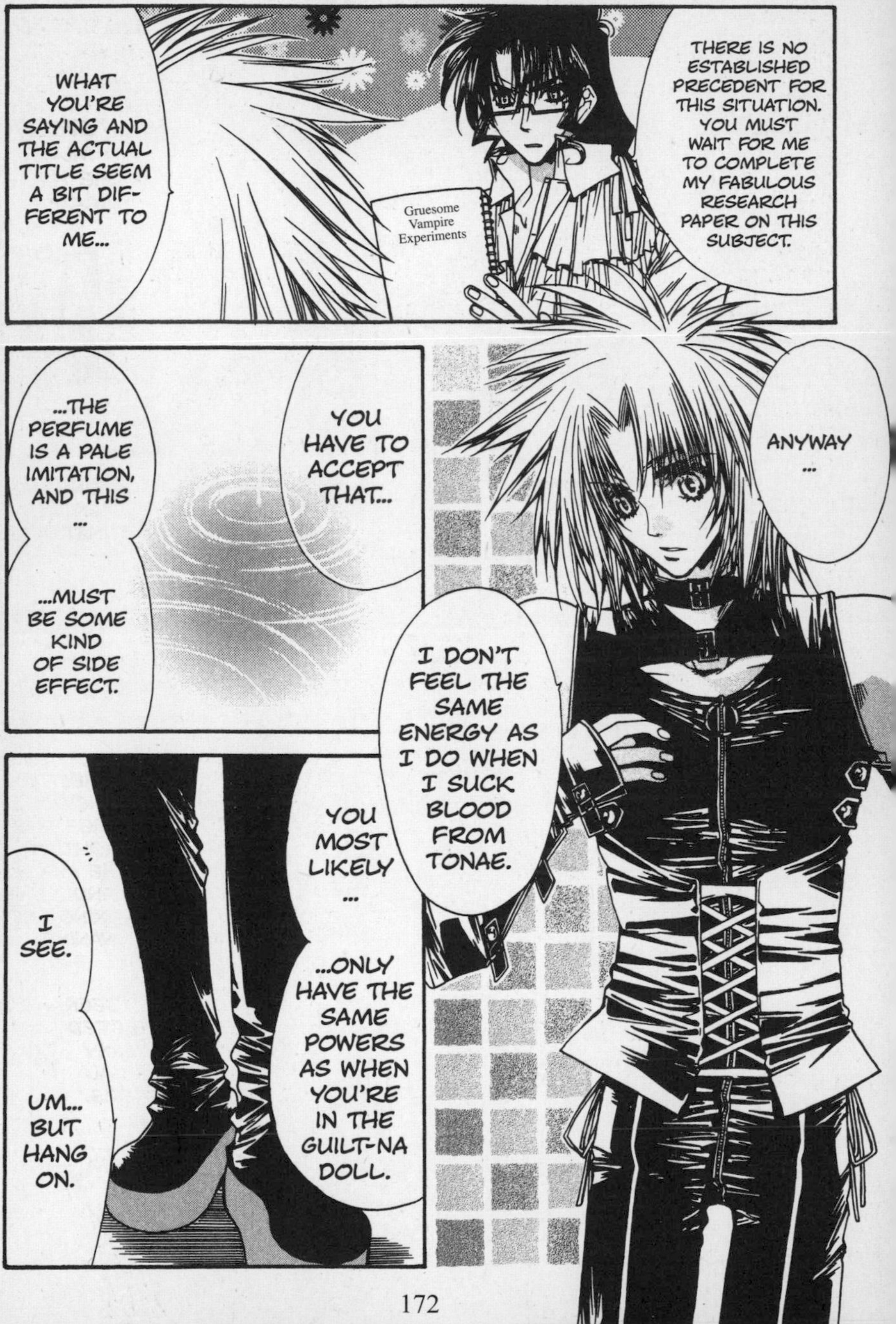
THERE IS NO ESTABLISHED PRECEDENT FOR THIS SITUATION. YOU MUST WAIT FOR ME TO COMPLETE MY FABULOUS RESEARCH PAPER ON THIS SUBJECT.
Gruesome Vampire Experiments
WHAT YOU'RE SAYING AND THE ACTUAL TITLE SEEM A BIT DIF-FERENT TO ME...
ANYWAY ...
I DON'T FEEL THE SAME ENERGY AS I DO WHEN I SUCK BLOOD FROM TONAE.
YOU HAVE TO ACCEPT THAT...
...THE PERFUME IS A PALE IMITATION, AND THIS ...
...MUST BE SOME KIND OF SIDE EFFECT.
YOU MOST LIKELY ...
...ONLY HAVE THE SAME POWERS AS WHEN YOU'RE IN THE GUILT-NA DOLL.
I SEE.
UM... BUT HANG ON.

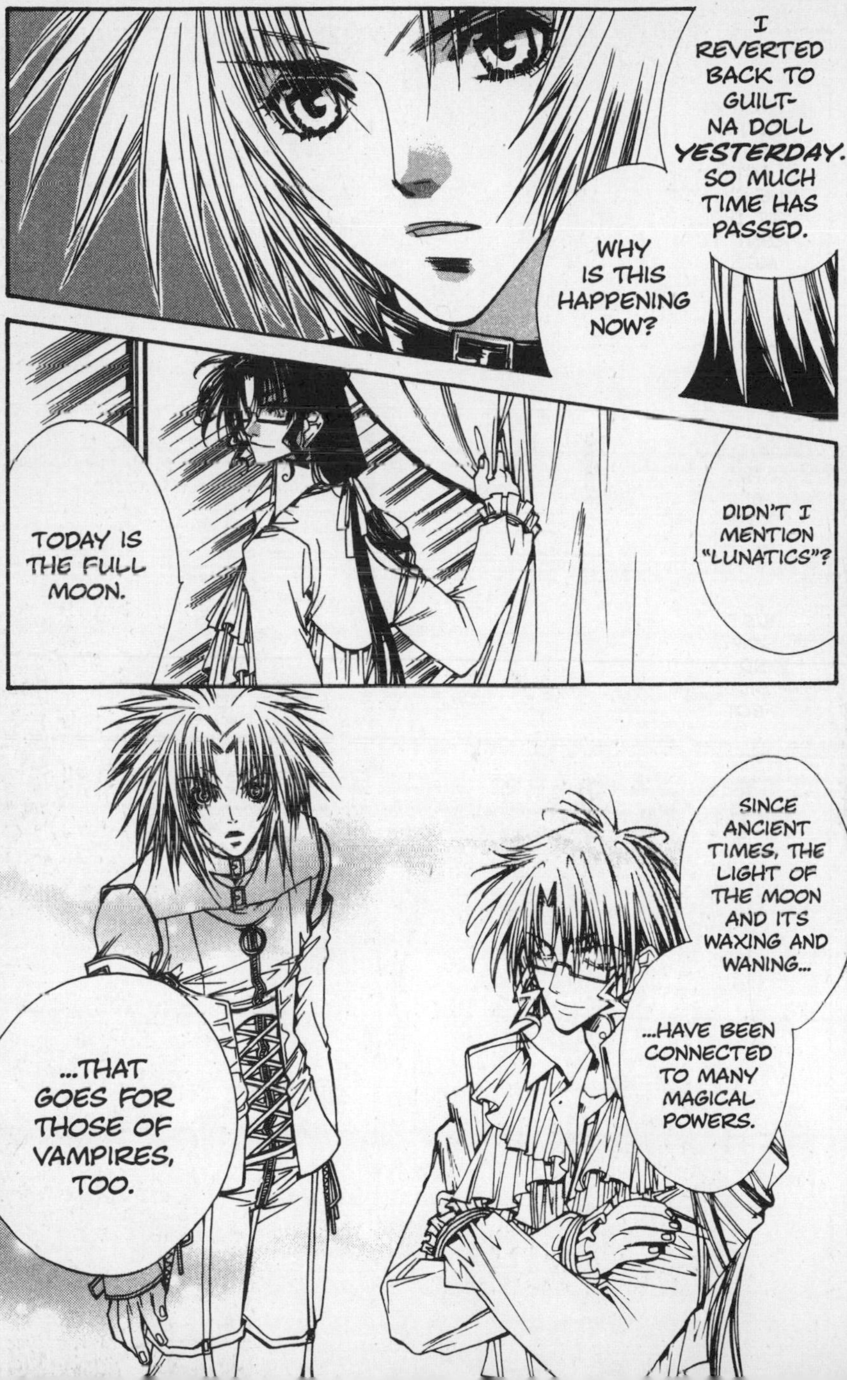
I REVERTED BACK TO GUILT-NA DOLL YESTERDAY. SO MUCH TIME HAS PASSED.
WHY IS THIS HAPPENING NOW?
DIDN'T I MENTION "LUNATICS"?
TODAY IS THE FULL MOON.
SINCE ANCIENT TIMES, THE LIGHT OF THE MOON AND ITS WAXING AND WANING...
...HAVE BEEN CONNECTED TO MANY MAGICAL POWERS.
...THAT GOES FOR THOSE OF VAMPIRES, TOO.

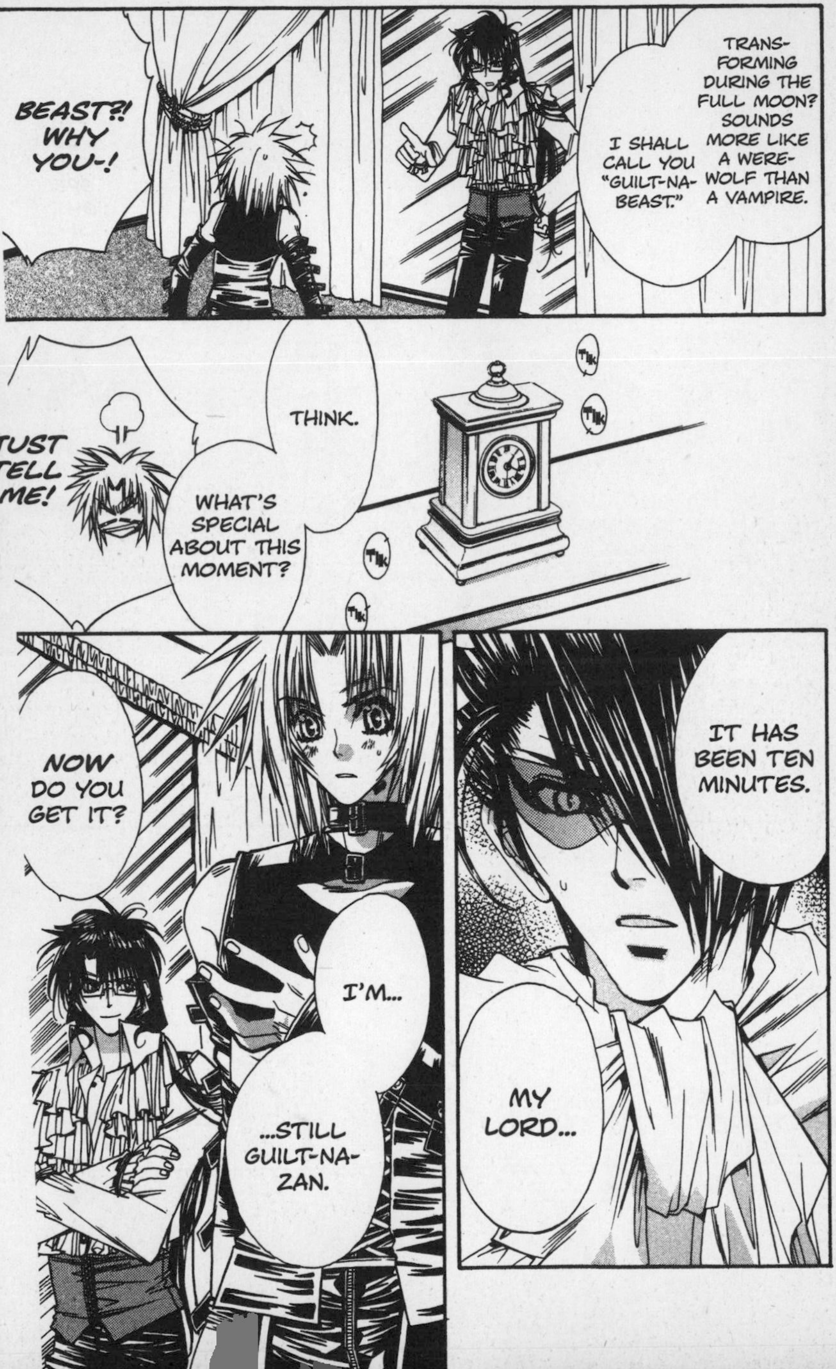
TRANS-FORMING DURING THE FULL MOON? SOUNDS MORE LIKE A WERE-WOLF THAN A VAMPIRE.
I SHALL CALL YOU "GUILT-NA-BEAST."
BEAST?! WHY YOU-!
TIK
TIK
THINK.
WHAT'S SPECIAL ABOUT THIS MOMENT?
JUST TELL ME!
TIK
TIK
IT HAS BEEN TEN MINUTES.
MY LORD...
NOW DO YOU GET IT?
I'M...
...STILL GUILT-NA-ZAN.

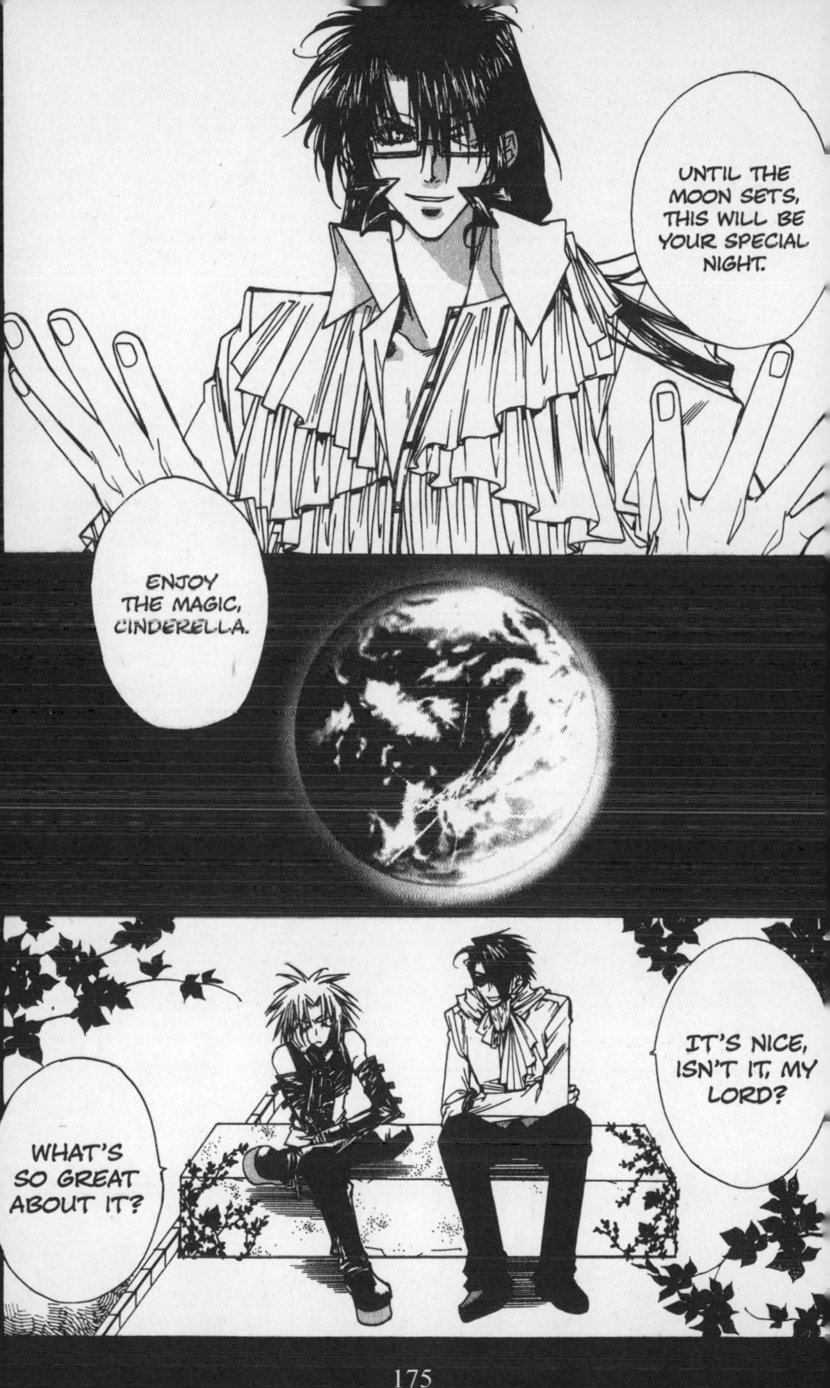
UNTIL THE MOON SETS, THIS WILL BE YOUR SPECIAL NIGHT.
ENJOY THE MAGIC, CINDERELLA.
IT'S NICE, ISN'T IT, MY LORD?
WHAT'S SO GREAT ABOUT IT?

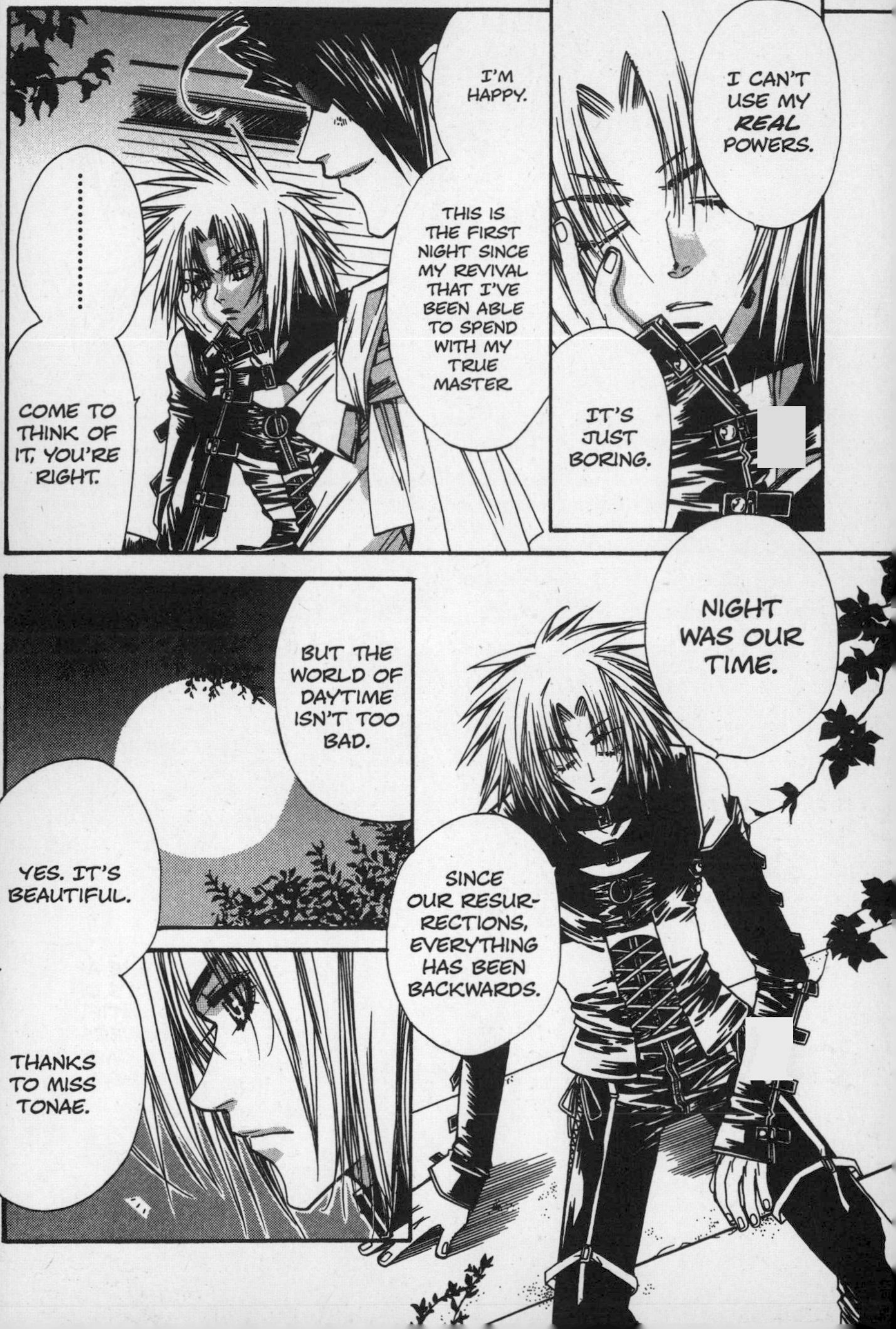
I CAN'T USE MY *REAL* POWERS.
IT'S JUST BORING.
I'M HAPPY.
THIS IS THE FIRST NIGHT SINCE MY REVIVAL THAT I'VE BEEN ABLE TO SPEND WITH MY TRUE MASTER
....
COME TO THINK OF IT, YOU'RE RIGHT.
NIGHT WAS OUR TIME.
SINCE OUR RESUR-RECTIONS, EVERYTHING HAS BEEN BACKWARDS.
BUT THE WORLD OF DAYTIME ISN'T TOO BAD.
YES. IT'S BEAUTIFUL.
THANKS TO MISS TONAE.

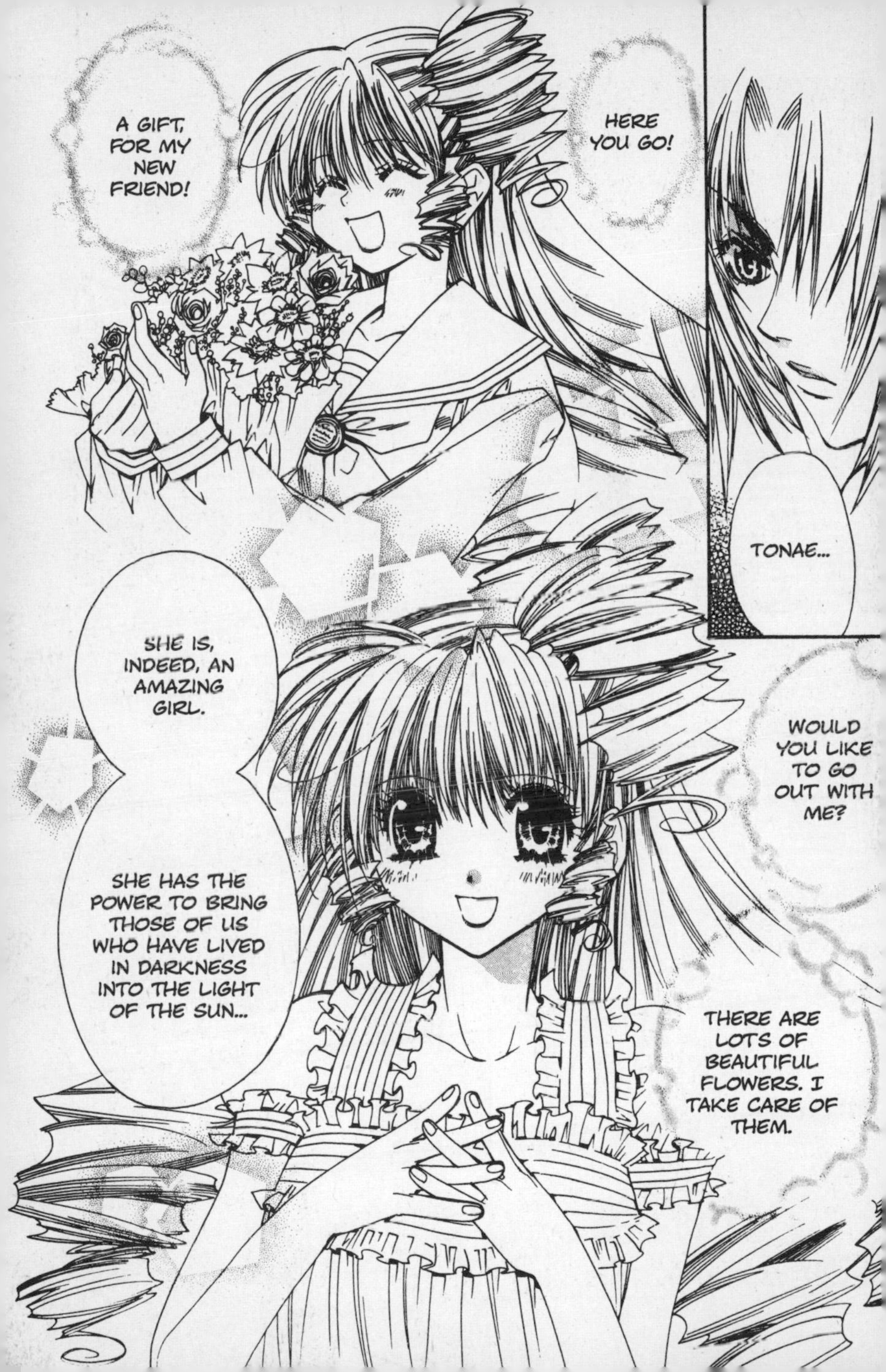
TONAE...
HERE YOU GO!
A GIFT, FOR MY NEW FRIEND!
WOULD YOU LIKE TO GO OUT WITH ME?
SHE IS, INDEED, AN AMAZING GIRL.
THERE ARE LOTS OF BEAUTIFUL FLOWERS. I TAKE CARE OF THEM.
SHE HAS THE POWER TO BRING THOSE OF US WHO HAVE LIVED IN DARKNESS INTO THE LIGHT OF THE SUN...

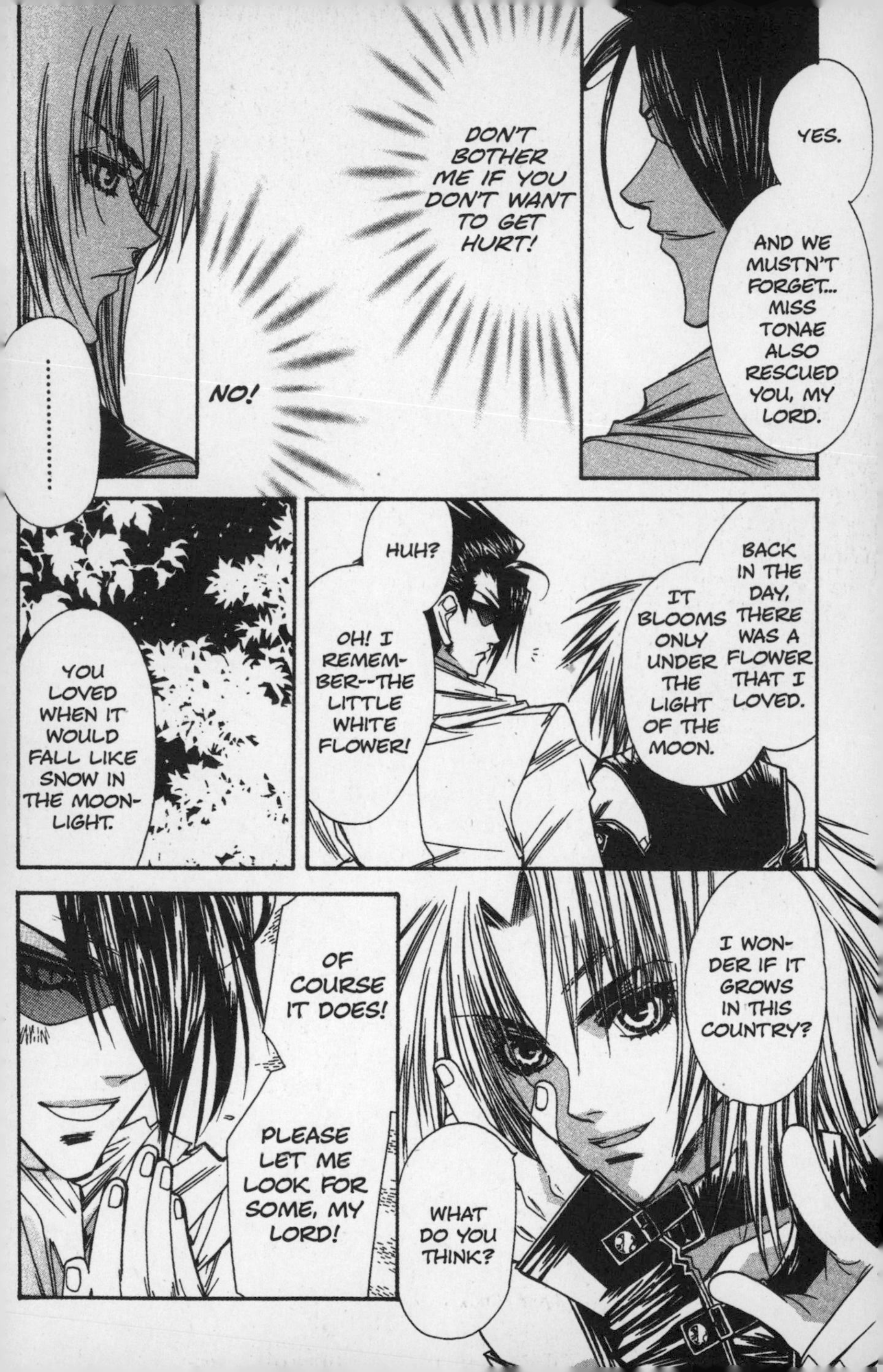
YES.
AND WE MUSTN'T FORGET... MISS TONAE ALSO RESCUED YOU, MY LORD.
DON'T BOTHER ME IF YOU DON'T WANT TO GET HURT!
NO!
......
BACK IN THE DAY, THERE WAS A FLOWER THAT I LOVED.
IT BLOOMS ONLY UNDER THE LIGHT OF THE MOON.
HUH?
OH! I REMEMBER--THE LITTLE WHITE FLOWER!
YOU LOVED WHEN IT WOULD FALL LIKE SNOW IN THE MOONLIGHT.
I WONDER IF IT GROWS IN THIS COUNTRY?
WHAT DO YOU THINK?
OF COURSE IT DOES!
PLEASE LET ME LOOK FOR SOME, MY LORD!

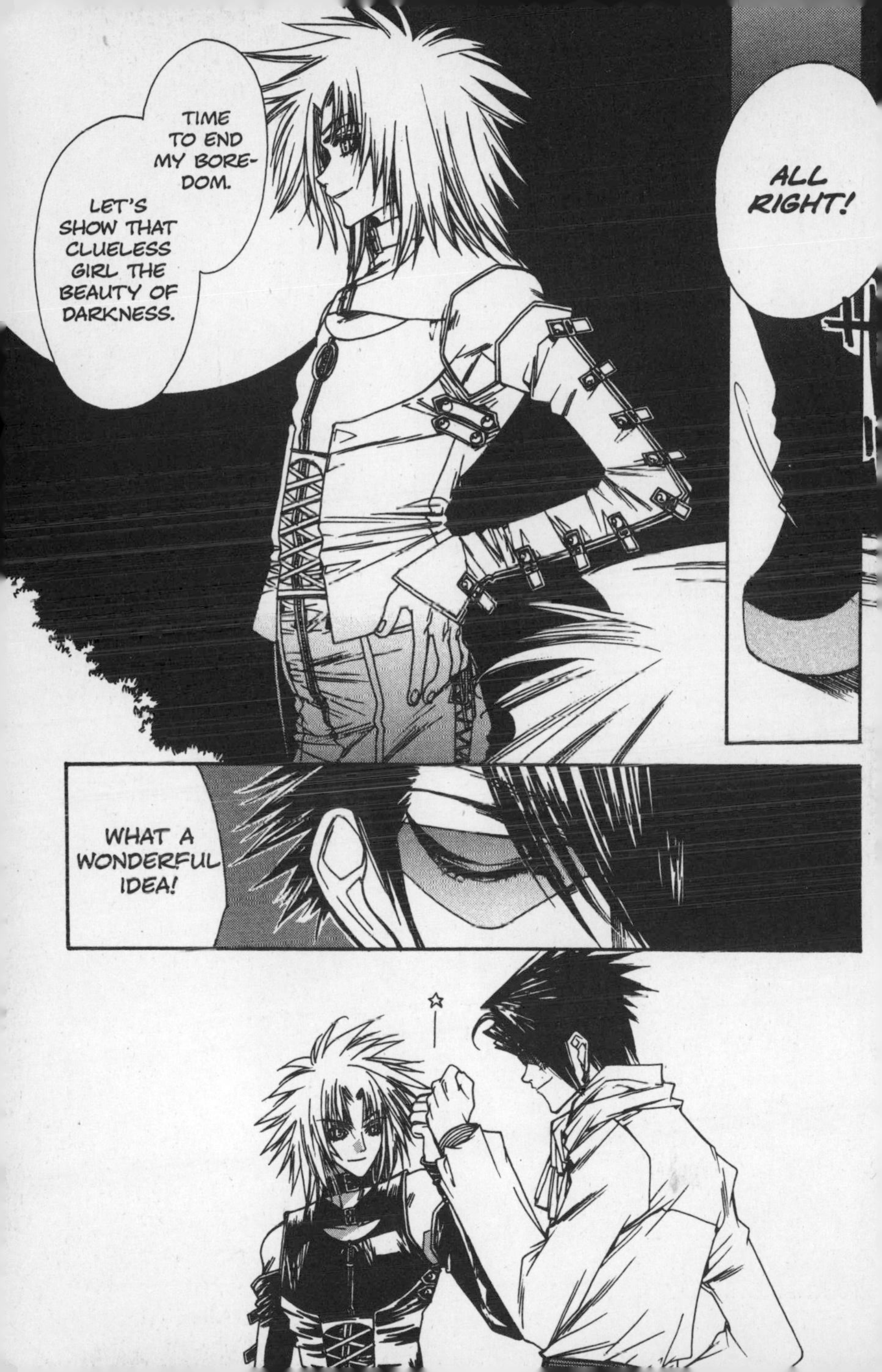
ALL RIGHT!
TIME TO END MY BORE-DOM.
LET'S SHOW THAT CLUELESS GIRL THE BEAUTY OF DARKNESS.
WHAT A WONDERFUL IDEA!

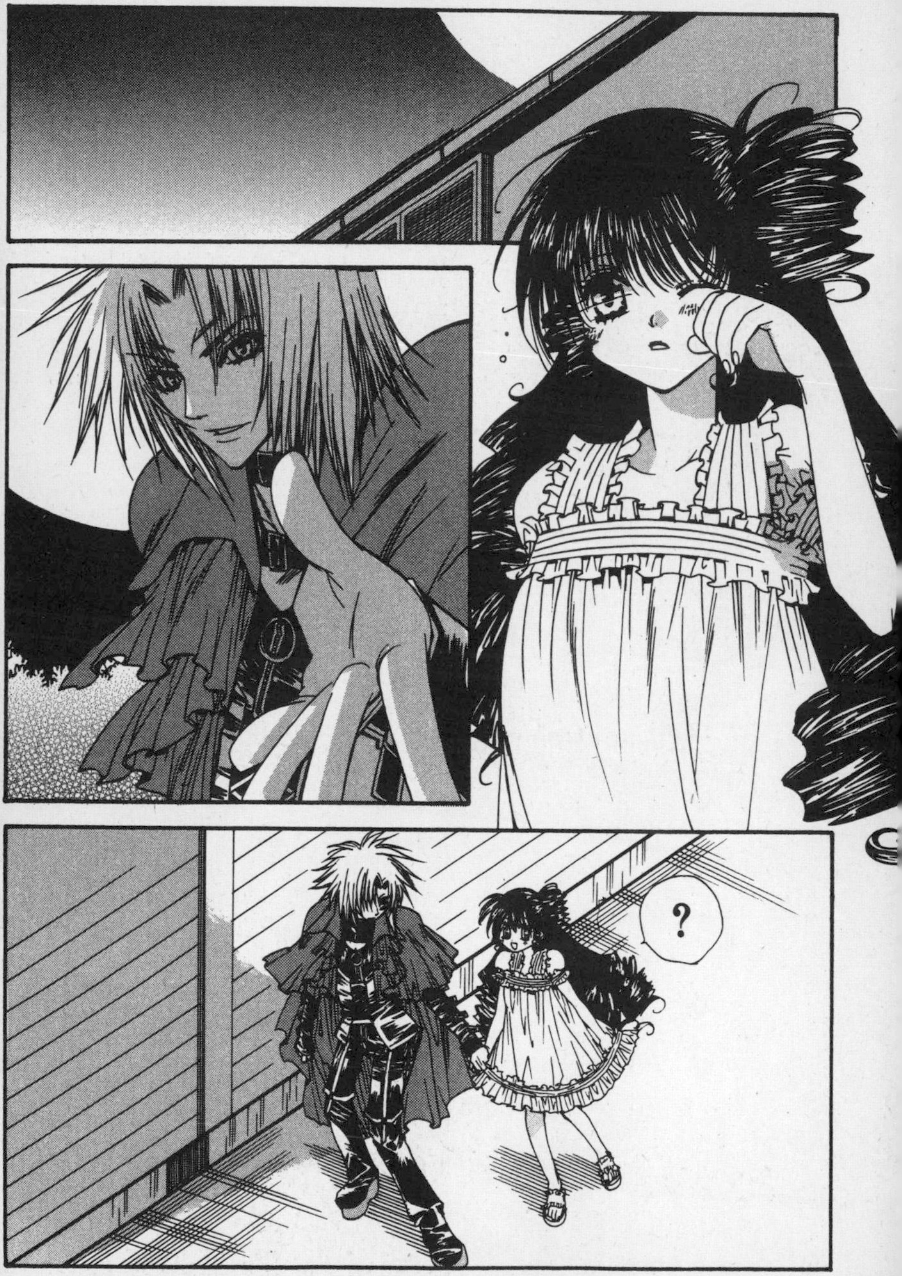
?

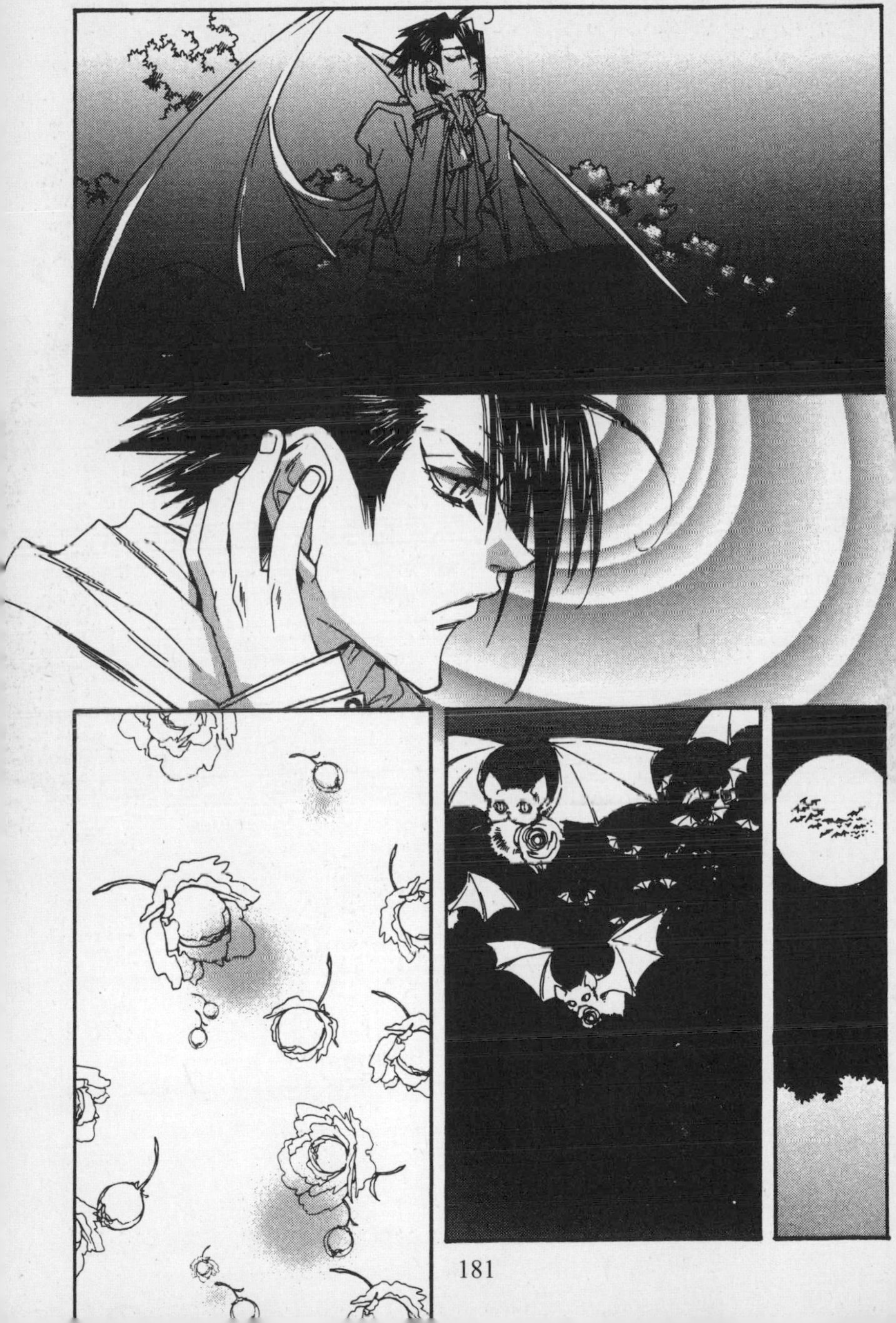

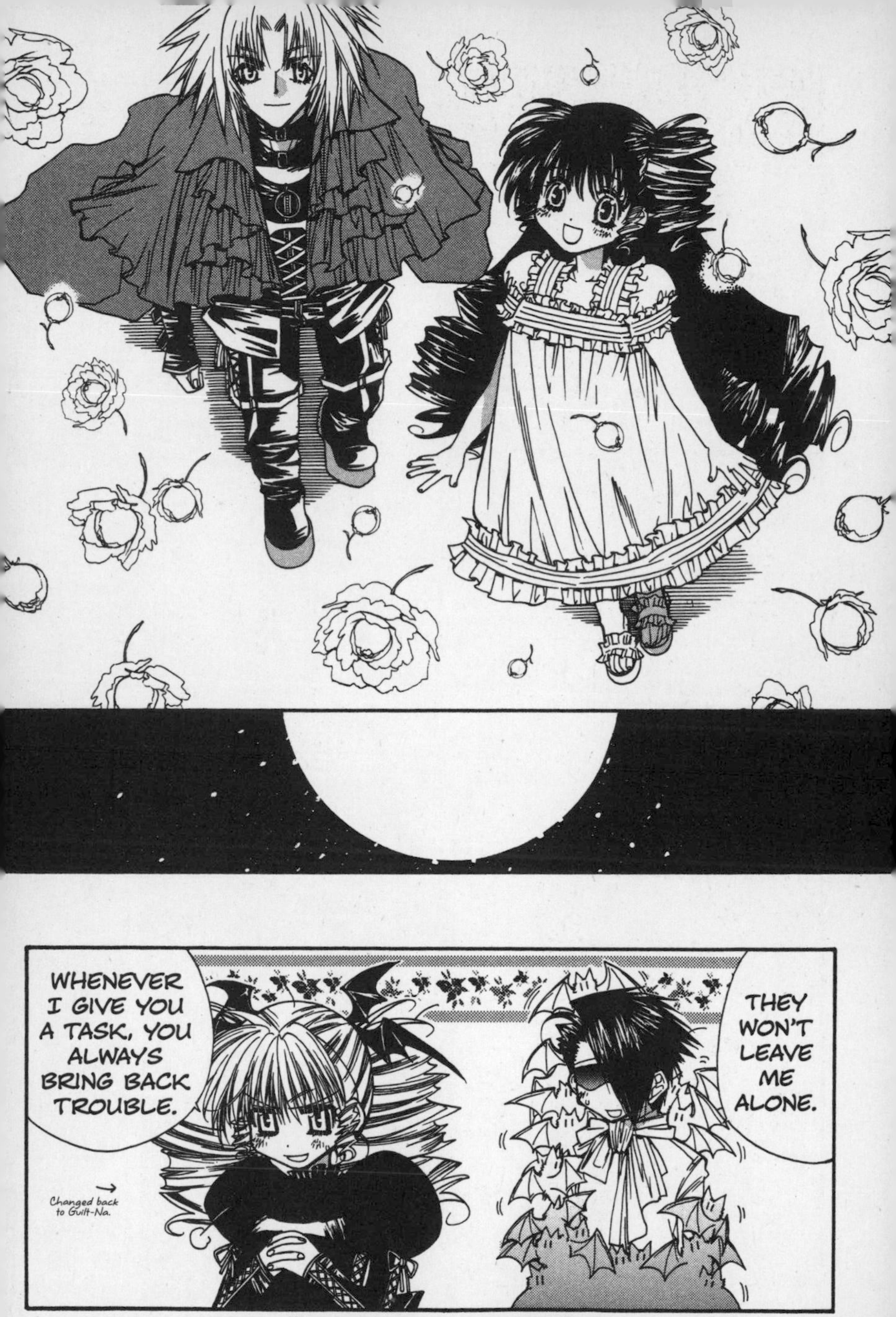
THEY WON'T LEAVE ME ALONE.
WHENEVER I GIVE YOU A TASK, YOU ALWAYS BRING BACK TROUBLE.
Changed back to Guilt-Na.

To be continued in vol. 2

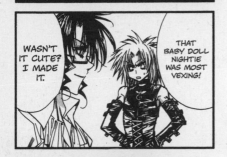

Lunatics

Bonus Comic Strip

THAT BABY DOLL NIGHTIE WAS MOST VEXING!
WASN'T IT CUTE? I MADE IT.
IT WASN'T SHOWN, BUT UNDERNEATH ...
...THERE ARE MATCHING BLOOMERS. TONAE'S CAUSAL CLOTHES ARE OF SIMILAR DESIGN.
COULD YOU MAKE SOME CLOTHES FOR WHEN I TRANSFORM INTO A MAN?
ALL RIGHT.
WHY ARE THEY SUCH SIMPLE DESIGNS?
I DON'T CARE ABOUT MEN'S CLOTHES.
Tank.
Trunks.

VAMPIRE DOLL

REFLECTIONS

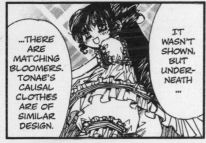

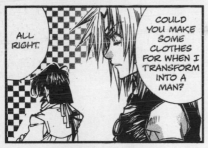

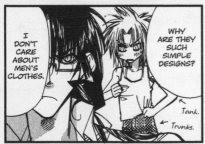

Kyoji

Vampire Doll
Guilt-na-Zan

Bonus Comic Strip

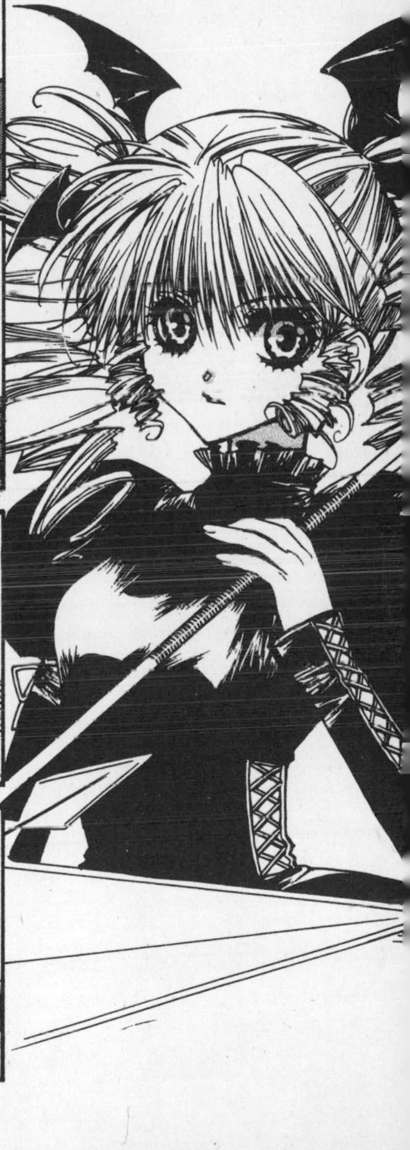

Breaking point

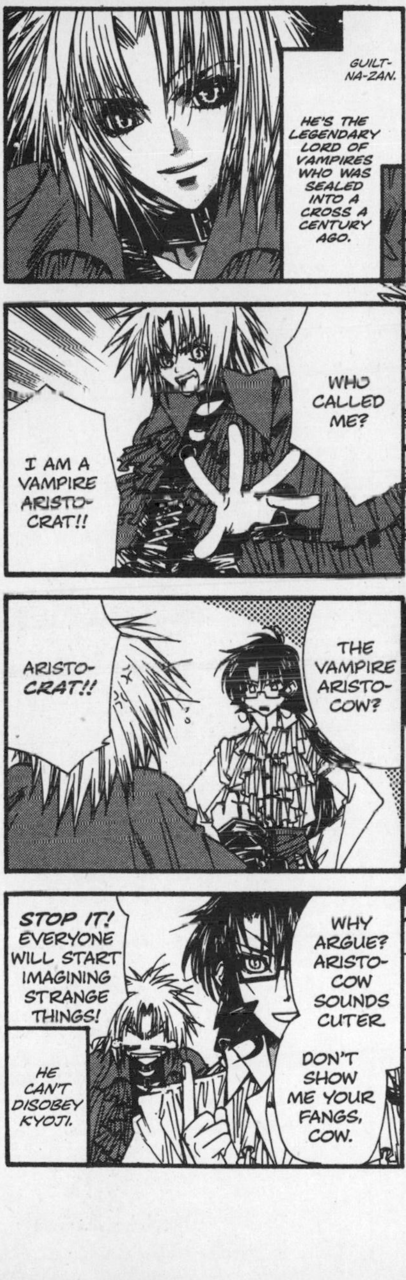
GUILT-NA-ZAN.
HE'S THE LEGENDARY LORD OF VAMPIRES WHO WAS SEALED INTO A CROSS A CENTURY AGO.
WHO CALLED ME?
I AM A VAMPIRE ARISTO-CRAT!!
THE VAMPIRE ARISTO-COW?
ARISTO-CRAT!!
WHY ARGUE? ARISTO-COW SOUNDS CUTER
STOP IT! EVERYONE WILL START IMAGINING STRANGE THINGS!
DON'T SHOW ME YOUR FANGS, COW.
HE CAN'T DISOBEY KYOJI.

Author's Notes: "Dare ga yonda ka?": (Who called me?) Said twice in a row, it's supposed to be a spell to bring luck with money. Synonym: "Kyo mo kimete no!" (Today I'll win!)

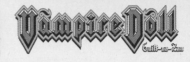

Author's Notes: WAX DOLL: A carefully sculpted figure made out of wax. There are many of them around Tokyo Tower and in creepy, foggy forests. **GAL ALPHABET:** Bizarre signs and characters that are used by high school girls.

Others

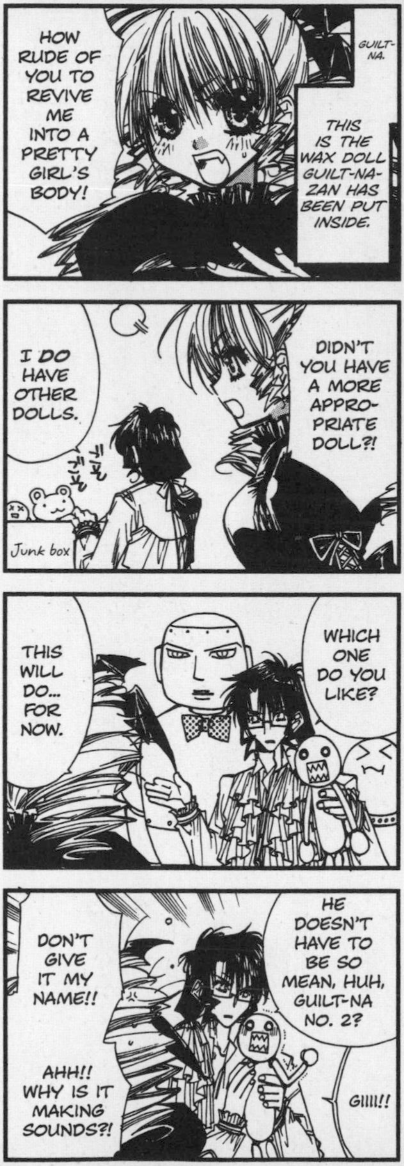
GUILT-NA.
THIS IS THE WAX DOLL GUILT-NAZAN HAS BEEN PUT INSIDE.
HOW RUDE OF YOU TO REVIVE ME INTO A PRETTY GIRL'S BODY!
DIDN'T YOU HAVE A MORE APPROPRIATE DOLL?!
I DO HAVE OTHER DOLLS.
Junk box
WHICH ONE DO YOU LIKE?
THIS WILL DO... FOR NOW.
HE DOESN'T HAVE TO BE SO MEAN, HUH, GUILT-NA NO. 2?
DON'T GIVE IT MY NAME!!
GIIII!!
AHH!! WHY IS IT MAKING SOUNDS?!

Attribute

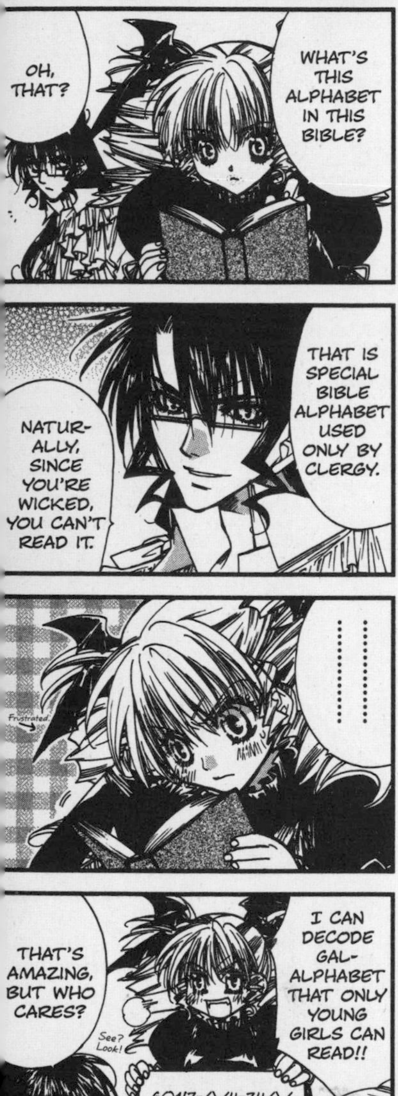
WHAT'S THIS ALPHABET IN THIS BIBLE?
OH, THAT?
THAT IS SPECIAL BIBLE ALPHABET USED ONLY BY CLERGY.
NATURALLY, SINCE YOU'RE WICKED, YOU CAN'T READ IT.
....
Frustrated.
I CAN DECODE GAL-ALPHABET THAT ONLY YOUNG GIRLS CAN READ!!
THAT'S AMAZING, BUT WHO CARES?
See? Look!
6O1!7-/\/4-Z4/\/

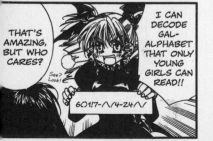

Vampire Doll Guilt-na-Zan

BONUS COMIC STRIP

Super

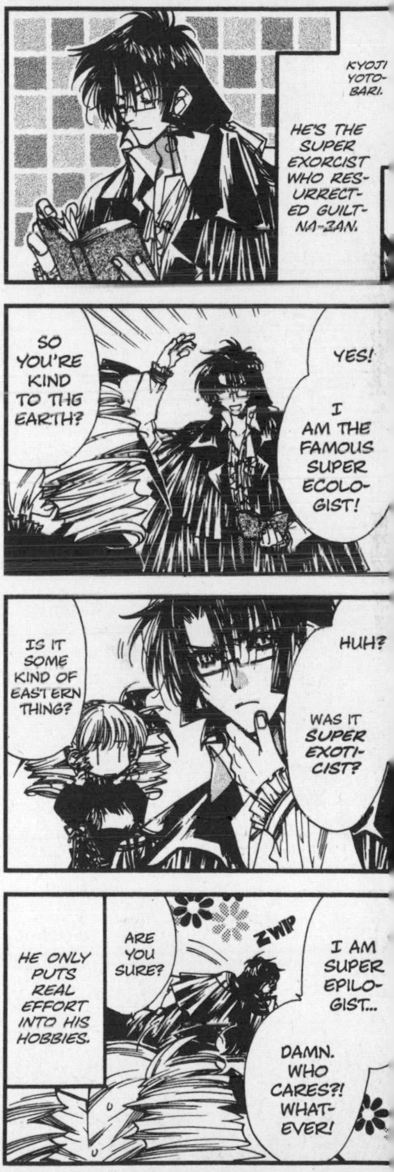
KYOJI YOTOBARI.
HE'S THE SUPER EXORCIST WHO RESURRECTED GUILT-NA-ZAN.
YES! I AM THE FAMOUS SUPER ECOLOGIST!
SO YOU'RE KIND TO THE EARTH?
HUH? WAS IT SUPER EXOTICIST?
IS IT SOME KIND OF EASTERN THING?
I AM SUPER EPILOGIST...
ZWIP
ARE YOU SURE?
DAMN. WHO CARES?! WHATEVER!
HE ONLY PUTS REAL EFFORT INTO HIS HOBBIES.

Income

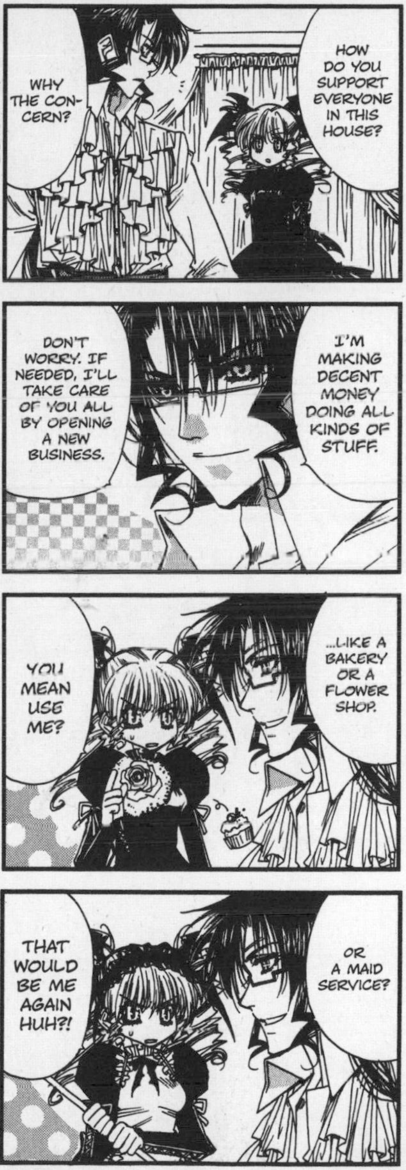
HOW DO YOU SUPPORT EVERYONE IN THIS HOUSE?
WHY THE CONCERN?
I'M MAKING DECENT MONEY DOING ALL KINDS OF STUFF.
DON'T WORRY. IF NEEDED, I'LL TAKE CARE OF YOU ALL BY OPENING A NEW BUSINESS.
...LIKE A BAKERY OR A FLOWER SHOP.
YOU MEAN USE ME?
OR A MAID SERVICE?
THAT WOULD BE ME AGAIN HUH?!

Author's Notes:

EXORCIST: There's a movie called, The Exorcist. The main character, father Demian Karras, was a serious man...unlike Kyoji. He was also good at boxing.

MAGIC: Guilt-Na's magic can only create flowers and sweets because Kyoji wants Guilt-Na to have "Magical Girlish" powers, but those aren't really common magical girl powers.

Author's Notes:

MADAGASCAR BAT: Big ones don't suck blood; they live by eating fruit and nectar. They also don't have very powerful ultrasonic waves.

MODERN TIMES: In Chaplin's famous 1936 film, human cynicism was revealed by the progressively mechanized world in which we live.

Rescue

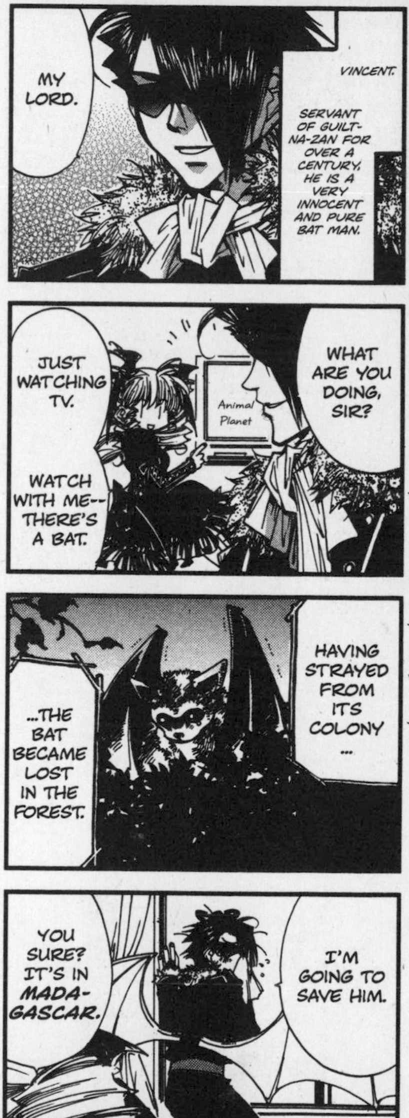
VINCENT.
SERVANT OF GUILT-NA-ZAN FOR OVER A CENTURY, HE IS A VERY INNOCENT AND PURE BAT MAN.
MY LORD.
WHAT ARE YOU DOING, SIR?
Animal Planet
JUST WATCHING TV.
WATCH WITH ME--THERE'S A BAT.
HAVING STRAYED FROM ITS COLONY ...
...THE BAT BECAME LOST IN THE FOREST.
I'M GOING TO SAVE HIM.
YOU SURE? IT'S IN MADAGASCAR.

Modern Times

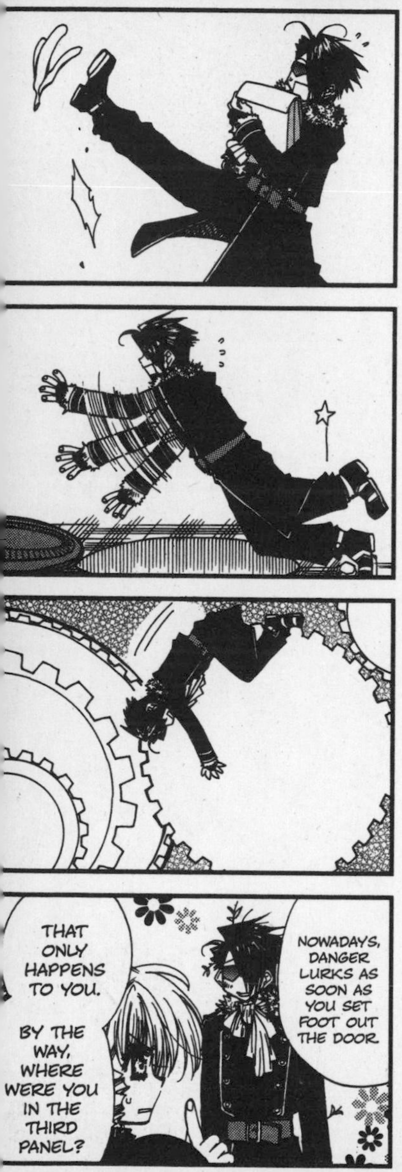
NOWADAYS, DANGER LURKS AS SOON AS YOU SET FOOT OUT THE DOOR
THAT ONLY HAPPENS TO YOU.
BY THE WAY, WHERE WERE YOU IN THE THIRD PANEL?

Vampire Doll Guilt-na-Zaw

BONUS COMIC STRIP

The Stooge

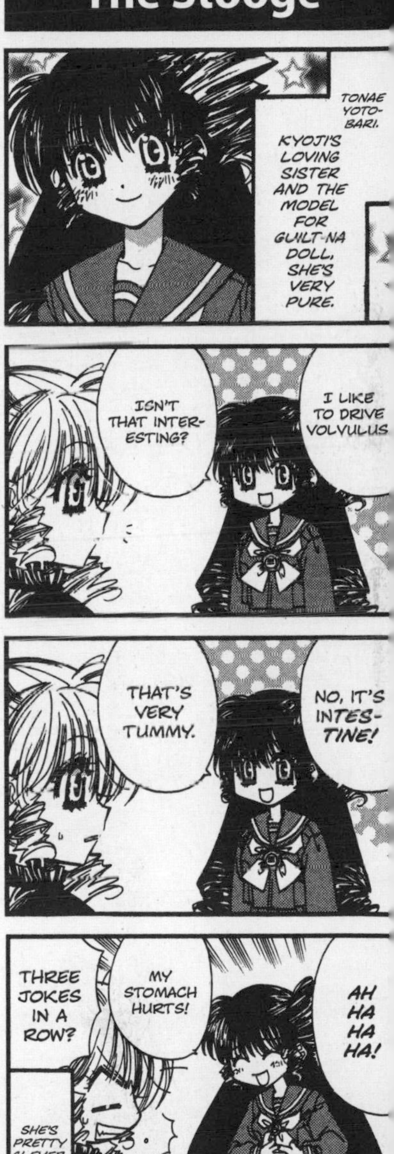
TONAE YOTO-BARI.
KYOJI'S LOVING SISTER AND THE MODEL FOR GUILT-NA DOLL, SHE'S VERY PURE.
I LIKE TO DRIVE VOLVULUS
ISN'T THAT INTER-ESTING?
NO, IT'S INTES-TINE!
THAT'S VERY TUMMY.
AH HA HA HA!
MY STOMACH HURTS!
THREE JOKES IN A ROW?
SHE'S PRETTY CLEVER.

Socksweater

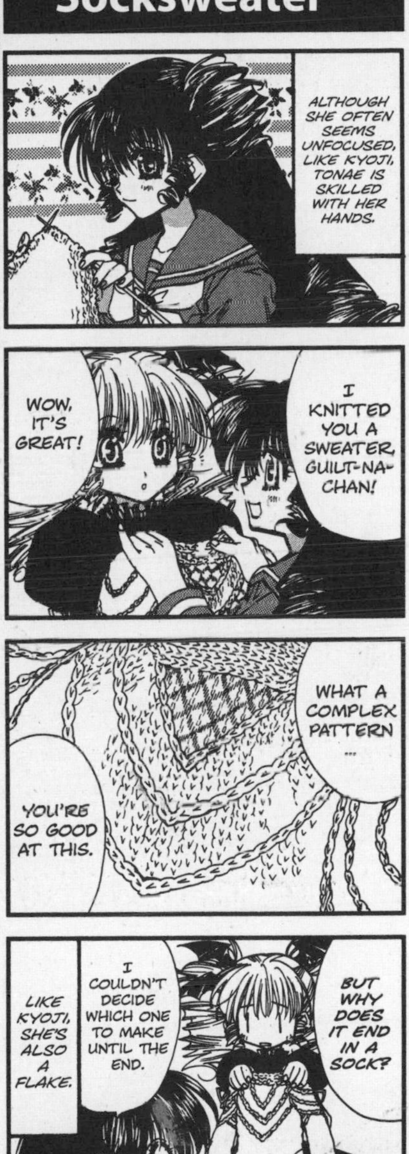
ALTHOUGH SHE OFTEN SEEMS UNFOCUSED, LIKE KYOJI, TONAE IS SKILLED WITH HER HANDS.
I KNITTED YOU A SWEATER, GUILT-NA-CHAN!
WOW, IT'S GREAT!
WHAT A COMPLEX PATTERN ...
YOU'RE SO GOOD AT THIS.
BUT WHY DOES IT END IN A SOCK?
I COULDN'T DECIDE WHICH ONE TO MAKE UNTIL THE END.
LIKE KYOJI, SHE'S ALSO A FLAKE.

Author's Notes:

VOLVULUS: It's is a condition in which the bowel becomes twisted. It's dangerous and can be stress induced. Also, "Tokyo Cho-Nen-Ten" (Tokyo Volvulus) is the name of a pair of comedians.

KNITTING: Anyone can make a scarf, but it takes a bit of skill to do sweaters and socks!

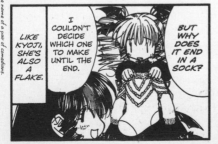

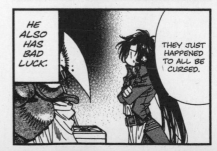

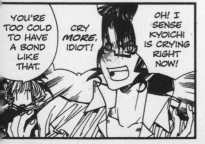

Author's Notes:

NIGHT VEIL: This is English translation of "Yotobari." I assume in English speaking countries I'd be laughed at if I introduced myself as Night Veil.

MING-LI: This is a Chinese term for the connection between twins. I learned this word from a popular video game.

Bad

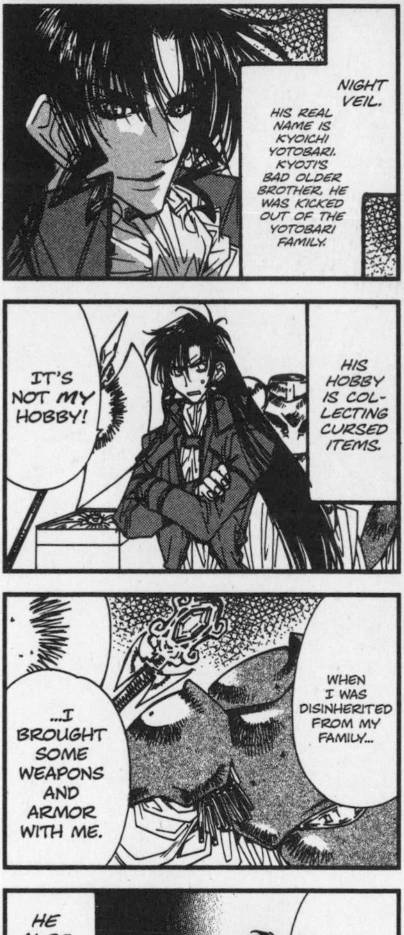
NIGHT VEIL.
HIS REAL NAME IS KYOICHI YOTOBARI. KYOJI'S BAD OLDER BROTHER. HE WAS KICKED OUT OF THE YOTOBARI FAMILY.
HIS HOBBY IS COL-LECTING CURSED ITEMS.
IT'S NOT MY HOBBY!
WHEN I WAS DISINHERITED FROM MY FAMILY...
...I BROUGHT SOME WEAPONS AND ARMOR WITH ME.
THEY JUST HAPPENED TO ALL BE CURSED.
HE ALSO HAS BAD LUCK.

Ming Li

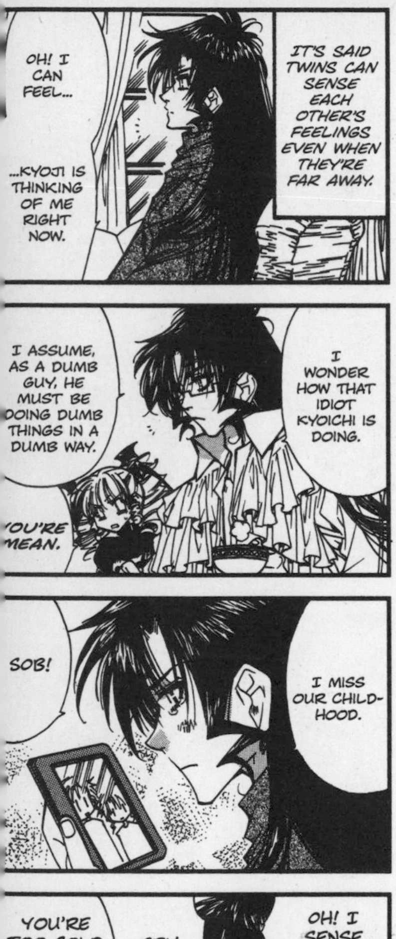
IT'S SAID TWINS CAN SENSE EACH OTHER'S FEELINGS EVEN WHEN THEY'RE FAR AWAY.
OH! I CAN FEEL...
...KYOJI IS THINKING OF ME RIGHT NOW.
I WONDER HOW THAT IDIOT KYOICHI IS DOING.
I ASSUME, AS A DUMB GUY, HE MUST BE DOING DUMB THINGS IN A DUMB WAY.
OU'RE MEAN.
I MISS OUR CHILD-HOOD.
SOB!
OH! I SENSE KYOICHI IS CRYING RIGHT NOW!
CRY MORE, IDIOT!
YOU'RE TOO COLD TO HAVE A BOND LIKE THAT.

Vampire Doll

Guilt-na-Zaw

BONUS COMIC STRIP

Again

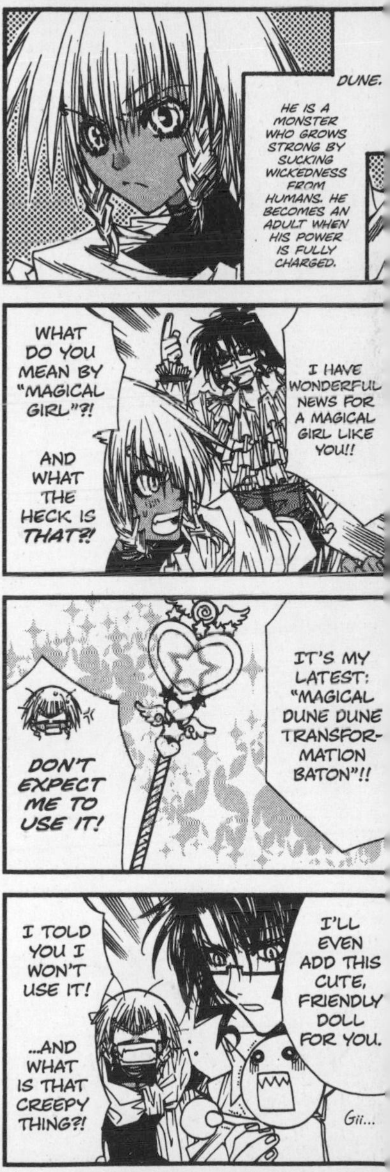
DUNE.
HE IS A MONSTER WHO GROWS STRONG BY SUCKING WICKEDNESS FROM HUMANS. HE BECOMES AN ADULT WHEN HIS POWER IS FULLY CHARGED.
I HAVE WONDERFUL NEWS FOR A MAGICAL GIRL LIKE YOU!!
WHAT DO YOU MEAN BY "MAGICAL GIRL"?!
AND WHAT THE HECK IS *THAT*?!
IT'S MY LATEST: "MAGICAL DUNE DUNE TRANSFORMATION BATON"!!
DON'T EXPECT ME TO USE IT!
I'LL EVEN ADD THIS CUTE, FRIENDLY DOLL FOR YOU.
Gii...
I TOLD YOU I WON'T USE IT!
...AND WHAT IS THAT CREEPY THING?!

Innocent

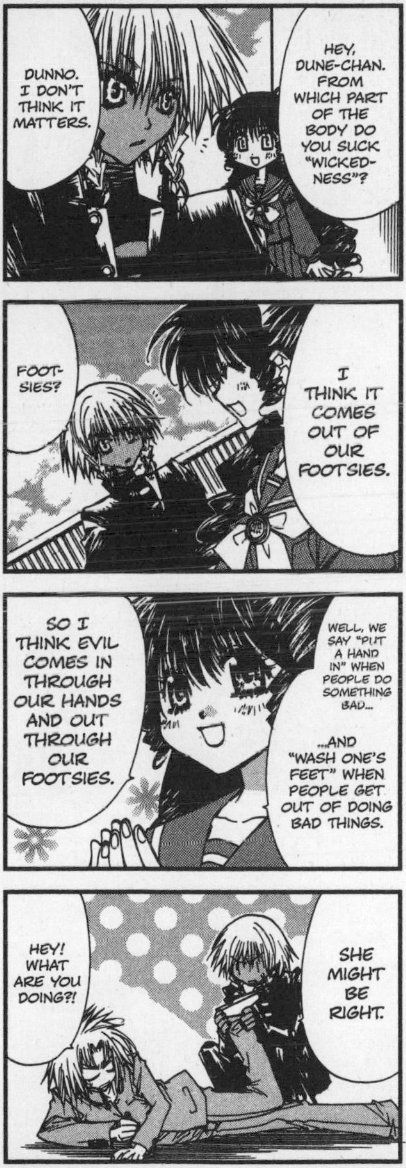
HEY, DUNE-CHAN. FROM WHICH PART OF THE BODY DO YOU SUCK "WICKEDNESS"?
DUNNO. I DON'T THINK IT MATTERS.
I THINK IT COMES OUT OF OUR FOOTSIES.
FOOTSIES?
WELL, WE SAY "PUT A HAND IN" WHEN PEOPLE DO SOMETHING BAD...
...AND "WASH ONE'S FEET" WHEN PEOPLE GET OUT OF DOING BAD THINGS.
SO I THINK EVIL COMES IN THROUGH OUR HANDS AND OUT THROUGH OUR FOOTSIES.
SHE MIGHT BE RIGHT.
HEY! WHAT ARE YOU DOING?!

Author's Notes:

MAGICAL GIRL: Generic term of a girl who has supernatural power or witchcraft. Mainly this word is used for a girl who is good at transforming.

FOOTSIE: It's a child's word for foot. My mother still uses words like "Footsie" and "Go night-night."

Author's Notes:

SWEATER: Part of the Mitsuhachi Academy uniform is a black sweater. They're long and come with V-necks and long sleeves.

DUNE INOUE: He was a band member who was good at playing the tambourine. The truth is...that was all he could play.

Class President

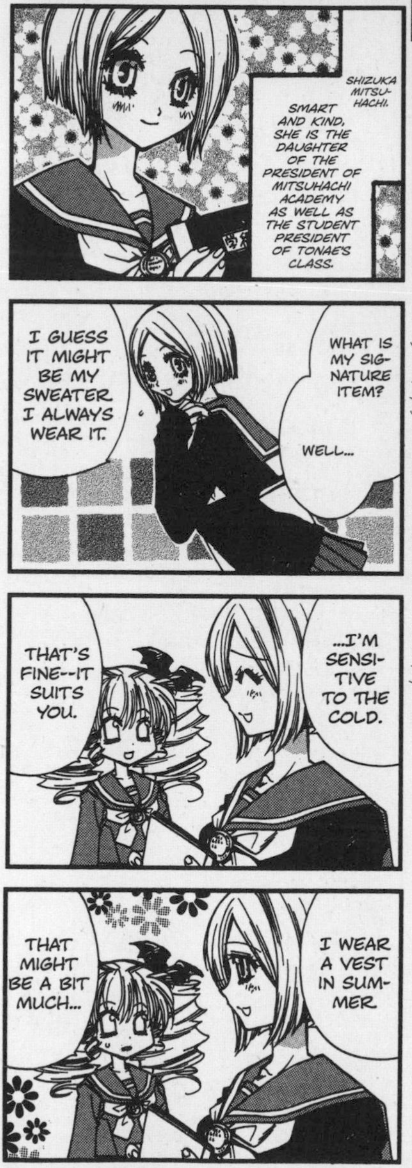

SHIZUKA MITSUHACHI.
SMART AND KIND, SHE IS THE DAUGHTER OF THE PRESIDENT OF MITSUHACHI ACADEMY AS WELL AS THE STUDENT PRESIDENT OF TONAE'S CLASS.
WHAT IS MY SIGNATURE ITEM?
WELL...
I GUESS IT MIGHT BE MY SWEATER I ALWAYS WEAR IT.
...I'M SENSITIVE TO THE COLD.
THAT'S FINE--IT SUITS YOU.
I WEAR A VEST IN SUMMER
THAT MIGHT BE A BIT MUCH...

Dune

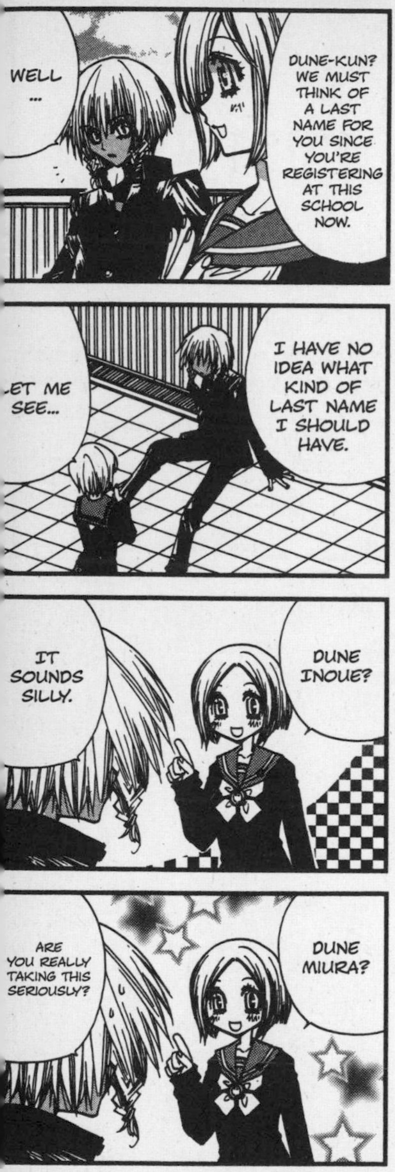

DUNE-KUN? WE MUST THINK OF A LAST NAME FOR YOU SINCE YOU'RE REGISTERING AT THIS SCHOOL NOW.
WELL ...
I HAVE NO IDEA WHAT KIND OF LAST NAME I SHOULD HAVE.
ET ME SEE...
DUNE INOUE?
IT SOUNDS SILLY.
DUNE MIURA?
ARE YOU REALLY TAKING THIS SERIOUSLY?

POSTSCRIPT

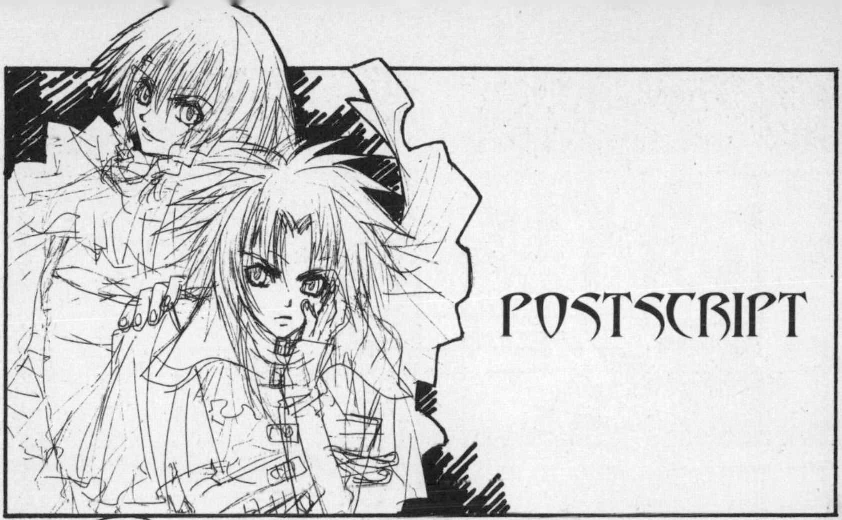

Another sketch.

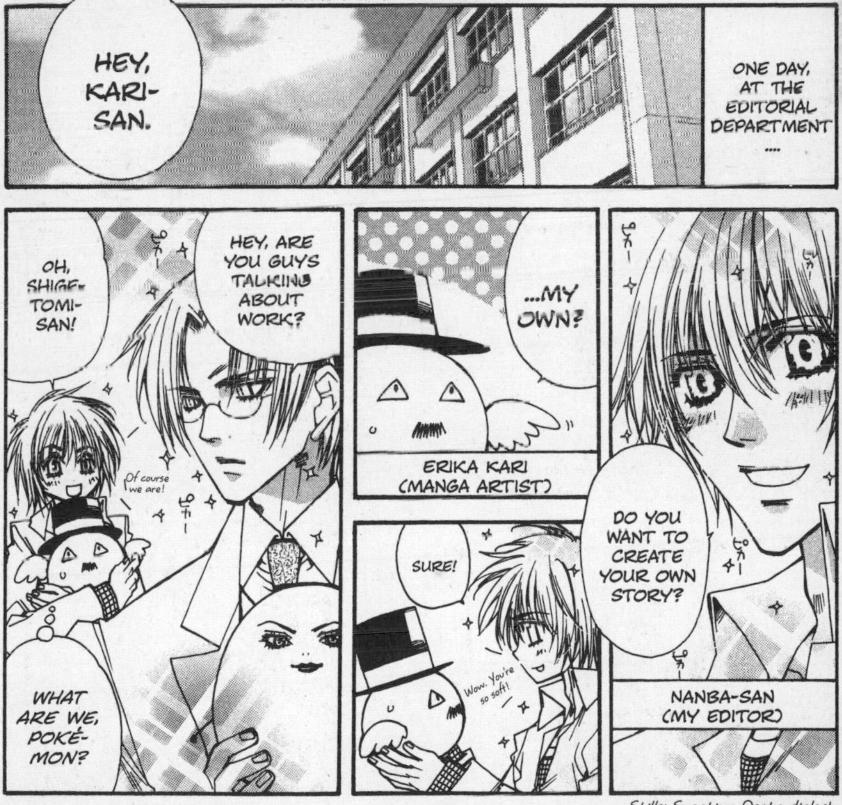
ONE DAY, AT THE EDITORIAL DEPARTMENT ....
HEY, KARI-SAN.
DO YOU WANT TO CREATE YOUR OWN STORY?
NANBA-SAN (MY EDITOR)
...MY OWN?
ERIKA KARI (MANGA ARTIST)
SURE!
Wow. You're so soft!
HEY, ARE YOU GUYS TALKING ABOUT WORK?
OH, SHIGE-TOMI-SAN!
Of course we are!
WHAT ARE WE, POKÉMON?

<Skills: Speaking Osaka dialect, eating a lot, being too nice.>

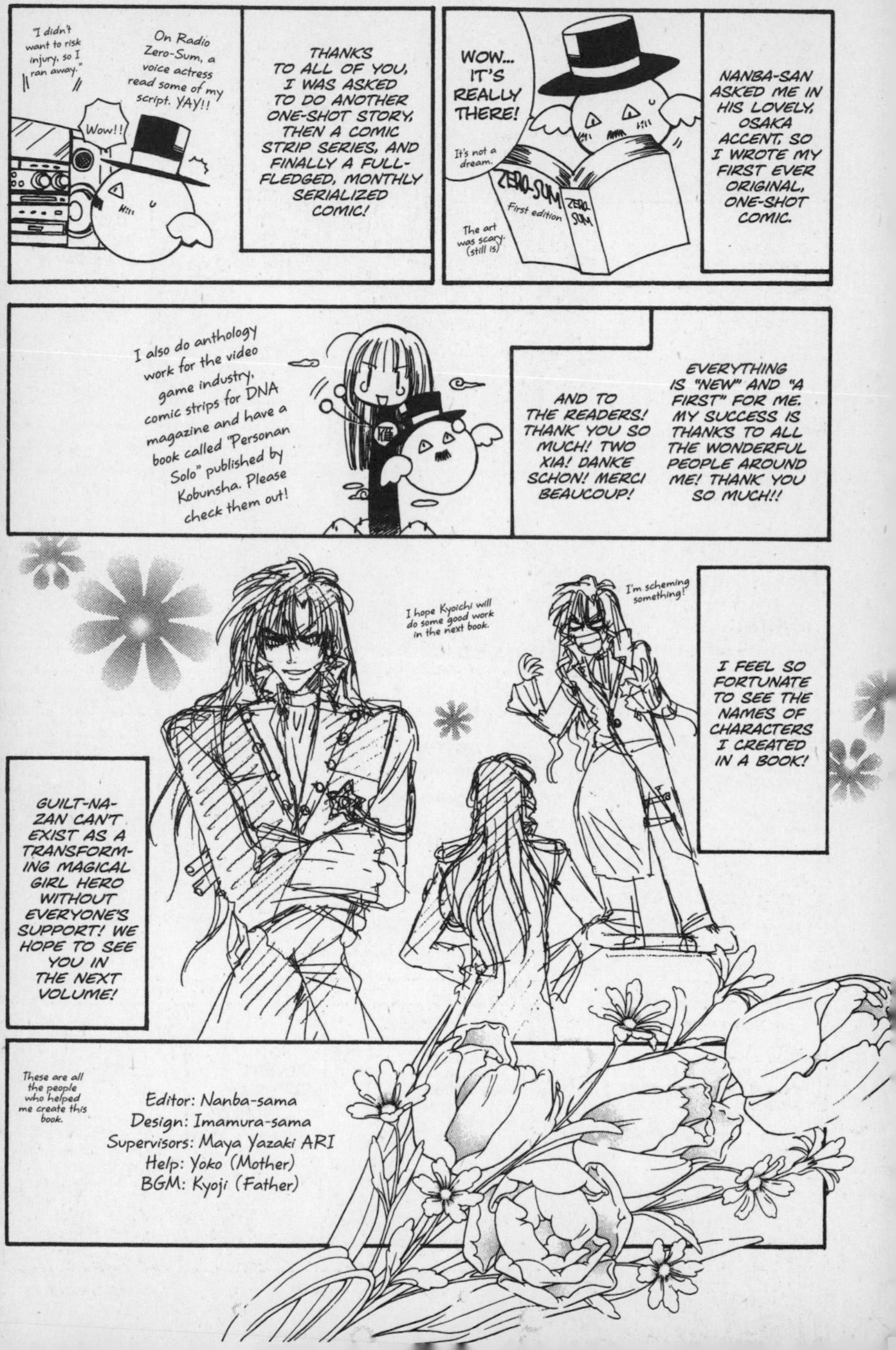
NANBA-SAN ASKED ME IN HIS LOVELY, OSAKA ACCENT, SO I WROTE MY FIRST EVER ORIGINAL, ONE-SHOT COMIC.
WOW... IT'S REALLY THERE!
It's not a dream.
ZERO-SUM
First edition
ZERO-SUM
The art was scary. (still is)
THANKS TO ALL OF YOU, I WAS ASKED TO DO ANOTHER ONE-SHOT STORY, THEN A COMIC STRIP SERIES, AND FINALLY A FULL-FLEDGED, MONTHLY SERIALIZED COMIC!
On Radio Zero-Sum, a voice actress read some of my script. YAY!!
"I didn't want to risk injury, so I ran away."
Wow!!
EVERYTHING IS "NEW" AND "A FIRST" FOR ME. MY SUCCESS IS THANKS TO ALL THE WONDERFUL PEOPLE AROUND ME! THANK YOU SO MUCH!!
AND TO THE READERS! THANK YOU SO MUCH! TWO XIA! DANKE SCHON! MERCI BEAUCOUP!
I also do anthology work for the video game industry, comic strips for DNA magazine and have a book called "Personan Solo" published by Kobunsha. Please check them out!
I FEEL SO FORTUNATE TO SEE THE NAMES OF CHARACTERS I CREATED IN A BOOK!
I'm scheming something!
I hope Kyoichi will do some good work in the next book.
GUILT-NA-ZAN CAN'T EXIST AS A TRANSFORMING MAGICAL GIRL HERO WITHOUT EVERYONE'S SUPPORT! WE HOPE TO SEE YOU IN THE NEXT VOLUME!
These are all the people who helped me create this book.
Editor: Nanba-sama
Design: Imamura-sama
Supervisors: Maya Yazaki ARI
Help: Yoko (Mother)
BGM: Kyoji (Father)

BONUS PAGE

SWEETS & ME

CHAPTER 1: HATEFUL

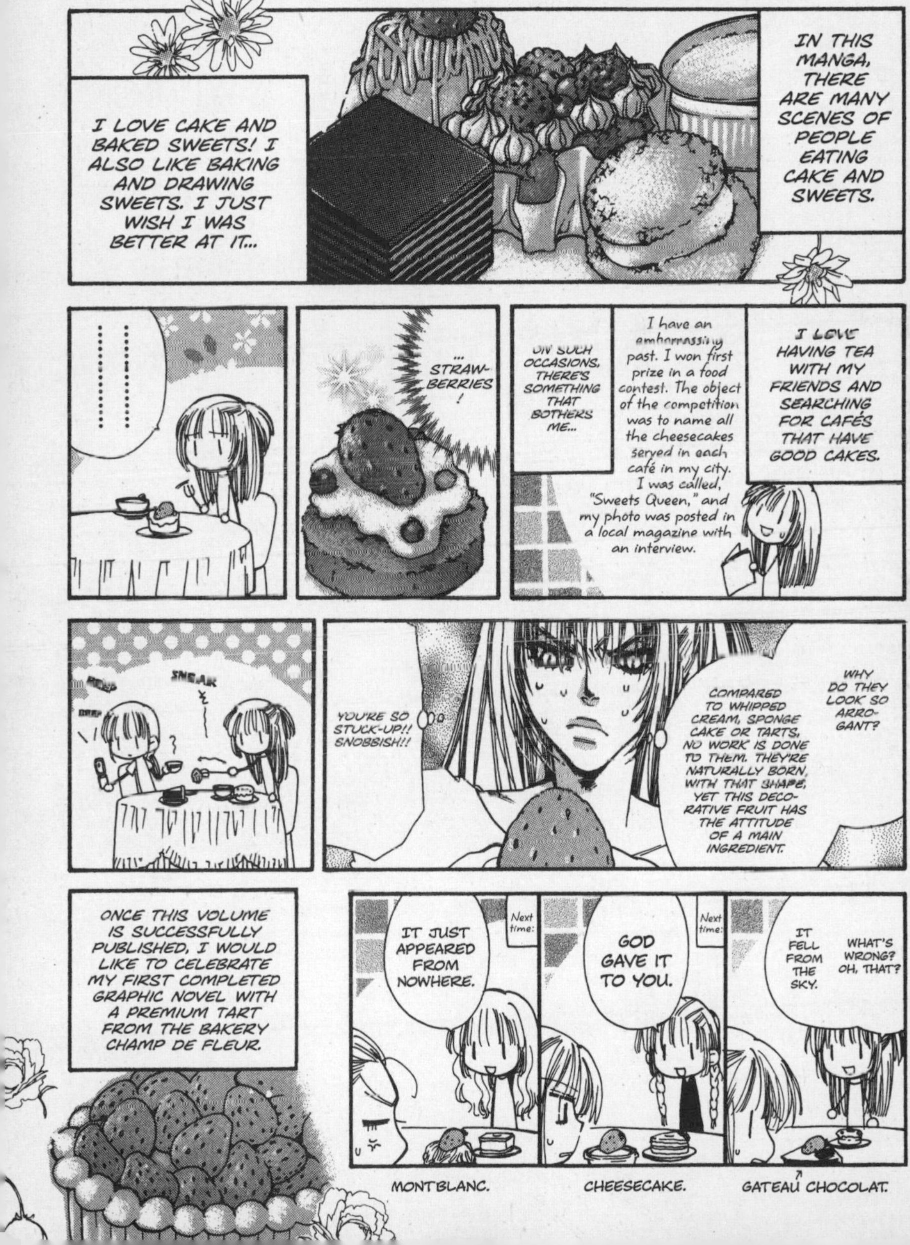

IN THIS MANGA, THERE ARE MANY SCENES OF PEOPLE EATING CAKE AND SWEETS.
I LOVE CAKE AND BAKED SWEETS! I ALSO LIKE BAKING AND DRAWING SWEETS. I JUST WISH I WAS BETTER AT IT...
I LOVE HAVING TEA WITH MY FRIENDS AND SEARCHING FOR CAFÉS THAT HAVE GOOD CAKES.
I have an embarrassing past. I won first prize in a food contest. The object of the competition was to name all the cheesecakes served in each café in my city. I was called, "Sweets Queen," and my photo was posted in a local magazine with an interview.
ON SUCH OCCASIONS, THERE'S SOMETHING THAT BOTHERS ME...
... STRAWBERRIES !
......
WHY DO THEY LOOK SO ARROGANT?
COMPARED TO WHIPPED CREAM, SPONGE CAKE OR TARTS, NO WORK IS DONE TO THEM. THEY'RE NATURALLY BORN, WITH THAT SHAPE, YET THIS DECORATIVE FRUIT HAS THE ATTITUDE OF A MAIN INGREDIENT.
YOU'RE SO STUCK-UP!! SNOBBISH!!
SMEAR
WHAT'S WRONG? OH, THAT?
IT FELL FROM THE SKY.
GATEAU CHOCOLAT.
Next time:
GOD GAVE IT TO YOU.
CHEESECAKE.
Next time:
IT JUST APPEARED FROM NOWHERE.
MONTBLANC.
ONCE THIS VOLUME IS SUCCESSFULLY PUBLISHED, I WOULD LIKE TO CELEBRATE MY FIRST COMPLETED GRAPHIC NOVEL WITH A PREMIUM TART FROM THE BAKERY CHAMP DE FLEUR.

Vampire Doll

Guilt-na-Zan

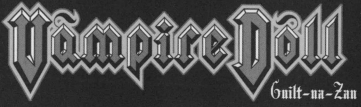

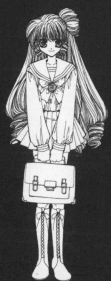

IN THE NEXT WACKY VOLUME!

KYOJI AND KYOICHI MAY BE VICIOUS RIVALS NOW BUT THEY WERE ONCE ACTUALLY CLOSE! WHAT DARK SECRETS IN THEIR PAST RESULTED IN SO MUCH HATRED AND JUVENILE NAME-CALLING BETWEEN THEM? COULD THEIR ANIMOSITY ALL BE BASED ON A SIMPLE MISUNDERSTANDING? WILL THEY BE ABLE TO OVERCOME THE DEMONS THAT HAVE TORN THESE LOVING BROTHERS APART? OR WILL THINGS ONCE AGAIN END IN THE GREAT NIGHT VEIL RUNNING OFF WHILE BEING CALLED A MORON? AND WHAT'S THIS? IS THAT THE VAMPIRE LORD DRESSING UP IN COSTUME FOR HALLOWEEN? GUILT-NA AND TONOE WILL HAVE TO TRACK DOWN A MYSTERIOUS OPPONENT THAT MAY POSE A GREAT TREAT!! HILARIOUS TRICKS AND TREATS AWAIT IN THE NEXT BLOOD-SUCKING VOLUME OF VAMPIRE DOLL: GUILT-NA-ZAN!

TO BE CONTINUED IN *VAMPIRE DOLL GUILT-NA-ZAN* VOL.2

TOKYOPOP.com

WHERE MANGA LIVES!

JOIN THE TOKYOPOP COMMUNITY!

Come and preview the hottest manga around!

CREATE...
UPLOAD...
DOWNLOAD...
BLOG...
CHAT...
VOTE...
LIVE!!!!

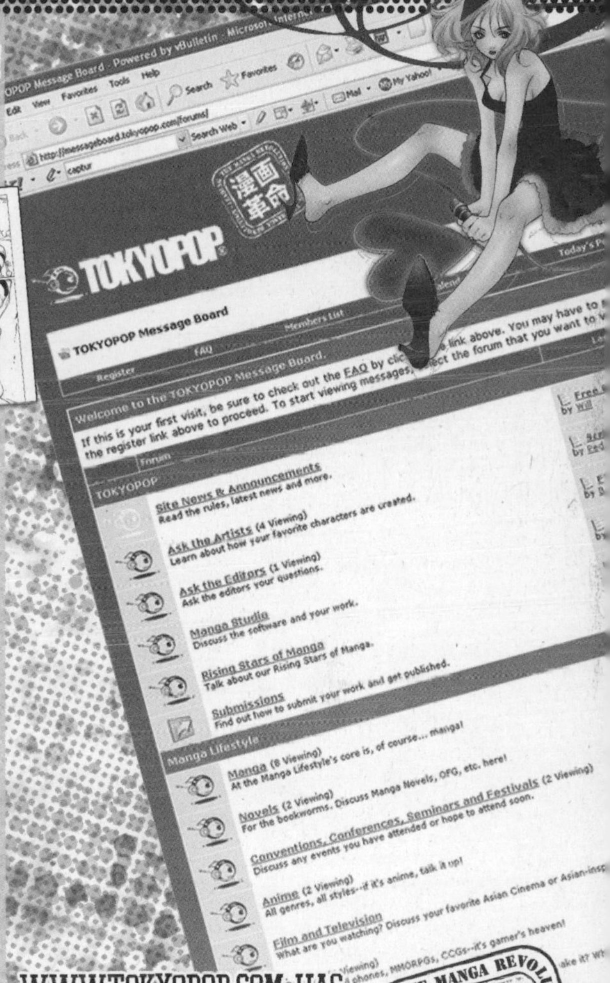

TOKYOPOP Message Board

Register   FAQ   Members List

Welcome to the TOKYOPOP Message Board.
If this is your first visit, be sure to check out the FAQ by clicking the link above. You may have to register before you can post: click the register link above to proceed. To start viewing messages, select the forum that you want to v

Forum

TOKYOPOP

Site News & Announcements
Read the rules, latest news and more.

Ask the Artists (4 Viewing)
Learn about how your favorite characters are created.

Ask the Editors (1 Viewing)
Ask the editors your questions.

Manga Studio
Discuss the software and your work.

Rising Stars of Manga
Talk about our Rising Stars of Manga.

Submissions
Find out how to submit your work and get published.

Manga Lifestyle

Manga (8 Viewing)
At the Manga Lifestyle's core is, of course... manga!

Novels (2 Viewing)
For the bookworms. Discuss Manga Novels, OFG, etc. here!

Conventions, Conferences, Seminars and Festivals (2 Viewing)
Discuss any events you have attended or hope to attend soon.

Anime (2 Viewing)
All genres, all styles—if it's anime, talk it up!

Film and Television
What are you watching? Discuss your favorite Asian Cinema or Asian-insp

WWW.TOKYOPOP.COM HAS:

Manga-on-Demand • News
Anime Reviews • Manga Reviews
Movie Reviews • Music Reviews
and more...

LEADING • THE MANGA REVOLUTION • LEADING • THE MANGA REVOLUTION

漫画革命

STOP!

This is the back of the book.
You wouldn't want to spoil a great ending!

This book is printed "manga-style," in the authentic Japanese right-to-left format. Since none of the artwork has been flipped or altered, readers get to experience the story just as the creator intended. You've been asking for it, so TOKYOPOP® delivered: authentic, hot-off-the-press, and far more fun!

DIRECTIONS

If this is your first time reading manga-style, here's a quick guide to help you understand how it works.

It's easy... just start in the top right panel and follow the numbers. Have fun, and look for more 100% authentic manga from TOKYOPOP®!